Aims of the E...

A READER AND GUIDE

Don Knefel

Loras College

ALLYN AND BACON

Boston   London   Toronto   Sydney   Tokyo   Singapore

Series Editor: Joseph Opiela
Production Administrator: Rowena Dores
Editorial-Production Service: Editorial Inc.
Text Designer: Pat Torelli
Cover Administrator: Linda Dickinson
Manufacturing Buyer: Louise Richardson

Library of Congress Cataloging-in-Publication Data

Aims of the essay : a reader and guide / Don Knefel.
   p.   cm.
  Includes index.
  ISBN 0-205-12655-3
  1. College readers. 2. English language—Rhetoric. I. Knefel,
Don.
  PE1417.A35 1991
  808'.0427—dc20   90-1107
                                         CIP

Printed in the United States of America

10 9 8 7 6 5 4 3 2 1   95 94 93 92 91 90

Credits

Chapter 1
Page 4. Jim Zimmerman, "Starting Small." Reprinted by permission of the author.
Credits continued on page 394, which constitutes an extension of the copyright page.

For Molly, John, and Mary Anne

Contents

6   Writing to Criticize or Evaluate: Arguing Meaning and Merit   219

Preface

Aims of the Essay, an aims-based reader, introduces the spectrum of purposes that shapes everything we write, and my own aim for it is to offer an alternative focus and design for freshman composition.

Instead of placing the rhetorical modes at the center, the book is built upon seven of the practical and common reasons for which people write anything: to express themselves, to inform others, to analyze or explain, to argue, to criticize, to persuade, and to entertain. The assumption is that purpose is the dominant influence in any writing task, affecting all the writer's choices, whether of content, structure, language, or style.

Aims of the Essay is meant to answer the frustration many writing teachers feel toward traditional rhetoric, with its blurring of purpose and method (seeing description, comparison, definition, and so on, as both ends and means). The rhetorical modes are treated here as tools among many others serving fundamental aims or purposes, offering essay-writing situations that I believe are engaging and realistic for students to study and practice.

Special Features

Throughout *Aims of the Essay,* you will encounter everyday examples of real-world writing, topical pieces as well as more academic works, treating subjects across the college curriculum. My goal has been to find models that are interesting for college students, readable, and possible to emulate. At the same time, I recognize that a new text cannot, and this one need not, depart radically from teachers' experience, and so you will find here familiar works and authors as well as newer, previously unanthologized essays.

The book considers the entire range of public writing from the perspective of purpose—from the personal or literary essay to the more practical forms of exposition and persuasion. The readings include classic, contemporary, and student pieces, written with specific aims for defined audiences. Throughout, you will notice consistent emphasis on the writing process, and on the ways in which purpose, strategy, content, and audience meet as that process unfolds.

Aims of the Essay has several features designed to make it flexible and easy to use:

- Its nine chapters include an introduction to the essay form and to the writing process; seven aims-based writing units; and a closing selection, "Writers on Writing," with essays composed for varied aims.
- Each unit includes a full discussion of purpose and strategy; a checklist to guide students through discovery, design, and execution; and model professional essays and follow-up student examples.
- The readings are balanced, including short, simple selections and others with greater complexity.
- A three-part sequence on argumentative and persuasive writing includes a longer chapter on argument and a unit on criticism.
- Study apparatus includes review questions on meaning, purpose, strategy, audience, style, and language; marginal notes for the first in each pair of student readings; and dozens of suggested writing topics.
- Alternate tables of contents at the back of the book arrange readings according to rhetorical mode and subject.

Aims of the Essay offers support for all the principles writing teachers emphasize. It is intended to help enliven the creative process for students, to let it more clearly approximate the one they actually face in college writing and in the working world—a process shaped by our goals and the strategies we use to achieve them.

Organization

Why these aims?

The ones that form the core of this book come from observation of the real world of writing—in academia, the professions, journalism, private life—and from a corresponding acknowledgment of these facts in recent rhetorical theory. Scholarship and experience tell us that there are several essential aims of discourse. Those which occur most frequently, and which make most sense, include:

- self-expression
- informing and explaining
- persuasion
- entertainment
- creation of poetry and fiction.

(Because this book deals only with the nonfiction prose most students read and write as freshmen, the last aim is beyond our scope here.)

In *Aims* I give detailed consideration to each of these, but also divide persuasion into more specific purposes, using traditional distinctions among logical, ethical, and emotional appeals, and include a second chapter on argumentative writing aimed at practical criticism. Here is an outline of the writing units as they relate to the general aims of discourse:

General Aim	*Chapter Number and Content*
	[1. Introduction: Writing Essays (form, aims, and process)]
Self-expression	2. Self-expression and reflection (subjective emphasis)
Informing and explaining	3. Informing and reporting (factual, objective emphasis)
	4. Analyzing and explaining (emphasis on meaning and interpretation)
Persuasion	5. Arguing and proving (emphasis on logic, evidence, reason)
	6. Criticism (applying argument to created works)
	7. Persuasion (emphasis on emotional and ethical appeals)
Entertainment	8. Humor (emphasis on writing to amuse and delight)
	[9. Further reading: Writers on writing]

In the real world, of course, the aims of discourse, like the modes and strategies we use to achieve them, are not completely isolated or detached from one another. Writing always takes place in a context of related purposes, which we may emphasize singly or in combination, depending on the job at hand.

- Expressive writing can use informative or explanatory strategies to help reveal the self.
- Informative and explanatory aims are closely related; although we may convey facts without explaining them, explanation always includes an informative, factual foundation.
- Argument, too, uses factual evidence, analysis, and explanatory justification to build logical, convincing cases.
- Criticism always includes information and analysis for support.
- Persuasion may rest on a logical or rational footing but isn't limited to it; we may intend to argue logically, on the one hand, or we may intend to persuade by other or additional means, by appealing to feelings, values, or self-interest.
- Writing to entertain can, at the same time, include other aims.

Aims of the Essay is an attempt to integrate the complex issues of teaching writing in a way that is realistic and useful, to illustrate some of the dominant influences every writer faces. These chapters are intended to encompass the wide world of the essay and to offer an introduction to its great utility, breadth, power, and beauty.

Acknowledgments

I would very much like to thank those who have helped this book see the light of day.

Among many who reviewed the manuscript, I am especially indebted to Chris Anson, University of Minnesota; George Miller, University of Delaware; William Pixton, Oklahoma State University; Eileen Schwartz, Purdue University Calumet; Robert Schwegler, University of Rhode Island; and Nancy Walker, Southwest Missouri State University. Their suggestions were unfailingly intelligent and useful.

Also, I wish to express my gratitude to the Loras College administration and English department for their generous support in the sabbatical year during which the first draft was written, and to the students who have so graciously allowed their work to appear here.

For their abundant editorial help, many thanks also to Marilyn Rash of Editorial Inc., Carolynne Lathrop, and my wife, Mary Anne Knefel.

Lastly, heartfelt thanks to Joe Opiela, the series editor at Allyn and Bacon, whose ideas, encouragement, and good cheer have been invaluable in bringing the book to its current form.

– 1 –

Writing Essays

The American author William Styron once was asked what it was like to write a novel. "Writing a novel," he said, "is like walking from Paris to Madrid—on your knees."

For most of us, spending months or years writing a book may seem an impossible job. It's hard enough, sometimes, just to compose a good one-page letter. Still, as we imagine ourselves trudging across Europe a knee at a time, we understand Styron's metaphor. Writing anything—a novel, a research paper, a short essay—*can* be a difficult, frustrating struggle. But there's also something else in this image of the writing process: a sense of devotion to the work and of how important it is to have a goal or purpose in mind—to know where we want to go, and why.

The task of writing may never be *easy*—anything worthwhile usually requires some effort—but it can be *made much easier* if we acknowledge a few simple principles about the way in which good writing comes about.

Whenever we write, we do undertake a kind of journey—a walk from here to there. Every phrase, sentence, and paragraph we write is another step toward the goal. Often we'll *retrace* those steps, change them, even start over, but eventually we'll arrive at our destination: a

1

finished piece of writing for our readers. The quality in that product will depend on a lot of things: our seriousness and intelligence, our ability to focus and organize our material, our patience to stay with the project until we're happy with it. The journey from start to finish will take time, but if we begin with a *purpose* in mind, and pay attention to what happens along the way, *achieving* that purpose can be enormously satisfying and rewarding. Moreover, we can learn to become better at taking the walk with each new challenge.

One way to visualize the situation in which writing takes place is to think of ourselves as moving through a field of subjects with certain destinations in mind. In writing we use many strategies and methods to meet our goals for ourselves and our readers. Depending upon the complexity of the task before us and our relationship with our audience, our aims may be one or several, but some clear purpose should be present if the writing is to have any value.

The aim in this book is to make writing less mysterious for you, to make it more manageable, productive, and enjoyable—to help writing become second nature as thoroughly as walking. We'll look at writing as an ordinary part of life, from a commonsense, practical perspective. We'll consider

- the basic *aims* or goals toward which we write
- the step-by-step *nature* of writing and how our aims influence it
- the specific *strategies* that writers use to achieve their goals
- the importance of the *reader* in the writer's plans
- the *language* writers use; how and why they say what they say

You'll study these guiding ideas by reading works by student and professional writers and by writing your own essays. In fact, careful reading of good writing may be the strongest influence in improving your own work.

Can you become a better writer?

By the time you began your freshman year of college, you may have read hundreds of pieces of writing and written a great many of your own. You may have a distinct image of yourself as this or that kind of writer, with certain skills and strong feelings about what you like, and don't like, to read and write. You may feel at times that you've reached your limits as a writer, that nothing more is to be gained from your writing education, or that each new writing task puts you back at square one, with a huge obstacle to overcome and not a clue about how to do it. Even though you've been reading and writing for years, in other words, how well you write may still depend more on luck than on your own intentions or sense of control.

If writing gives you this touch of stage fright, it may be helpful to know you're not alone. Even seasoned, successful professionals—journalists, novelists, poets, essayists—are not strangers to such anxiety. Still, every moment in the act of writing is different from every other, and though some may be less than joyful, others will give us wonderful surprises, striking and useful ideas, and phrases and sentences that seem just right. As we gain experience as writers, just as we become accomplished at any other undertaking, those moments of anxiety or fear diminish; instead we feel a relaxed sense of confidence, a clear-headed and self-assured knowledge of what we're doing. Eventually we come to *enjoy* writing because we understand how it works, and how we work with it. We learn to recognize and accept the gifts writing offers us. We find real, enduring satisfaction in our accomplishments and become eager for another session with the typewriter, word processor, or legal pad.

This book is designed to give you greater experience in the kind of reading and writing you'll encounter in college and beyond. In it we consider one of the basic, practical, and flexible forms of everyday writing: *the essay*. The readings in these chapters—many of them from popular, contemporary sources—are meant to serve not only as models of good essay writing for study, but as inspirations for your work.

Writing never occurs in a vacuum. It's always a response to something *real* in the world: a need for personal expression, a body of information, an unanswered question or unsolved problem, a pressing issue or dispute. Frequently, writing is a response to writing, as we read, think, and write in the continuing discourse of our school, our workplace, and the larger community.

The essayists whose work you'll read in the coming weeks will inform and entertain you, explain and clarify varied subjects for you, attempt to persuade you to change your opinions or actions, and give you insight into others' minds and hearts. And they should prompt your own written responses to your world, the essays you'll contribute to your community of fellow readers and writers.

The Essay

One problem we all face is making sense of the bewildering array of types or forms of writing. In one day we might encounter news stories, business letters, college research papers, critical reviews, maga-

zine articles, poems, short stories and novels, plays, nonfiction narratives (such as biographies and autobiographies), speeches, editorials,
reports—and the list goes on. Despite this enormous variety, however,
we can understand the world of writing better according to two broad
categories.

The one basic distinction we should be aware of is the difference
between *fiction* (and other kinds of imaginative literature, such as
poetry and drama) and *nonfiction*. Stories, poems, and plays may be
based on fact, of course, but they need not be limited by it. Nonfiction, on the other hand, whatever its form, always refers to the actual
world in which we live.

You may write fiction, poetry, or drama in creative-writing
classes, but most of your college writing will be nonfiction, such as
reports, papers, and essays about your course subjects and related interests. Certainly the bulk of your college writing will be *essays*: answers
to exam questions, analytical essays, critical essays, and research-based
essays varying in length and scope.

But what *are* essays, exactly? What are some of the characteristics we find in them?

Here is a brief example from a student:

STARTING SMALL

Jim Zimmerman

If you don't own a personal computer, you probably have a   1
good reason--the expense. Most advertised systems cost thousands of dollars, too high an investment for those who don't
know what they want. It's easy for many first-timers to make
the mistake of buying a computer much more powerful (and expensive) than they need. What's the best way to plunge
into the computer field? Try stepping in slowly, with a small
computer.

Small computers, those with 128K of memory or less, are   2
much less expensive than their more powerful cousins. Depending on the model and manufacturer, you can buy a basic
unit, use an old black-and-white television set as a monitor,
and have a perfectly functional little computer system for
about $200.

The major difference between smaller and larger com-   3
puters is the amount of memory (described as K, or kilobytes)
available in each. The more memory, the more information the

computer can store as programs, data, or written documents.
Smaller machines can handle fewer data at any one time, but
unless you're working on huge amounts of material, 128K
should be plenty to start with.

What can you learn from a small computer? First, you can   4
begin to see what a computer will do for you: experiment with
its functions and learn its characteristics. Also, it's easier to learn on a small, simple machine. You can learn com-
mands, common software, and technical jargon as easily on a
$200 computer as on a $2,000 one.

Small computers do have drawbacks, though, the biggest   5
one being a lack of software, or programs. Still, even simple
machines have basic software packages—word processors,
data bases, and spread sheets—that will give you an inexpensive introduction to these programs. More exotic software,
however, such as games, may be unavailable.

For most first-time users, a small, cheap computer is   6
just the right thing for getting started. If you just want to
find out what computers are all about, or discover what your
specific needs might be, don't spend your money blindly on a
lot of memory and functions you'll never use. Try a small computer first.

What do we notice about this piece of writing?

- *It presents a clear, specific main idea, or thesis* (called a *claim* or *proposition* when the purpose is argumentative), usually a direct state-ment of the author's essential point (though sometimes the thesis is left unstated or implied). Here, Zimmerman's thesis comes at the end of the first paragraph: "Try stepping in slowly, with a small computer."
- *The thesis likewise implies the writer's primary aim and gives us a sense of the content to follow.* What is Zimmerman's aim? To give us information and advice: to inform and to convince. In his content he will consider the virtues of the small computer.
- *It keeps a unified focus on its subject, without unrelated or unneeded material.* Here, the author limits himself to aspects of the small com-puter as a starter machine.
- *It supports its point with detailed discussion, explanation, or evi-dence.* Zimmerman defines terms in paragraph 2, explains with com-parison in paragraph 3, and gives supporting evidence in paragraphs 4 and 5.
- *It has a clear pattern of organization, including introduction, body,*

and conclusion. Here, paragraph 1 introduces the subject, paragraphs 2–5 develop the body, and paragraph 6 concludes.

• *The introduction opens the subject to readers and appeals to their interest and curiosity.* Zimmerman addresses his readers directly ("If you don't own a personal computer . . ."), appeals to their interest in saving money, and offers his suggestion.

• *The body of the essay develops the thesis with subpoints or topics, each directly related to the main point and supported by specific detail.* Zimmerman's topics are a definition of small computers (paragraph 2), differences between small and large machines (paragraph 3), benefits of small machines (paragraphs 4–5), and a drawback (paragraph 5).

• *The essay unfolds in a logical, coherent way so that the reader can follow from idea to idea without getting lost.* The author's topic sentences flow smoothly and clearly from his thesis and connect to each other in a pattern that makes sense.

• *It is written in a clear, direct style, without wasted words.* Here, Zimmerman's style is economical, clean, and precise throughout.

• *The essay concludes with an overall assessment of the subject or a final point of emphasis.* Zimmerman ends his essay by stressing his essential advice: that small computers are good for learning what computers can do and what you may need them for.

• *The essay reveals the writer's unique perspective on, or attitude toward, the subject.* Throughout, Zimmerman writes as an advocate for inexpensive machines, against the prevailing wisdom that one's first car should be a Rolls Royce.

In other words, every essay gives us an individual writer's unique engagement with *selection, design, and emphasis,* resulting in prose that asserts and supports specific ideas. The word *essay* is also a verb, meaning to try, to attempt, to put to a test. No matter what *aim(s)* you have in mind—whether your thesis is a point of information, explanation, argument, criticism, or personal expression (or some combination of these)—every finished essay, whatever its length, displays your attempts to *discover, select, shape, support,* and *present* a clear and unified view.

Basic Essay Aims

People naturally communicate with each other in writing—from jotting notes to writing multivolume histories of their cultures—to compose and record such structures of language for future use. Writing, especially, helps us to give form and substance to our thoughts, helps us to discover what we know, think, and feel about ourselves and the things that interest us. It encourages us to confront our own minds and to test what we say (our information and ideas) for truth, common sense, originality, and honesty.

Our reasons for writing essays at all, of course, are as basic as our reasons for writing or saying anything: we need to communicate with others, usually for one or more specific purposes. When we write anything, we usually do so to achieve general *aims,* all grounded in the demands made by everyday experience. We write in order to *do* something. What do essays do? In our written communication with others, we find it necessary to

- *express* ourselves to others about our feelings, thoughts, and experiences
- *report* information—to relay important or necessary facts or knowledge
- *analyze* or *explain* subjects for greater understanding, both for ourselves and others
- *convince* others that they should believe or act in some new way, to argue logically for or against specific ideas, values, or courses of action
- *criticize* and evaluate the nature or merit of works of art, music, film, or literature
- *persuade* others by means that aren't limited to perfect rationality or logic
- *entertain* others with wit or humor
- *combine several aims* in a piece of writing for greater complexity and richness.

Most of the prose we see in everyday life, such as essays, articles, books, is controlled or greatly influenced by one or more such fundamental aims. In your college writing, too, and in the writing you'll produce in your job or profession, many of these overriding purposes determine much about what you'll include and exclude, how you'll go about it, and which strategies you'll choose to make your work clear, understandable, and interesting for your readers.

The aims listed above are the focus for the rest of this book. In each chapter, you'll find a group of essays illustrating a general goal of the writing process, the aim or purpose that motivates the writer or calls the essay into being. These works are finished products, of course, but they also reveal much about *how* they were written. Essays, like all other forms of writing, arise from our active encounters with subjects, through discovery and decision. The points we wish to make and the ways that we choose to support those points often come to us as we wrestle with our material. Writing always takes place within a context, within limits or boundaries, and our overall aims exert perhaps the strongest influence on us as we work.

The Writing Process

The situation in which we write includes other forces that limit us, too. Whenever we write, we're motivated by an overall purpose, but that purpose is part of the larger context of *subject* and *audience*: *what* we're writing about, and for *whom*. These three limits—our aim, our subject, and our intended readers—give us the necessary bounds that help us to control what we're doing. If we write without such limits, or if we misunderstand them, our words are much more likely to be without focus or shape—unfinished, muddled—without good reason to be read.

The first step in any of our writing, then, is to understand the context, the nature of the task:

- *Why* are we writing?
- *What* are we going to write about?
- *Whom* are we writing to?

Sometimes we may not know the essay's precise topic, the "what" part of the task, at this early stage, and we must write to discover it. (See "Exploring and Collecting," below.) Even when we do know our aim, our specific subject, and our audience, however, that's only the beginning. Once we've established the context, we take steps to:

- *generate* useful material
- *focus* that material to a clear, manageable thesis
- *design* an appropriate structure
- *draft* a working version of our essay
- *react critically* to our draft and *revise* it (for greater clarity, better design, more detailed development)
- *commit* ourselves to the final product (the whole essay: its paragraphs, sentences, words, and the accepted standards for grammar, usage, and mechanics)

Our writing *rarely* forms a straight line, however. Instead, we shift back and forth among these steps, recursively, in multiple loops—

designing, drafting, digging up more material, modifying the design, doing further drafting, and so on—more an exploratory walk than a forced march.

Now let's examine all this in detail, remembering that *you may visit each stage several times* as you work toward your goal.

One: The Task

We've said that first we must determine the kind of work we intend to do; we take the lay of the land. What is our general aim? Which subject will we address? Who will read our work?

In college writing, tasks may be quite narrowly defined by *subject* or course content, *length, audience*, and the *specific goal* in the assignment (to analyze the causes behind the Great Depression for an economics class, or to write a critical interpretation of a poem or story for a literature course). Just as often, however, and especially in writing courses, tasks may be just generally defined, leaving you the freedom to choose among aims, subjects, and audiences. When searching for a topic, or an angle on an assignment, then, ask yourself a few questions:

- What am I really *interested* in?
- How can I make the subject interesting for my *readers*?
- How can I *limit* my treatment to an essay of manageable size?

Each of us writes in a unique way, and your methods for choosing topics may differ from mine. Still, if we think of our writing as a *bridge* between subject and audience, and try to make it accomplish a specific goal, we'll be likely to choose lively, compelling topics that interest us as much as they do our readers. As a rule:

- Always try to write along the lines of your genuine interest; choose subjects that appeal to your honest curiosity—things you know well or want to know more about.
- Remember that essays are a form of "public" writing, that they're designed to be read by others. What will your readers want to know about your subject?
- Keep your topics limited in size and scope so that you can give them detailed treatment in a few pages. A two- or three-page essay (500–750 words) must be focused sharply on one specific feature of a general subject:

Subject: popular music (very broad)
Narrowed subjects (pick one):
    rock ✓
    country
    jazz
Specific angles on rock music:
    current themes in rock lyrics
    new electronic instruments in rock
    innovative bands

When you begin exploring your working topics, of course, you may find even further narrowing necessary, which will be much easier to do if you've already started planning.

Whether the subject is assigned or is one you've chosen, be sure you understand the task and its limits *before* you begin to write.

Task checklist

General aim(s): To express, inform, explain, persuade, entertain?

Subject: Narrowed to manageable size?

Reader: Common ground of interest? Reader's needs?

Estimated length: Brief, moderate, extended?

Specific purpose: Assigned? Self-determined?

Two: Exploring and Collecting

Once you've gauged the task and settled on a tentative topic, it's time to start gathering the material from which you'll build your working draft. Your goal at this stage is to open the subject to detailed view, to *explore your subject* for ideas that you and your readers want to know more about, and to *generate ideas* and information that will be useful in supporting and developing your essay.

Open writing

One of the most-used ways to develop material is free or spontaneous writing—an informal, open-ended exploration. Such open writing employs varied methods: jotting notes, making lists, asking questions, clustering ideas in groups, writing whatever comes to mind to uncover potentially useful thoughts, facts, and details. Being able to write openly is essential at *all* stages in writing, but it's especially valuable in the early ones. When we write as freely as possible—without considering yet the finer points such as form, grammar, and style—we allow ourselves to be open to our own creativity in thought and expression, and likewise to our subject's possibilities. As we write we *explore, discover, invent;* we *consider various angles* of approach, *look for gaps* in our knowledge, and *assemble the foundation* for the more careful writing to follow. Such a sense of open-endedness is essential if our work is to be fresh, lively, engaging. Exploration is always a part of all the writing we do.

Also remember that open writing is *writing,* not just thinking. Writing *as* we think, as if we were speaking in a conversation, we find that our thoughts flow through our words, and that the writing itself opens up *new* thoughts as we work. Then, when we're able to see those thoughts in written form, we can evaluate their potential use.

Let's look at a brief example of open writing in action:

Suppose, like the writer on page 4, that you're knowledgeable about personal or home computers, and you want to work up an informative essay for fellow students unfamiliar with the subject. Your task checklist:

General aim: To inform
Subject: Home computers—not narrowed yet
Readers: Fellow students
Estimated length: Brief—2–3 pages

It's obvious that the subject is huge, and must be cut down to size. You might approach it from any number of angles, each one a narrower or more limited view. You start writing, listing such narrowed topics as the following:

Uses of the home computer
Types of personal computers
Computers that are "user-friendly"
Problems in choosing a personal computer

Even this brief list gives you clear possibilities for several essays; you must decide. As you think, you write:

Which one of these would be the most interesting? Which might be most practical or informative for readers who don't know much about computers? Actually, three of the four look pretty good: uses, types, and problems. The first two might be awfully dry, though. How about problems? That might get people's attention.

You decide to isolate some of the problems would-be buyers might face in selecting their first machine. An interesting topic, probably narrow enough for now. You write, *What are the problems?* You start another list:

> Problems in selecting a personal computer:
> — getting educated, knowing what you need to know
> — incompatibility of different systems
> — expenses
> — the right software
> — the right hardware
> — buying a system that won't become obsolete tomorrow

You've named some specific problems, and you're eager to start writing about them in detail. You decide to choose the ones you think most interesting or promising and write a paragraph on each to see if you have something worthwhile to say. You start with "getting educated, knowing what you need to know":

> Where's a good place to start with this? I got educated about personal computers the hard way—buying before I knew what I was doing (maybe I can use this?). There's so much information to learn. One thing would be to read some of the popular computing magazines—only they may be too technical. You could talk to salespeople at your local computer store (they'll be biased). Or you can find a friend who knows something about computers and ask a bunch of questions (or read my essay!). I'd say getting educated means a couple of things: knowing what you need the computer for (you may not need one at all), <u>knowing how much you can afford to spend, and maybe knowing how involved you want to get with the whole thing</u> . . .

As the underscored words in this paragraph show, it may take a bit of writing before you discover a useful train of thought. When you uncover specific, potentially valuable ideas, however, hold them for later reference—they will come in handy, perhaps as key points or topics to develop in the essay.

As you continue to write, you'll learn whether you have enough material, whether the paragraphs can become building blocks for your essay-in-progress. With further writing, too, you may decide to drop some subtopics and expand others. Only by *writing your way into the subject*, however, will you be able to discover its possibilities. Then you'll be prepared for the next phase: achieving a specific focus for your essay (the point you want to make), *your working thesis*.

We'll say more in later chapters about other methods for collecting information at all stages in writing.

Exploring and collecting checklist

Open writing: Ideas, connections, possibilities, problems?
Topic: Moving toward a specific angle on the subject?
Subtopics: Looking for good support and development?
Material: Solid facts and details? Enough depth?

Three: Finding Your Thesis

As you write with a sense of openness and exploration, you'll begin to see one or more *key ideas* appearing in your material, almost as if it were telling you what it wanted to say. Such controlling ideas *synthesize* the material; they *put it together* and help it to make sense. They are the sources of your tentative thesis, the idea that eventually you'll place at the heart of your essay.

In any writing task, it's likely that more than one main idea may present itself. In your informative essay about personal computers, several potential thesis ideas might arise from your preliminary work:

— Home computers can do many things, but they are expensive investments that can become outmoded as soon as you buy one.
— Despite the ad writers' claims, not all personal computers are easy to operate.
— Sometimes people overestimate the usefulness of personal computers and discover that what they've bought is just an expensive toy.

Your writing has rewarded you with several possible points around which to build your essay. How do you choose the right one?

Again, a few guiding questions:

- Which focus is likely to be most interesting or useful?
- Which one comes closest to stating my understanding of the subject?
- Which thesis best fulfills the essay's purpose?
- Which one best commits me to a concrete, specific line of thought?

When you select a working thesis, of course, you further limit your essay's possibilities, but you also open the way to solid content: saying something *definite and meaningful* about your subject. The thesis firmly plants you in a particular place, gives your material a specific direction, and helps keep you on track. As you develop the thesis in a working draft of the essay, you may find that your main point must be revised, made clearer, or, sometimes, thrown out for a new one. Don't panic. The working thesis is your best guess at this stage—a kind of experiment. Chances are that your *final* thesis won't be identical to the one you started with, and it won't be possible at all unless you make a start somewhere.

Thesis checklist

A good working idea that focuses my material?

Suits the essay's main purpose?

Makes a clear, meaningful point?

Commits the essay to a specific line of thought?

Four: Designing

As you settle on a working thesis, you'll naturally consider how best to support and develop it. You've already uncovered enough material to give your essay a direction. What's the best way to arrange those ideas so that the reader understands and accepts your point? Your goal is to design a structure that makes your thesis and the essay that supports it clear, complete, and logical.

We've seen that essays have three essential parts: the introduction, the body, and the conclusion. Although some essays are quite informal in their design, most of the ones you'll write in college should follow this fundamental plan—not only because the reader will expect it, but because following the plan makes writing essays much easier. If we acknowledge the general form, we can use it to our advantage.

Just as narrowing your topic helps you to gain control over your material, considering the parts of the essay helps you to control its overall form and content. Why? Instead of trying to write essays in one fell swoop, you'll work on smaller, more manageable sections, building the whole essay from them. In *specific* structure each essay will be unique, but the underlying pattern will be similar from one to another:

Introduction: ¶ Opening for reader's interest
                  Thesis—your main point

        Body: ¶ Supporting topic
                  Detailed development

               ¶ Supporting topic
                  Detailed development

               ¶ Supporting topic
                  Detailed development

  Conclusion: ¶ Closing remarks for emphasis

The parts of an essay may have *any number of paragraphs,* of course, although shorter essays usually have single-paragraph introductions and conclusions. The body of the essay, too, may have more than three paragraphs, and the kinds of supporting topics it includes will depend on the writer's choice of content, development strategies, and overall aim. Keeping this general format in mind, however, will help you assemble your essay according to the requirements in each part, with your thesis as the thread that connects them all.

Let's consider each part in more detail.

The introduction

The first part of the essay has two jobs to do: it opens the subject to the reader, and usually it states the writer's thesis.

When we introduce one person to another, we say, "I'd like you to meet someone." Similarly, when we introduce an essay, we say, "I'd like you to meet some*thing.*" That is, we make an opening gesture to our readers, inviting them to get acquainted with our subject. Successful introductions arrest the readers' attention or appeal to their interest, encouraging them to read on.

Several introductory strategies are popular:

The direct approach.   Sometimes it's best to open with a blunt statement of the problem, issue, or subject you will address in the essay. You don't mince words. Here's how a point of argument, here a call for action, might be introduced (thesis statement in italics):

> For years students have been complaining about the grading system, saying that it's too subjective and often unfair. *If they want to make the system fairer, students should organize to petition the administration to publish specific grading policies and standards.*

The intriguing quotation.   Someone else's words often get your reader interested, especially if the person being quoted is an authority or witness, or if the remark itself arouses our curiosity. In this example, the aim is informative, the thesis a point of fact:

> "Grades? I don't believe in them," says one of our campus's most respected professors. "At best they're a necessary evil—at worst, a downright hoax." *Many students would agree, and some of them have formed a group to study possible revisions in grading policy.*

The rhetorical question.   One of the best ways to capture attention is by asking a question. When authors pose questions, they don't expect readers to answer, but to be curious about where the question might lead. Here the aim is to analyze and explain:

> Is it fair for teachers to grade papers according to personal feelings about students? Is it fair for teachers to give higher grades to papers whose arguments they agree with? *These are just two of the problems many consider obstacles in making the grading system even-handed and objective.*

The illustrative anecdote.   An anecdote is a brief story, usually one that bears directly on the subject at hand. It's vital to keep the story short, to the point, and appropriate to the essay's tone and subject. In this example, the aim is also explanatory:

> When I left for college, my father told me to study hard, have fun, and get straight A's. I asked him what would happen if I didn't get the four-point. He said I shouldn't worry—we could always cut the "have fun" part. He was kidding (I think), but his remarks say a lot about how much people, especially parents, value good grades. *In a crowded, competitive world, a high grade-*

point average is a shorthand way to judge someone's intelligence, achievement, and potential.

Other introductory strategies include:

- defining or clarifying terms
- listing revealing or startling facts
- sketching background or historical information.

As you read the essays in this book and in your other reading, notice the kinds of openings writers use. You may not always write the introduction first, but you'll come to it sooner or later.

The body

The second part of the essay is the longest and the most complex (it's not called the body for nothing), and in it you do a very specific job: you develop, explain, argue, or otherwise give detailed support for your thesis. It must fit together in a unified, logical, coherent way—like any healthy body, whose various systems must support one another.

Depending on your purpose and topic, the body may be organized in any number of ways. You'll see detailed examples of design strategies in subsequent chapters and readings. In brief, here are several methods or rhetorical tools that turn up repeatedly in the essay:

- *Narration*—telling a brief or extended story
- *Description*—writing to create a vivid impression by appealing to our sense of sight, smell, hearing, and so on
- *Using example or illustration*—providing samples, instances, or specific cases for support
- *Definition*—telling what something is or is not
- *Process analysis*—explaining the step-by-step way in which something happens or can be made to happen
- *Comparison and contrast*—pointing up meaningful similarities and differences
- *Division and classification*—dividing subjects into smaller parts, or grouping related things or ideas into useful categories
- *Cause-and-effect analysis*—showing relationships and links between events
- *Analogy and metaphor*—explaining one subject in terms of another.

Throughout these chapters we will refer to these methods or tools as *ways of opening subjects to investigation* and of *presenting material* to your readers. Remember that such rhetorical strategies are among many available to you, that they can be used alone or in combination with others, and that they can help shape sentences and paragraphs (including introductions and conclusions) as well as whole essays.

No matter what strategies you use, however, the body of any well-written essay will have these general characteristics:

- All the body paragraphs should *relate directly to the thesis*, by giving either background information or specific support. That is, each part of the body should fit the overall *unity* of the essay, keeping it focused on your main point.
- Body paragraphs should progress in a *logical, coherent pattern* that makes the thesis clearly and completely understandable to the reader. The flow of thought from one part to the next, in other words, should allow the reader to follow what you're saying without wondering what you mean.
- Body paragraphs should provide enough *specific, detailed evidence* (examples, illustration, explanation, or reasoning) to give the thesis *backing*—to give it substance or weight and to confirm it in the reader's mind.
- Body paragraphs should be *unified,* each limited in focus and content by a *topic sentence* (often the first or second sentence) stating the paragraph's main idea.
- Each new body paragraph should build upon the preceding one, with *key words* and clear *transitions* or connecting phrases that remind readers where they've been, where they are, and where they're going next.

Here's a sample middle paragraph from our essay on grading policy. Thesis: The grading system has several fundamental flaws. Notice that the paragraph begins with a *transitional* phrase that both connects it to the preceding one and reminds us of the subject ("Another major flaw . . ."); that a *topic sentence* controls the paragraph's focus (" . . . flaw in the grading system is inconsistent standards from class to class") and relates it directly to the thesis; and that the paragraph gives detailed *backing* to the topic.

Another major flaw in the grading system is inconsistent standards from class to class. An A in a math or computer science course may be much harder to achieve than the same grade in some of the "skate" courses we know about. It is possible, and even customary, for students to avoid difficult classes and maintain a higher grade-point average than they otherwise might. I talked to a random sample of fifteen students on my door floor, and twelve (or 80 percent) said they would avoid math and science classes because it was so hard to get above a C. Some of those students said they even liked math and science but couldn't afford the damage to their average.

The body of an essay grows from thoughtful interaction between author and material, and, like persons, each body is unique. Still, we have some strategies for organizing the middle of the essay, and we'll consider them in other chapters as we investigate essay aims.

The conclusion

Like every other part of the essay, the conclusion must support the thesis and flow naturally from the preceding paragraphs. The conclusion, however, also brings your discussion to a close, ties your essay together, and makes a final, forceful statement that confirms your point.

For conclusions we can use some of the same strategies as for introductions:

- Closing with a direct, blunt remark—often a restatement of the thesis in stronger language or a brief summary of the essay's subpoints. In argument, often, the thesis or claim is withheld until the conclusion, giving it special emphasis.
- Using a fitting or pointed quotation for emphasis.
- Ending with a question—one that the essay has implicitly answered or that captures the essay's overall direction.
- Concluding with an anecdote that illustrates the essay's content.

In essays that have an explanatory or argumentative aim, it sometimes makes sense to end with a *prediction* of what may happen—supported, of course, by what you have said:

Although some students are working to eliminate the inequities in the grading system, it seems likely that most of us will continue to accept the system as it is, without doing much to change it.

In persuasive essays, too, ending with a *recommendation*, which really may be the essay's essential point, can give your ideas added weight:

> It's time for all of us to stand up for reform of the grading system. We must petition the administration for uniform, published standards, and regular evaluation of departmental grading policies. Let's make the system fair for all of us.

The outline

Writers have different ways of visualizing their designs—of drawing a blueprint for the essay they intend to write. One of the best methods, and one every writer must learn to use, is the outline: a list of parts in order of their appearance, divided by major and minor ideas. We've already seen a brief, all-purpose essay outline in our discussion of essay structure. The outlines we develop should reflect both the general format and the specific pattern and content of our essays. Here is a possible outline for an essay supporting our "policy flaws" thesis:

I. Introduction: ¶ Anecdote—Illustration of problem
Thesis: The grading system has several fundamental flaws

II. Body:
   A. ¶ (Topic 1) First flaw: Subjective judgment among teachers
   B. ¶ (Topic 2) Second flaw: Inconsistent standards
   C. ¶ (Topic 3) Third flaw: Inadequate oversight by administration

III. Conclusion: ¶ Recommendation

Remember that the working outline is a *draft*, subject to change as you continue to write. It's a necessary part of getting started, but it's not the last word on your design. As new and better ideas come to you, revise your outline to reflect them. The outline and the essay that grows from it will continue to change—either a little or a lot—until finished writing.

Designing checklist

General format: All parts represented?

Specific outline: Each part designed for its task?

   Introduction: Gesture to reader and thesis statement?

   Body: Subtopics: All related to thesis?

   Support: Detailed, specific?

   Conclusion: Forceful? Supports and confirms whole
   essay?

Overall design: Unified by one focus?

              Logical pattern of development?

              Parts fit and flow together?

Five: Drafting

You've chosen a subject, narrowed it, developed enough material to give you a preliminary thesis, and designed a working outline. Now comes the moment you've been waiting for: your first draft.

Why not avoid all the groundwork and just *start* with the first draft? Some writers do prefer to start writing and see what happens, but sooner or later every essayist must come to a sense of the bigger picture, the essay's overall content and design, its thesis and the way in which that thesis should be developed. No matter what your individual writing habits, you'll arrive eventually at the stage when you first make a stab at the whole essay—beginning, middle, and end. With the plan that grew from your earlier work, however, you'll have better control over what you're doing, and you'll be likely to avoid wasting time on drafts that don't go anywhere because they have no guiding limits.

You may want to write your draft from start to finish, beginning with the introduction and writing through each body paragraph until you reach the conclusion. Or you may want to draft the body first and worry about the introduction and conclusion later. Whichever you choose, remember that a draft is an attempt to get something down in reasonable shape, not the finished version. For the moment, you may wish to worry less about grammar, mechanics, and spelling, knowing that you'll make repairs later. Try to write freely and openly, and as clearly as you can—but within the bounds you've established with your working thesis and outline. Stay focused on your essential aim, the point you want to make, and the specific development you'll give that point. If, as you write, clearer, more convincing ideas or details come to mind, use them. Put them in and don't worry yet if they make a perfect fit. Try to get a complete sense of your ideas and information, using the material you've selected from your earlier writing and adding to it.

Your goal in the drafting stage is to put together a working version of the whole essay—one that holds most of the ideas you think you'll need, in an arrangement that makes sense. This version will be the foundation for your later drafts, the necessary object that you'll continue to refine. Without it, you won't be able to approach a final, polished version of your work.

Drafting checklist

Plan: Makes sense overall?

Content: Includes all useful material in logical order?

Flow: Whole essay fits together in one coherent, continuous line of thought?

Six: Critical Reading and Rewriting

Each general stage in writing paves the way for the next. We need a first draft to react to—to evaluate and criticize—in order to see strengths and weaknesses: what to keep and what to change. You may see much in the first draft that you'll want to keep, but you'll also see things that no longer fit your plan or that need to be made smaller or larger, cut out, added, or said in a better way.

Revision isn't something you relegate to one stage in the procedure, however. Really, you've been revising all along, perhaps without being aware of it. Even in the midst of composing a sentence, we sort through countless possibilities, often unconsciously, looking for the right word, the right phrase, the right structure or order for our thoughts. Revision as we mean it here, coming after the first draft, is *conscious* rethinking and review of what you've written. It is *reading* as a clear-eyed critic of your own work, trying to see it objectively, as someone else might, and *rewriting* to make the improvements your critical judgment advises.

Before you begin rereading and rewriting, it helps to take some time off. If you can, put your work aside for a while and do something else. When you return to it, even after an hour or two, you'll be better able to see it with fresh eyes, to see its strengths and weaknesses plainly, and to perform the necessary surgery.

Because revision means *seeing again*, you'll want to take a good look at your work again on *every level:* the whole essay, the parts and paragraphs, the sentences and words.

The whole essay

First reread the entire draft, and ask yourself if its overall content, focus, and organization seem right. Does the essay make the *exact* point you want it to? Does the essay develop and support that point with appropriate subtopics? Do you begin the essay by appealing to the reader's interest and end with emphasis?

Write any new or revised material you need until you're satisfied. Don't rush. You may find yourself recomposing sentences or paragraphs, perhaps substituting whole new passages or parts.

Parts and paragraphs

When you've done all you want to with the overall essay, look again at each of the parts (introduction, body, conclusion) and the paragraphs that make them up. Is the introduction the most appealing gesture you can make to your readers? Does it give them reason to go on? Is your thesis stated clearly, concisely, accurately?

Do the body paragraphs develop the thesis in detail? Do the paragraphs flow in a straightforward, commonsense way? Can you read the topic sentences in the body paragraphs and follow the essay's line of thought? Do the paragraphs support their topic sentences without shifting to new or unrelated information?

Does your conclusion make a logical, natural closing? Does it reinforce the thesis in strong, memorable words?

Sentences and words

Is each sentence the best you can make it? Are the sentences completely clear, logical, accurate? Are they connected in a smooth, continuous line? Are they written without wasted words and unnecessary or trite phrases? Are the words as specific as possible? Are there words, phrases, or sentences that can be made even better, deleted, added, or moved to another spot?

Critical reading and rewriting checklist

The whole essay: Unified content and focus? Logical, coherent organization?

Parts and paragraphs: Effective introduction? Body paragraphs developed and detailed? Emphatic conclusion?

Sentences and words: Clear? Specific? Concise? Accurate?

Seven: The Final Draft

At last, when your essay is as nearly complete and as well designed as you can make it, you'll execute the final, finished manuscript. You may find that even at this stage you're still revising—clarifying here, adding information there, cutting needless language somewhere else. As you prepare the final typescript or computer printout, you'll use a dictionary and an English handbook to check spelling, grammar, punctuation and mechanics, and style—all the nuts and bolts—one more time, proofreading your work so that it is as clean and correct as you can make it, absolutely the best you can do. You've invested a lot of effort in your essay. Now it's time to present it to the world.

Final-draft checklist

Spelling: All doubts satisfied?

Grammar: Sentence fragments? Comma splices? Tenses? Agreement?

Punctuation and mechanics: Commas? Semicolons? Apostrophes? Quotation marks? Capitalization? Abbreviations?

Style: Direct? Smooth? Economical? Honest?

Reading and Writing

Becoming an Apprentice

Certainly one of the best ways to become a better writer is by being a more careful and attentive reader—by really taking the time to listen to a writer's words. Studying the works of others helps us understand not only the concrete results of the writing process, the goals toward which we all work, but also that good writing is well within our grasp.

Students of any undertaking—whether in athletics, the arts, the sciences, or the professions—learn by observings others' behavior and by emulating it. We may imitate the styles of favorite musicians or sports figures, or we may model ourselves, in part, after those we admire. Likewise, as we read essays by other writers, observing how they've approached their subjects, we learn to practice the strategies of design, development, and style that will contribute to our own works. We learn the ways of good writing by *apprenticing* ourselves to others, both students and professionals, who've mastered it before us.

As an apprentice writer, then, take the opportunity to learn from these teachers. Have a *conversation** with them. Read slowly, read aloud, and stop to write your questions, comments, and observations. Join them as they explore and reveal their subjects. Notice how they establish limits; appeal to your interest and curiosity; set forth their ideas clearly and directly; develop those ideas in a logical, orderly pattern; support them with detailed discussion, explanation, or argument; and conclude them with emphatic language. Read and reread these essays—not as a passive audience but as an *active observer and fellow writer,* with a questioning mind and an energetic desire to learn. You'll find that these writers have much to say to you. As you watch and listen, you'll find yourself wanting to join the conversation—to write. *Wanting* to write, and wanting to join the community of people who write well, that will provide the spark for your essays and for your continued, self-directed writing education.

For easy reference, here is a final checklist for the essay-writing process, from task to finished draft:

*Thanks to Robert DiYanni for this idea.

Writing-process checklist

The task

General aim(s): To express, inform, explain, persuade, entertain?

Subject: Narrowed to manageable size?

Reader: Common ground of interest? Reader's needs?

Estimated length: Brief, moderate, extended?

Specific purpose: Assigned? Self-determined?

Exploring and collecting

Open writing: Ideas, connections, possibilities, problems?

Topic: Moving toward a specific angle on the subject?

Subtopics: Looking for good support and development?

Material: Solid facts and details? Enough depth?

Finding your thesis

A good working idea that focuses my material?

Suits the essay's main purpose?

Makes a clear, meaningful point?

Commits the essay to a specific line of thought?

Designing

General format: All parts represented?

Specific outline: Each part designed for its task?

   Introduction: Gesture to reader and thesis statement?

   Body: Subtopics related to thesis?

   Support: Detailed, specific?

   Conclusion: Forceful? Supports and confirms whole essay?

Overall design: Unified by one focus? Logical pattern of development? Parts fit and flow together?

Drafting

Plan: Makes sense overall?

Content: Includes all useful material in logical order?

Flow: Whole essay fits together in one coherent, continuous line of thought?

Writing-process checklist (*continued*)

Critical reading and rewriting

The whole essay: Unified content and focus? Logical organization?

Parts and paragraphs: Effective introduction? Body paragraphs developed and detailed? Emphatic conclusion?

Sentences and words: Clear? Specific? Concise? Accurate?

The final draft

Spelling: All doubts satisfied?

Grammar: Sentence fragments? Comma splices? Tenses? Agreement?

Punctuation and mechanics: Commas? Semicolons? Apostrophes? Quotation marks? Capitalization? Abbreviations?

Style: Direct? Smooth? Economical? Honest?

– 2 –

> # Writing to Express or Reflect
>
> ## Shaping Thoughts, Feelings, Experiences

The Expressive Aim

Throughout this book we will see a range of essay aims—writing to inform, explain, argue, criticize, and persuade. All these purposes, though they may employ differing strategies, share one goal: to accomplish specific kinds of practical work. Such aims control, or greatly influence, much of the prose we see in everyday life, and each kind of writing can be evaluated according to how well it achieves its purpose.

Practical prose designed to accomplish practical work has an essential place in the world of writing. Probably it dominates that world—at least in education, business, the sciences, and the news media—and the educated writer certainly must master it. But practical prose is not the *whole* world. Other kinds of writing also have a part in our everyday life, and are just as valuable. One of these is the writing we do to express ourselves—whether privately, as in journals or diaries, or publicly, in personal essays—in order to give shape to our thoughts, feelings, and experiences. We'll look now at expressive essay writing as a foundation for the aims that follow.

What is expressive writing? How is it different from other kinds of prose?

When we write to express ourselves, it is usually because we feel a strong impulse to say something, to "get it down on paper," to vent powerful feelings or record impressions, ideas, or moments that seem important to us. Although such writing may also become informative, explanatory, critical, or persuasive, our main goal isn't to deliver a commodity to the reader. Rather, expressive prose is focused more on the writer, on the self or the self's interaction with the world; it puts the writer in the *foreground* rather than the background. All essays are somewhat personal, of course: they show us the unique encounter between writer and subject. In expressive or reflective essays, however, our thoughts, emotions, or experiences *are* the subject. We write about ourselves directly, and our essays are directly self-revealing.

We may think of expressive writing in two ways: private or public. The private words that we commit to our journals or in letters to friends are not intended for public consumption; they are among our most intimate possessions. Although we often use private writing for personal matters, self-expression needn't *remain* private. In fact, some of the most enduring prose in our culture is expressive writing designed for a broad or public audience. In autobiography, memoir, and personal or reflective essays, people in all walks of life (not only professional writers) express themselves to interested, curious, or sympathetic readers; they shape private matters into suitable public forms.

Building a bridge between the private and public worlds isn't always easy. We risk a larger part of ourselves when we address personal subjects; we are more than reporter, instructor, advocate, or critic. Instead, we speak directly as ourselves, about ourselves or about the things that deeply interest us. We must be confident that what we say matters, and that if we say it with honesty and conviction our reader will acknowledge its value.

All good writing must be honest; our readers must know that we're telling the truth as best we can. In expressive writing, however, it's essential to be honest not only with your reader but with yourself. Writing with an expressive aim means trying to uncover what you *really* think and feel—though it may be painful, unsettling, unconventional. It means choosing subjects that compel us to express ourselves, that need working out. We say what we need to say, not what we think we *should* say. We acknowledge how complex our thoughts, emotions, or experiences are—that our feelings may be mixed, our ideas at odds with each other. Being frank with ourselves will help us compose essays that are honest, personal, and compelling to our readers.

Expression in a Paragraph

In this example, author Maya Angelou voices her childhood sense of hopelessness and fury at the cruelty of the white world. Notice Angelou's blunt, forthright honesty; her expression of painful emotions; her powerful, visual language. Here is expressive writing at its purest.

> It was awful to be Negro and have no control over my life. It was brutal to be young and already trained to sit quietly and listen to charges brought against my color with no chance of defense. We should all be dead. I thought I should like to see us all dead, one on top of the other. A pyramid of flesh with the whitefolks on the bottom, as the broad base, then the Indians with their silly tomahawks and teepees and wigwams and treaties, the Negroes with their mops and recipes and cotton sacks and spirituals sticking out of their mouths. The Dutch children should all stumble in their wooden shoes and break their necks. The French should choke to death on the Louisiana Purchase (1803) while silkworms ate all the Chinese with their stupid pigtails. As a species, we were an abomination. All of us.
>
> —Maya Angelou, *I Know Why the Caged Bird Sings**

Expressive Strategies

Writing to express or reflect means engaging the creative process face-to-face. We are the primary source of material. Through memory, we recall vital details in our lives; we consider ideas and beliefs that matter deeply to us. We explore and collect; we find a focus; we plan a design; we write, think, shape, seeking clarity, coherence, structure, and emphasis. As we write, moreover, we'll want to use methods or devices that can help us express ourselves vividly and concretely—so that our readers will feel the full worth of our thoughts, emotions, and experiences.

Many of the strategies we'll see in later chapters are equally well suited to expressive writing. Among the most useful are those listed here.

*(New York: Random House, 1969): 176.

Narration: Telling a Story

Often, one of the best ways to develop your expressive point is by telling a story, either about yourself (adopting a *subjective* point of view) or about someone else (the *objective* stance). You can use narration as your overall design for the essay, or you can combine it with other methods of development.

Sometimes, especially when you're trying to capture the *feeling* of an experience (the first time you fell in love, say, or your most frightening or embarrassing moment), your focus will be on the story itself, and your whole essay will follow that shape, with a beginning, middle, and end. Perhaps falling in love that first time was also your most frightening experience; if so, your story should *illustrate* that idea. Just as often, however, your main point will be unstated or *implied.* That is, you may tell a story for its own sake, because it's a good story or because it expresses a number of ideas, or themes, without being limited to just one.

Stories often have built-in tension or suspense that makes us want to keep reading or listening. When developing an expressive essay with narration, then, don't let the cat out of the bag too soon. Without confusing us, try to keep your readers wondering how your story will turn out.

Narration usually uses a time-line or chronological structure, with the story unfolding from beginning to end. Other narrative patterns are possible, however: revealing the end, then telling the story from the beginning; interrupting the narrative with flashbacks to earlier moments; opening with a dramatic scene from the middle, then starting at the beginning. As in any form of writing, of course, narrative must be unified and logical. Include only relevant details or dialogue, and make sure that everything you say has a job to do.

Narration also can be a useful way to develop shorter parts of an essay, even if the whole design isn't that of a story. You can introduce your essay with a brief narrative passage, or *anecdote,* use narration in a body paragraph for *support* or *illustration,* or *conclude* with narrative for emphasis.

Whether your narration is brief or extended, however, remember that narrative should give us the *texture* of experience—specific details about real life, people, places, events, and passing time. You can make your narrative more lifelike with concrete, detailed *description,* and by including individual *scenes* and *dialogue* that dramatize events. Here, in a passage from a journalist's autobiography, the author describes his start in the profession at age eight.

With my load of magazines I headed toward Belleville Avenue. That's where the people were. There were two filling stations at the intersection with Union Avenue, as well as an A&P, a fruit stand, a bakery, a barber shop, Zuccarelli's drugstore, and a diner shaped like a railroad car. For several hours I made myself highly visible, shifting position now and then from corner to corner, from shop window to shop window, to make sure everyone could see the heavy black lettering on the canvas bag that said THE SATURDAY EVENING POST. When the angle of the light indicated it was suppertime, I walked back to the house.

"How many did you sell, Buddy?" my mother asked.

"None."

"Where did you go?"

"The corner of Belleville and Union Avenues."

"What did you do?"

"Stood on the corner waiting for somebody to buy a *Saturday Evening Post.*"

"You just stood there?"

"Didn't sell a single one."

"For God's sake, Russell!"

Uncle Allen intervened. "I've been thinking about it for some time," he said, "and I've about decided to take the *Post* regularly. Put me down as a regular customer." I handed him a magazine and he paid me a nickel. It was the first nickel I earned.

—Russell Baker, *Growing Up**

Baker might have written, instead: "On my first day selling magazines, I stood around on the corner but found no customers and went home." That's what happened, of course, but readers don't see or hear anything in that flat statement. By *showing* the moment as a detailed scene, and by letting us *hear* his mother's exasperation and his uncle's sympathy, Baker lets us relive the experience with him.

Dramatizing portions of your narrative with scenes and dialogue can make your experiences come alive on the page. A couple of guiding hints, however: Choose moments that are particularly outstanding, exciting, or in some way essential to the story; and avoid scenes in which little happens, or in which people make small talk ("How are you today?" I said. "Fine," she replied. "That's good," I said.) Likewise, make sure your dialogue does useful work—that it reveals someone's character or response to a situation, or otherwise

*(New York: Congdon & Weed, 1982): 13.

helps to move the story forward. And though it's easier said than done, try to make your conversations sound realistic. People usually talk in fragments, sometimes interrupting each other, often speaking more about what's on their own minds than about what the other person is saying.

Description: Appealing to the Senses

Descriptive writing appeals to our senses, lets us see, hear, touch, taste, and smell with specific, vivid, concrete language. You'll find writing effective narration almost impossible without it. Telling what happened may give us the bare bones of a story, but descriptive language adds flesh to those bones; it helps us to re-create experience by putting the reader in the writer's shoes—sometimes inside his or her skin.

Here's a brief narrative passage with descriptive language omitted. The author, essayist E. B. White, tells about taking his son fishing, and feeling that he is reliving a moment from his own childhood, when he fished the same lake with his father:

> We went fishing the first morning. I . . . saw the dragonfly alight on the tip of my rod. . . . It was the arrival of this fly that convinced me beyond any doubt that everything was as it always has been, that the years were a mirage and that there had been no years. . . . The small waves were the same . . . and the boat was the same boat. . . .

Now here's the passage with White's original descriptive language restored (in italics):

> We went fishing the first morning. I *felt the same damp moss covering the worms in the bait can,* and saw the dragonfly alight on the tip of my rod *as it hovered a few inches from the surface of the water.* It was the arrival of this fly that convinced me beyond any doubt that everything was as it always had been, that the years were a mirage and that there had been no years. The small waves were the same, *chucking the rowboat under the chin as we fished at anchor,* and the boat was the same boat, *the same color green and the ribs broken in the same places, and under the floorboards the same fresh-water leavings and debris—the dead hellgrammite, the wisps of*

moss, the rusty discarded fishhook, the dried blood from yesterday's catch.

—E. B. White, "Once More to the Lake"*

Notice how much more *expressive* the second (original) version is. Instead of merely reporting that he felt no time had passed, White describes the moment in sensory detail—feeling with his hands "the same damp moss covering the worms in the bait can," seeing with his eyes the "rusty discarded fishhook, the dried blood from yesterday's catch." And as we read, we too feel and see, with the hands and eyes of our imagination.

Description, of course, needn't be used only to aid narration. It can stand on its own as an expressive strategy when you want to give readers the sense of persons, places, things—or personal feelings about them.

Like narration, descriptive language can be *objective* or *subjective*, that is, slanted toward either an impartial view, or one that stresses the writer's unique perceptions. In expressive writing you're likely to use both kinds—objective description for necessary information ("the subway car was filled with commuters, the aisle blocked by passengers standing shoulder to shoulder"), and subjective description for self-expression ("and when the lights went out, I felt buried alive, surrounded by growling, shadowy human forms in an airless grave"). Subjective description, in fact, will be one of your handiest tools in expressive prose.

Structure and Style

Expressive writing may be more *informal* than some of the other kinds of prose, in both design and language. Expressive essays sometimes depart from a strict thesis-and-support format, playing more freely with the possibilities of the essay form. Likewise, the kind of language we use in expressive writing may be more flexible or wideranging, including slang words and phrases, a conversational tone and style, or humor. (For more on humor writing, see Chapter 8.)

Such informality can help us to give a more personal account of our feelings and experiences, as in our private writing in letters, journals, or diaries. Remember, however, that expressive writing, like all good writing for a public audience, must be *controlled* and *focused*.

*Essays of E. B. White (New York: Harper & Row, 1977): 198–199.

You'll want your expressive essays to be unified, coherent, complete, and polished, despite their informality—compelling reading not only for you, but for your audience as well.

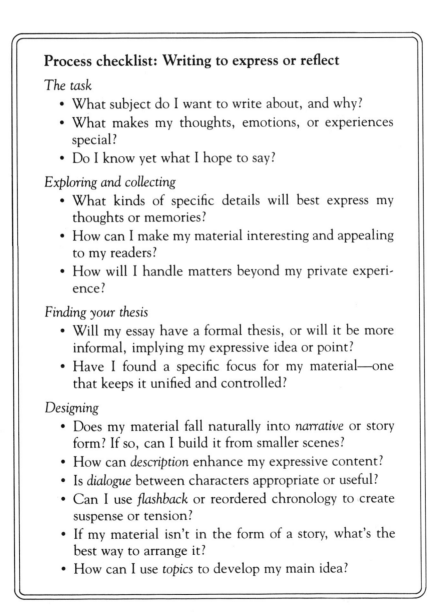

Process checklist: Writing to express or reflect

The task
- What subject do I want to write about, and why?
- What makes my thoughts, emotions, or experiences special?
- Do I know yet what I hope to say?

Exploring and collecting
- What kinds of specific details will best express my thoughts or memories?
- How can I make my material interesting and appealing to my readers?
- How will I handle matters beyond my private experience?

Finding your thesis
- Will my essay have a formal thesis, or will it be more informal, implying my expressive idea or point?
- Have I found a specific focus for my material—one that keeps it unified and controlled?

Designing
- Does my material fall naturally into *narrative* or story form? If so, can I build it from smaller scenes?
- How can *description* enhance my expressive content?
- Is *dialogue* between characters appropriate or useful?
- Can I use *flashback* or reordered chronology to create suspense or tension?
- If my material isn't in the form of a story, what's the best way to arrange it?
- How can I use *topics* to develop my main idea?

Process checklist: Writing to express or reflect (*continued*)

Drafting
- Am I satisfied with the overall shape of my working draft? If not, how might I make it clearer or more effective?
- Does it illustrate or support my stated or implied thesis?
- Have I discovered useful new material for my essay?

Critical reading and rewriting
- Have I reviewed all the parts of the essay—introduction, body, conclusion?
- Can I expand, revise, or delete material for more clarity and emphasis?
- Have I used concrete language and detail?

The final draft
- Have I polished and proofread my essay for spelling, punctuation, mechanics?

In the readings that follow, notice how the writers shape their expressive or reflective interests; how they involve us in material that may be quite private or personal; and how they make their ideas, feelings, and experiences compelling for a wide audience.

— Adam Liptak —

Adam Liptak is a former staff member of The New York Times. *Born in 1960 in Stamford, Connecticut, he studied at Columbia University and Yale Law School. He has been a college intern at* The New Yorker *and* Business Week, *a* New York Times *copyboy, and a summer associate in the legal department of that newspaper. He has published articles in* Vanity Fair, Business Week, Publisher's Weekly, *and* Rolling Stone.

Playing Air Guitar

In an essay from the "About Men" series in The New York Times Magazine, *Liptak here expresses a private side of himself—but one he no doubt shares with almost everyone who likes rock music. In this essay he says something, too, about the place of rock in our lives, and about growing older with an undiminished craving to play loud music "first thing in the morning."*

1   When I hear a song on the radio that I really like, or that used to be a favorite, I sometimes dance around a little bit and pretend to play guitar. I play air guitar. It probably looks dumb to an outsider, but to the man who plays, it is quite serious—a primal and private dance. Men identify with the great rock guitarists the way they do with sports legends, and we mimic their gestures and attitudes in an instinctive quest for grace.

2   What you do is: extend your left arm sort of crookedly, faking chord changes on the neck of an invisible electric guitar, rhythmically. Your right hand strums. Your head bobs. Your hips twitch. A nearby mirror reflects your grimaces. There is loud music on.

3   When I was a teen-ager, I used to play all the time. The impulse arose at odd moments. Just walking around, in an empty, late-afternoon school hallway, say, I might be seized by the inner music, drop to a crouch and let loose a devastating solo, the whole thing over in 10 seconds. A favorite song on the car radio, I am embarrassed to recount, could make me take my hands from the wheel and imitate a Stones riff—stopping only to keep my father's car from drifting into the next lane.

Certainly air guitar was handy at parties, where by stiffening and 4
lowering the arms a little it passed for dancing. Countless men still
dance this way.

But the true essence of air guitar is intensely personal and a little 5
embarrassing, a strange conflation of fantasy and desire. I remember
summer dusks in anticipation of parties—this at a time when a party
was a promise of wonder, of a life transformed—climbing out of the
shower, the evening's first beer lodged precariously on the soap tray,
and hearing the perfect song. Here was pleasure: a long swig, a half-
turn on the volume knob, the hallucinatory rush of adrenaline, followed by mindless dancing around in front of the fogged-up mirror.

As with anything, it is possible to play air guitar well or poorly, 6
but it has nothing at all to do with being able to play guitar, which is in
fact a drawback. One is after an image, a look; technical proficiency is
distracting. The choice of role model is important, but what one
copies is stance, attitude and character. Virtuosity is for the most part
irrelevant. Only the electric guitar counts; there is no such thing as
playing acoustic air guitar. Years of practice help, and so does an
appreciation for loud, dumb music.

I am certain that the success of the movie "Risky Business" had a 7
great deal to do with the scene in which Tom Cruise bounds about the
living room in a shirt, socks and underpants. His parents are out of
town, of course. He turns up the stereo and indulges in a whole array
of rock-star moves and prancing.

Talking with friends afterward, I discovered that our enjoyment 8
of the scene—of its celebratory tone—was tempered by an uneasy
feeling of having somehow been found out. A kind of reverse identification had taken place, and we saw ourselves not as guitar heroes but
as slightly absurd kids from the suburbs. This shock of recognition was
followed by a shudder.

In college, I played less often but more openly. Sometimes, at the 9
end of a beery night, my friends and I would put together a whole
band—it was always the Stones, and I always wanted to be Keith
Richards—and clamber up onto the furniture and play, each of us with
his eyes closed, in a way alone. It sounds like a silly and slightly
aggressive scene, and it was.

At the same time, this was a way men could dance with other 10
men without compromising their version of masculinity. At parties,
dancing with women, my best friend and I might step away and take a
moment to jam, leaning on each other this way and that, falling over
and playing incredible dual solos on our invisible Fenders. The women
we abandoned were generally not amused.

We joked about it, air guitar being a perfect subject for my genera- 11
tion's mode of discourse, which is a mix of the intimate and the ironic.
Here we could say just what we meant, confessing to the odd habit in a
deadpan way, so that no listener could be quite sure if we really meant
it. Or we could go beyond our own experience—admit to playing
naked on city rooftops, say—and then double back and make fun of
anyone taken in or, worse, who admitted to doing the same thing.

I have noticed lately the attempt to institutionalize air guitar, in 12
the form of "concerts" at colleges, "lip-sync" contests at certain night-
clubs in the boroughs of New York and on television shows. There is
something peculiarly American about making the intimate public and
competitive, something reassuring at first but in the long run repulsive.

This is not to say that an air guitar contest is without humor. To 13
see four or five people aping the movements of an entire band with the
appropriate music in the background can be hilarious. An ensemble
called Men Without Instruments, at Princeton University, is funny
even to contemplate.

I don't know if teen-agers today find in Prince and Bruce 14
Springsteen adequate idols. I suspect they do. And I suppose they
know the moves better than we ever did, thanks to music videos.

These days, I find myself at some emotional distance from most 15
of the popular music I hear, and going to rock concerts has lost its
appeal. I still put on loud music first thing in the morning, though,
loud enough to hear in the shower, which is down the hall from my
stereo. And sometimes, as I start to dress, barefoot, my shirt unbut-
toned and my tie loose around my neck, I play a couple of notes if it
feels right. And then, refreshed, I finish dressing and go to work.

Questions for Study and Discussion

Meaning and Purpose

1. What is it about playing air guitar that is so appealing or exhilarating?
   Why do you think Liptak portrays playing air guitar as an exclusively
   male pastime?
2. How much does Liptak risk embarrassing himself in writing about this
   secret passion? Would he have been as likely to write about it in
   earlier years, when it was a bigger part of his life? Why or why not?
3. In paragraph 11, Liptak refers to air guitar as "a perfect subject for my
   generation's mode of discourse, which is a mix of the intimate and the
   ironic." What does he mean?

Strategy and Audience

1. How is Liptak's essay organized? How do his introduction and conclusion fit together, and what principle helps him to structure the body of the essay? Why does he choose this structure?
2. What role does description have in Liptak's essay? Find examples of description that seem particularly fresh or vivid to you.
3. Does Liptak's essay appeal only to a male audience? What might female readers find useful or interesting in his words?

Style and Language

1. Throughout the essay, Liptak's style mixes abstract language ("we mimic their gestures and attitudes in an instinctive quest for grace") and concrete detail ("the evening's first beer lodged precariously on the soap tray"). Why does he employ this range of diction? What does each kind of language allow Liptak to express about his subject?
2. Vocabulary: primal (paragraph 1); conflation, hallucinatory (5); proficiency, virtuosity (6).

Writing Ideas

1. Write an expressive essay about one of your own current or past secret passions—singing along with a favorite band, being obsessed with a screen or television star, or in some way pretending to be someone or something other than the person you really are.
2. Write an expressive-reflective essay about something that used to be a very big part of your life but which you've since outgrown. What was it about the pastime that was so compelling, and why have you fallen away from it? Are there times when you miss it or feel you've lost something you can't get back?

— Maxine Hong Kingston —

Maxine Hong Kingston has devoted much of her writing career to the conflicts of living in a divided culture. The daughter of Chinese immigrants, Kingston was born in California in 1940 and grew up among other Chinese in Stockton, learning English when she attended school. A graduate of the University of California at Berkeley, she taught high school in her home state and later moved to Hawaii. Her two books of autobiography, The Woman Warrior: Memories of a Girlhood Among Ghosts *(1976), and* China Men *(1980), won critical acclaim and wide readership. Her most recent book is a novel,* Tripmaster Monkey: His Fake Book *(1989), set in California in the 1960s.*

A Shame of Silence

In this excerpt from The Woman Warrior, *Kingston recalls her childhood frustrations at being asked to speak in English, her second language. Kingston's prose is infused with an expressive, poetic power that draws much from her ability to re-create past moments with vivid detail and an acute memory for the feelings these moments produced.*

When I went to kindergarten and had to speak English for the first time, I became silent. A dumbness—a shame—still cracks my voice in two, even when I want to say "hello" casually, or ask an easy question in front of the check-out counter, or ask directions of a bus driver. I stand frozen, or I hold up the line with the complete, grammatical sentence that comes squeaking out at impossible length. "What did you say?" says the cab driver, or "Speak up," so I have to perform again, only weaker the second time. A telephone call makes my throat bleed and takes up that day's courage. It spoils my day with self-disgust when I hear my broken voice come skittering out into the open. It makes people wince to hear it. I'm getting better, though. Recently I asked the postman for special-issue stamps; I've waited since childhood for postmen to give me some of their own accord. I am making progress, a little every day.

My silence was thickest—total—during the three years that I covered my school paintings with black paint. I painted layers of black over houses and flowers and suns, and when I drew on the blackboard, I put a layer of chalk on top. I was making a stage curtain, and it was the moment before the curtain parted or rose. The teachers called my parents to school, and I saw they had been saving my pictures, curling and cracking, all alike and black. The teachers pointed to the pictures and looked serious, talked seriously too, but my parents did not understand English. ("The parents and teachers of criminals were executed," said my father.) My parents took the pictures home. I spread them out (so black and full of possibilities) and pretended the curtains were swinging open, flying up, one after another, sunlight underneath, mighty operas.

During the first silent year I spoke to no one at school, did not   3
ask before going to the lavatory, and flunked kindergarten. My sister also said nothing for three years, silent in the playground and silent at lunch. There were other quiet Chinese girls not of our family, but most of them got over it sooner than we did. I enjoyed the silence. At first it did not occur to me I was supposed to talk or to pass kindergarten. I talked at home and to one or two of the Chinese kids in class. I made motions and even made some jokes. I drank out of a toy saucer when the water spilled out of the cup, and everybody laughed, pointing at me, so I did it some more. I didn't know that Americans don't drink out of saucers.

I liked the Negro students (Black Ghosts) best because they   4
laughed the loudest and talked to me as if I were a daring talker too. One of the Negro girls had her mother coil braids over her ears Shanghai-style like mine; we were Shanghai twins except that she was covered with black like my paintings. Two Negro kids enrolled in Chinese school, and the teachers gave them Chinese names. Some Negro kids walked me to school and home, protecting me from the Japanese kids, who hit me and chased me and stuck gum in my ears. The Japanese kids were noisy and tough. They appeared one day in kindergarten, released from concentration camp, which was a tic-tac-toe mark, like barbed wire, on the map.

It was when I found out I had to talk that school became a   5
misery, that the silence became a misery. I did not speak and felt bad each time that I did not speak. I read aloud in first grade, though, and heard the barest whisper with little squeaks come out of my throat. "Louder," said the teacher, who scared the voice away again. The other Chinese girls did not talk either, so I knew the silence had to do with being a Chinese girl.

Reading out loud was easier than speaking because we did not   6
have to make up what to say, but I stopped often, and the teacher would think I'd gone quiet again. I could not understand "I." The Chinese "I" has seven strokes, intricacies. How could the American "I," assuredly wearing a hat like the Chinese, have only three strokes,

the middle so straight? Was it out of politeness that this writer left off strokes the way a Chinese has to write her own name small and crooked? No, it was not politeness; "I" is a capital and "you" is lower-case. I stared at that middle line and waited so long for its black center to resolve into tight strokes and dots that I forgot to pronounce it. The other troublesome word was "here," no strong consonant to hang on to, and so flat, when "here" is two mountainous ideographs. The teacher, who had already told me every day how to read "I" and "here," put me in the low corner under the stairs again, where the noisy boys usually sat.

When my second grade class did a play, the whole class went to the auditorium except the Chinese girls. The teacher, lovely and Hawaiian, should have understood about us, but instead left us behind in the classroom. Our voices were too soft or nonexistent, and our parents never signed the permission slips anyway. They never signed anything unnecessary. We opened the door a crack and peeked out, but closed it again quickly. One of us (not me) won every spelling bee, though.

I remember telling the Hawaiian teacher, "We Chinese can't sing 'land where our fathers died.' " She argued with me about politics, while I meant because of curses. But how can I have that memory when I couldn't talk? My mother says that we, like the ghosts, have no memories.

After American school, we picked up our cigar boxes, in which we had arranged books, brushes, and an inkbox neatly, and went to Chinese school, from 5:00 to 7:30 P.M. There we chanted together, voices rising and falling, loud and soft, some boys shouting, everybody reading together, reciting together and not alone with one voice. When we had a memorization test, the teacher let each of us come to his desk and say the lesson to him privately, while the rest of the class practiced copying or tracing. Most of the teachers were men. The boys who were so well behaved in the American school played tricks on them and talked back to them. The girls were not mute. They screamed and yelled during recess, when there were no rules; they had fistfights. Nobody was afraid of children hurting themselves or of children hurting school property. The glass doors to the red and green balconies with the gold joy symbols were left wide open so that we could run out and climb the fire escapes. We played capture-the-flag in the auditorium, where Sun Yat-sen and Chiang Kai-shek's pictures hung at the back of the stage, the Chinese flag on their left and the American flag on their right. We climbed the teak ceremonial chairs and made flying leaps off the stage. One flag headquarters was behind the glass door and the other on stage right. Our feet drummed on the hollow stage. During recess the teachers locked themselves up in their office with the shelves of books, copybooks, inks from China. They drank tea and warmed their hands at a stove. There was no play supervision. At recess we had the school to ourselves, and also we could roam as far as we could go—downtown, Chinatown stores, home—as long as we returned before the bell rang.

At exactly 7:30 the teacher again picked up the brass bell that sat   10
on his desk and swung it over our heads, while we charged down the stairs, our cheering magnified in the stairwell. Nobody had to line up.

Not all of the children who were silent at American school   11
found voice at Chinese school. One new teacher said each of us had to get up and recite in front of the class, who was to listen. My sister and I had memorized the lesson perfectly. We said it to each other at home, one chanting, one listening. The teacher called on my sister to recite first. It was the first time a teacher had called on the second-born to go first. My sister was scared. She glanced at me and looked away; I looked down at my desk. I hoped that she could do it because if she could, then I would have to. She opened her mouth and a voice came out that wasn't a whisper, but it wasn't a proper voice either. I hoped that she would not cry, fear breaking up her voice like twigs underfoot. She sounded as if she were trying to sing though weeping and strangling. She did not pause or stop to end the embarrassment. She kept going until she said the last word, and then she sat down. When it was my turn, the same voice came out, a crippled animal running on broken legs. You could hear splinters in my voice, bones rubbing jagged against one another. I was loud, though. I was glad I didn't whisper.

Questions for Study and Discussion

Meaning and Purpose

1. Why did Kingston have trouble speaking when she first went to school? Why did she feel ashamed? How has her attitude toward this problem changed over the years?
2. What are some other especially strong pressures or differences Kingston felt as a young person growing up in a foreign culture?
3. What sense of time, place, or social setting grows from this recollection? From what you know about American history, how important is this background to the emotions and events Kingston is expressing?

Strategy and Audience

1. Kingston wants us to feel her experiences powerfully. Point out how she uses narration, dialogue, and scene setting to make her memories memorable for us.
2. Descriptive language is also valuable for expressive prose. Is Kingston's description mainly objective, subjective, or a mixture? Find examples to support your view.
3. How did you respond to this memoir? If you felt sympathy for the author, can you say why? If not, why not? Which passages had the greatest effect on you?

Style and Language

1. Throughout her work, Kingston employs a lyrical, metaphorical, poetic style: "A dumbness—a shame—still cracks my voice in two. . . ." What is the effect of such language? Can you find other examples in "Silence"?
2. Like all other good writers, however, Kingston varies her style, and is as much at home with the plain, blunt statement as with poetry. Find some sentences that are especially clear, straightforward, elegant— expressed in plain, literal language.

Writing Ideas

1. Recall a period in your youth when you felt out of place, awkward, afraid, embarrassed. Try to pinpoint some specific, concrete moments that really illustrate what you were going through. Think about how you coped and what finally happened. Then write an expressive essay capturing your feelings and struggles. (Remember your audience: your private pains must have some meaning for your readers. In Kingston's essay, for example, she speaks for all who feel themselves to be strangers.)
2. As above, recall a period of test or trial when you were especially challenged. Try to render the experience dramatically as a story or memoir. (See the first student essay in this chapter, "The Score," for an example.)

— James Baldwin —

James Baldwin was one of this country's most distinguished men of letters—a novelist, short-story writer, essayist, autobiographer, playwright, and screenwriter. Born in New York in 1924, Baldwin grew up in Harlem, the oldest of nine children, and spent his teen years as a preacher (his father was a clergyman). He graduated from DeWitt Clinton High School and worked odd jobs for several years before publishing his first novel, Go Tell It on the Mountain, *in 1953. Baldwin had a varied and controversial career, and wrote such enduring works as* Notes of a Native Son *(1955);* Nobody Knows My Name *(1961);* Another Country *(1962);* The Fire Next Time *(1963);* Tell Me How Long the Train's Been Gone *(1968);* Just Above My Head *(1980);* The Evidence of Things Not Seen *and* The Price of the Ticket *(both 1985). Long an impassioned advocate of racial equality, Baldwin was influential in bringing attention to the plight of blacks in the United States. One critic said of him that "Many of Baldwin's best insights illuminate our national psychology," and that some of his works are of "rare distinction in contemporary American writing." He died in 1987.*

Autobiographical Notes

In this classic essay, the introduction to Notes of a Native Son, *Baldwin reflects on his past, on being a black writer, and on contemporary society in the mid-1950s. Baldwin's language is particularly expressive; read him slowly and carefully to fully appreciate this powerful voice.*

I was born in Harlem thirty-one years ago. I began plotting novels at about the time I learned to read. The story of my childhood is the usual bleak fantasy, and we can dismiss it with the restrained observation that I certainly would not consider living it again. In those days my mother was given to the exasperating and mysterious habit of having babies. As they were born, I took them over with one hand and held a book with the other. The children probably suffered, though they have since been kind enough to deny it, and in this way I read *Uncle Tom's Cabin* and *A Tale of Two Cities* over and over and over again; in this way, in fact, I read just about everything I could get my hands on—except the Bible, probably because it was the only book I was encouraged to read. I must also confess that I wrote—a great deal—and my first professional triumph, in any case, the first effort of mine to be seen in print, occurred at the age of twelve or thereabouts, when a short story I had written about the Spanish revolution won some sort of prize in an extremely short-lived church newspaper. I remember the story was censored by the lady editor, though I don't remember why, and I was outraged.

Also wrote plays, and songs, for one of which I received a letter   2
of congratulations from Mayor La Guardia, and poetry, about which the less said, the better. My mother was delighted by all these goings-on, but my father wasn't; he wanted me to be a preacher. When I was fourteen I became a preacher, and when I was seventeen I stopped. Very shortly thereafter I left home. For God knows how long I struggled with the world of commerce and industry—I guess they would say they struggled with *me*—and when I was about twenty-one I had enough done of a novel to get a Saxton Fellowship. When I was twenty-two the fellowship was over, the novel turned out to be unsalable, and I started waiting on tables in a Village restaurant and writing book reviews—mostly, as it turned out, about the Negro problem, concerning which the color of my skin made me automatically an expert. Did another book, in company with photographer Theodore Pelatowski, about the storefront churches in Harlem. This book met exactly the same fate as my first—fellowship, but no sale. (It was a Rosenwald Fellowship.) By the time I was twenty-four I had decided to stop reviewing books about the Negro problem—which, by this time, was only slightly less horrible in print than it was in life—and I packed my bags and went to France, where I finished, God knows how, *Go Tell It on the Mountain.*

Any writer, I suppose, feels that the world into which he was   3
born is nothing less than a conspiracy against the cultivation of his talent—which attitude certainly has a great deal to support it. On the other hand, it is only because the world looks on his talent with such a frightening indifference that the artist is compelled to make his talent important. So that any writer, looking back over even so short a span of time as I am here forced to assess, finds that the things which hurt him and the things which helped him cannot be divorced from each other; he could be helped in a certain way only because he was hurt in a certain way; and his help is simply to be enabled to move from one conundrum to the next—one is tempted to say that he moves from one disaster to the next. When one begins looking for influences one finds them by the score. I haven't thought much about my own, not enough anyway; I hazard that the King James Bible, the rhetoric of the store-front church, something ironic and violent and perpetually understated in Negro speech—and something of Dickens' love for

bravura—have something to do with me today; but I wouldn't stake my life on it. Likewise, innumerable people have helped me in many ways; but finally, I suppose, the most difficult (and most rewarding) thing in my life has been the fact that I was born a Negro and was forced, therefore, to effect some kind of truce with this reality. (Truce, by the way, is the best one can hope for.)

One of the difficulties about being a Negro writer (and this is not special pleading, since I don't mean to suggest that he has it worse than anybody else) is that the Negro problem is written about so widely. The bookshelves groan under the weight of information, and everyone therefore considers himself informed. And this information, furthermore, operates usually (generally, popularly) to reinforce traditional attitudes. Of traditional attitudes there are only two—For or Against—and I, personally, find it difficult to say which attitude has caused me the most pain. I am speaking as a writer; from a social point of view I am perfectly aware that the change from ill-will to good-will, however motivated, however imperfect, however expressed, is better than no change at all. 4

But it is part of the business of the writer—as I see it—to examine attitudes, to go beneath the surface, to tap the source. From this point of view the Negro problem is nearly inaccessible. It is not only written about so widely; it is written about so badly. It is quite possible to say that the price a Negro pays for becoming articulate is to find himself, at length, with nothing to be articulate about. ("You taught me language," says Caliban to Prospero, "and my profit on't is I know how to curse.") Consider: the tremendous social activity that this problem generates imposes on whites and Negroes alike the necessity of looking forward, of working to bring about a better day. This is fine, it keeps the waters troubled; it is all, indeed, that has made possible the Negro's progress. Nevertheless, social affairs are not generally speaking the writer's prime concern, whether they ought to be or not; it is absolutely necessary that he establish between himself and these affairs a distance which will allow, at least, for clarity, so that before he can look forward in any meaningful sense, he must first be allowed to take a long look back. In the context of the Negro problem neither whites nor blacks, for excellent reasons of their own, have the faintest desire to look back; but I think that the past is all that makes the present coherent, and further, that the past will remain horrible for exactly as long as we refuse to assess it honestly. 5

I know, in any case, that the most crucial time in my own development came when I was forced to recognize that I was a kind of bastard of the West; when I followed the line of my past I did not find myself in Europe but in Africa. And this meant that in some subtle 6 way, in a really profound way, I brought to Shakespeare, Bach, Rembrandt, to the stones of Paris, to the cathedral at Chartres, and to the Empire State Building, a special attitude. These were not really my creations, they did not contain my history; I might search in them in vain forever for any reflection of myself. I was an interloper; this was not my heritage. At the same time I had no other heritage which I could possibly hope to use—I had certainly been unfitted for the jungle or the tribe. I would have to appropriate these white centuries, I would have to make them mine—I would have to accept my special attitude, my special place in this scheme—otherwise I would have no place in *any* scheme. What was the most difficult was the fact that I was forced to admit something I had always hidden from myself, which the American Negro has had to hide from himself as the price of his public progress; that I hated and feared white people. This did not mean that I loved black people; on the contrary, I despised them, possibly because they failed to produce Rembrandt. In effect, I hated and feared the world. And this meant, not only that I thus gave the world an altogether murderous power over me, but also that in such a self-destroying limbo I could never hope to write.

One writes out of one thing only—one's own experience. Every-   7
thing depends on how relentlessly one forces from this experience the last drop, sweet or bitter, it can possibly give. This is the only real concern of the artist, to recreate out of the disorder of life that order which is art. The difficulty then, for me, of being a Negro writer was the fact that I was, in effect, prohibited from examining my own experience too closely by the tremendous demands and the very real dangers of my social situation.

I don't think the dilemma outlined above is uncommon. I do   8
think, since writers work in the disastrously explicit medium of language, that it goes a little way towards explaining why, out of the enormous resources of Negro speech and life, and despite the example of Negro music, prose written by Negroes has been generally speaking so pallid and so harsh. I have not written about being a Negro at such length because I expect that to be my only subject, but only because it was the gate I had to unlock before I could hope to write about anything else. I don't think that the Negro problem in America can be even discussed coherently without bearing in mind its context; its context being the history, traditions, customs, the moral assumptions and preoccupations of the country; in short, the general social fabric. Appearances to the contrary, no one in America escapes its effects and everyone in America bears some responsibility for it. I believe this the more firmly because it is the overwhelming tendency to speak of this problem as though it were a thing apart. But in the work of Faulkner,

in the general attitude and certain specific passages in Robert Penn
Warren, and, most significantly, in the advent of Ralph Ellison, one
sees the beginnings—at least—of a more genuinely penetrating search.
Mr. Ellison, by the way, is the first Negro novelist I have ever read to
utilize in language, and brilliantly, some of the ambiguity and irony of
Negro life.

About my interests: I don't know if I have any, unless the morbid   9
desire to own a sixteen-millimeter camera and make experimental
movies can be so classified. Otherwise, I love to eat and drink—it's my
melancholy conviction that I've scarcely ever had enough to eat (this
is because it's *impossible* to eat enough if you're worried about the next
meal)—and I love to argue with people who do not disagree with me
too profoundly, and I love to laugh. I do *not* like bohemia, or bohemi-
ans, I do not like people whose principal aim is pleasure, and I do not
like people who are *earnest* about anything. I don't like people who
like me because I'm a Negro; neither do I like people who find in the
same accident grounds for contempt. I love America more than any
other country in the world, and, exactly for this reason, I insist on the
right to criticize her perpetually. I think all theories are suspect, that
the finest principles may have to be modified, or may even be pulver-
ized by the demands of life, and that one must find, therefore, one's
own moral center and move through the world hoping that this center
will guide one aright. I consider that I have many responsibilities, but
none greater than this: to last, as Hemingway says, and get my work
done.

I want to be an honest man and a good writer.   10

Quesions for Study and Discussion

Meaning and Purpose

1. Baldwin isolates several major influences that shaped his character.
   What are these? Which is the most difficult and rewarding, according
   to him?
2. What was "the most crucial time" in Baldwin's development, and
   why was it so?
3. Baldwin's essay is as revealing of himself as it is of the racial issues
   facing the United States in 1955 (before the full flowering of the Civil
   Rights movement). What do you glean from this essay about the
   problem then and Baldwin's feelings about it?

Strategy and Audience

1. As his title indicates, Baldwin's essay may not be entirely controlled by one thesis. What are the controlling forces or principles in "Autobiographical Notes"? What overall focus is implied by Baldwin's material?
2. Why does Baldwin conclude with a seemingly random list of likes and dislikes? Are all his statements consistent with what he has said throughout the essay?
3. Baldwin writes openly of being black, and of being a writer. For those readers who are neither black nor struggling writers, what does this essay offer?

Style and Language

1. Baldwin's prose is rich in sentence variety and diction, from short, blunt remarks, such as "In effect, I hated and feared the world," to much longer, more complex, and abstract statements: "Nevertheless, social affairs are not generally speaking the writer's prime concern, whether they ought to be or not; it is absolutely necessary that he establish between himself and these affairs a distance which will allow, at least, for clarity, so that before he can look forward in any meaningful sense, he must first be allowed to take a long look back" (5). What do Baldwin's style and language reveal about his experience, his character, his sense of himself? (Notice his remark, in paragraph 8, about most black prose being "so pallid and so harsh.")
2. Vocabulary: exasperating (paragraph 1); conundrum, bravura (3); pallid (8).

Writing Ideas

1. Chronicle your own artistic, intellectual, or athletic development in an autobiographical essay. Focus on what you think are the primary factors that shaped your character—such influences as parents, inborn interests or passions, race or gender, and economic class.
2. Write an expressive-reflective essay about awakening to a sense of what the world was like—when you first realized, for instance, that people had strengths and weaknesses, that most of us must work for a living, that friendships could end without warning, that your desires were limited by reality.

— Annie Dillard —

Annie Dillard is one of our most accomplished nonfiction writers, winning the Pulitzer Prize in 1974 for her widely praised Pilgrim at Tinker Creek, *the story of a year spent observing nature at very close range. More than a nature writer, however, Dillard combines her stunningly detailed knowledge of the natural world with a genuine sense of awe, so that her work often has a religious or philosophical depth unusual in much contemporary writing. Dillard is also a poet (her* Tickets for a Prayer Wheel *appeared in 1973), critic (a collection of critical essays,* Living by Fiction, *was published in 1982), and writing teacher. Her most recent book is* The Writing Life *(1989). Dillard's autobiography,* An American Childhood *(1987), from which this essay is taken, has been called a "classic story of the dawning of an American Consciousness."*

The Chase

In this chapter from her autobiography, Dillard recounts an event from one winter day long ago, when she and some friends were throwing snowballs at passing cars. In re-creating the drama that followed, Dillard not only captures the feeling of childhood adventure but uses the story to illustrate an expressive point about what she learned from the experience.

Some boys taught me to play football. This was fine sport. You   1
thought up a new strategy for every play and whispered it to the others.
You went out for a pass, fooling everyone. Best, you got to throw
yourself mightily at someone's running legs. Either you brought him
down or you hit the ground flat out on your chin, with your arms empty
before you. It was all or nothing. If you hesitated in fear, you would miss
and get hurt: you would take a hard fall while the kid got away, or you
would get kicked in the face while the kid got away. But if you flung
yourself wholeheartedly at the back of his knees—if you gathered and
joined body and soul and pointed them diving fearlessly—then you
likely wouldn't get hurt, and you'd stop the ball. Your fate, and your
team's score, depended on your concentration and courage. Nothing
girls did could compare with it.

Boys welcomed me at baseball, too, for I had, through enthusias-   2
tic practice, what was weirdly known as a boy's arm. In winter, in the
snow, there was neither baseball nor football, so the boys and I threw

snowballs at passing cars. I got in trouble throwing snowballs, and have seldom been happier since.

On one weekday morning after Christmas, six inches of new   3
snow had just fallen. We were standing up to our boot tops in snow on a front yard on trafficked Reynolds Street, waiting for cars. The cars traveled Reynolds Street slowly and evenly; they were targets all but wrapped in red ribbons, cream puffs. We couldn't miss.

I was seven; the boys were eight, nine, and ten. The oldest two   4
Fahey boys were there—Mikey and Peter—polite blond boys who lived near me on Lloyd Street, and who already had four brothers and sisters. My parents approved Mikey and Peter Fahey. Chickie McBride was there, a tough kid, and Billy Paul and Mackie Kean too, from across Reynolds, where the boys grew up dark and furious, grew up skinny, knowing, and skilled. We had all drifted from our houses that morning looking for action, and had found it here on Reynolds Street.

It was cloudy but cold. The cars' tires laid behind them on the   5
snowy street a complex trail of beige chunks like crenellated castle walls. I had stepped on some earlier; they squeaked. We could have wished for more traffic. When a car came, we all popped it one. In the intervals between cars we reverted to the natural solitude of children.

I started making an iceball—a perfect iceball, from perfectly   6
white snow, perfectly spherical, and squeezed perfectly translucent so no snow remained all the way through. (The Fahey boys and I considered it unfair actually to throw an iceball at somebody, but it had been known to happen.)

I had just embarked on the iceball project when we heard tire   7
chains come clanking from afar. A black Buick was moving toward us down the street. We all spread out, banged together some regular snowballs, took aim, and, when the Buick drew nigh, fired.

A soft snowball hit the driver's windshield right before the   8
driver's face. It made a smashed star with a hump in the middle.

Often, of course, we hit our target, but this time, the only time   9
in all of life, the car pulled over and stopped. Its wide black door opened; a man got out of it, running. He didn't even close the car door.

He ran after us, and we ran away from him, up the snowy Reyn-   10
olds sidewalk. At the corner, I looked back; incredibly, he was still after us. He was in city clothes: a suit and tie, street shoes. Any normal adult would have quit, having sprung us into flight and made his point. This man was gaining on us. He was a thin man, all action. All of a sudden, we were running for our lives.

Wordless, we split up. We were on our turf; we could lose our-   11

selves in the neighborhood backyards, everyone for himself. I paused
and considered. Everyone had vanished except Mikey Fahey, who was
just rounding the corner of a yellow brick house. Poor Mikey, I trailed
him. The driver of the Buick sensibly picked the two of us to follow.
The man apparently had all day.

He chased Mikey and me around the yellow house and up a   12
backyard path we knew by heart: under a low tree, up a bank, through
a hedge, down some snowy steps, and across the grocery store's delivery driveway. We smashed through a gap in another hedge, entered a
scruffy backyard and ran around its back porch and tight between
houses to Edgerton Avenue; we ran across Edgerton to an alley and up
our own sliding woodpile to the Halls' front yard; he kept coming. We
ran up Lloyd Street and wound through mazy backyards toward the
steep hilltop at Willard and Lang.

He chased us silently, block after block. He chased us silently   13
over picket fences, through thorny hedges, between houses, around
garbage cans, and across streets. Every time I glanced back, choking
for breath, I expected he would have quit. He must have been as
breathless as we were. His jacket strained over his body. It was an
immense discovery, pounding into my hot head with every sliding,
joyous step, that this ordinary adult evidently knew what I thought
only children who trained at football knew: that you have to fling
yourself at what you're doing, you have to point yourself, forget yourself, aim, dive.

Mikey and I had nowhere to go, in our own neighborhood or out   14
of it, but away from this man who was chasing us. He impelled us
forward; we compelled him to follow our route. The air was cold; every
breath tore my throat. We kept running, block after block; we kept
improvising, backyard after backyard, running a frantic course and
choosing it simultaneously, failing always to find small places or hard
places to slow him down, and discovering always, exhilarated, dis-
mayed, that only bare speed could save us—for he would never give
up, this man—and we were losing speed.

He chased us through the backyard labyrinths of ten blocks be-   15
fore he caught us by our jackets. He caught us and we all stopped.

We three stood staggering, half blinded, coughing, in an obscure   16
hilltop backyard: a man in his twenties, a boy, a girl. He had released
our jackets, our pursuer, our captor, our hero: he knew we weren't
going anywhere. We all played by the rules. Mikey and I unzipped our
jackets. I pulled off my sopping mittens. Our tracks multiplied in the
backyard's new snow. We had been breaking new snow all morning.
We didn't look at each other. I was cherishing my excitement. The
man's lower pants legs were wet; his cuffs were full of snow, and there

was a prow of snow beneath them on his shoes and socks. Some trees bordered the little flat backyard, some messy winter trees. There was no one around: a clearing in a grove, and we the only players.

It was a long time before he could speak. I had some difficulty at   17
first recalling why we were there. My lips felt swollen; I couldn't see out of the sides of my eyes; I kept coughing.

"You stupid kids," he began perfunctorily.   18

We listened perfunctorily indeed, if we listened at all, for the   19
chewing out was redundant, a mere formality, and beside the point. The point was that he had chased us passionately without giving up, and so he had caught us. Now he came down to earth. I wanted the glory to last forever.

But how could the glory have lasted forever? We could have run   20
through every backyard in North America until we got to Panama. But when he trapped us at the lip of the Panama Canal, what precisely could he have done to prolong the drama of the chase and cap its glory? I brooded about this for the next few years. He could only have fried Mikey Fahey and me in boiling oil, say, or dismembered us piecemeal, or staked us to anthills. None of which I really wanted, and none of which any adult was likely to do, even in the spirit of fun. He could only chew us out there in the Panamanian jungle, after months or years of exalting pursuit. He could only begin, "You stupid kids," and continue in his ordinary Pittsburgh accent with his normal right-eous anger and the usual common sense.

If in that snowy backyard the driver of the black Buick had cut   21
off our heads, Mikey's and mine, I would have died happy, for nothing has required so much of me since as being chased all over Pittsburgh in the middle of winter—running terrified, exhausted—by this sainted, skinny, furious redheaded man who wished to have a word with us. I don't know how he found his way back to his car.

Questions for Study and Discussion

Meaning and Purpose

1. What is the apparent subject of the "The Chase"? Does Dillard address another subject that may be less obvious? How do the two relate to each other?
2. What is it about the encounter with the man in the black Buick that made Dillard so happy? Why does she speak of the chase as "glory," and why does she want this feeling to last?

3. What did Dillard learn from her experience? What does the chase have to do with her thoughts about playing boys' sports, especially football?

Strategy and Audience

1. One of Dillard's expressive strategies is description. Where does she use descriptive language to evoke the texture of childhood and to illustrate her ideas?
2. Dillard structures her essay as a narrative. Why is this the most effective shape for her material? How does she use scenes and dialogue (or lack of it) to develop the story?
3. Dillard writes for the general reader. How does she make her story, a personal memory, appeal to a wider audience?

Style and Language

1. Dillard's essay is about almost continual physical movement. How does she use the style and rhythm of her sentences to capture this sense of physical action (especially in paragraphs 9–16)? How does her use of repetition help create an atmosphere of panic, fear, headlong flight?
2. Suggestions for vocabulary study: perfunctorily (paragraph 18); redundant (19); exalting, righteous (20).

Writing Ideas

1. Write an expressive essay about an event that is especially memorable or important to you. What makes it special? What feelings does it bring forth? What did you take from it? Try to find objective details (such as Dillard's clanking tire chains on the snowy street [7]) that embody your feelings and impressions for your audience.
2. Write a reflective essay in which you consider a special time in your life. What kinds of feelings—sadness, joy, regret, exhilaration—do the memories stir in you? How does this time in your past continue to influence you? What do you remember most vividly about it?

— Henry David Thoreau —

Henry David Thoreau (1817–1862) has come to be regarded as one of the seminal writers of the American nineteenth century, a unique voice and a man whose ideas are as timely today as when he first expressed them. Thoreau was educated at Harvard but shunned a formal career, working at odd jobs for most of his life and preferring to spend his days writing in his journal and observing the everyday world. A rebel in his attitudes, Thoreau argued in his influential essay "Civil Disobedience" (1849) that citizens could break the law for a higher moral purpose. His most famous work, Walden *(1854), recounts his time spent living alone in the woods of Concord, Massachusetts.*

Life Without Principle

In this lecture, which he reworked for many years under a number of titles, Thoreau speaks about the values of his time and expresses his disdain for the pursuit of money and business. Moreover, he expresses his devout belief in our right to live by our own lights, to determine for ourselves, and according to our nature, our notion of the good life.

Let us consider the way in which we spend our lives. 1

This world is a place of business. What an infinite bustle! I am 2
awaked almost every night by the panting of the locomotive. It inter-
rupts my dreams. There is no sabbath. It would be glorious to see
mankind at leisure for once. It is nothing but work, work, work. I
cannot easily buy a blankbook to write thoughts in; they are commonly ruled for dollars and cents. An Irishman, seeing me making a
minute in the fields, took it for granted that I was calculating my
wages. If a man was tossed out of a window when an infant, and so
made a cripple for life, or scared out of his wits by the Indians, it is
regretted chiefly because he was thus incapacitated for—business! I
think that there is nothing, not even crime, more opposed to poetry,
to philosophy, ay, to life itself, than this incessant business.

There is a coarse and boisterous money-making fellow in the 3
outskirts of our town, who is going to build a bank-wall under the hill
along the edge of his meadow. The powers have put this into his head
to keep him out of mischief, and he wishes me to spend three weeks
digging there with him. The result will be that he will perhaps get

58

some more money to hoard, and leave for his heirs to spend foolishly. If I do this, most will commend me as an industrious and hard-working man; but if I choose to devote myself to certain labors which yield more real profit, though but little money, they may be inclined to look on me as an idler. Nevertheless, as I do not need the police of meaning-less labor to regulate me, and do not see anything absolutely praisewor-thy in this fellow's undertaking any more than in many an enterprise of our own or foreign governments, however amusing it may be to him or them, I prefer to finish my education at a different school.

If a man walk in the woods for love of them half of each day, he is   4
in danger of being regarded as a loafer; but if he spends his whole day as a speculator, shearing off those woods and making earth bald before her time, he is esteemed an industrious and enterprising citizen. As if a town had no interest in its forests but to cut them down!

Most men would feel insulted if it were proposed to employ them   5
in throwing stones over a wall, and then in throwing them back, merely that they might earn their wages. But many are no more wor-thily employed now. For instance: just after sunrise, one summer morn-ing, I noticed one of my neighbors walking beside his team, which was slowly drawing a heavy hewn stone swung under the axle, surrounded by an atmosphere of industry—his day's work begun, his brow com-menced to sweat—a reproach to all sluggards and idlers—pausing abreast the shoulders of his oxen, and half turning round with a flour-ish of his merciful whip, while they gained their length on him. And I thought, Such is the labor which the American Congress exists to protect—honest, manly toil—honest as the day is long—that makes his bread taste sweet, and keeps society sweet—which all men respect and have consecrated: one of the sacred band, doing the needful but irksome drudgery. Indeed, I felt a slight reproach, because I observed this from a window, and was not abroad and stirring about a similar business. The day went by, and at evening I passed the yard of another neighbor, who keeps many servants, and spends much money fool-ishly, while he adds nothing to the common stock, and there I saw the stone of the morning lying beside a whimsical structure intended to adorn this Lord Timothy Dexter's premises, and the dignity forthwith departed from the teamster's labor, in my eyes. In my opinion, the sun was made to light worthier toil than this. I may add that his employer has since run off, in debt to a good part of the town, and, after passing through Chancery, has settled somewhere else, there to become once more a patron of the arts.

The ways by which you may get money almost without exception   6
lead downward. To have done anything by which you earned money *merely* is to have been truly idle or worse. If the laborer gets no more

than the wages which his employer pays him, he is cheated, he cheats himself. If you would get money as a writer or lecturer, you must be popular, which is to go down perpendicularly. Those services which the community will most readily pay for, it is most disagreeable to render. You are paid for being something less than a man. The state does not commonly reward a genius any more wisely. Even the poet laureate would rather not have to celebrate the accidents of royalty. He must be bribed with a pipe of wine; and perhaps another poet is called away from his muse to gauge that very pipe. As for my own business, even that kind of surveying which I could do with most satisfaction my employers do not want. They would prefer that I should do my work coarsely and not too well, ay, not well enough. When I observe that there are different ways of surveying, my employer commonly asks which will give him the most land, not which is most correct. I once invented a rule for measuring cordwood, and tried to introduce it in Boston; but the measurer there told me that the sellers did not wish to have their wood measured correctly—that he was already too accurate for them, and therefore they commonly got their wood measured in Charlestown before crossing the bridge.

The aim of the laborer should be, not to get his living, to get "a   7
good job," but to perform well a certain work; and, even in a pecuniary sense, it would be economy for a town to pay its laborers so well that they would not feel that they were working for low ends, as for a livelihood merely, but for scientific, or even moral ends. Do not hire a man who does your work for money, but him who does it for love of it.

It is remarkable that there are few men so well employed, so   8
much to their minds, but that a little money or fame would commonly buy them off from their present pursuit. I see advertisements for *active* young men, as if activity were the whole of a young man's capital. Yet I have been surprised when one has with confidence proposed to me, a grown man, to embark in some enterprise of his, as if I had absolutely nothing to do, my life having been a complete failure hitherto. What a doubtful compliment this to pay me! As if he had met me halfway across the ocean beating up against the wind, but bound nowhere, and proposed to me to go along with him! If I did, what do you think the underwriters would say? No, no! I am not without employment at this stage of the voyage. To tell the truth, I saw an advertisement for able-bodied seamen, when I was a boy, sauntering in my native port, and as soon as I came of age I embarked.

The community has no bribe that will tempt a wise man. You   9
may raise money enough to tunnel a mountain, but you cannot raise money enough to hire a man who is minding *his own* business. An efficient and valuable man does what he can, whether the community

pay him for it or not. The inefficient offer their inefficiency to the higest bidder, and are forever expecting to be put into office. One would suppose that they were rarely disappointed.

Perhaps I am more than usually jealous with respect to my free-   10
dom. I feel that my connection with and obligation to society are still very slight and transient. Those slight labors which afford me a liveli-hood, and by which it is allowed that I am to some extent serviceable to my contemporaries, are as yet commonly a pleasure to me, and I am not often reminded that they are a necessity. So far I am successful. But I foresee that if my wants should be much increased, the labor required to supply them would become a drudgery. If I should sell both my forenoons and afternoons to society, as most appear to do, I am sure that for me there would be nothing left worth living for. I trust that I shall never thus sell my birthright for a mess of pottage. I wish to suggest that a man may be very industrious, and yet not spend his time well. There is no more fatal blunderer than he who consumes the greater part of his life getting his living. All great enterprises are self-supporting. The poet, for instance, must sustain his body by his poetry, as a steam planing-mill feeds its boilers with the shavings it makes. You must get your living by loving. But as it is said of the merchants that ninety-seven in a hundred fail, so the life of men generally, tried by this standard, is a failure, and bankruptcy may be surely prophesied.

Merely to come into the world the heir of a fortune is not to be   11
born, but to be stillborn, rather. To be supported by the charity of friends, or a government pension—provided you continue to breathe— by whatever fine synonyms you describe these relations, is to go into the almshouse. On Sundays the poor debtor goes to church to take an account of stock, and finds, of course, that his outgoes have been greater than his income. In the Catholic Church, especially, they go into chancery, make a clean confession, give up all, and think to start again. Thus men will lie on their backs, talking about the fall of man, and never make an effort to get up.

As for the comparative demand which men make on life, it is an   12
important difference between two, that the one is satisfied with a level success, that his marks can all be hit by point-blank shots, but the other, however low and unsuccessful his life may be, constantly ele-vates his aim, though at a very slight angle to the horizon. I should much rather be the last man, though, as the Orientals say, "Greatness doth not approach him who is forever looking down; and all those who are looking high are growing poor."

It is remarkable that there is little or nothing to be remembered   13
written on the subject of getting a living; how to make getting a living not merely honest and honorable, but altogether inviting and glorious;

for if *getting* a living is not so, then living is not. One would think, from looking at literature, that this question had never disturbed a solitary individual's musings. Is it that men are too much disgusted with their experience to speak of it? The lesson of value which money teaches, which the Author of the Universe has taken so much pains to teach us, we are inclined to skip altogether. As for the means of living, it is wonderful how indifferent men of all classes are about it, even reformers, so called—whether they inherit, or earn, or steal it. I think that Society has done nothing for us in this respect, or at least has undone what she has done. Cold and hunger seem more friendly to my nature than those methods which men have adopted and advise to ward them off.

The title *wise* is, for the most part, falsely applied. How can one   14
be a wise man, if he does not know any better how to live than other men?—if he is only more cunning and intellectually subtle? Does Wisdom work in a treadmill? or does she teach how to succeed *by her example?* Is there any such thing as wisdom not applied to life? Is she merely the miller who grinds the finest logic? It is pertinent to ask if Plato got his *living* in a better way or more successfully than his contemporaries—or did he succumb to the difficulties of life like other men? Did he seem to prevail over some of them merely by indifference, or by assuming grand airs? or find it easier to live, because his aunt remembered him in her will? The ways in which most men get their living, that is, live, are mere makeshifts, and a shirking of the real business of life—chiefly because they do not know, but partly because they do not mean, any better.

The rush to California, for instance, and the attitude, not merely   15
of merchants, but of philosophers and prophets, so called, in relation to it, reflect the greatest disgrace on mankind. That so many are ready to live by luck, and so get the means of commanding the labor of others less lucky, without contributing any value to society! And that is called enterprise! I know of no more startling development of the immorality of trade, and all the common modes of getting a living. The philosophy and poetry and religion of such a mankind are not worth the dust of a puffball. The hog that gets his living by rooting, stirring up the soil so, would be ashamed of such company. If I could command the wealth of all the worlds by lifting my finger, I would not pay *such* a price for it. Even Mahomet knew that God did not make this world in jest. It makes God to be a moneyed gentlemen who scatters a handful of pennies in order to see mankind scramble for them. The world's raffle! A subsistence in the domains of Nature a thing to be raffled for! What a comment, what a satire, on our institutions! The conclusion will be, that mankind will hang itself upon a

tree. And have all the precepts in all the Bibles taught men only this? and is the last and most admirable invention of the human race only an improved muck-rake? Is this the ground on which Orientals and Occidentals meet? Did God direct us so to get our living, digging where we never planted—and He would, perchance, reward us with lumps of gold?

God gave the righteous man a certificate entitling him to food   16
and raiment, but the unrighteous man found a facsimile of the same in God's coffers, and appropriated it, and obtained food and raiment like the former. It is one of the most extensive systems of counterfeiting that the world has seen. I did not know that mankind was suffering for want of gold. I have seen a little of it. I know that it is very malleable, but not so malleable as wit. A grain of gold will gild a great surface, but not so much as a grain of wisdom. . . .*

Questions for Study and Discussion

Meaning and Purpose

1. Thoreau's essay is a personal statement about his own values and ambitions. To what extent does the essay transcend this personal focus to become a reflection about the larger world? Explain.
2. What are Thoreau's objections to the world of business and work? What does he mean when he says, "The community has no bribe that will tempt a wise man"?
3. Thoreau claims that the ways in which most of us "get" our living "are mere makeshifts, and a shirking of the real business of life." What *is* the real business of life, according to him?

Strategy and Audience

1. Thoreau's subject—"the ways in which we spend our lives"—is abstract. How does he avoid being vague or cloudy in treating this very large subject? Cite examples.
2. How do you respond to Thoreau's ideas? Is he impractical or excessively idealistic? Are his ideas applicable to today's world? Is he correct? Explain.

*Henry David Thoreau, excerpted from "Life Without Principle," originally in the *Altantic Monthly* (October 1863).

3. "Life Without Principle" is perhaps as much an argument as it is a piece of personal reflection. Of what may Thoreau be trying to convince us?

Style and Language

1. Thoreau, like many philosophers, is fond of writing in *aphorisms*— terse, pithy statements of feelings or ideas. An example from paragraph 7: "The aim of the laborer should be, not to get his living, to get 'a good job,' but to perform well a certain work. . . ." Find other examples of such aphorisms. Which ones seem particularly sharp or insightful to you?
2. Vocabulary: consecrated, irksome (paragraph 5); pecuniary (7); prophesied (10); almshouse (11); raiment, facsimile, malleable (16).

Writing Ideas

1. Like Thoreau, write an essay in which you reflect upon contemporary life. Some questions you might consider: What values and ambitions do you hold? How do these mesh with the values and ambitions in the world around you? How much does money matter in your world view? How vital is meaningful work?
2. What does wisdom mean to you? Write an essay in which you reflect on the meaning and value of wisdom in your own life.

— *Student Essays* —

Author Daniel T. Graham recounts, in story form, a turning point in his life. In this dramatic retelling he keeps his focus on the event itself, letting his feeling about it and its aftermath arise naturally from concrete details. The essay is almost completely narrative, but the author does frame his story with a brief introduction and a concluding assessment of what this moment meant to him. The expressive quality of the essay comes not just from Graham's final remarks, however, but from his way of telling the story, maintaining a sense of tension or anticipation throughout and narrating from a perspective that reveals how he felt both during the event and afterward. The author's relaxed, informal style enhances the simple expressiveness of the essay.

Following Graham's essay is another student piece, with questions and suggestions for writing.

Daniel T. Graham

The Score

Introduction: Implies expressive subject, establishes dramatic context for story

The October of my senior year of high school seemed an unlikely time for me to discover my outlook on life. My football career was ending, and I had yet to carry the ball across the goal line. After the last game, there would be no more practices and no more chances.

Story begins

Expressive language—the game as war

Description

The Tigers were fighting their final battle. My stomach, more than my head, knew it was game day. Sitting in the locker room, putting on the equipment of warfare, I prayed for a score and an injury-free afternoon. The "31" slipped down over my shoulderpads, and I knew I'd never wear it again.

Our coach entered the locker room and ordered silence. After some last-minute instruc-

65

Description

Author explains why moment is important

Withholds some information— increases dramatic tension

Story moves to central action

Author lets us inside his mind

Sense of drama— time running out

Description throughout lets us feel author's experience ourselves

tions and a team prayer, we all roared into a frenzy and rushed out onto the field. These guys were my family, and we all wondered why it had to end.

I realized this was it, my last chance to claim my part of team history. I wanted to be a hero just once. I had waited four years; I'd sweated through the drudgery of countless practices, had been chewed up and spit out. Where and when would it be my time to shine?

As the duel began, all my pregame jitters vanished, and I remembered why I was out there. Jason, our star player, scored easily on the first two drives, and it was already obvious that we were going to win. I thought I would trade my right arm just to cross the goal with the ball, and as the game progressed I grew more worried. Everything seemed to be going against me.

On offense I had my first chance. We were on the opposing team's thirty-yard line, and Coach called a pass play to me. I thought, *I'm finally going to do it!* (Our team usually ran the ball, and so this was a rare occasion.) Racing down to the goal line, I had my man beaten. *Please let the ball be there,* I said to myself, and as I turned there it was—I couldn't have been more wide open. My luck was holding. But then, the ball started to die. Just as I saw it coming into my hands, some total idiot on the other team batted it away.

There was still another chance. I could intercept a pass and try to run with it. Soon enough, the other team began to pass more frequently. They were now behind by three touchdowns and desperate for a score. Third down approached, and our secondary was poised for a pass. As the offense unleashed its attack, we checked its every move, but still the quarterback passed. *How easy this is,* I thought. Standing in perfect position to make the interception, I waited. Then, in a flash, a few yards in front of me a red jersey darted between the ball and my

4

5

6

7

hands. One of my own teammates had stolen the pass!

It was getting late in the game. We had our second-string offense in. I knew that my high-school career was finishing rapidly. A few more plays and I would have ended years of misery without anything to show for it. 8

I was on defense just one last set of downs before the second string was going to take over that, too. Third down came fast, and I figured the next play for a pass. I picked out my designated receiver to cover. 9

Description

"Set, hut!" As I was running I heard someone yell "Pass!" and caught a glimpse of the ball coming toward my man. *Why was this guy so tall? I'll never get the ball!* He reached for the pigskin hesitantly—I think he knew I was right behind him, ready for a crunch tackle. Then, to my astonishment, the ball flipped lazily out of his grasp and into the air. This just couldn't be happening. The ball plopped into my hands. 10

*Concrete language
lets us see the action*

Thirty yards—it looked like miles—and eleven blue jerseys separated me from the end zone. Sprinting as fast as I could, I angled for the corner. Four players were cutting me off at the same point, but there was no way I was going to be denied. I went airborne at about the time three of them hit me, tumbling us out of bounds. We lay there, peering at each other, wondering if the ball had crossed the goal. As we looked up, a referee came jogging over. 11

Dialogue

"What the hell is it!" I screamed. 12

"A touchdown," he said, "and don't swear." 13

Conclusion: final assessment of what the moment meant

Controlling idea placed at the end

Focusing so much importance on that one goal probably seems absurd, but I now realize its consequences are forever going to affect my life. I'll never forget the pride, the feeling of accomplishment, the *relief* of my moment finally coming. *For me, that score was the ultimate in mental and physical achievement. It will always remain in my memory as the moment in my life when I knew I* 14

*could achieve any goal, as long as I wanted it badly
enough and worked hard to get it.*

Student Cindy LaLoggia addresses one of our most difficult subjects from a personal point of view. In this narrative essay, she reflects
on the loss of her brother and expresses the experience of coming to
accept his death.

Cindy LaLoggia

Transitions

> All we secure of beauty is its evanescence.
>
> —*Emily Dickinson*

At 8:30 P.M. on May 17, 1979, my family learned that my   1
brother Vito had been involved in a boating accident while fishing in a
northern Michigan lake near the border of Canada. At eight that
morning, the canoe had capsized when it hit an undercurrent. All the
men in the boat, except Vito, had made it safely to shore, swimming
through the cold spring waters. After the party searched the entire
lake and surrounding land, they still had found no trace of him, and by
eight that evening they were quite certain that he could not have
survived the cold lost and in wet clothes (if, that is, he was even on
land). The search party reported it was probable that Vito had gone
into shock in the icy water and had drowned.

Never had my emotions taken such a strong hold over me as   2
when my mother told me they thought he was dead. When first I had
heard about the accident, I automatically assumed that my brother was
injured but alive. Now I was faced with the possibility of never seeing
him again.

The shock was different from anything I could have imagined. It   3
was a strange sort of high: Things went past me without my noticing.
As family and friends paraded through our house that night, I tried to
shut myself out from the rest. I wanted to be alone with my thoughts
and memories of Vito. The last time I had seen him, he was getting out
of the car, fishing pole in hand, while my mother tried to make him

feel guilty. "You just finish a second year in college, and you can't even spend two days with your family?" she'd said. Vito had leaned over, given her a kiss, and said he'd see us in a week.

Now, suddenly, our household was in a frenzy. I went to my room 4 and shut the door. I searched my closet for anything that reminded me of him, but found only the Cubs hat he had bought for me on my last birthday.

Later that night, when most of our supporters had gone home, I 5 sat on the porch outside, listening through the screen door to my mother's quiet crying. Suddenly, I heard faint sobs from around the back of the house. Thinking it was one of my sisters, I followed the sound to the side of the garage. As I peered around the corner, I saw my father facing the wall, his head buried in his hands. Watching him cry like that, I forgot my own sorrow. I saw him as a real person for the first time.

I was beginning to see the other members of my family in that 6 same way. Because we were all going through this experience together, we leaned most on each other for support.

By June 20, Vito's body still had not been found. We all had 7 prepared ourselves for the day when it would be, but deep down we each had a flicker of surviving hope. My family had never been closer than during that month. In that time, we learned how important the family was to each of us. We all grew up quickly.

Although I was only fourteen then, I knew I had matured as I 8 became aware of some things in the world around me. I was struck with the realization of how dependent we are on others as human beings and how little control we have over our destinies.

Vito's body was found June 26, 1979. Although we had antici- 9 pated feeling relief on hearing the news, we were faced instead by a new emotion. The flickers of hope were blown out and replaced with great spaces of hopelessness. In the end, I realized I had just gone through one of the most trying times of my life. As Vito had made his ultimate transition from life to death, I had gone through a smaller one of my own.

Questions for Study and Discussion

Meaning and Purpose

1. According to LaLoggia, what effect did her brother's death have on her? On her family? What complex idea lies at the heart of this story?

2. How much does the author risk something of herself in writing this work? Explain.
3. Some readers might claim that this essay's subject is unoriginal. Do you agree? If not, how would you defend the author's treatment of it?

Strategy and Audience

1. What principal strategy does LaLoggia use to structure her essay? Why is her choice especially appropriate?
2. How does the author support her main method?
3. Must readers have suffered a death in the family to fully appreciate LaLoggia's memoir? What does the work offer for those who've escaped such an experience?

Style and Language

1. How would you describe LaLoggia's style—plain or fancy, quiet or loud, simple or complex?
2. Why do you think the author shies away from overtly emotional statements? What effect does her language have on you as you read?

Writing Ideas

1. If you've ever lost a beloved relative or friend, recall your immediate reactions and those which followed. How did your feelings change? How did you come to accept the death? Write an expressive memoir about your experience.
2. Write a reflective essay about a subject that seems troubling or mysterious to you. Try to keep your language concrete, using narration, description, and example to illustrate your ideas. Sample topics: conflict, aging, failure, injustice, luck, talent, goodness.

— Additional Writing Ideas —

Write an expressive-reflective essay on a topic about which you feel you need to say something, addressing your words to a general audience. Try to confront your honest feelings about the subject (don't limit yourself to a clinical description or definition) in either essay or story form. Sample topics:

- Your philosophy of life
- Success or failure
- Love
- Beauty
- Being alone
- Hope or fear
- Family life
- God or mystery
- Leaving home
- Bravery and cowardice
- Moral choices
- Death
- Loss of innocence
- Surviving tragedy
- Knowing oneself
- The good life
- The past or future
- Honesty and cheating
- Responsibility
- The natural world
- Job and careers
- Personal values
- Self and society
- Seeking status or material possessions
- Fame, honor, glory
- Ambition
- Media images and influences
- Politics
- A sense of place

— 3 —

Writing to Inform or Report

Conveying Useful Knowledge

The Informative Aim

Essays can do a lot of things. In Chapter 2, we saw how they can be a vehicle for personal expression. Now we'll turn to another of their jobs: relaying information beyond the writer's personal experience.

Expressive writing, of course, has an informative core, as we tell others about our lives and thoughts, but the reader's need for that information may be less than our need to express it. Writing that is *primarily* informative, on the other hand, has a stronger *practical* slant for readers: it tells them what may be useful, regardless of its connection to the author. When you send a letter home to warn the family about an impending tuition increase ("Just wanted to let you know a rumor is going around campus about a 10 percent hike for next year. . . ."), you're writing with an informative aim, reporting facts that are objectively valid despite your opinion about them.

Likewise, when you write essays and papers for your college courses, much of your work is to communicate the factual knowledge you've acquired by reading and discussion, to show that you've mastered course content. When you write on the job, too, many of your letters, memos, reports, evaluations, and proposals will include specific information that your readers need.

It's almost impossible to imagine a writing task that does not require at least *some* informing or reporting, even though you may use the facts to support an additional aim, such as explaining or persuading. Learning to write essays whose chief aim is to convey information, then, will help in all your other personal, academic, or occupational writing.

Informative essays share some characteristics with a kind of writing we all know: the news report. When we read newspaper stories or articles, we expect the content to be *clear, accurate, objective, concrete.* In other words, we expect the information to be able to stand on its own as truthful—*independent* of the writer's personal view. Many kinds of essays are not purely objective reports, of course, but works whose main purpose is to present information give less emphasis to personal views and much more to the facts themselves.

Although every essay reveals something about the author's attitude toward a subject, the reader must be able to *trust the essay's factual substance.* When writing with an informative aim, our main goal is to present vital or useful information, not necessarily to evaluate its meaning.

Informative prose is common in everyday writing—from your college textbooks, which include explanation and analysis, to newspaper and magazine journalism and general nonfiction. Let's define its qualities in detail:

Clarity

We see things clearly when they are sharp and distinct. When your writing is clear, both you and your reader understand exactly what you're saying, without question or uncertainty. Your language is precise, your style direct and economical, your design logical and complete. Your essay's informative thesis and factual support present a unified case—difficult, even impossible, to misinterpret.

> *Vague or ambiguous language:*   The agency includes many people, along with writers and artists.
> *Clearer language:*   The agency employs a staff of twelve and represents dozens of writers and artists as its clients.

Accuracy

An accurate shot is one that hits its intended mark. Accuracy in prose, likewise, means that you know what you're talking about, and that your reader trusts your authority. Your work is as error-free as you can make it—from the meanings of the words you choose to your factual claims. Accurate information is *verifiable*, able to be checked by others, not invented or imagined. We avoid unwarranted speculation (guesswork) and hearsay (taking someone else's word for it).

> *Inaccurate:*   To stay healthy, everybody must get at least 30 minutes of vigorous exercise daily.
>
> *Accurate:*   According to many sports-medicine experts, even people who are cleared by their doctors for vigorous workouts should try them only three or four times a week.

Objectivity

An object stands apart from us, something separate. When our writing is objective, it is not distorted by private feelings. As honestly as possible, we give a balanced or unbiased view. We consider the facts independently of our feelings about them, and, if we include opinion at all, we keep it distinct from fact. (Opinion will be a larger part of our writing in later chapters.) When our aim is strictly informative, we avoid language that implies opinion—connotative language, loaded words—in favor of more neutral diction.

> *Opinionated:*   The off-campus living policy is a disgrace, implying that only seniors are mature and that all underclassmen and women are stupid or irresponsible.
>
> *Neutral:*   Many students object to the "seniors only" off-campus apartment policy, claiming that it discriminates against underclassmen (and women).

Concreteness

Concrete things are solid, real, seeable. Concrete writing, similarly, uses specific details, examples, and illustrations to support general or abstract statements, and keeps the latter to a minimum. Concrete diction names the thing itself whenever possible, not the category to which it belongs.

> *Abstract or general:*   My job interview was in a big building downtown.
>
> *Concrete:*   I interviewed at XYZ corporate headquarters, a thirty-five-story steel and glass office tower overlooking the Chicago River.

Learning to write clear, accurate, objective, and concrete prose will be useful to you whatever your aims.

Information in a Paragraph

Here's a brief passage by an author known for his excellent reporting. Notice that this prose has all the qualities we've discussed; it's clear, accurate, objective, and concrete. The writer gives us detailed, objective fact:

> The taste and aroma of oranges differ by type, season, county, state, and country, and even as a result of the position of the individual orange in the framework of the tree on which it grew. Ground fruit—the orange that one can reach and pick from the ground—is not as sweet as fruit that grows high on the tree. Outside fruit is sweeter than inside fruit. Oranges grown on the south side of a tree are sweeter than oranges grown on the east or west sides, and oranges grown on the north side are the least sweet of the lot. The quantity of juice in an orange, and even the amount of Vitamin C it contains, will follow the same pattern of variation. Beyond this, there are differentiations of quality inside a single orange. Individual segments vary from one another in their content of acid and sugar. But that is cutting it pretty fine. Orange men, the ones who actually work in the groves, don't discriminate to that extent. When they eat an orange, they snap out the long, thin blades of their fruit knives and peel it down, halfway, from the blossom end, which is always sweeter and juicier than the stem end. They eat the blossom half and throw the rest of the orange away.
>
> —John McPhee, *Oranges**

Informative Strategies

Your informative essays will share the general format outlined in Chapter 1. They'll start with an interesting, engaging introduction that leads logically to the thesis; they'll develop your point with smaller topics and ample body paragraphs for support; they'll conclude with emphasis and resolution. Also, when writing with an informative

---

*(New York: Farrar, Straus and Giroux, 1967): 8–9.

aim, as with any purpose, you'll want to consider strategies for realizing your goal. Here we'll look at ways of gathering the information you need, and at how best to present it. Keep the following discussion in mind, too, as you read subsequent chapters, because gathering and presenting information deeply influences writing for other aims.

Collecting Information

The facts, statistics, quoted remarks, and observations with which you form the core of your essay may be gathered from many sources in several ways. Remember that open, exploratory writing at all stages in composing is essential to uncovering potentially useful information and ideas. When we write to explore a subject, we try to discover what we know or need to know, and to get a sense of direction and boundaries—a sort of rough map of the terrain we expect to investigate more thoroughly. Apart from this vital part of writing, we have three other main methods for collecting material. Each is like a river feeding our work, each a valuable resource. In any informative writing task, and in many others as well, you may find yourself using any, or all, of them.

Looking and listening

Observing the world at first hand has always been our primary way of knowing. As we observe, we absorb a torrent of information, much of it unconsciously. Good writing, however, demands that we become *conscious*, that we deliberately become aware of what we see and hear. Accurate, detailed looking and listening give our work truthfulness, an impression of being rooted in concrete reality. If your subject calls for it, leave your desk and take your eyes and ears to the action. Observe details of place, behavior, physical appearance, styles of speech and dress. Listen for the sound of voices, nature, crowded streets. In your open writing, likewise, try to recall those concrete, specific visual details, images, and sounds which can enliven your work with the texture of experience.

Asking questions

Often, one of the best ways of getting information is to talk to people—experts, knowledgeable participants, or those with informed or interesting opinions. Interviews can provide your essay with background material, color or immediacy, and quoted statements as support. When gathering information by interviewing, try to learn something about your subject (the person you're questioning) beforehand, or at least before the formal interview begins. Prepare several questions likely to elicit the facts you're looking for. Use these as a guide, but be alert for unexpected turns as the interview progresses. Follow up on unanswered or incompletely answered questions. Stay close to the focus you've established, but pursue related issues if the material seems useful. Take careful notes, or use a tape recorder, but only with your subject's permission.

Reading

Finally, don't forget the wealth of sources available in libraries. In college, and in the wider world, reading research is an essential way of gathering information, ideas, and opinions on almost any subject we can name. Reading printed sources—books, newspapers, magazines and journals, and reference books—can help to put your topic in perspective, narrow its scope, sharpen its focus, and provide substantial background and support. Certainly some of your assignments will call for extended research for a longer paper. When we use such material, however, we must observe rules, depending on the field of study, about how to integrate it with our own work and to give proper credit to the source. Ask your instructor or consult your handbook for appropriate guidance. In general, we must always make it clear to our readers (1) *when* we use research material, (2) *how* we use it (as direct quotation or rephrased in our own words), and (3) *where* it came from.

Presenting Information

However you collect information, you'll want to design the body of your essay to present it appropriately and effectively. When your aim is to inform or report without significant explanation or interpretation, to tell *what* or *that,* the methods listed here can be especially useful.

Citing instances: examples and illustrations

One of the most frequent ways of lending substance to a factual point is by giving the reader a "for instance." *It's a fact that seat belts save lives. For instance, my friend Bob was in a head-on collision recently, and the paramedics told him he would have been killed if he hadn't worn his shoulder harness.* One example or illustration usually won't be enough to fully support a thesis, but several of them can give it weight or

backing. Citing such evidence for your points will be necessary whatever your aim.

Description

Another useful way of developing an informative essay is with
description—giving a concrete, detailed picture—especially if you're
writing about people, places, or physical objects (for more about description, see Chapter 2). *You wouldn't know it was the same man when
you see Professor Hall perform comedy in the faculty talent show. Dressed in
a brown suit that's at least three sizes too small, he paces the stage with the
wild-eyed look of a mad scientist, his arms twitching, his voice like a nail
scratching metal, his jokes so strange that your sides ache from laughing.*
Descriptive writing appeals to our senses and gives the reader that
sensory information vividly.

We saw in Chapter 2 that descriptive language can be either
objective or *subjective*. Objective description is neutral—an attempt to
give an unbiased or detached view. Subjective description, on the
other hand, pays more attention to the writer's own attitudes, and may
include emotionally charged language. Here are two descriptions of an
event. Which is objective? Which subjective?

> The elevator held fifteen passengers, all of whom stood still,
> faced the front, and looked either at the floor or the lighted
> numbers above the door. When the car stalled and the lights
> went off, a few riders expressed concern, but none panicked.

> The passengers stood still and silent, clutching their purses
> and briefcases, as the elevator slowly rose. All of us stared into
> empty space, preoccupied with our private thoughts. Suddenly
> the car jerked to a halt. Black darkness engulfed us. My throat
> began to tighten, and I felt cool beads of sweat at my temples.

In most of your informative writing, objective description may be
more appropriate, in keeping with the general objectivity in such
prose. Subjective description, likewise, may be more useful in persuasive or expressive writing.

As with citing instances, you can use description for small parts
of an essay or as a design strategy for the whole. If you use *extended*
description for most or all of your essay, the way in which you organize
it will depend on what you're describing. Places and physical objects
often imply a *spatial* order for descriptive details (starting at one end
and moving toward the other, say). Other descriptive patterns treat

details by their *order of importance* or their *sequence* (if the subject is a process). Of course, always try to find the most clear-cut, logical way to set forth your descriptive material.

Narration

Certainly one of our fundamental ways of conveying information is by telling what happened, the story of an event or circumstance (see also Chapter 2). *We were in the library when it caught fire. We smelled smoke upstairs, and someone shouted down that the roof was burning. Joan pulled the alarm, and we ran outside. We could see the thick gray smoke billowing up from the roof. We heard sirens, then, and the fire trucks started arriving almost immediately.* Narration isn't just a method of development, however; extended narration is a distinct form of writing, like the essay, with its own characteristics: separate scenes, dialogue between characters, and dramatic structure. Still, essay writers often use narration within the essay form, especially in personal or expressive prose, sometimes letting the story structure dominate if appropriate for the subject.

Definition

Last, one of the handiest strategies for keeping information clear is definition, telling our readers the essential features of a thing, idea, or word: *Democratic governments aren't identical, but they have qualities in common: majority rule, political power vested in the people, and free election of representatives.* Definition asserts *what* something is or isn't, the characteristics that set it apart.

Definition may be used briefly, to provide essential vocabulary or to clarify language or ideas, or it may be extended to control longer sections, from paragraphs to whole essays. The brief definition above might also be the thesis for an extended and much more detailed definition of democratic government, including such topics as majority rule and free elections.

Whenever you write with an informative aim, keep in mind these ways of presenting information: *giving examples, describing, narrating,* and *defining.* Illustration, description, narration, and definition may be useful in achieving many other aims, too, as we'll see. Practice using them in your informative writing and you'll find they become second nature as your writing grows in complexity.

When you write an informative essay, you'll engage the writing process to determine your task, collect facts, find a focus and suitable shape, and revise for your best content and audience response. Here are some questions to guide you through your informative writing.

Process checklist: Writing to inform or report

The task

- How can I make my essay interesting and informative reading?
- Is my subject concrete and factual instead of general or abstract?
- Who will read my essay, and what will they want or need to know?
- Does my task have a specific purpose besides the general one of providing information?

Exploring and collecting

- Have I discovered a specific angle and narrowed it to workable size?
- Have I developed enough supporting ideas, and do I have sufficient information on each?
- Have I collected material from all useful sources?

Finding your thesis

- What does the information tell me? What main ideas or points seem especially valuable, interesting, really worth making?
- Can I focus the information in one concept or sentence?
- Will that statement commit me to a unified line of thought and tie my material together in the best arrangement?

Designing

- How can I best use the general essay form (introduction, body, conclusion) to suit my informative aim?
- What are potential introductory strategies for my material?
- How should I organize the body of my essay? Should I use *examples* or *illustrations*, *descriptive passages*, *narration*, *definition*, or some *combination* of these?

Process checklist: Writing to inform or report (*continued*)

- Is my design the clearest and most logical way to present my information? Have I focused my essay on making an informative point, with all the parts related to and supporting that point?
- Do my strategies support my aim?

Drafting

- Have I followed my working thesis and outline?
- If my draft has led me in a new direction, is it better than my original decision? Why?
- Have I used all useful material in an appropriate spot?
- Does my draft hang together at this stage?

Critical reading and rewriting

- Am I satisfied that I present my informative point as clearly and completely as I can?
- If not, which parts of my essay need further work?
- Are my paragraphs unified and concrete in use of facts?
- Are my sentences and words as clear, specific, concise, and accurate as I can make them?
- Can I read my essay aloud so that a listener can follow and completely understand it?

The final draft

- Have I satisfied myself that this is the best essay I can write on this topic?
- Have I checked my spelling, grammar, punctuation, and style?

The following readings give you further illustrations of informative writing in the essay form. Study them carefully, especially the way in which they are focused, designed, and developed. Read aloud whole essays, or passages from them, to hear the clarity, concreteness, and objectivity of informative prose. Then, try your hand at your own informative writing, using the suggestions to get started.

— Stephen Crane —

Stephen Crane (1871–1900), perhaps best known for his classic Ameri-can novel, The Red Badge of Courage, *was also a poet and journalist, and one of our notable nineteenth-century writers. The son of a Methodist preacher, Crane was a rebel, a social critic who preferred to live the artist's life. His first novel,* Maggie, a Girl of the Streets, *which in its realism went against the conventional fiction of the day, was critically praised but sold poorly. In the following year, still in his early twenties, Crane achieved worldwide acclaim for* Red Badge. *In his brilliant but short career, Crane was enormously prolific. He died of tuberculosis only a few years after his auspicious beginning.*

War Dispatch

In a piece that appeared in the New York Journal *in May 1897, Crane here reports on Greek-Turkish fighting, with penetrating detail, with exact and telling observation. Crane's primary purpose is to inform, placing his readers vividly on the scene. As in much war reporting, however, the brutal facts inevitably affect the writer's tone.*

Athens, May 22 (On Board the St. Marina, Which Left Chalkis, 1
Greece, May 18.)—We are carrying the wounded away from Domokos.
There are eight hundred bullet-torn men aboard, some of them dead.
This steamer was formerly used for transporting sheep, but it was taken
by the Government for ambulance purposes. It is not a nice place for a
well man, but war takes the finical quality out of its victims, and the
soldiers do not complain. The ship is not large enough for its dreadful
freight. But the men must be moved, and so 800 bleeding soldiers are
jammed together in an insufferably hot hole, the light in which is so
faint that we cannot distinguish the living from the dead.

Near the hatch where I can see him is a man shot through the 2
mouth. The bullet passed through both cheeks. He is asleep, with his
head pillowed on the bosom of a dead comrade. He had been awake for
days, doubtless, marching on bread and water, to be finally wounded at
Domokos and taken aboard this steamer. He is too weary to mind
either his wound or his awful pillow. There is a breeze on the gulf and
the ship is rolling, heaving one wounded man against the other.

Some of the wounded were taken off at Chalkis; the others will   3
be taken to Athens, because there is not room for them in the
Chalkis hospitals. Already we have travelled a night and a day under
these cheerful circumstances that war brings to some of those that
engage in it.

When we with our suffering freight arrived at Piraeus they were   4
selling the newspaper extra, and people were shouting, "Hurrah!
Hurrah for war!" And while they shouted a seemingly endless proces-
sion of stretchers proceeded from the ship, the still figures upon
them.

There is just enough moaning and wailing to make a distinct   5
chorus above the creaking of the deck timbers over that low hole
where the lamps are smoking.

This is Wednesday, I think. We are at Stylidia. All day there   6
have been clouds of dust upon the highroad over which Smolenski's
division is retreating toward Thermopylae. The movement completely
uncovers this place, and the Turks are advancing from Halmyros.

One long line of dust marked the road across the green plain   7
where Smolenski marched away. And the people stared at this and
then at the great mountains in back of the town, whence the Turks
were coming. All the household goods of the city were piled on the
pier. The town was completely empty, except for two battalions of
Smolenski's rear guard, who slept in the streets, worn out, after a
twenty hours' march. We loaded the steamer and schooner with
women and children, and household goods. The anchor was raised by
two man-of-war's men, three fugitives, and one Greek Red Cross
nurse.

The refugees seemed dazed. The old women particularly, up-   8
rooted from the spot they had lived so long, kept their red eyes turned
toward the shore as they sat on their rough bundles of clothes and
blankets.

Our deck looked like an emigrant quarter of an Atlantic liner,   9
except for the sick soldiers. The Journal steamer then went to St.
Marina and landed the hospital stores.

Lieutenant-Colonel Caracolas came aboard there, much dis-   10
turbed because some bread had been left at Stylidia. He was at the
head of the commissary department of Smolenski's division. He asked
us if we would try to get the bread. We agreed and found another
schooner. We told the captain we were going to take him to Stylidia
and he flatly refused to go. There was no time for argument; our extra
bluejackets, seven in number, promptly stormed the schooner and
took it by assault. I guess the captain of the schooner is talking of the

outrage yet. The bluejackets got us a hawser, raised the anchor, and we towed the protesting schooner back to Stylidia, with the captain on the bow, gesticulating violently throughout the voyage. Incidentally we never found the bread.

We steamed back to St. Marina and found Dr. Belline, chief 11 surgeon of the Greek army. He was worried about the safety of the hospital at St. Marina, but no orders had been issued for its removal. The obvious thing to do was to get orders from Thermopylae headquarters, and we carried the doctor across the gulf. He got the orders promptly and we took him back to St. Marina and took aboard the wounded men and Red Cross nurses of the hospital. The last boat had left the shore when a soldier came and said something to the interpreter, who shook his head negatively. The soldier turned quietly away.

On board the steamer your correspondent idly asked the inter- 12 preter what the soldier had said, and he answered that the soldier had asked for transportation to Chalkis on the ground that he was sick. The interpreter thought the man too well to go on a boat containing wounded men.

We sent ashore and after some trouble found the soldier. He was 13 ill with fever, was shot through the calf of the leg and his knees were raw from kneeling in the trenches.

There is more of this sort of thing in war than glory and heroic 14 death, flags, banners, shouting and victory. *

Questions for Study and Discussion

Meaning and Purpose

1. Crane's dispatch from the war zone is grimly detailed. To what extent do such details support the author's informative purpose? Why?
2. Some readers might argue that Crane wants to do more than merely report the facts. Do you find evidence that he might have additional aims in mind? Cite passages to support your answer.
3. Does Crane's report include a thesis or main idea? If so, is it stated explicitly or implied? Explain.

*Stephen Crane, "War Dispatch," originally in the New York Journal, May 23, 1897.

Strategy and Audience

1. How and where does Crane use informative strategies, such as description and narration, in his essay? Give examples.
2. What is the effect of Crane's writing in the first person? Overall, how objective, or subjective, are Crane's observations? What's the effect, for instance, of phrases such as "awful pillow" (2) or "cheerful circumstances" (3)?
3. Crane's article was aimed at newspaper readers. Does it share characteristics with today's typical newspaper or television reporting for a large audience? Explain.

Style and Language

1. Why do you think Crane uses the present tense in the early paragraphs? Why does he change to the past tense in paragraph 7?
2. Vocabulary: finical (paragraph 1); hawser, gesticulating (10).

Writing Ideas

1. Write a "report from the scene" about a recent event you witnessed and can recall vividly. Like Crane, keep your language concrete and specific, including details that create a unified impression and give your readers a sense of being at your side.
2. If time permits, attend a local or campus event and file an eyewitness report, as above, about what you saw and heard.

— Sandra Schocket —

Sandra Schocket is assistant director of career services at the New Jersey Institute of Technology. Born in Amityville, New York, Schocket grew up in Meriden, Connecticut, and attended Mount Holyoke College and Rutgers University, where she took her master's in counseling and personnel. She has worked for both the business and academic worlds, including Drew University, the College of Saint Elizabeth, Metropolitan Life Insurance, and Allied Corporation. Schocket is the author of many articles on employment, is a regular contributor to The New York Times, *and has published two volumes:* Summer Jobs Resource Book *(1979) and* Summer Jobs: Finding Them, Getting Them, Enjoying Them *(1985).*

Making the Summer Job a Career Launching Pad

In her essay from the annual New York Times *Spring Survey of Education, Schocket takes an inside look at summer internships and provides readers with useful, concrete information about how such programs can open the way to careers. By talking to current and former students, and to internship administrators, Schocket is able to give us a balanced view based on their firsthand experience.*

"I don't think I would be here today if it were not for that summer job," said Mary Pisano, a staff accountant at Deloitte, Haskins & Sells, a Big Eight accounting concern. Miss Pisano, a 1984 graduate of Villanova University, worked as an accounting intern for the New Jersey Board of Public Utilities during the summer before her senior year. The experience she gained there gave her an edge over other candidates when she sought permanent employment.

Summer jobs have traditionally helped to finance college. But increasingly, students are seeking work that offers them not only a salary but also—or sometimes instead—career-related experience that they can list on their résumés, and in some cases, college credit. Internships, in which the student holds a preprofessional position, working closely with a supervisor or mentor, offer such experience. Interns frequently become integral members of a department, contributing ideas and expertise. Some are required to submit a writen report to their employer at the end of the summer.

There is a growing trend toward career-related summer intern- 3
ships, as students increasingly worry about getting an edge that will help them obtain a good job or admission to graduate school. A study last year published by the Washington Center, a public-service educa- tion organization in Washington, D.C., and funded by the National Endowment for the Humanities, indicated that nearly two-thirds of college or university departments sponsoring internships started their programs in the last 10 years, and that 25 percent of them were initiated since 1980. Last year the National Society for Internships and Experiential Education, in Raleigh, N.C., received almost 15,000 requests for information, more than double the number received two years earlier, according to Jane C. Kendall, the executive director. At the Xerox Corporation, technical internships have increased by 10 percent a year in the last two years.

Employers and interns find the summer a good time to evaluate 4
one another without making a commitment. "Internships help stu- dents to see if the company culture is right," said Alan Merry, manager of corporate employment and college relations for the Xerox Corpora- tion, which offers technical internships to electrical- and mechanical- engineering students. "We organize a program for them," he said, "including meaningful work assignments, tours of the area, social events and housing arrangements." Students are given projects to de- velop, and their recommendations are considered along with those of regular employees.

The American Telephone and Telegraph Company's Bell Labora- 5
tories sponsors summer research programs open to women and to male members of minority groups that are underrepresented in science and engineering. The objectives of the programs are to identify talent and stimulate interest in advanced technical research. Working one-to- one with a senior scientist, each student pursues a research project on the topic of interest to both student and mentor, such as spectroscopy, stereovision or robotics. "Each summer, students become co-authors of patents and publications," said Susan Fahrenholtz, administrator of the program. Norris Hobbins, an analytical chemist who interviews candidates, looks for academic achievement, curiosity, enthusiasm, relevant courses and a demonstrated ability to conduct research. Bell Laboratories recruits at 80 colleges nationwide for this program, and typically hires 15 percent of the applicants.

For the student, working in a corporation adds a dimension to 6
classroom study. "I was in awe—seeing the equipment," said Richard

Miller, who worked at Fairchild Communications and Electronics Company in Germantown, Md. "Instead of just looking at textbooks, I now know what to expect."

Mr. Miller, an electrical-engineering major at the Johns Hopkins   7
University, worked as an assembly technician on the A-10 fighter airplane. He also worked on armament-control indicators for helicopters. He believes that the hands-on experience he gained in soldering component parts for aircraft will help him to become a better design engineer.

"The material that students find boring in the classroom is fasci-   8
nating when they see it on the job," said Hans Pawel, a professor at the New Jersey Institute of Technology, in Newark. "It is important for them to see that things go wrong in the real world, and that everything doesn't fit into neat pigeonholes. They can also make valuable contacts in their field."

Most colleges grant credit for academically valid work experi-   9
ence. Laure Paul, director of the field-work program at Drew University, in Madison, N.J., stressed the importance of such experience for liberal-arts students. "Students have become more career-oriented," she said. "An internship can be the bridge between the academic and the professional world." At most colleges, internship projects must be evaluated for educational content and receive prior approval by a faculty adviser. Credit is usually granted after the student has submitted a written report on the project.

Some students, when they are unable to find paying jobs in a   10
chosen field, volunteer their services. Hospitals, social-service agencies, environmental centers, museums, radio stations, newspapers and theaters are among employers that use unpaid interns.

Summer internships cover a wide variety of interests. Martha   11
Lipson, a Drew senior, was a teaching assistant in a high school for mentally disturbed teenagers. Tenley Phillips of Vassar College searched for Etruscan artifacts at a dig site in northern Italy. Both earned academic credit for their work. Daniel Polisar prepared speeches, wrote press releases and researched issues for a 1984 Congressional candidate. After submitting an in-depth report, he will receive credit for a semester's work at Princeton.

David Kau, a senior art major at Harvard, has used internships to   12
explore careers in design. Last summer he worked in the creative department of Benton & Bowles, the New York advertising agency. The position was part of a minority-internship program sponsored by the American Association of Advertising Agencies, which selected 27 students from the 600 who applied.

An early career decision is sometimes changed as a result of   13
summer work. As a sophomore at the University of Rochester,
Christopher Swersey was considering a major in biomedical engineering and obtained an internship in the biomedical-sciences division
of the Exxon Corporation in East Millstone, N.J. As a result, he
decided against a career in engineering and instead chose a major in
chemistry.

Students can locate internships through college placement of-   14
fices and academic departments, newspaper want ads, personal contacts, employment agencies and by direct application to an organization. Application deadlines range from November to May, but an early
start is often the key to finding a position. While some highly selective
programs require lengthy applications, essays and several interviews,
others ask only completion of an application and an interview. Christopher Swersey obtained his job at Exxon after mailing in an application
and being interviewed by telephone.

Because there are not enough established internships to fill the   15
need, many students create their own. Any organization can be approached with an internship proposal. When applying, students
should be specific about the work they want to do, the benefits to the
employer and the obligations and goals of both employer and em-
ployee. For academic credit, an agreement should be made with the
appropriate office on campus.

Information on internships can be obtained from the National   16
Society for Internships and Experiential Education, 122 St. Mary's
Street, Raleigh, N.C. 27605.

"Internships helped me determine the direction I wanted to   17
move," said Mr. Kau. "If you want to learn about a career, an internship is an ideal way to do it."

Questions for Study and Discussion

Meaning and Purpose

1. According to Schocket, what are some of the reasons students give
    for finding summer internships attractive? Why do employers gain
    from those internships?
2. What alternatives do students have who can't find paying internships
    or ones that suit their interests?
3. Does this informative essay have a potential second purpose? If so,
    what might it be? (Cite passages to explain your answer.)

Strategy and Audience

1. What methods for gathering information has the author used, and where has she included the collected material? (Cite specific paragraphs.) How does she use it to support her informative point?
2. What general strategy (example, description, narration, definition) does Schocket employ to structure the body of her essay? What subtopics help to control the flow of her ideas?
3. How does the author appeal directly to her student audience? Does she aim her essay beyond students to a larger group? Who else might be interested in this subject?

Style and Language

1. Schocket keeps her language objective throughout, often letting students and employers speak for themselves. Find passages in which her commentary adds information without including personal opinion.
2. Schocket's style is direct and concise. Point out passages that seem particularly clear, specific, and well written.

Writing Ideas

1. Put together your own interview-based essay about students' experience with internships or summer jobs. Before you conduct your interviews, make a working list of questions that you want to address in your essay: What did you hope to gain from your summer work? Why did you take that job and not another? What did you learn in your job?—and so on. Using your interview material as support, aim your informative essay at a student audience, and focus it on the specific facts you learned during your interviews.
2. As in suggestion 1, conduct interviews with students about other subjects—high-school sports, classes, volunteer activities, romance, and so on—aiming to give an informative portrait of these shared experiences.

— Margaret Mead —

Margaret Mead (1901–1978) was a renowned anthropologist and author who helped to popularize the study of primitive cultures. She was curator of ethnology at the American Museum of Natural History in New York, a Columbia University professor, and author of many widely read books. While still in her twenties, she made her reputation with a study of the South Sea Islanders, Coming of Age in Samoa *(1928), and spent much of her career studying the people of the Pacific. She was especially interested in cultural evolution—changes and adaptations from one generation to the next. Margaret Mead was a revolutionary in her field, expanding anthropology to incorporate insights from psychology and economics, and writing for the general reader as well as the scientific community. Throughout her life Mead was an active and influential intellectual, outspoken on public issues such as feminism and the arms race.*

A Day in Samoa

In this second chapter of Coming of Age in Samoa, *Mead gives us a remarkably vivid and detailed glimpse of native daily life. Mead's description and meticulous observation throughout have an almost cinematic effect; we feel the hot sand and the sun's heat, and seem to be quietly walking among the people in this serene community.*

The life of the day begins at dawn, or if the moon has shown 1 until daylight, the shouts of the young men may be heard before dawn from the hillside. Uneasy in the night, populous with ghosts, they shout lustily to one another as they hasten with their work. As the dawn begins to fall among the soft brown roofs and the slender palm trees stand out against a colourless, gleaming sea, lovers slip home from trysts beneath the palm trees or in the shadow of beached canoes, that the light may find each sleeper in his appointed place. Cocks crow, negligently, and a shrill-voiced bird cries from the breadfruit trees. The insistent roar of the reef seems muted to an undertone for the sounds of a waking village. Babies cry, a few short wails before sleepy mothers give them the breast. Restless little children roll out of their sheets and wander drowsily down to the beach to freshen their faces in the sea. Boys, bent upon an early fishing, start collecting their tackle and go to rouse their more laggard companions. Fires are lit, here and there, the white smoke hardly visible against the paleness of the dawn. The whole village, sheeted and frowsy, stirs, rubs its eyes, and stumbles towards the beach. "Talofa!" "Talofa!" "Will the journey start to-day?" "Is it bonito fishing your lordship is going?" Girls stop to giggle over some young ne'er-do-well who escaped during the night from an angry father's pursuit and to venture a shrewd guess that the daughter knew more about his presence than she told. The boy who is taunted by another, who has succeeded him in his sweetheart's favour, grapples with his rival, his foot slipping in the wet sand. From the other end of the village comes a long drawn-out, piercing wail. A messenger has just brought word of the death of some relative in another village. Half-clad, unhurried women, with babies at their breasts, or astride their hips, pause in their tale of Losa's outraged departure from her father's house to the greater kindness in the home of her uncle, to wonder who is dead. Poor relatives whisper their requests to rich relatives, men make plans to set a fish trap together, a woman begs a bit of yellow dye from a kinswoman, and through the village sounds the rhythmic tattoo which calls the young men together. They gather from all parts of the village, digging sticks in hand, ready to start inland to the plantation. The older men set off upon their more lonely occupations, and each household, reassembled under its peaked roof, settles down to the routine of the morning. Little children, too hungry to wait for the late breakfast, beg lumps of cold taro which they munch greedily. Women carry piles of washing to the sea or to the spring at the far end of the village, or set off inland after weaving materials. The older girls go fishing on the reef, or perhaps set themselves to weaving a new set of Venetian blinds.

In the houses, where the pebbly floors have been swept bare with   2
a stiff long-handled broom, the women great with child and the nursing mothers, sit and gossip with one another. Old men sit apart, unceasingly twisting palm husk on their bare thighs and muttering old tales under their breath. The carpenters begin work on the new house, while the owner bustles about trying to keep them in a good humour. Families who will cook to-day are hard at work; the taro, yams and bananas have already been brought from inland; the children are scuttling back and forth, fetching sea water, or leaves to stuff the pig. As the sun rises higher in the sky, the shadows deepen under the thatched roofs, the sand is burning to the touch, the hibiscus flowers wilt on the hedges, and little children bid the smaller ones, "Come out of the sun." Those whose excursions have been short return to the village, the women with strings of crimson jelly fish, or baskets of shell fish, the men with cocoanuts, carried in baskets slung on a shoulder pole. The women and children eat their breakfasts, just hot from the oven,

if this is cook day, and the young men work swiftly in the midday heat, preparing the noon feast for their elders.

It is high noon. The sand burns the feet of the little children, who leave their palm leaf balls and their pin-wheels of frangipani blossoms to wither in the sun, as they creep into the shade of the houses. The women who must go abroad carry great banana leaves as sun-shades or wind wet cloths about their heads. Lowering a few blinds against the slanting sun, all who are left in the village wrap their heads in sheets and go to sleep. Only a few adventurous children may slip away for a swim in the shadow of a high rock, some industrious woman continues with her weaving, or a close little group of women bend anxiously over a woman in labour. The village is dazzling and dead; any sound seems oddly loud and out of place. Words have to cut through the solid heat slowly. And then the sun gradually sinks over the sea.

A second time, the sleeping people stir, roused perhaps by the cry of "a boat," resounding through the village. The fishermen beach their canoes, weary and spent from the heat, in spite of the slaked lime on their heads, with which they have sought to cool their brains and redden their hair. The brightly coloured fishes are spread out on the floor, or piled in front of the houses until the women pour water over them to free them from taboo. Regretfully, the young fishermen separate out the "Taboo fish," which must be sent to the chief, or proudly they pack the little palm leaf baskets with offerings of fish to take to their sweethearts. Men come home from the bush, grimy and heavy laden, shouting as they come, greeted in a sonorous rising cadence by those who have remained at home. They gather in the guest house for their evening kava drinking. The soft clapping of hands, the high-pitched intoning of the talking chief who serves the kava echoes through the village. Girls gather flowers to weave into necklaces; children, lusty from their naps and bound to no particular task, play circular games in the half shade of the late afternoon. Finally the sun sets, in a flame which stretches from the mountain behind to the horizon on the sea, the last bather comes up from the beach, children straggle home, dark little figures etched against the sky; lights shine in the houses, and each household gathers for its evening meal. The suitor humbly presents his offering, the children have been summoned from their noisy play, perhaps there is an honoured guest who must be served first, after the soft, barbaric singing of Christian hymns and the brief and graceful evening prayer. In front of a house at the end of the village, a father cries out the birth of a son. In some family circles a face is missing, in others little runaways have found a haven! Again quiet settles upon the village, as first the head of the household, then the women and children, and last of all the patient boys, eat their supper.

After supper the old people and the little children are bundled off to bed. If the young people have guests the front of the house is yielded to them. For day is the time for the councils of old men and the labours of youth, and night is the time for lighter things. Two kinsmen, or a chief and his councillor, sit and gossip over the day's events or make plans for the morrow. Outside a crier goes through the village announcing that the communal breadfruit pit will be opened in the morning, or that the village will make a great fish trap. If it is moonlight, groups of young men, women by twos and threes, wander through the village, and crowds of children hunt for land crabs or chase each other among the breadfruit trees. Half the village may go fishing by torchlight and the curving reef will gleam with wavering lights and echo with shouts of triumph or disappointment, teasing words or smothered cries of outraged modesty. Or a group of youths may dance for the pleasure of some visiting maiden. Many of those who have retired to sleep, drawn by the merry music, will wrap their sheets about them and set out to find the dancing. A white-clad, ghostly throng will gather in a circle about the gaily lit house, a circle from which every now and then a few will detach themselves and wander away among the trees. Sometimes sleep will not descend upon the village until long past midnight; then at last there is only the mellow thunder of the reef and the whisper of lovers, as the village rests until dawn.

Questions for Study and Discussion

Meaning and Purpose

1. Does Mead's essay have a specific thesis or controlling idea? If so, where is it stated? If not, why do you think she may have omitted it? Does this essay *imply* a main point?
2. The author intends to give a factual account of ordinary life in Samoan culture, without obvious explanation or interpretation. How would you characterize the life she describes? In other words, using her facts as a base, how would you interpret their significance?
3. Which features in Mead's description of Samoan life remind you of life in contemporary culture? What do you think are the main differences?

Strategy and Audience

1. What methods has Mead used to gather her information? Point out passages that reveal how material was collected.
2. Mead includes a wealth of factual detail. How does she organize this material? What is the overall structure of the essay, and of the individual paragraphs? Why do you think Mead chose such a design?
3. For whom is Mead writing this informative portrait? An audience of fellow professionals? The general reader? Both? How do you know?

Style and Language

1. Mead evokes the rich texture of daily life in Samoa to let us see through her eyes and hear through her ears. Point out descriptive passages in the essay that are particularly vivid or striking, and read them aloud. Then analyze specific nouns, verbs, adjectives, and adverbs—and ask yourself why Mead chose them instead of other possibilities.
2. Would you say that Mead's descriptive language and style are mostly subjective or objective? That is, does she give a neutral, unbiased view of Samoan life, or does she imply personal judgment or feeling in her words? Explain by citing specific passages.

Writing Ideas

1. Using Mead's essay as a model, write an anthropological sketch of a day among people whom you're familiar with—fellow students, family, coworkers, teammates, and so on. Write as a detached observer, however, not as a member or participant, and keep your language impartial and neutral (yet vividly descriptive). Your goal is to report daily life for an audience of people from another culture.
2. Observe at first hand a group of people engaged in an activity that's new to you: tape-watchers at the local stockbroker's office, players of a sport you don't know well, students in the chemistry lab, and so on. As does Mead, give a detailed, objective view of such behavior for unschooled readers.

— David Mamet —

David Mamet is one of the United States' most popular and successful playwrights, as well as being a theatrical director and screenwriter (The Verdict, The Untouchables, We're No Angels) and filmmaker (House of Games, Things Change). A native of Chicago, Illinois, born in 1947, Mamet has been called "a language playwright," and himself has said that his aim is to "bring out the poetry in the plain, everyday language people use." He is author of such works as Sexual Perversity in Chicago (1974, adapted for film in 1986 as About Last Night); American Buffalo (1975); Glengarry Glen Ross (1983), for which he won the Pulitzer Prize; and Speed-the-Plow (1988). Mamet is known for his gritty realism and his vivid, compelling characters. Writing in Restaurants, a collection of essays from which this piece is taken, appeared in 1986. Mamet's latest book is Some Freaks (1989).

Things I Have Learned Playing Poker on the Hill

Here Mamet considers his nearly lifelong attachment to poker with an eye toward telling us what it has taught him. Although Mamet writes openly from a first-person perspective, he focuses on the game rather than on himself, observing and then reporting the way in which poker reveals its players' character.

In 20 years of playing poker, I have seen very few poor losers. Poker is a game of skill and chance. Playing poker is also a masculine ritual, and, most times, losers feel either sufficiently chagrined or sufficiently reflective to retire, if not with grace, at least with alacrity. 1

I have seen many poor winners. They attribute their success to divine intervention and celebrate either God's good sense in sending them lucky cards or God's wisdom in making them technically superior to the others at the table. Most are eventually brought back to reality when the cards begin to even out. 2

Any poker player knows that, despite what mathematicians say, there are phenomenal runs of luck that defy explanation. The poker player learns that sometimes both science and common sense are 3 wrong. There is such a thing as absolute premonition of cards, a rock bottom *surety* of what will happen next. A good poker player knows that there is a time to push your luck and a time to retire gracefully, that all roads have a turning.

What do you do when you are pushing your luck beyond its limits? You must behave like a good philosopher and ask what axiom you must infer that you are acting under. Having determined that, you ask if this axiom, in the long run, will leave you a winner. For instance, you are drawing to a flush. You have a 1-in-4½ chance. The pot is offering you money odds of 5-to-1. It seems a close thing, but if you did it all day, you must receive a 10 percent return.

If the axiom you are acting under is not designed to make you money, you may discover that your real objective at the game is something else: you may be trying to prove yourself beloved of God. You *then* must ask yourself if—financially and emotionally—you can afford the potential rejection. For the first will certainly, and the second will most probably, ensue.

Poker is boring. If you sit down at the table to experience excitement, you will, consciously and subconsciously, do things to make the game exciting. You will take long-odds chances, you will create emergencies, and they will lose you money. The poker players I admire most are like that wise old owl who sat on the oak and kept his mouth shut and his eye on the action.

When you are proud of having made the correct decision (that is, the decision which, in the long run, *must* eventually make you a winner), you are inclined to look forward to the results of that decision with some degree of impassivity. When you are so resolved, you become less fearful and more calm. You are less interested in yourself and more naturally interested in the other players: now *they* begin to reveal themselves. Is their nervousness feigned? Is their hand made already? Are they bluffing? These elections are impossible to make when you are afraid, but they become easier the more content you are with your own actions.

Poker reveals to the frank observer something else of import—it will teach him about his own nature. Many bad players do not improve because they cannot bear self-knowledge. The bad player will not deign to determine what he thinks by watching what he does. To do so might, and frequently would, reveal a need to be abused (in calling what must be a superior hand); a need to be loved (in staying for "that one magic card"); a need to have Daddy relent (in trying to bluff out the obvious best hand), etc. It is painful to observe this sort of thing about oneself. Many times we'd rather suffer on than fix it.

The pain of losing is diverting. So is the thrill of winning. Winning, however, is lonelier, because those you've taken money from are not apt to commiserate with you. Winning takes some getting used to.

Many of us, and most of us from time to time, try to escape a   10
blunt fact that may not tally with our self-image. When we are de-pressed, we recreate the world around us to rationalize our mood. We are then apt to overlook or misinterpret happy circumstances. At the poker table, this can be expensive, for opportunity may knock, but it seldom nags. Which brings us to a crass thought many genteel players cannot grasp: poker is about money.

The ability of a poker player is judged solely by the difference   11
between his stack when he sits down and his stack when he gets up. The point is not to win the most hands, the point is not even to win the most games. The point is to win the most money. This probably means playing fewer hands than the guy who has just come for the action; it means not giving your fellow players a break because you value their feelings; it means not giving some back at the end of the night because you feel embarrassed by winning; it means taking those steps and creating those habits of thought and action that, in the long run, must prevail.

The long run for me—to date—has been those 20 years. One day   12
in college I promoted myself from the dormitory game to the *big* poker game in town, up on the Hill. After graduation, I would occasionally come back for visits. I told myself my visits were to renew friendships, to use the library, to see the leaves. But I was really coming back to play in the Hill game.

Last September, one of the players pointed out that five of us at   13
the table that night had been doing this for two decades. As a group, we have all improved. Some of us have improved drastically. Because the facts, the statistics, the tactics are known to us all, and because we are men of equal intelligence, that improvement can be due to only one thing: to character, which, as I finally begin to improve a bit myself, I see that the game of poker is all about.

Questions for Study and Discussion

Meaning and Purpose

1. Mamet makes a number of informative points in "Things I Have Learned." What does the author want us to know most about poker? Does he state this main idea directly, or imply it?
2. What are some of the other things Mamet has learned? Why are these also important?

3. In paragraph 10, Mamet says poker is about money, and in paragraph 13 he says it is about character. Is this a contradiction? Why or why not?

Strategy and Audience

1. What would you say is Mamet's principal method in revealing his subject? Does he support this strategy with any others? If so, which ones?
2. Does anything in Mamet's essay tell us why he's been attached to the game for twenty years?
3. Poker traditionally has been a male pastime, and Mamet refers to the game as a "masculine ritual." Can "Things" be as interesting to a female audience? Does Mamet attempt to appeal to female readers?

Style and Language

1. Some of Mamet's discussion is framed in abstract language—paragraph 7, for instance: "When you are proud of having made the correct decision (that is, the decision which, in the long run, *must* eventually make you a winner), you are inclined to look forward to the results of that decision with some degree of impassivity." Such language may seem to be at odds with the gritty subject of poker playing. Why do you think Mamet decided to use abstraction and generality? Is it appropriate?
2. What do these words mean? Chagrined, alacrity (paragraph 1); premonition (3); axiom (4); impassivity, feigned (7); commiserate (9).

Writing Ideas

1. For an audience that includes the opposite sex, write your own informative essay on a favorite recreation, game, hobby, or sport, emphasizing its significant or revealing qualities: "Things I Have Learned ____." Some suggestions: video games, baseball, painting, running, dancing, juggling.
2. What are some other pastimes that reveal character? Write an informative essay in which you observe an ordinary activity and what it tells us about people: watching soap operas, dressing in specific ways, eating or drinking habits.

— Daniel J. Boorstin —

Daniel J. Boorstin is a historian and former Librarian of Congress. Educated at Harvard, Oxford, and Yale, he has been a teacher, museum director, and Pulitzer Prize-winning author. Long associated with the University of Chicago, Boorstin has published widely in popular and academic outlets. Among his books: The Americans, *a three-volume history of the United States, published between 1958 and 1973;* Democracy and Its Discontents *(1974);* The Exploring Spirit *(1976);* The Discoverers *(1983); and* Hidden History *(1987). Professor Boorstin has also served as editor of American history for* Encyclopaedia Britannica.

An American Diaspora

In this selection from The Americans: The Democratic Experience, *the third volume of his trilogy, Boorstin considers the Irish who came to the United States in an extended illustration of the emigrant experience. Boorstin packs his essay with information: statistics, specific names of persons and places, and quoted observations of witnesses and participants. As a transitional reading to the next chapter, "An American Diaspora" includes some explanatory material along with its dominant informative aim.*

The Old World expanded across the United States in one of the 1
great migrations of history. In the century after the close of the Napoleonic Wars in 1815 there was a mass exodus from Europe. About 50 million people emigrated and, of these, 35 million came to the United States. Had it not been so, when would this continent have been peopled? While immigration statistics are crude before 1820 when the federal government first began to record the immigrants' places of origin, only about 250,000 immigrants arrived here in the three and a half decades between the close of the American Revolution and 1819. Thereafter, although there were fluctuations, the annual influx increased spectacularly. By 1832 the annual figure exceeded 60,000; by 1850 it was more than 350,000. Not until 1858 did the annual immigration figure again fall below 200,000.

And the United States would somehow meld these miscellaneous 2
peoples into a nation. This was the more remarkable because these peoples had come from an Old World that was overwhelmingly rural,

and the great bulk of them were peasants, farmers, or villagers who had lived close to the land. When they were being drawn into American life, in the century after the Civil War, the nation every year was becoming more urban; and most of them had to find a place in an urban wilderness.

Of course, many times before in history, population had migrated   3
from one part of the world to another. Britain herself, as Jefferson and others reminded the British at the time of the Revolution, had been peopled by immigrants. In the long run in most countries the immigrants tended to become assimilated to the earlier residents; and so it was in America. But what was most remarkable about the American immigrant experience in the late nineteenth and early twentieth centuries was not that in a single nation American immigrants became assimilated, but that so many different peoples somehow retained their separate identities. The United States never entirely lost the flavor of Diaspora. Other nations had dissolved peoples into one. This nation became one by finding ways of allowing peoples to remain several. While the United States took for its motto the Latin cliché *E pluribus unum,* a more appropriate motto might have been *E pluribus plura.*

American national politics would remain a politics of regions and   4
of groups of different immigrant origin. "Hyphenated Americans"—Italian-Americans, German-Americans, Irish-Americans, and so on—would include a substantial part of the population. The successful manipulation of these groups was a distinctive requirement for the successful American politician on the national stage. Immigrant groups continued to play as important a role here as did religious sects or economic or social classes in Europe. But there were important distinctions between the migrations which had peopled the United States during the colonial period and those which brought the largest numbers in the first century of national life.

In the age of *colonists,* large numbers of immigrants had been led   5
by men with a vision who aimed to build a certain kind of community. Others had come to found a "colony" in the simple dictionary sense: "a group of people who leave their native country to form in a new land a settlement subject to, or connected with, the parent state." For the considerable number that came with visions of a City upon a Hill, an Inward Plantation, a Charity Colony, a Transplanted English Country life, or some other definable type of society, their recollections of the old were less compelling than their visions of the new. Different visions made at least thirteen different loyalties. And these made American federalism, the United States of America.

Afterward came the age of *emigrants.* This was the word first   6
commonly used here in the era of our Revolution to describe those

who *left* a foreign country to come and settle. "Emigrant" was then gradually replaced by "immigrant" (emphasizing not the leaving but the coming) or by "refugee" (emphasizing the flight and the asylum). While the American arrivals in the colonial age were dominated by those people who came with a purpose, later arrivals were dominated by those who had left for a reason and were in search of a purpose. The colonist's vision was dominated by his destination, the emigrant's by his place of departure. The colonist had been attracted, the refugee had been expelled. This is not to say that in the first age many colonists were not driven by persecution and poverty, nor that in the second age many emigrants did not have a vision of a "Golden Land." But the earlier were mainly in pursuit, the latter mainly in flight. The Pilgrim Fathers struck the keynote of the first age of peopling, the Emigrant Fathers of the second. The first era made the states, the later made the nation. The first era created an American federalism; the second created a new kind of national politics.

In the twentieth century no other nation of comparable size had   7 been so dominated by memories of its origins. Groups which came from Europe in the nineteenth century were held together into the twentieth by their family memories, and even by nostalgia for the places from which they had fled. And their later American experience, their place in American life and American politics were permanently shaped by the peculiar circumstances of their immigration. Although the Old World experience of each immigrant group—of the Irish, Germans, Italians, Jews, Poles, and others—had been different, the opportunities that the New World offered them were quite similar. Each group in its own way kept its identity, and by keeping its identity secured a place in the nation.

Of course no group was typical. But the Irish were the largest   8 single group to arrive in the half-century before the Civil War. And after the war, too, their experience continued to illustrate how this New Nation would open opportunities for people to remain themselves while they somehow joined the search for nationality. Of all the millions who came to the United States in the century after 1820, about one fourth came from Ireland. Between 1820 and 1840, Irish immigrants totaled nearly three quarters of a million, an average of about 35,000 a year. This number skyrocketed in the '40's, reaching a peak in 1851 of nearly a quarter-million. Partly as a consequence of this movement to America, the total population of Ireland had decreased by about 2.5 million in the twenty years before the American Civil War.

Many found that they had changed their locale but not their   9 fortunes. Irish paupers became American paupers. But what was re-markable was that so many of these victims of centuries of oppression actually attained power and respectability in a strange country. To those who were lucky and energetic and ambitious, America did offer a new life, first to a few leaders, then to more and more of the anony-mous thousands.

When Joyce's Stephen Dedalus said, "History is a nightmare from   10 which I am trying to awake," he summed up Irish history. And the United States was to be the place of awakening. Irish history in Ireland and Irish history in America were a set of beautifully symmetrical antitheses. While America was a land of immigration, Ireland was a land of invasions. Beginning with Henry II of England and his Nor-man followers in the twelfth century, efforts were made forcibly to assimilate the Irish to the ways of the invaders. Yet, however often the land was invaded, the people were never really conquered. The En-glish came to call them "barbarians" because they held on to their own ways, refusing, for example, to become Protestant. During the seven-teenth century, Irish sufferings reached a climax. On a single occasion at Drogheda, Cromwell, in what he called a "marvellous great mercy," massacred 2,800 Irish, including priests and civilians as well as sol-diers. In the decade before 1652, over 600,000 Irish (one third of the population) died by pestilence, war, and famine. Cromwell redistrib-uted most of the land to his followers, and sold thousands of Irishmen into slavery on the West Indian plantations. English rule fastened on the island.

During the eighteenth century the Irish lived not under a govern-   11 ment so much as under a penal code. Irish Catholics, rightless in their own country, could not own a horse worth over five guineas, they could not vote or serve on a jury or carry firearms or teach school or enter the army or navy or practice law or become government officials. If they were tradesmen they could not have more than two appren-tices. Catholic churches could not have spires.

In the early nineteenth century, landlords seeking to "improve"   12 their lands and consolidate their holdings evicted tenants by the thou-sands. An American evangelist, Mrs. Asenath Nicholson, described a common sight in Galway in the 1840's:

> I saw a company of men assembled in a square, and supposed
> something new had gathered there; but drawing nearer found it
> was a collection of poor countrymen from distant parts, who had
> come hoping on the morrow to find a little work. Each man had
> his space, and all were standing in waiting posture, in silence,
> hungry and weary, for many, I was told, had walked fifteen miles

without eating, nor did they expect to eat that day. Sixpence a
day was all they could get, and they could not afford food on the
Sabbath, when they could not work. Their dress and their desponding looks told too well the tale of their suffering.

Then came the potato rot, bringing still more evictions, famine, and
starvation. Crop failures in 1845 and 1846 sent whole families wander-
ing the countryside in futile search of food. While the weaker died
along the roads, the more resigned sat by their fireside until death
relieved their hunger. This Irish Famine lasted five years, during which
the population of the country declined from about 8.5 million to about
6.5 million. No one knows exactly how many died of starvation, but
the combined effects of malnutrition, "famine fever" (a form of typhus
induced by undernourishment), dysentery (from food scavenged or
eaten raw), and scurvy brought death to hundreds of thousands.

It was a scene, Captain Robert F. Forbes of Boston wrote from   13
Cork, "to harrow up your hearts." And the Boston *Pilot* pleaded: "In
God's name, give us this generation out of the mouth of the Irish
grave, to feed them, that they may live and not die!" And they came.
Through all ports from Boston to New Orleans, their numbers swelled
American immigration from Europe to an unprecedented high in the
fifteen years before the Civil War. Between May 1847, when the New
York Commissioners of Emigration first kept accurate records, and the
end of 1860, some 2.5 million immigrants entered the United States
through the port of New York alone. More than one million of these,
by far the largest single group, were natives of Ireland.

As the demand for passage to America increased, the price of   14
passage from Ireland went up. Still, helped by American philanthropy
and by the self-interest of Irish landlords, the impoverished Irish found
the means to come. Some used remittances from American relatives,
sent at the rate of about $1 million annually in the 1840's, firmly
establishing historian Marcus Lee Hansen's principle that "Emigration
begets emigration."

One recently arrived Irishman, according to the traveling French   15
economist Michel Chevalier, showed his American employer a letter he
had just written to his family back in Ireland. "But Patrick," the employer asked, "why do you say that you have meat three times a week,
when you have it three times a day?" And Patrick replied, "It is because
they wouldn't believe me, if I told them so." No wonder that Father
John T. Roddan, editor of the Boston *Pilot*, boasted that the Irish, like
the Jews, were indestructible, with "more lives than the blackest
cat . . . killed so many times that her enemies are tired of killing
her. . . . God made Ireland need America and he made America an

asylum for Ireland." America's reward, Father Roddan prophesied, was eventual conversion to the True Faith: "a majority of Americans in the year 1950 will be Catholics."

Their emigrant frame of mind was peculiarly open to new oppor-   16
tunities. The practicality of the Puritans had come from their conviction that they were on the right track. Their main problem, then, was
not to discover a purpose or to develop an ideology, but to apply and
fulfill their orthodoxy in America. The practicality and adaptability of
the Irish came from quite opposite causes. Determined simply to escape the Old World they knew, they were anxious to discover any and
all opportunities of a New World. And so they were ready to do
whatever had to be done. In a word, the Puritans had been colonists,
the Irish were emigrants.

Much of American vitality came from the fact that so many of   17
the newcomers brought this emigrant frame of mind. A peculiar
strength of the Irish and other nineteenth-century emigrants was their
lack of a clear limiting purpose. Held together by recollections, sometimes of a past that never was, the Irish "remembered" the rural delights of their Emerald Isle, just as the Jews "remembered" the cozy
community of the ghetto, as the Italians "remembered" the musical
and culinary charms of their villages under Mediterranean skies.

The American nation, then, would be a confederation among   18
past and present: a federal union of emigrant groups, memory-tied and
sentiment-bound. And these groups would produce new national institutions by their very ways of remaining distinct.

Questions for Study and Discussion

Meaning and Purpose

1. According to Boorstin, what does the Irish emigrants' experience in
    the United States illustrate about the emigrant experience in general?
2. In your own words, what is the leading fact that Boorstin asserts in his
    essay? Where does he state it? What other major, closely related
    points does he make?
3. Although Boorstin's aim here is mainly informative, do you find any
    instances in which the author also explains or interprets his facts? If
    so, where? How might these remarks make the information clearer or
    more understandable?

Strategy and Audience

1. Which informative methods does Boorstin use in his essay, and where does he use each? Which one(s) does he rely on most?
2. What is the principal source of Boorstin's facts? Where does he refer specifically to his source material?
3. Critics have called Boorstin a "popularizer," someone who writes for a wide audience, rather than an academic historian. What clues do you find that the author is aiming beyond a narrow or professional readership?

Style and Language

1. For the most part, Boorstin's language is concrete and specific, but he does generalize now and then. Point out some instances of abstract language. Are these phrases or sentences clear to you? Why or why not?
2. Some potential dictionary words: exodus (paragraph 1); assimilated (3); nostalgia (7); pestilence (10).

Writing Ideas

1. Write a brief informative essay on a historical subject that you know well without major research. Assert a fact, and illustrate, describe, narrate, or define to support your thesis. For example:

    *   The Vietnam war continues to be an unresolved issue in the minds of many citizens, especially veterans.
    *   My community reflects Boorstin's thesis about taking one's identity at least partly from an emigrant group.
    *   People in my generation seem to have weak ties to their emigrant roots, often ignoring them completely.

2. Interview an older relative or friend and compose an informative portrait of what life was like years ago. Frame your questions around several subjects, such as transportation, eating habits, consumer goods, or leisure activities.

— *Student Essays* —

Here author James Barr presents clear informative advice for readers unfamiliar with the pitfalls in buying personal computers. He has collected his material from first-hand experience and has organized it as a list of specific examples or instances of such problems (paragraphs 2–4): hidden costs, hardware and software incompatibility, and obsolescence. He introduces the essay with a direct statement of his topic that leads to his informative thesis. He concludes with a rhetorical question and answers it with a general statement summarizing the essay's aim. He treats the topic objectively throughout and includes enough details to keep his general information specific and concrete.

Following Barr's essay is an informative narrative by another student author, with questions and suggestions for writing.

James Barr

The Computer Jungle

Introduction: Direct approach, establishes context for essay

Transition to thesis

Thesis statement makes a point— implies points to follow

Topic 1 introduced with appropriate transition

Material collected by first-hand experience—specific examples

In the past few years, the personal computer industry has grown at a phenomenal rate. The power and capabilities of personal computers have vastly increased, and the machines have become much smaller and faster—and inexpensive enough for the average person. The affordability of home computers can open the door to many new and exciting vistas, but *it can also bring many unforeseen problems that almost all computer companies neglect to tell their customers.*

One of the first things you must consider when purchasing a personal computer is the price of a complete system. Most advertisements, if they do show a price, do so only for the computer itself. The ads usually don't mention the "hidden" costs—those for a means of permanent storage (a disk drive or hard disk), a video

1

2

108

display unit, a printer, and the necessary software (the programs that allow you to work on your computer). Aside from the computer itself, these extra necessities can raise your total system cost by hundreds of dollars.

Another problem a new computer user might face is incompatibility—meaning that a particular computer may not be able to use software and hardware designed for other computers of different brands, or, for that matter, older and newer models from the same company. Users thus may be unable to take advantage of industry advancements (more versatile software, faster disk drives, larger memory) with their older machines. This is not to say that when you buy a computer you won't be satisfied with it, but for those, especially businesses, who want to keep up with the latest and the best equipment, it becomes a losing battle.

Finally, it never fails that when you buy a computer system that seems right for you, a new and better one soon becomes available, sometimes at a lower price. You face the problem of buying the computer you like and risking obsolescence, or waiting until you find something better—when you still risk being stuck with an outmoded machine. Fortunately, some companies are starting to keep what is called *upward compatibility*, which means that software and hardware from older models will generally work with newer machines, but not usually the reverse.

Is all this just a lesson in futility? Perhaps not—if prospective buyers take more time to think before they buy and realize that there can be some unforeseen vines in the computer jungle.

In "Revenge on the Street," student Sharon Hayden recounts events that led to the death of an innocent bystander. With expert control throughout, Hayden tells the story she has pieced together from her own and others' knowledge, maintaining her objectivity despite her closeness to the subject, and allowing these powerful and disturbing facts to speak for themselves.

Sharon Hayden

Revenge on the Street

The article on the front page of the *Daily Calumet* said that Nacho and Carlos had turned themselves in to the police after a shooting at the park. The word from the street said that Nacho had been driving by the park in his car when he saw a group of people playing softball. One of them was the guy Nacho had been looking for. Nacho pulled out a gun and shot. He missed his target and hit a fifteen-year-old in the head.

Like the rest of us, Nacho had come up through the ranks at the YMCA. We had elected him vice president of our Junior Leaders club. He had coached a basketball team, taught swimming, worked as a day camp counselor, and been a member of our volleyball and swim teams. He had been honored often at the yearly YMCA banquets.

Yet, over the last two years, he had changed dramatically. During his senior year at an all-male Catholic high school on the South Side, he had formed some new friendships and did not come around as often as he used to. We always kept our ears open, however, for word of how he was doing and rejoiced when we heard that he had received a scholarship to IIT (Illinois Institute of Technology).

As the year progressed, the news grew less and less joyful. The group of new friends had evolved into a gang, with Nacho at its head. The gang's name began appearing on viaduct walls, parked cars, garage doors, and school buildings. These writings proclaimed that they had chosen South Chicago as their territory. They were an open invitation to fight any other gang who disputed this rule, and several did.

At the beginning of the second semester, Nacho dropped out of school. Although his family persuaded him to return, he put no effort into his studies during the rest of that year, barely graduating. He relished telling us this story when he dropped by for one of his very rare visits and topped it off with another:

On graduation day he had gone to the church with a knife concealed beneath his robe. (He now carried a knife with him no matter where he went.) When he received his diploma, he just took it and walked away, refusing to shake hands with the principal.

The summer following his graduation, things grew even worse. 7
In an effort to bring Nacho out into the open, a rival gang attacked his sister as she walked home one evening. Eventually they found Nacho and beat him up. We gathered in the pool at the Y to discuss the latest development.

"Did you hear what happened to Nacho?" 8

"Yeah, I heard. Hey, he's been asking for it for a long time." 9

"I know but . . . still; I didn't want him to get hurt." With this 10
we were all in agreement.

By the end of the summer, Nacho carried a gun with him at all 11
times. He had enemies everywhere, even among his old friends, and his mother was drawing closer to a nervous breakdown each day. The family was forced to move.

Something else happened that summer, but only Nacho and his 12
two closest friends, Carlos and Jose, knew what it was. Although we spent many hours talking about it at the Y, we were never able to put all the pieces together. Its effects, however, were very plain.

That fall, Nacho became a target. His enemies were at first 13
frustrated by the fact that the family had moved. When they did happen to run across him, their attempts to kill him were unsuccessful, until one winter night.

Nacho had walked his girlfriend into her house, leaving Jose 14
waiting in the car. Nacho and Jose were in their enemy's home territory, and Jose recognized the occupants of a passing car. Jose started up Nacho's car and drove away. No one is really sure why he did it. Maybe he was attempting to lead them away from Nacho. In any case, the other car chased him and forced him off the road. Nacho's car slammed into a telephone pole, and Jose was dead. They had killed him, not realizing that it was Jose who had been driving the car.

The news hit us hard. Before the accident our relationship with 15
Nacho had improved a little. Just the weekend before some of us had gone to Carlos's birthday party. Nacho and Jose were both there.

Now it was Nacho's and Carlos's turns to hate. When one of the 16
people from the Y went to the wake, he approached Carlos.

"Hey, man, I'm real sorry about what happened." At this he 17
extended his hand, but Carlos turned around and walked away.

Angry at this snub, the guy mumbled something obscene under 18
his breath. Unfortunately, Carlos heard him, and a fight broke out.

I suppose it was guilt that controlled Nacho from then on. He fell 19
apart during the funeral and from that moment all he could think about was revenge. After the funeral, he and his gang went through

their enemy's neighborhood shooting at anything they could see. The fight was on again.

I saw Nacho a couple months later. He looked very different; he 20
was pale and thin and looked as if he was dying of some terminal disease. We talked a while. He asked what everyone from the Y was doing and I brought him up to date. Eventually, however, the conversation turned to revenge. He swore that he would have it.

That's what led him to the park on that early summer afternoon. 21

Questions for Study and Discussion

Meaning and Purpose

1. As an impartial observer, Hayden relates the events leading to a tragic accident. What does her story imply about the facts of life in her neighborhood?
2. Does Hayden claim to understand why Nacho did what he did? Is her purpose to explain his actions or only to report them and to leave interpretation to the reader? Why do you say so?
3. Would this story be improved if Hayden had included more of her own views and opinions? Why or why not?

Strategy and Audience

1. Although it's clear that the author's chief organizational strategy is narration, she varies the chronological order in one vital place. Where is that, and why does she do so?
2. How much does Hayden use other narrative techniques (scenes, dialogue, description)? Where does she employ them, and why?
3. Who do you think is the intended audience for Hayden's narrative essay? Why?

Style and Language

1. Hayden uses a very low-key, matter-of-fact style in her story. Why do you think she avoids emotional or highly descriptive language? Does the story suffer for being too neutral in its tone?
2. Where do you consider the author's prose to be particularly strong, and where would you revise it? Why?

Writing Ideas

1. Like Hayden, tell the story of a person well known to you. Try to select material that has some dramatic focus: a problem that needed to be solved, a good situation ruined, a tragedy averted. If necessary, talk to people who were involved or who witnessed the events. Then try to write a compact but sharply pointed version of the story, including description and dialogue where useful.

2. Interview a classmate for an interesting, informative story about his or her life. Ask questions that will help you get a first-hand feeling for the other's experience, and use the interview material as a base for your narrative. Be concise in your language, specific in your detail.

— *Additional Writing Ideas* —

Write an informative essay about one of these subjects for an audience of your fellow students. You may need to supplement facts you already know with further research, by interviewing, observing, or reading. Keep your essay objective, emphasizing the information rather than your feelings or opinions about it. Some suggested topics:

- Good, or bad, places to eat
- A day on the job
- Your home town, place of employment, or church
- Good, or bad, vacation spots
- A short history of a remarkable person you know
- Things to look for (or avoid) when buying a stereo, a used car, new clothes, athletic shoes, and so on
- Qualifications for success in a specific sport, academic subject, or career
- Student attitudes toward a current domestic or foreign-policy issue
- The most beautiful (or ugliest) place you know
- The story of an unusual or important event you witnessed
- Your organization's goals, accomplishments, activities, and general philosophy
- Tips for repairing household objects, cars, electronic equipment
- Student views on a recent film, record album, concert, or campus event
- How to live on a tight budget
- Using time productively
- Finding good summer jobs
- Making the college search less painful

— 4 —

Writing to Analyze or Explain

Weighing Facts for Meaning

The Analytical-Explanatory Aim

If I tell you that fewer college students are smoking cigarettes or drinking alcohol today, that's a piece of information. I might write an essay based on observed behavior, interviews with students who claim to be smoking and drinking less, or published research, using such material to support my informative point. If I wanted to go beyond reporting information, however, to explaining *why* students were cutting back on or avoiding smoking and drinking, I would be changing my aim to a more complex one. Instead of just reporting something, I would be trying to *analyze* students' habits in greater depth, for my own or my readers' increased understanding. I'd be trying to *make sense* of my subject, weighing facts for their significance or meaning.

Writing to analyze or explain goes hand in hand with writing to inform. Just as we're called upon to communicate facts clearly and impartially, we often need to *interpret* information, to probe it for answers and solutions, to place it in a context of meaning, to see why facts are important. In college, especially, but also in the larger world as well, our ability to analyze what we see, hear, read, or experience, and to explain it clearly to others, affects every aspect of life. Explanatory writing builds from a foundation of information, broadens our communicative skills, and helps to prepare us for the even more complex tasks of constructing sound, convincing arguments.

When we write to analyze or explain information, we want our work to be just as clear, accurate, and concrete as when we write with an informative aim. As we write toward greater insight or understanding, however, we also try to draw meaningful distinctions, to break down or separate our subject according to basic ways of analytical writing and thinking. We can use these strategies both in developing our essay—as approaches to thinking about and writing about a subject, discovering what we can say about it—and as useful ways to organize and present what we've learned.

Take our smoking and drinking topic. We might, among other possibilities, try to understand *cause and effect,* investigating the reasons for a kind of behavior in addition to reporting that it exists. Why are students smoking or drinking less? Perhaps they've become worried about the health hazards in using tobacco and alcohol. Perhaps it's more a matter of peer pressure or style—such things may be out of favor these days. Perhaps students simply can't afford such expensive habits. Or perhaps all three reasons contribute to students' decisions. When we've satisfied ourselves that we have enough material to offer a reasonable explanation, the essay we write will use (at least in part) the same cause-and-effect strategy for setting forth our findings. If our thesis is that students are smoking and drinking less because of health hazards, peer pressure, and the high cost of these habits, our working outline may look like this:

I.   Introduction: Anecdote about student trying to quit habits, and thesis

II. First reason: health hazards
     A. Review of hazards
     B. Students' comments about avoiding hazards

III. Second reason: peer pressure
     A. How peer pressure influences students
     B. Testimony about peer pressure

IV. Third reason: high cost
     A. Examples of costs
     B. Students' comments about costs

V.   Conclusion: Overall assessment: Like many others in our society, students are adopting healthier habits for several practical reasons.

Cause-and-effect analysis is only one of several analytical methods suitable for this, or any, subject. We might *compare or contrast* current behavior to that of another day; we might analyze *how* people change habitual behavior; we might *classify* types of habits according to their consequences for health or their addictive power; or we might explain our subject by setting it alongside something else, using *metaphor* or *analogy*. A longer treatment of the subject, moreover, might apply several analytical strategies for a full explanation.

We find examples of explanatory-analytical essays throughout the world of nonfiction writing: as analysis of current events (why someone may have won or lost an election, why inflation has increased or decreased); as science writing (how acid rain damages crops and forests, how supercomputers solve problems); as interpretations of history (why the United States entered World War II, how the 1980s compared to the 1920s); and in countless other forms, addressing every subject imaginable.

In explanatory or analytical prose, because it always includes information, we should be clear, accurate, objective, and concrete in presenting facts. As we interpret or explain information, however, we have greater room for *interpretation*—the writer's own understanding of what the facts may mean.

Analytical or explanatory writing shows us *how* or *why* things are true; it points out meaningful similarities or differences, causes and effects, parts or categories, steps or stages. It should move us beyond mere awareness of information toward awareness of the meaning that information carries.

Explanation in a Paragraph

Here's an example from a science writer. Notice that the author analyzes a process *and* its causes to explain her topic. Her language is concrete, detailed, factual, to better support clarity in that explanation, but she ends with a more personal sense of her fascination with the subject:

> If air is warmed by the sun and contains a large amount of moisture in the form of water vapor, it rises. This occurs for two reasons—because it is warm and because moist air is actually lighter than dry air. . . . As the air reaches higher altitudes it expands and cools; and the water vapor begins to condense into cloud droplets. This process releases heat and the air rises again. Borne aloft to even colder regions of the troposphere, the water

droplets are chilled to the point where freezing takes place, forming crystals of ice and snow. The freezing again releases heat energy and the column of air rises still higher. This self-augmenting process enables currents of moist air to defy gravity and rise twenty or thirty thousand feet above the earth's surface, carrying water first as a gas, then as droplets, then as snow or ice crystals that form at the top of a thunderhead. A storm has been created, a storm with fantastic amounts of energy squeezed from countless billions of those tiny simple molecules of water.

—Louise B. Young, *Earth's Aura**

Analytical and Explanatory Strategies

Whenever we inspect a subject to gain greater understanding, we find ourselves asking questions, seeking answers. The questions we ask and the answers we seek can be grouped according to distinct rhetorical strategies—ways of examining subjects or opening them to scrutiny. In Chapter 3, we saw that citing examples or illustrations, describing, and narrating are useful ways to convey information. When we write to explain or analyze, several other methods can help us explore subjects and organize the facts we've found.

Analyzing and Explaining Processes

When we inspect or explain how things work, or happen, or can be made to happen, we use *process analysis*. With process analysis we examine the step-by-step unfolding of an action, distinguish between stages or phases, slow the action so that it can be more clearly understood. We can describe processes from our perspective as *observers*, analyzing *how* things take place (the changing of the seasons, the flow of money through the banking system, the process of learning), or we can describe them as *instructors*, explaining *how to* carry out actions (building a model airplane, writing a computer program, growing prize-winning tomatoes). And, of course, we can use process analysis or explanation as part of our essay or as a way of organizing most or all of the essay's body.

In the passage by Louise Young, above, we saw an example of process observed—how storms form. Here's a sample of the other

*(New York: Knopf, 1977): 26–27.

kind of process writing—instruction (a training program for beginning runners):

> Step 1: Start walking daily. Gradually increase the tempo until you are able to walk briskly for ten minutes a day. It's all right to walk so vigorously that you have to breathe deeply.
>
> Step 2: Jog a few steps, then walk a few steps. Do this for ten minutes each day. Be careful not to push yourself beyond mild breathlessness. Gradually decrease the walking and increase the jogging until you can jog continuously for ten minutes. Distance and speed are not important.
>
> If you are in poor shape, it may take weeks or even months to achieve this level of fitness. But don't become impatient. Years of neglect can't be cured with a few weeks of exercise. . . .
>
> Step 3: Jog daily for ten minutes for several weeks. Don't worry about distance or speed. Ten minutes of jogging is the minimum amount of time needed to condition you.
>
> —Gabe Mirkin, M.D., and Marshall Hoffman,
> *The Sportsmedicine Book* *

Comparing and Contrasting

Another very useful way of thinking and writing is to look for clear similarities and differences within a subject. When you chose a college, for instance, you almost certainly compared schools to make sense of the options available to you. Probably, you had specific *points* with which to organize your comparison (size of school, tuition, scholarships, academic standards or emphasis)—common characteristics or grounds upon which to base your analysis. Probably, you ignored obvious similarities or differences and looked for vital or significant distinctions or shared qualities. (Two large state schools might have similarly low tuition, but one school might have a much better reputation.) Any time you analyze or explain with comparison or contrast, you'll follow a similar line of thought—looking for a common basis of comparison and for meaningful similarities and differences.

You can use comparison and contrast within a sentence, within a paragraph, or as a way to structure a whole essay. When writing longer

* (Boston: Little, Brown, 1978): 184.

passages of such analysis or explanation, you'll find two patterns helpful—subject by subject, and point by point:

Subject pattern: Subject A
                                  Characteristics
                            Subject B
                                  Similarities or differences

Point-by-point pattern: First characteristic
                                  Subject A
                                  Subject B
                            Second characteristic
                                  Subject A
                                  Subject B
                            Third, and so on

In comparison and contrast, you may want either to stress important similarities or differences, or to balance your analysis. Whichever strategy you choose, emphasize information your reader doesn't already know, so that your explanation is original and useful.

Dividing and Classifying

Just as we can separate a process into stages, or similar subjects into points of comparison and contrast, another typical way to examine information is to divide it into parts or to classify it according to distinct categories. We *divide* subjects into smaller elements or components (houses into living, sleeping, working, and recreational areas, for instance); we *classify* subjects by common qualities or characteristics (movies as thrillers, comedies, mysteries, romances, or fantasies).

Whether we're dividing, or classifying, or using a combination of the two, our purpose is to point out valuable distinctions between parts or classes, and so it's especially necessary to avoid blurring or overlapping them. If we were to classify television programs as "good," "mediocre," and "terrible," we'd find all kinds of confusion in our system. Not only are the categories hard to define, but each one could include everything under the sun: "good" situation comedies and mysteries, and "terrible" situation comedies and mysteries. It would make more sense to classify programs by type—comedies, dramas, talk shows—and then evaluate quality within each category. Division and classification work best when parts or categories are clearly separate from one another and consistent within themselves.

In this example from a guide to personal finance, the author divides the broad range of incomes into five segments, each one a distinct class or category (dollar figures are from a few years ago).

Where does your income rank?

Are you rich? You are if you have a household income of $50,000 and over. This is the class of the rich and there are only about 800,000 homes in it. But while you make up 1 percent of our nation's population, you get 6 percent of our entire personal income.

Are you affluent? You are if your household income is $25,000 to $50,000, and if so, you are also in a skinny minority of 10 percent of our households. But if you are in this class you have at your disposal some 26 percent of our nation's total earnings. . . .

Are you upper-middle? Your household income is $15,000 to $25,000 and some 18 million—or about one out of every four of the nation's families—are in this class. Your per capita income exceeds $5,000, which is a third again as much as the national average.

Are you average? Then your household income is $10,000 to $15,000 and you join nearly one fifth of all American homes. What's more, in contrast to the affluent and the rich, many of you are thirty-four years of age or younger and less than 25 percent of you are over fifty-five.

Are you below par? That's you, if your household income is $5,000 to $10,000, and you represent one of every five homes. Your per capita income is only $2,600 a year. . . .

—*Sylvia Porter's New Money Book for the 80's**

Studying Cause and Effect

We saw in our opening example that looking for cause-and-effect relationships can be a useful strategy in analysis or explanation. When we study cause and effect, we look for connections: Why did something happen in the way it did? What brought it about? What effects does one thing have on another?

Because such relationships usually are complex, however, we have to be careful not to oversimplify or jump to conclusions. The distinctions we make in cause-and-effect writing must be just as sharp as in other kinds of analysis and explanation. Here are some types to be aware of:

*(New York: Doubleday, 1979): 8.

Necessary versus sufficient causes

A *necessary* cause is always needed to produce a particular effect, but it may not be able to do so on its own. A *sufficient* cause, however, can produce the effect without other, contributing causes being present. To become a superb athlete, you must have talent; it's a necessary cause. But talent alone is not enough; you must train, stay healthy, avoid serious injury, and so on. Talent isn't a sufficient cause of athletic success.

Main versus secondary causes

Main causes are the most important ones, and should receive greatest emphasis in your explanation; *secondary* or contributing causes are less important, and should receive less emphasis. It's not always easy to tell which is which, however, and you may find no overriding main cause. If your team loses a game, it may have been the result of many small things (a few bad plays, a few missed opportunities), or one major cause (your star player and team leader was in bed with the flu).

Immediate versus remote causes

Immediate causes are close in time or distance to their effect(s); *remote* causes are further away in time or distance and sometimes harder to pinpoint. Remote causes may be quite important, and immediate ones need not be main causes. For instance, an athlete's ability to perform may be linked to a decision years ago to develop a routine for training and practice. Likewise, a player's having been bawled out by the coach that morning may affect the game but be of little final consequence.

Sequence versus cause

Causes always come before effects, but one thing preceding another doesn't automatically make it a cause. Events may follow others but be unrelated to them. If I sell my stock in a company and the next day the stock rises 20 percent, I may be tempted to attribute cause, but doing so would be superstition, not logic.

Using Analogy and Metaphor

One other very useful way to think and write for analysis or explanation is to make figurative comparisons between basically dissimilar things. A country isn't a ship, but when we talk about "the ship of state," we make a *metaphor* that helps us understand or perceive the concept of "state" in a different way (we have a leader at the helm, we're all in the same boat, and so on). Metaphors and *analogies* talk about one thing in terms of another, usually to make an unfamiliar or complex subject clearer. Such *figurative* or nonliteral comparisons are fragile, however, and may collapse if we lean too hard on them. Clichés like "life is a game of winners and losers" won't get us very far if we try to extend them into a full explanation. Even the "ship of state" metaphor will sink if we load it with too much freight. The most useful metaphors and analogies include several meaningful points of comparison, and they continue to provide insight as we explore them.

Any of these strategies may be used to structure entire essays, of course, but it's more likely that you'll find more than one of them useful in any analytical or explanatory task. Think of them as tools or instruments to be selected whenever they're appropriate, whenever they can help you make your points clearer, easier to grasp, more distinct and sharp. And remember that these methods are also ways of *exploring* topics for potential points of focus and emphasis. Use them to pry subjects open to closer view, and then use them to help shape your discoveries into clear, fully developed explanations.

Process checklist: Writing to analyze or explain

The task
- What is the problem or question that I attempt to answer in my analysis or explanation?
- How much do I and my readers already know about the subject?
- What kinds of new, interesting, or helpful information and explanation might I look for?

Exploring and collecting
- How can I use rhetorical tools in this chapter to uncover potentially useful material for my essay?
- What additional information may I need to find to support my analysis?
- What are some likely sources?

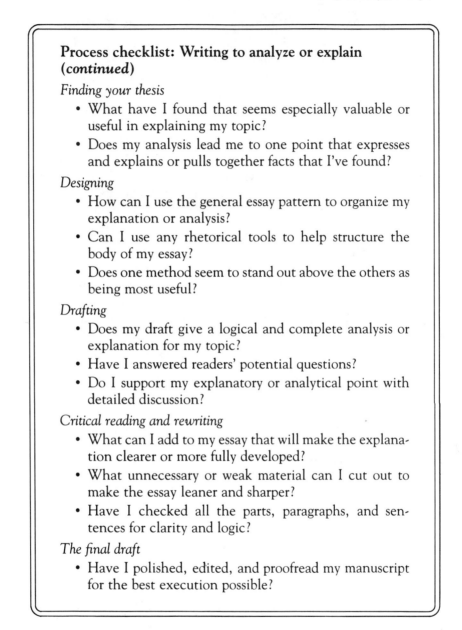

Process checklist: Writing to analyze or explain (*continued*)

Finding your thesis
- What have I found that seems especially valuable or useful in explaining my topic?
- Does my analysis lead me to one point that expresses and explains or pulls together facts that I've found?

Designing
- How can I use the general essay pattern to organize my explanation or analysis?
- Can I use any rhetorical tools to help structure the body of my essay?
- Does one method seem to stand out above the others as being most useful?

Drafting
- Does my draft give a logical and complete analysis or explanation for my topic?
- Have I answered readers' potential questions?
- Do I support my explanatory or analytical point with detailed discussion?

Critical reading and rewriting
- What can I add to my essay that will make the explanation clearer or more fully developed?
- What unnecessary or weak material can I cut out to make the essay leaner and sharper?
- Have I checked all the parts, paragraphs, and sentences for clarity and logic?

The final draft
- Have I polished, edited, and proofread my manuscript for the best execution possible?

The readings that follow further illustrate writing to explain or analyze information. The authors typically use more than one strategy to help their material make sense. As you read, look for the general essay characteristics we've discussed in earlier chapters, and notice how these writers build from an informative base toward their explanatory or analytical aims.

— Bruce Catton —

Bruce Catton (1899–1978) was one of America's most widely read writers on the Civil War, and his many books on the subject continue to find a large audience. Born in Michigan, Catton worked as a newspaperman and later as editor of American Heritage *magazine. His* A Stillness at Appomattox *(1953) won both the Pulitzer Prize and the National Book Award. Other works include* Mr. Lincoln's Army *(1951),* This Hallowed Ground *(1956),* The Coming Fury *(1961),* Terrible Swift Sword *(1963), and* The Final Fury *(1974).*

Grant and Lee: A Study in Contrasts

In this selection, which first appeared in The American Story, *a collection of historical essays by a number of writers, Catton analyzes the similarities, and significant differences, between the two Civil War generals whose meeting at Appomattox symbolized one of the grand moments in nineteenth-century American history.*

When Ulysses S. Grant and Robert E. Lee met in the parlor of a 1 modest house at Appomattox Court House, Virginia, on April 9, 1865, to work out the terms for the surrender of Lee's Army of Northern Virginia, a great chapter in American life came to a close, and a great new chapter began.

These men were bringing the Civil War to its virtual finish. To be 2 sure, other armies had yet to surrender, and for a few days the fugitive Confederate government would struggle desperately and vainly, trying to find some way to go on living now that its chief support was gone. But in effect it was all over when Grant and Lee signed the papers. And the little room where they wrote out the terms was the scene of one of the poignant, dramatic contrasts in American history.

They were two strong men, these oddly different generals, and 3 they represented the strengths of two conflicting currents that, through them, had come into final collision.

Back of Robert E. Lee was the notion that the old aristocratic 4 concept might somehow survive and be dominant in American life.

Lee was tidewater Virginia, and in his background were family, 5 culture, and tradition . . . the age of chivalry transplanted to a New

World which was making its own legends and its own myths. He embodied a way of life that had come down through the age of knighthood and the English country squire. America was a land that was beginning all over again, dedicated to nothing much more complicated than the rather hazy belief that all men had equal rights, and should have an equal chance in the world. In such a land Lee stood for the feeling that it was somehow of advantage to human society to have a pronounced inequality in the social structure. There should be a leisure class, backed by ownership of land; in turn, society itself should be keyed to the land as the chief source of wealth and influence. It would bring forth (according to this ideal) a class of men with a strong sense of obligation to the community; men who lived not to gain advantage for themselves, but to meet the solemn obligations which had been laid on them by the very fact that they were privileged. From them the country would get its leadership; to them it could look for the higher values—of thought, of conduct, of personal deportment—to give it strength and virtue.

Lee embodied the noblest elements of this aristocratic ideal.   6
Through him, the landed nobility justified itself. For four years, the Southern states had fought a desperate war to uphold the ideals for which Lee stood. In the end, it almost seemed as if the Confederacy fought for Lee; as if he himself was the Confederacy . . . the best thing that the way of life for which the Confederacy stood could ever have to offer. He had passed into legend before Appomattox. Thousands of tired, underfed, poorly clothed Confederate soldiers, long since past the simple enthusiasm of the early days of the struggle, somehow considered Lee the symbol of everything for which they had been willing to die. But they could not quite put this feeling into words. If the Lost Cause, sanctified by so much heroism and so many deaths, had a living justification, its justification was General Lee.

Grant, the son of a tanner on the Western frontier, was every-   7
thing Lee was not. He had come up the hard way, and embodied nothing in particular except the eternal toughness and sinewy fiber of the men who grew up beyond the mountains. He was one of a body of men who owed reverence and obeisance to no one, who were self-reliant to a fault, who cared hardly anything for the past but who had a sharp eye for the future.

These frontier men were the precise opposites of the tidewater   8
aristocrats. Back of them, in the great surge that had taken people over the Alleghenies and into the opening Western country, there was a deep, implicit dissatisfaction with a past that had settled into grooves. They stood for democracy, not from any reasoned conclusion about the proper ordering of human society, but simply because they had grown up in the middle of democracy and knew how it worked. Their society

might have privileges, but they would be privileges each man had won for himself. Forms and patterns meant nothing. No man was born to anything, except perhaps a chance to show how far he could rise. Life was competition.

Yet along with this feeling had come a deep sense of belonging to   9
a national community. The Westerner who developed a farm, opened a shop or set up in business as a trader, could hope to prosper only as his own community prospered—and his community ran from the Atlantic to the Pacific and from Canada down to Mexico. If the land was settled, with towns and highways and accessible markets, he could better himself. He saw his fate in terms of the nation's own destiny. As its horizons expanded, so did his. He had, in other words, an acute dollars-and-cents stake in the continued growth and development of his country.

And that, perhaps, is where the contrast between Grant and Lee   10
becomes most striking. The Virginia aristocrat, inevitably, saw himself in relation to his own region. He lived in a static society which could endure almost anything except change. Instinctively, his first loyalty would go to the locality in which that society existed. He would fight to the limit of endurance to defend it, because in defending it he was defending everything that gave his own life its deepest meaning.

The Westerner, on the other hand, would fight with an equal   11
tenacity for the broader concept of society. He fought so because everything he lived by was tied to growth, expansion, and a constantly widening horizon. What he lived by would survive or fall with the nation itself. He could not possibly stand by unmoved in the face of an attempt to destroy the Union. He would combat it with everything he had, because he could only see it as an effort to cut the ground out from under his feet.

So Grant and Lee were in complete contrast, representing two   12
diametrically opposed elements in American life. Grant was the modern man emerging; beyond him, ready to come on the stage, was the great age of steel and machinery, of crowded cities and a restless, burgeoning vitality. Lee might have ridden down from the old age of chivalry, lance in hand, silken banner fluttering over his head. Each man was the perfect champion of his cause, drawing both his strengths and his weaknesses from the people he led.

Yet it was not all contrast, after all. Different as they were—in   13
background, in personality, in underlying aspiration—these two great soldiers had much in common. Under everything else, they were marvelous fighters. Furthermore, their fighting qualities were really very much alike.

Each man had, to begin with, the great virtue of utter tenacity   14
and fidelity. Grant fought his way down the Mississippi Valley in spite

of acute personal discouragement and profound military handicaps. Lee hung on in the trenches at Petersburg after hope itself had died. In each man there was an indomitable quality . . . the born fighter's refusal to give up as long as he can still remain on his feet and lift his two fists.

Daring and resourcefulness they had, too; the ability to think   15 faster and move faster than the enemy. These were the qualities which gave Lee the dazzling campaigns of Second Manassas and Chancellorsville and won Vicksburg for Grant.

Lastly, and perhaps greatest of all, there was the ability, at the   16 end, to turn quickly from war to peace once the fighting was over. Out of the way these two men behaved at Appomattox came the possibility of a peace of reconciliation. It was a possibility not wholly realized, in the years to come, but which did, in the end, help the two sections to become one nation again . . . after a war whose bitterness might have seemed to make such a reunion wholly impossible. No part of either man's life became him more than the part he played in their brief meeting in the McLean house at Appomattox. Their behavior there put all succeeding generations of Americans in their debt. Two great Americans, Grant and Lee—very different, yet under everything very much alike. Their encounter at Appomattox was one of the great moments of American history.

Questions for Study and Discussion

Meaning and Purpose

1. According to Catton, which two "conflicting currents" in American history did Grant and Lee represent? Why was the collision of these forces so significant? How did each man embody the specific qualities of his respective tradition?
2. Is Catton balanced in his comparison of Grant and Lee, or does he appear to admire one man more than the other? Explain.
3. In what ways were the two generals similar? Why does Catton include this material, when his major focus is on their differences?

Strategy and Audience

1. Catton's obvious controlling strategy is to contrast the two men. What structure does the contrast take (point-by-point or subject-by-

subject)? Does the author use any other rhetorical methods to explain the significance of his material? If so, which ones?

2. This famous and widely reprinted essay is an especially clear model of effective organization. Map or outline the major sections in the essay and explain why Catton uses the structure he does.

3. Does the audience for this essay appear to be the general reader or a more highly knowledgeable group of historians? What clues indicate Catton's apparent target?

Style and Language

1. Because of his subject, Catton is almost forced to generalize, to make broad, abstract statements. How does he keep these declarations from becoming vague or unconnected to the facts? Where does he add specific, detailed support with description or example to help justify his generalities?

2. Although Catton's language overall is plain, direct, and very clear, his vocabulary is challenging at times. Some words to check: poignant (paragraph 2); aristocratic (4); chivalry, deportment (5); obeisance (7); indomitable (14).

Writing Ideas

1. Using comparison/contrast and plenty of specific detail, explain the major similarities or differences between two well-known figures in the same field who represent different traditions beyond their individual accomplishments in business, entertainment, history, sports, or education. Be sure to consider your audience and to point out generally unnoticed qualities rather than obvious ones.

2. As above, analyze and explain important similarities or differences in conflicting values or traditions: East/West, North/South, urban/rural, individual/community, freedom/responsibility.

— Judith Viorst —

Judith Viorst is a contributing editor and columnist for Redbook *magazine, a poet, prose writer, and children's book author. She was born in 1936 in Newark, New Jersey, and is a graduate of Rutgers University. Her book* It's Hard to Be Hip Over Thirty, and Other Tragedies of Married Life *(1968) was a national bestseller and helped to launch her career. Viorst has published two sequels,* How Did I Get to Be Forty . . . and Other Atrocities *(1976) and* Forever Fifty . . . and Other Negotiations *(1989).*

Friends, Good Friends—and Such Good Friends

In this, a good example of informal or "occasional" writing for a wide audience, Viorst considers her own experience and explains her understanding of adult friendships among women through a series of types or categories.

Women are friends, I once would have said, when they totally   1
love and support and trust each other, and bare to each other the
secrets of their souls, and run—no questions asked—to help each
other, and tell harsh truths to each other (no, you can't wear that dress
unless you lose ten pounds first) when harsh truths must be told.

Women are friends, I once would have said, when they share the   2
same affection for Ingmar Bergman, plus train rides, cats, warm rain,
charades, Camus, and hate with equal ardor Newark and Brussels
sprouts and Lawrence Welk and camping.

In other words, I once would have said that a friend is a friend all   3
the way, but now I believe that's a narrow point of view. For the friendships I have and the friendships I see are conducted at many levels of
intensity, serve many different functions, meet different needs and
range from those as all-the-way as the friendship of the soul sisters
mentioned above to that of the most nonchalant and casual playmates.

Consider these varieties of friendship: 4

1. Convenience friends. These are the women with whom, if our   5
paths weren't crossing all the time, we'd have no particular reason to
be friends: a next-door neighbor, a woman in our car pool, the mother

of one of our children's closest friends or maybe some mommy with whom we serve juice and cookies each week at the Glenwood Co-op Nursery.

Convenience friends are convenient indeed. They'll lend us their cups and silverware for a party. They'll drive our kids to soccer when we're sick. They'll take us to pick up our car when we need a lift to the garage. They'll even take our cats when we go on vacation. As we will for them.   6

But we don't, with convenience friends, ever come too close or tell too much; we maintain our public face and emotional distance. "Which means," says Elaine, "that I'll talk about being overweight but not about being depressed. Which means I'll admit being mad but not blind with rage. Which means I might say that we're pinched this month but never that I'm worried sick over money."   7

But which doesn't mean that there isn't sufficient value to be found in these friendships of mutual aid, in convenience friends.   8

2. Special-interest friends. These friendships aren't intimate, and they needn't involve kids or silverware or cats. Their value lies in some interest jointly shared. And so we may have an office friend or a yoga friend or a tennis friend or a friend from the Women's Democratic Club.   9

"I've got one woman friend," says Joyce, "who likes, as I do, to take psychology courses. Which makes it nice for me—and nice for her. It's fun to go with someone you know and it's fun to discuss what you've learned, driving back from the classes." And for the most part, she says, that's all they discuss.   10

"I'd say that what we're doing is *doing* together, not being together," Suzanne says of her Tuesday-doubles friends. "It's mainly a tennis relationship, but we play together well. And I guess we all need to have a couple of playmates."   11

I agree.   12

My playmate is a shopping friend, a woman of marvelous taste, a woman who knows exactly *where* to buy *what*, and furthermore is a woman who always knows beyond a doubt what one ought to be buying. I don't have the time to keep up with what's new in eyeshadow, hemlines and shoes and whether the smock look is in or finished already. But since (oh, shame!) I care a lot about eyeshadow, hemlines and shoes, and since I don't *want* to wear smocks if the smock look is finished, I'm very glad to have a shopping friend.   13

3. Historical friends. We all have a friend who knew us when . . . maybe way back in Miss Meltzer's second grade, when our family lived in that three-room flat in Brooklyn, when our dad was out of work for seven months, when our brother Allie got in that fight where they had to call the police, when our sister married the endodontist from Yonkers   14

and when, the morning after we lost our virginity, she was the first, the only, friend we told.

The years have gone by and we've gone separate ways and we've   15
little in common now, but we're still an intimate part of each other's past. And so whenever we go to Detroit we always go to visit this friend of our girlhood. Who knows how we looked before our teeth were straightened. Who knows how we talked before our voice got un-Brooklyned. Who knows what we ate before we learned about arti-chokes. And who, by her presence, puts us in touch with an earlier part of ourself, a part of ourself it's important never to lose.

"What this friend means to me and what I mean to her," says   16
Grace, "is having a sister without sibling rivalry. We know the texture of each other's lives. She remembers my grandmother's cabbage soup. I remember the way her uncle played the piano. There's simply no other friend who remembers those things."

4. Crossroads friends. Like historical friends, our crossroads   17
friends are important for *what was*—for the friendship we shared at a crucial, now past, time of life. A time, perhaps, when we roomed in college together; or worked as eager young singles in the Big City together; or went together, as my friend Elizabeth and I did through pregnancy, birth and that scary first year of new motherhood.

Crossroads friends forge powerful links, links strong enough to   18
endure with not much more contact than once-a-year letters at Christ-mas. And out of respect for those crossroads years, for those dramas and dreams we once shared, we will always be friends.

5. Cross-generational friends. Historical friends and crossroads   19
friends seem to maintain a special kind of intimacy—dormant but always ready to be revived—and though we may rarely meet, when-ever we do connect, it's personal and intense. Another kind of intimacy exists in the friendships that form across generations in what one woman calls her daughter-mother and her mother-daughter relationships.

Evelyn's friend is her mother's age—"but I share so much more   20
than I ever could with my mother"—a woman she talks to of music, of books and of life. "What I get from her is the benefit of her experience. What she gets—and enjoys—from me is a youthful perspective. It's a pleasure for both of us."

I have in my own life a precious friend, a woman of 65 who has   21
lived very hard, who is wise, who listens well; who has been where I am and can help me understand it; and who represents not only an ultimate ideal mother to me but also the person I'd like to be when I grow up.

In our daughter role we tend to do more than our share of self-   22 revelation; in our mother role we tend to receive what's revealed. It's another kind of pleasure—playing wise mother to a questing younger person. It's another very lovely kind of friendship.

6. Part-of-a-couple friends. Some of the women we call our friends we never see alone—we see them as part of a couple at couples' parties. And though we share interests in many things and respect each other's views, we aren't moved to deepen the relationship. Whatever the reason, a lack of time or—and this is more likely—a lack of chemistry, our friendship remains in the context of a group. But the fact that our feeling on seeing each other is always, "I'm *so* glad she's here" and the fact that we spend half the evening talking together says that this too, in its own way, counts as a friendship.

(Other part-of-a-couple friends are the friends that came with the marriage, and some of these are friends we could live without. But sometimes, alas, she married our husband's best friend; and sometimes, alas, she *is* our husband's best friend. And so we find ourself dealing with her, somewhat against our will, in a spirit of what I'll call *reluctant friendship*.)

7. Men who are friends. I wanted to write just of women friends, but the women I've talked to won't let me—they say I must mention man-woman friendships too. For these friendships can be just as close and as dear as those that we form with women. Listen to Lucy's description of one such friendship:

"We've found we have things to talk about that are different from what he talks about with my husband and different from what I talk about with his wife. So sometimes we call on the phone or meet for lunch. There are similar intellectual interests—we always pass on to each other the books that we love—but there's also something tender and caring too."

In a couple of crises, Lucy says, "he offered himself, for talking and for helping. And when someone died in his family he wanted me there. The sexual, flirty part of our friendship is very small, but *some*— just enough to make it fun and different." She thinks—and I agree— that the sexual part, though small is always *some*, is always there when a man and a woman are friends.

It's only in the past few years that I've made friends with men, in the sense of a friendship that's *mine*, not just part of two couples. And achieving with them the ease and the trust I've found with women friends has value indeed. Under the dryer at home last week, putting on mascara and rouge, I comfortably sat and talked with a fellow named Peter. Peter, I finally decided, could handle the shock of me minus mascara under the dryer. Because we care for each other. Because we're friends.

8. There are medium friends, and pretty good friends, and very 29 good friends indeed, and these friendships are defined by their level of intimacy. And what we'll reveal at each of these levels of intimacy is calibrated with care. We might tell a medium friend, for example, that yesterday we had a fight with our husband. And we might tell a pretty good friend that this fight with our husband made us so mad that we slept on the couch. And we might tell a very good friend that the reason we got so mad in that fight that we slept on the couch had something to do with that girl who works in his office. But it's only to our very best friends that we're willing to tell all, to tell what's going on with that girl in his office.

The best of friends, I still believe, totally love and support and 30 trust each other, and bare to each other the secrets of their souls, and run—no questions asked—to help each other, and tell harsh truths to each other when they must be told.

But we needn't agree about everything (only 12-year-old girl 31 friends agree about *everything*) to tolerate each other's point of view. To accept without judgment. To give and to take without ever keeping score. And to *be* there, as I am for them and as they are for me, to comfort our sorrows, to celebrate our joys.

Questions for Study and Discussion

Meaning and Purpose

1. What is the essential point of explanation or analysis Viorst wishes to make here? Is it stated in one sentence? Where?
2. In considering the varieties of friendship, the author establishes several categories. What are they? To what extent are they distinct from one another?
3. How have the author's views on friendship changed? Does she say *why* her ideas are different now?

Strategy and Audience

1. Why does classification seem an especially appropriate method here? Does Viorst support this strategy with any others? Which ones?
2. Viorst uses the first-person point of view in "Friends." Does such an open presence in the essay contribute to, weaken, or have little effect on her explanatory aim?

3. The audience for Viorst's essay (first published in *Redbook* magazine) was women under thirty-five. What clues reflect the author's awareness of her female readers? What's here for a male or older female audience?

Style and Language

1. Magazine journalism often employs a punchy, breezy style, sometimes using very brief sentences or fragments (incomplete sentences) and short paragraphs for easy reading. Look for instances of such techniques in this essay. How do you respond to them?
2. Despite her very informal language, some of Viorst's words may need looking up: ardor (paragraph 2); nonchalant (3); endodontist (14); self-revelation (22).

Writing Ideas

1. Using Viorst as a model, do your own analysis of friendship, explaining what you see (or discover) to be significant distinctions. If you use classification, try to keep your categories or types from overlapping, and support each one with specific examples from your own experience.
2. Consider the varieties of other people in your life with an eye toward pointing out significant differences. Some possibilities: fellow students, coworkers, teachers, coaches, parents, and role models.

— Lewis Thomas —

Lewis Thomas is a physician, author, research scientist, and administrator. For many years Thomas has been associated with the Memorial Sloan-Kettering Cancer Center in New York. He has taught at the University of Minnesota and served as dean of the New York University-Bellevue Medical Center and as chairman of pathology at Yale Medical School. He won the National Book Award in 1974 for his first collection of essays, The Lives of a Cell, *and has gone on to publish extensively, almost always with a scientific bent, including* The Youngest Science *and* Late Night Thoughts on Listening to Mahler's Ninth Symphony *(both 1983). Thomas's most recent book,* A Long Line of Cells: Collected Essays, *was published in 1990.*

To Err Is Human

In this selection from The Medusa and the Snail *(1979), Thomas analyzes the learning process and explains why error is essential to it. Using several rhetorical strategies, such as cause-and-effect analysis, definition, and analogy, Thomas lets us see something we usually consider discouraging in a new and hopeful way.*

Everyone must have had at least one personal experience with a computer error by this time. Bank balances are suddenly reported to have jumped from $379 into the millions, appeals for charitable contributions are mailed over and over to people with crazy-sounding names at your address, department stores send the wrong bills, utility companies write that they're turning everything off, that sort of thing. If you manage to get in touch with someone and complain, you then get instantaneously typed, guilty letters from the same computer, saying, "Our computer was in error, and an adjustment is being made in your account."

These are supposed to be the sheerest, blindest accidents. Mistakes are not believed to be part of the normal behavior of a good machine. If things go wrong, it must be a personal, human error, the result of fingering, tampering, a button getting stuck, someone hitting the wrong key. The computer, at its normal best, is infallible.

I wonder whether this can be true. After all, the whole point of computers is that they represent an extension of the human brain, vastly improved upon but nonetheless human, superhuman maybe. A good computer can think clearly and quickly enough to beat you at chess, and some of them have even been programmed to write obscure verse. They can do anything we can do, and more besides.

It is not yet known whether a computer has its own conscious-   4
ness, and it would be hard to find out about this. When you walk into one of those great halls now built for the huge machines, and stand listening, it is easy to imagine that the faint, distant noises are the sound of thinking, and the turning of the spools gives them the look of wild creatures rolling their eyes in the effort to concentrate, choking with information. But real thinking, and dreaming, are other matters.

On the other hand, the evidences of something like an *uncon-*   5
scious, equivalent to ours, are all around, in every mail. As extensions of the human brain, they have been constructed with the same prop- erty of error, spontaneous, uncontrolled, and rich in possibilities.

Mistakes are at the very base of human thought, embedded   6
there, feeding the structure like root nodules. If we were not provided with the knack of being wrong, we could never get anything useful done. We think our way along by choosing between right and wrong alternatives, and the wrong choices have to be made as frequently as the right ones. We get along in life this way. We are built to make mistakes, coded for error.

We learn, as we say, by "trial and error." Why do we always say   7
that? Why not "trial and rightness" or "trial and triumph"? The old phrase puts it that way because that is, in real life, the way it is done.

A good laboratory, like a good bank or a corporation or govern-   8
ment, has to run like a computer. Almost everything is done flaw- lessly, by the book, and all the numbers add up to the predicted sums. The days go by. And then, if it is a lucky day, and a lucky laboratory, somebody makes a mistake: the wrong buffer, something in one of the blanks, a decimal misplaced in reading counts, the warm room off by a degree and a half, a mouse out of his box, or just a misreading of the day's protocol. Whatever, when the results come in, something is obviously screwed up, and then the action can begin.

The misreading is not the important error; it opens the way. The   9
next step is the crucial one. If the investigator can bring himself to say, "But even so, look at that!" then the new finding, whatever it is, is ready for snatching. What is needed, for progress to be made, is the move based on the error.

Whenever new kinds of thinking are about to be accomplished,   10
or new varieties of music, there has to be an argument beforehand. With two sides debating in the same mind, haranguing, there is an amiable understanding that one is right and the other wrong. Sooner or later the thing is settled, but there can be no action at all if there are not the two sides, and the argument. The hope is in the faculty of

wrongness, the tendency toward error. The capacity to leap across mountains of information to land lightly on the wrong side represents the highest of human endowments.

It may be that this is a uniquely human gift, perhaps even stipu-   11
lated in our genetic instructions. Other creatures do not seem to have DNA sequences for making mistakes as a routine part of daily living, certainly not for programmed error as a guide for action.

We are at our human finest, dancing with our minds, when there   12
are more choices than two. Sometimes there are ten, even twenty different ways to go, all but one bound to be wrong, and the richness of selection in such situations can lift us onto totally new ground. This process is called exploration and is based on human fallibility. If we had only a single center in our brains, capable of responding only when a correct decision was to be made, instead of the jumble of different, credulous, easily conned clusters of neurones that provide for being flung off into blind alleys, up trees, down dead ends, out into blue sky, along wrong turnings, around bends, we could only stay the way we are today, stuck fast.

The lower animals do not have this splendid freedom. They are   13
limited, most of them, to absolute infallibility. Cats, for all their good side, never make mistakes. I have never seen a maladroit, clumsy, or blundering cat. Dogs are sometimes fallible, occasionally able to make charming minor mistakes, but they get this way by trying to mimic their masters. Fish are flawless in everything they do. Individual cells in a tissue are mindless machines, perfect in their performance, as absolutely inhuman as bees.

We should have this in mind as we become dependent on more   14
complex computers for the arrangement of our affairs. Give the comput-ers their heads, I say; let them go their way. If we can learn to do this, turning our heads to one side and wincing while the work proceeds, the possibilities for the future of mankind, and computerkind, are limitless. Your average good computer can make calculations in an instant which would have taken a lifetime of slide rules for any of us. Think of what we could gain from the near infinity of precise, machine-made miscomputation which is now so easily within our grasp. We could begin the solving of some of our hardest problems. How, for instance, should we go about organizing ourselves for social living on a planetary scale, now that we have become, as a plain fact of life, a single commu-nity? We can assume, as a working hypothesis, that all the right ways of doing this are unworkable. What we need, then, for moving ahead, is a set of wrong alternatives much longer and more interesting than the short list of mistaken courses that any of us can think up right now. We need, in fact, an infinite list, and when it is printed out we need the

computer to turn on itself and select, at random, the next way to go. If it is a big enough mistake, we could find ourselves on a new level, stunned, out in the clear, ready to move again.

Questions for Study and Discussion

Meaning and Purpose

1. What is the implied question that Thomas seeks to answer in his essay? What answer does the author propose?
2. According to Thomas, why is error important to human learning? How does the capacity for making mistakes distinguish human beings from other creatures?
3. If Thomas is explaining human error, why does he devote so much attention to computers? What do computers have to do with his explanation?

Strategy and Audience

1. Thomas uses more than one rhetorical strategy to explain how significant error is in learning. Cite sample passages that illustrate these modes of analysis.
2. Although Thomas's essays usually appear first in a medical journal, they are aimed at a general audience. What in the author's explanatory approach tells you that he's writing for the ordinary reader?
3. Do you agree with Thomas's implication that "wrong alternatives" and "big enough" mistakes can lead to improvement in human society? Why or why not?

Style and Language

1. Do you have any trouble understanding Thomas's explanation? Upon rereading, where does the essay seem most, or least, clear to you? Why?
2. Thomas combines an engaging, informal style with a fairly sophisticated vocabulary. Cite several examples of phrases or sentences that have a conversational feel (such as "something is obviously screwed up" [8]). Then list the words you don't know and, if you haven't already done so, look them up.

Writing Ideas

1. Write an essay in which you explain Thomas's thesis by examining a specific activity. For instance, how may error lead to learning in playing a sport, mastering a skill, or acquiring a new language?
2. Analyze your own learning style from an objective viewpoint. Do you acquire knowledge best by first-hand experience, observation, study, or in some other way? Can classification, comparison, causal analysis, or analogy help explain how you learn?

— Robert B. Reich —

Robert B. Reich teaches political economy and management at Harvard's John F. Kennedy School of Government. Born in 1946 in Scranton, Pennsylvania, Reich studied at Dartmouth College, Oxford University, and Yale Law School. He has been a Rhodes Scholar, law clerk, assistant solicitor general of the United States, director of policy planning for the Federal Trade Commission, and adviser to presidential candidates. Reich is the author of Minding America's Business *(1982);* The New American Frontier *(1983);* New Deals: The Chrysler Revival and the American System *(coauthor, 1985);* Tales of a New America *(1987);* The Power of Public Ideas *(1987); and* The Resurgent Liberal *(1989).*

Political Parables for Today

In this essay, written at the height of the Reagan era, Reich examines "the central experiences of American history" and finds recurring patterns and themes in the stories we tell about American life. He discovers four such themes, illustrating each story type with striking examples that surprise us with insight about our common, public life.

The 1986 campaign season is almost upon us, a prelude to the 1988 Presidential race. In short order, we will be treated to a new round of speeches, debates and interviews concerning America's most pressing problems. Some of the proposals will be original, a few of the perspectives novel. But underlying the rhetoric will be stories we have heard many times before. They are the same stories we tell and retell one another about our lives together in America; some are based in fact, some in fiction, but most lie in between. They are our national parables.

These parables are rooted in the central experiences of American history: the flight from an older culture, the rejection of central authority and aristocratic privileges, the lure of the unspoiled frontier, the struggles for social equality. One can distill four central themes:

1. *The Rot at the Top.* This parable is about the malevolence of powerful elites, be they wealthy aristocrats, rapacious business leaders or imperious government officials. It is the story of corruption in

141

high places, of conspiracy against the public. At the turn of the century, muckrakers like Upton Sinclair and Ida Tarbell uncovered sordid tales of corporate malfeasance; their modern heirs are called investigative reporters. The theme arises from the American detective story whose hero—such as Sam Spade, Serpico or Jack Nicholson in "Chinatown"—traces the rot directly to the most powerful members in the community. The political moral is clear: Americans must not allow any privileged group to amass too much power.

2. *The Triumphant Individual.* This is the story of the little person   4
who works hard, submits to self-discipline, takes risks, has faith in himself, and is eventually rewarded with wealth, fame and honor. Consider Benjamin Franklin's "Autobiography," the first of a long line of American manuals on how to become rich through self-denial and diligence. The theme recurs in the tale of Abraham Lincoln, log-splitter from Illinois who goes to the White House; in the hundred or so novellas of Horatio Alger, whose heroes all rise promptly and predictably from rags to riches, and in modern success stories, such as *Rocky* and *Iacocca*. Regardless of the precise form, the moral is the same: Anyone can "make it" in America through hard work and perseverance.

3. *The Benign Community.* The third parable is about the Ameri-   5
can community. It is the story of neighbors and friends rolling up their sleeves and pitching in to help one another, of self-sacrifice, community pride and patriotism. The story is rooted in America's religious traditions, and its earliest formulations are found in sermons like John Winthrop's "A Model of Christian Charity," delivered on board ship in Salem Harbor just before the Pilgrims landed in 1630. He envisioned a "city set upon a hill" whose members would "delight in each other" and be "of the same body." Three hundred years later, these sentiments echoed in Robert Sherwood's plays, John Steinbeck's novels, Aaron Copland's music and Frank Capra's films. The last scene in *It's a Wonderful Life* conveys the lesson: Jimmy Stewart learns that he can count on his neighbors' generosity and goodness, just as they had counted on him. They are bound together in a spirit of dependence and compassion. The principle: We must nurture and preserve genuine community.

4. *The Mob at the Gates.* The fourth parable is about social   6
disintegration that lurks just below the surface of democracy. It is the tale of mob rule, violence, crime and indulgence—of society coming apart from an excess of democratic permissiveness. It gives voice to the fear that outsiders will exploit the freedom and openness of America. The story shows up in Federalist writings about the instabilities of democracy, in Whig histories of the United States and in the anti-immigration harangues of the late 19th and early 20th centuries. Its

most dramatic appearance in recent years has come in fictionalized accounts of vigilante heroes who wreak havoc on muggers—like Clint Eastwood's Dirty Harry or Charles Bronson in *Death Wish*—and in Rambo's messy eradication of platoons of Communist fighters. The lesson: We must impose social discipline, lest the rabble overrun us.

These four parables are completely familiar to most of us. They 7 shape our political discourse. They confirm our ideologies. Every American retells and listens repeatedly to all four stories; every politician and social commentator borrows, embellishes and seeks legitimacy from them.

But the parables can be linked together in different ways, each 8 arrangement suggesting a distinct political message. At any given time in our nation's history one particular configuration has been dominant, eventually to be replaced by another. The art of political rhetoric has been to reconfigure these stories in a manner that affirms and amplifies the changes already occurring in the way Americans tell the tales.

In the early part of the century, for example, leaders of the Progres- 9 sive era emphasized the link between the parables of Rot at the Top and the Triumphant Individual. Big business—the trusts—blocked worthy citizens from their rightful places in society; corruption at the top was thwarting personal initiative. Woodrow Wilson put the matter succinctly in a speech during the 1912 Presidential campaign, promising to wage "a crusade against the powers that have governed us . . . that have limited our development . . . that have determined our lives . . . that have set us in a straitjacket to do as they please." In his view, the struggle against the trusts would be nothing less than "a second struggle for emancipation."

By the 1930's, the parables had shifted. Now the key conceptual 10 link was between Rot at the Top and the Benign Community. The liberties of common people were under attack by leaders of big business and finance. In the 1936 Presidential campaign, Franklin D. Roosevelt warned against the "economic royalists" who had impressed the whole of society into "royal service."

"The hours men and women worked, the wages they received, the 11 conditions of their labor . . . these had passed beyond the control of the people, and were imposed by this new industrial dictatorship," he warned in one speech. "The royalists of the economic order have conceded that political freedom was the business of the Government, but they have maintained that economic slavery was nobody's business." What was at stake, he concluded, was the "survival of democracy."

The shift from the Progressives' emphasis on the Triumphant 12 Individual to the New Deal's Benign Community was more than an

oratorical device. It represented a change in Americans' understanding of social life. The Great Depression had provided a national lesson
in social solidarity; nearly every American family felt the effects of
poverty. The Benign Community became intimately relevant as relatives and neighbors sought to help one another, as Government became the insurer of last resort, and then as Americans turned together
to winning the "good war" against fascism. The Benign Community
embraced the entire nation.

In the decades following World War II, however, the Benign   13
Community became a less convincing parable. Much of the country's
middle class began to enjoy a scattered suburban affluence, far re-
moved from the experiences of mutual dependence that had characterized American life a generation before. The prewar images of the
common people and the forgotten man were less compelling now that
most Americans felt prosperous and not at all forgotten; the story of
Rot at the Top was less convincing now that life at the top was within
plain sight.

The descendant of the Benign Community was a feeble impulse   14
toward social altruism. Lyndon Johnson's War on Poverty was sold to
the American public as being relatively costless. The idea was that
proper Keynesian management of the economy required substantial
public expenditures, which might as well be for the benefit of the
poor. The economy was buoyant enough that America could afford to
enlarge its welfare state; the "fiscal dividend" could be spent on the less
fortunate. And in any event, "we" were only giving "them" an "equal
opportunity," simply allowing the Triumphant Individuals among
them to come forth and find their true potential. Under the banner of
civil rights and social justice, Triumphant Individuals joined the nation's Benign Community.

Once again, the configuration of stories Americans told one   15
another began to shift. As the economy slowed in the 1970's, a public
tired of belt tightening became less tolerant of social altruism.

Enter Ronald W. Reagan, master storyteller. His parables draw   16
upon the same four American tales, but substantially recast. This time
the Rot at the Top refers to career bureaucrats in government and
liberal intellectuals. The Triumphant Individuals are America's business entrepreneurs. The Benign Community comprises small, traditional neighborhoods in which people voluntarily help one another,
free from government interference. And the Mob at the Gates is filled
with criminals, pornographers, welfare cheats, illegal immigrants,
third-world debtors and revolutionaries, ornery trading partners and
Communist aggressors—all of them encouraged by liberal acquies-
cence. The Reagan Revolution will discipline "them," to liberate the

Triumphant Individuals in "us." Political choices in this story are cast as how "hard" or "soft" we should be on "them." Hard always emerges as the only decent American response.

Inevitably, the configuration of stories Americans tell one another   17
will change yet again. The "us" and "them" recountings of the present era eventually may be superseded by a new version that reflects a more complex, interdependent world. Perhaps, in the next version, the parable of the Benign Community will be expanded to include more of the earth's peoples, and that of the Triumphant Individual will embrace our collective aspirations for freedom and dignity. Indeed, it is just possible that Americans already are telling one another these sorts of stories, and are only waiting for a new set of political leaders to give them voice.

Questions for Study and Discussion

Meaning and Purpose

1. How is each of Reich's parables "rooted in the central experiences of American history"? From what specific experience does each parable arise?
2. In addition to explaining how the stories shape political rhetoric, what does Reich say about how their use has shifted over the years?
3. In your view, how accurate are Reich's political parables? How would you apply them to recent political campaigns or reform movements? Would you add any of your own? (See "Writing Ideas," below.)

Strategy and Audience

1. Apart from his classifying parables into four categories, what other rhetorical methods does Reich apply to his subject?
2. It's clear that Reich's audience is very large—the entire citizenry. How does the author make his subject appealing to such a diverse group?
3. Does Reich reveal any of his own liberal or conservative political sentiments in this essay? If so, where? What are they?

Style and Language

1. To illustrate his points, Reich refers often to United States history and the movies. How important is it that we understand such references (to

Ida Tarbell and Jack Nicholson, for instance)? Does Reich do anything to make unfamiliar names meaningful?

2. Some candidates for the dictionary: aristocratic (paragraph 2); malevolence, rapacious, imperious, muckrakers, malfeasance (3); benign (5); permissiveness, harangues, vigilante (6).

Writing Ideas

1. Construct your own version of political or social parables that seem to you to influence the way people think or behave—in college, in communities, in families, on the national scene, and so on. Or, try applying Reich's parables to current events, such as easing Cold War tensions, or the savings and loan crisis, or other political issues.

2. Analyze another phenomenon of contemporary life, looking for possible types or categories, causes or effects. Some examples: moral values, widespread hopes or fears, career paths, social pressures.

— Marie Winn —

Marie Winn was born in Czechoslovakia and was educated at Radcliffe College. The mother of two sons, she has written often on the subject of children and family life for a number of magazines. Among her books are The Plug-in Drug *(1977) and* Children Without Childhood *(1983), from which the following essay is taken. A follow-up volume to her 1977 book,* Unplugging the Plug-in Drug: Help Your Children Kick the TV Habit, *appeared in 1987.*

Something Has Happened

Like Daniel Boorstin's essay at the end of Chapter 3, which both informs and explains, this selection is meant to serve as a transition to the following chapter. Although Winn clearly analyzes contemporary childhood, from another perspective her discussion can be seen as support for an argument about facts—the claim that childhood in recent years has undergone a profound and unsettling change.

Once upon a time a fictional twelve-year-old from New England named Lolita Haze slept with a middle-aged European intellectual named Humbert Humbert and profoundly shocked American sensibilities. It was not so much the idea of an adult having sexual designs on a child that was appalling. It was Lolita herself, unvirginal long before Humbert came upon the scene. Lolita, so knowing, so jaded, so *unchildlike,* who seemed to violate something America held sacred. The book was banned in Boston. Even a sophisticated book reviewer of the *New York Times* called Nabokov's novel "repulsive" and "disgusting."

No more than a single generation after *Lolita's* publication Nabokov's vision of American childhood seems prophetic. There is little doubt that schoolchildren of the 1980s are more akin to Nabokov's nymphet than to those guileless and innocent creatures with their shiny Mary Janes and pigtails, their scraped knees and trusting ways, that were called children not so long ago.

Something has happened to the joys of childhood. The child of a generation ago, observes the satirical magazine *National Lampoon,* spent his typical Saturday afternoon "climbing around a construction site, jumping off a garage roof and onto an old sofa, having a crabapple war, mowing the lawn." The agenda for today's child, however, reads: "Sleep late, watch TV, tennis lesson, go to shopping mall and buy albums and new screen for bong, play electronic WW II, watch TV, get high." The bulging pockets of the child of the past are itemized: "knife, compass, 36¢, marble, rabbit's foot." The contemporary tot's pocket, on the other hand, contains "hash pipe, Pop Rocks, condom, $20.00, 'ludes, Merits."

Something has happened to the limits of childhood. An adver- 4 tisement for a new line of books called "Young Adult Books" defines a young adult as "a person facing the problems of adulthood." The books, however, which deal with subjects such as prostitution, divorce, and rape, are aimed at readers between the ages of ten and thirteen, "persons" who were formerly known as children.

Something has happened to the image of childhood. A full-page 5 advertisement in a theatrical newspaper showing a sultry female wearing dark lipstick, excessive eye-shadow, a mink coat, and possibly nothing else bears the legend: "Would you believe I'm only ten?" We believe it. For beyond the extravagances of show business lies the evidence of a population of normal, regular children, once clearly distinguishable as little boys and little girls, who now look and act like little grown-ups.

Something has happened to blur the formerly distinct boundaries 6 between childhood and adulthood, to weaken the protective membrane that once served to shelter children from precocious experience and sorrowful knowledge of the adult world. All over the country newly single mothers are sitting down with their children and making what has come to be known as The Speech: "Look, things are going to have to be different. We're all in this together and we're going to have to be partners." Things truly are different for great numbers of children today as the traditional, hierarchical structure of the family in which children are children and parents are adults is eroded and new partnerships are forged.

What's going on with children today? Is everything happening 7 too soon? There is nothing wrong with sex, the modern adult has come to understand well, but what about sex at age twelve? Marijuana and alcohol are common social accessories in today's society, but is sixth grade the right time to be introduced to their gratifications? Should nine-year-olds have to worry about homosexuality? Their parents hardly knew the word until their teens. Lassitude, indifference, cynicism, are understandable defenses against the hardships of modern adult life, but aren't these states antithetical to childhood? Shouldn't these kids be out at the old fishing hole or playing with their dolls or stamp albums instead of reading *Screw* and *Hustler,* or flicking the TV dial to see what's playing, just like weary adults after a hard day's work? Shouldn't childhood be special and different?

We are at the beginnings of a new era, and like every time of 8 transition from one way of thinking to another, ours is characterized by resistance, anxiety, and no small amount of nostalgia for those familiar landmarks that most contemporary adults still recall from their own "old-era" childhoods. And yet the change has occurred so swiftly that most adults are hardly aware that a true conceptual and behavioral revolution is under way, one that has yet to be clearly defined and understood. At the heart of the matter lies a profound alteration in society's attitude towards children. Once parents struggled to preserve children's innocence, to keep childhood a carefree golden age, and to shelter children from life's vicissitudes. The new era operates on the belief that children must be exposed early to adult experience in order to survive in an increasingly complex and uncontrollable world. The Age of Protection has ended. An Age of Preparation has set in.

Every aspect of contemporary children's lives is affected by this 9 change in the way adults think about children. Indeed, it is a change as consequential as the transformation in thinking and behaving that occurred at the end of the Middle Ages. Not until then was childhood recognized as a distinct entity and children perceived as special creatures with special needs, not miniature versions of adults. Today's integration of children into adult life marks a curious return to that old, undifferentiated state of affairs in which childhood and adulthood were merged into one.

To be sure, today's changed approach to children did not result 10 from some deliberate adult decision to treat kids in a new way; it developed out of necessity. For children's lives are always a mirror of adult life. The great social upheavals of the late 1960s and early 1970s—the so-called sexual revolution, the women's movement, the proliferation of television in American homes and its larger role in child rearing and family life, the rampant increase in divorce and single parenthood, political disillusionment in the Vietnam and post-Vietnam era, a deteriorating economic situation that propels more mothers into the work force—all these brought about changes in adult life that necessitated new ways of dealing with children.

No single societal change, however important, can account for 11 the end of a centuries-old conviction about childhood and the emergence of a brave new relationship between adults and children. It was the confluence of all these changes at one time, acting upon each other and upon society as a whole, that helped to alter long-established patterns within the course of a single decade. Only with the rise in two-career families and only with the mounting divorce rate, two factors to come up again and again in the course of this discussion, did parents have cause to withdraw their close, protective attention from children. Only with the fascinating presence of television in every home, mesmerizing and sedating normally unpredictable and demanding children, was the actual decrease in adult attention and supervision made possible. This conjunction occurred in the 1960s. Suddenly the idea of childhood as a special and protected condition came to seem inadvisable if not actually dangerous, and in any event, quite impossible to maintain.

Which came first, the unchildlike child or the unprotecting 12 adult? There is an intricate interconnection to be found between society's underlying concepts of childhood and children's perceivable behavior. A circular pattern always comes into view. For instance, as today's children impress adults with their sophisticated ways, adults begin to change their ideas about children and their needs; that is, they form new conceptions of childhood. Why, these tough little customers don't require protection and careful nurture! No longer need adults withhold information about the harsh realities of life from children. No longer need they hide the truth about their own weaknesses. Rather, they begin to feel it is their duty to prepare children for the exigencies of modern life. However, as adults act less protectively (not entirely as a reaction to the seeming worldliness of their children, of course, but also because of their own adult concerns, their work, their marital problems) and as they expose children to the formerly secret underside of their lives—adult sexuality, violence, injustice, suffering, fear of death—those former innocents grow tougher, perforce, less playful and trusting, more skeptical—in short, more like adults. We have come full circle. . . .

Questions for Study and Discussion

Meaning and Purpose

1. Winn makes several related points about the changes she sees in childhood. What are they? Can you summarize them in a sentence? Does Winn make such a statement anywhere in her essay?
2. Certainly Winn wants to convince us that her view of the new childhood is objectively correct. To what extent, however, does she con-

demn the changes she mentions? Do her feelings about her subject make her analysis appear biased or slanted? If so, do you think this attitude makes it less believable? Why or why not?

3. Do you agree with Winn's characterization of modern childhood? How much of what she says reflects your own experience? Where would your analysis of childhood differ from hers?

Strategy and Audience

1. How does Winn support her explanation? Does she rely most on factual evidence, her own interpretations, or a combination of both?
2. How does Winn employ such strategies as cause-and-effect analysis and comparison/contrast to explain her views? Cite sample passages.
3. How would you define Winn's intended audience? Is her essay's appeal limited to current or prospective parents? Why or why not?

Style and Language

1. Winn's style is at times objective ("At the heart of the matter lies a profound alteration in society's attitude towards children." [paragraph 8]), at times much more personal, even sarcastic ("Why, these tough little customers don't require protection and careful nurture!" [12]). Do such stylistic shifts seem inconsistent, or can they be justified? Why does Winn repeat her title phrase, "something has happened," at the start of paragraphs 3–6?
2. Some words to check: sensibilities, appalling, jaded (paragraph 1); prophetic, akin, guileless (2); sultry, extravagances (5); precocious, hierarchical (6).

Writing Ideas

1. Analyze your own childhood from an objective viewpoint. To what extent was it an "age of protection" or an "age of preparation"? Write an essay for your fellow students in which you explain why it was one or the other, or a bit of each. Try to keep your explanation based on concrete detail and objective analysis.
2. Write your own "Something Has Happened" analysis (with your own title), in which you explain how or why a change has taken place. Some areas to consider: education, political life, sports, the arts, fads or fashions, or the economy.

— Student Essays —

In this essay, author Kevin Costello concisely explains our complex legislative process to support his thesis that making American law is intentionally difficult. He organizes his material step by step after a paragraph of background (2) following his introduction, using transitional words and phrases ("when," "next," "finally," and so on) smoothly and often. Both introductory and concluding strategies are direct, appropriate for this technical discussion, with a concluding summary. Because this analytical essay also informs, the author maintains a generally objective attitude.

Following Costello's essay is another analytical piece, with questions and suggestions for writing.

Kevin Costello

Long Odds: How a Bill Becomes Law

Introduction: Opens subject with appeal to general reader

It may seem that every time we open a newspaper or watch the news on television, we learn of some new law that's been put on the books. Certainly the amount of legislation that has been enacted over the years is enormous, and some would say excessive. *But a closer look at the legislative process reveals that the Founding Fathers built a system designed to make it very hard for new laws to be passed.*

Thesis makes a point of explanation

Second paragraph provides useful background information as context for explanation

All the laws of the United States, except for those in the Constitution and its amendments, are created through the legislative process. Pieces of proposed legislation—bills—are taken through a series of complicated and difficult steps until eventually a very low percentage completes the process and becomes law. Four different sources can propose legislation: congresspersons, congressional committees, the execu-

1

2

152

Starts step-by-step
organization

Transitions within
paragraph keep
process clear

Transition to next
phase of process

Factual support

Additional informa-
tion and transition to
next step

tive branch of government (the President's programs), and private or public interest groups.

When legislation is proposed, either as a   3
bill or a resolution, the first step in the process
has occurred. Next, the bill is referred to the
appropriate committee, which in turn submits it
to one of its subcommittees, where most of the
work is done. The subcommittee studies and
holds hearings on the proposed legislation.
When the review is completed, the subcommittee reports the bill to the full committee. If it
gives a negative account, the bill is killed. If the
subcommittee okays it, the bill must then come
under further review by the full committee. Finally, the full committee reports to the parent
house, and only a positive recommendation will
keep the bill alive.

The legislation now reaches another stum-   4
bling block. It is placed on the calendar, or
scheduled for debate. Most bills never go beyond this point because the limited sessions in
Congress allow very little time to debate all the
bills that come up. Thus, it is typical for sessions to end with most bills never having
reached the floor for debate. Even if the bill
does reach the floor, however, the house may
vote not to consider it, in effect killing it. If the
house does debate the bill, it will make any
necessary amendments and put the whole pack-
age to a vote.

Since a bill must be ratified by both houses   5
of Congress before it can be sent to the President, legislation proposed in one house must un-
dergo virtually the same steps in the other. If
both houses ratify, a conference committee is set
up to settle the differences between the two versions. The bill then goes up for final passage by
both houses in identical form. The ratified bill is
then submitted to the President for its final test.
If he signs it, the bill becomes law; if he vetoes
the bill, it goes back to Congress. If in both
houses two-thirds of the members vote for the
bill, it becomes law over the President's veto—

Conclusion: Summa-
rizes overall content
with emphatic final
statement

which happens only about 10 percent of the
time.

One can see by the number of steps in-   6
volved in the legislative process that the odds are
very great against an average bill becoming law.
At almost every turn a bill may be killed. Hundreds of bills may start out, but only a few survive to become law.

Here student Brian Finnegan replies to a piece of science journalism whose author extols the possibilities of genetic technology. In his
analysis, Finnegan explains how the human condition imposes limits
on our ability to thwart the artificial constraints we wish to place on
aging and death.

Brian Finnegan

On Death and Nature

A recent issue of *OMNI* magazine contained an article about the   1
"supergene," a group of genes on the sixth human chromosome that
controls cell repair. The article maintained that if some stimulus could
be developed by which the genes, called the major histocompatibility
complex, would be induced to continually repair themselves, then the
cells whose repairs they control would remain healthy, and if this could
be done in enough cells the aging process would slow down. Theoreti-
cally, because aging and death are considered to be the results of the
deterioration of cells, it is conceivable that death itself could be pre-
vented. The prospect of manipulating the genes in that way in humans
is as yet only a distant possibility, although one technique has been
successful in extending the life span of paramecium. This manipulation would be a serious break from what nature has dictated to be a
natural process, however, and, aside from the technical difficulties
involved, certain problems of what life would be without death present
themselves as unavoidable obstacles to those who would seriously pursue the possibility.

Man has always wished for immortality, as the prospect of one's   2 own death, if not wholly unimaginable, certainly is repugnant. Religious conviction in an afterlife has served to lessen the fear with which we face death because it states explicitly that death is not actually an end to our lives, but merely a stage in life that usually leads to a happier state of being. Some men, however, look for immortality without death, such as the discoverer of Florida who searched for years for the Fountain of Youth. Mythology has many stories of people who had immortality conferred upon them, but there are as many stories of the tragedy that can be caused by a union of what are, essentially, the mortal and immortal aspects of human nature. The one fact of life is that it ends, and that fact is inescapable, as those stories, as well as the totality of man's experience, reveal. Nature simply does not allow immortality, and man's tampering with the basic processes of nature—life and death—may lead to consequences that will point out the reasons why nature has not made some kind of regrettable error in dictating that things must die.

The only things in nature that come close to immortality are   3
species, and they come close only because they change in order to survive changing conditions. A single member of a species, including man, is insignificant on the scale of species continuation because the changes to which species must adapt occur extremely slowly. A mutation occurring today may meet a need that will exist in 100,000 years, but today the mutation is an abnormality. Nature, in other words, is indifferent to the individual, and concerns itself only with itself, or the long-range continuance of existing life forms. And this continuance is never linear; that is, it is never accomplished by the prolonged existence of an individual. The continuance is cyclic—one generation produces another, and this new generation does the same, and this occurs endlessly. What also occurs—must occur endlessly is the death of previous generations. Applied to humanity, this means that if generations ceased to die the results would be as tortuous as mass unemployment and geometrically increasing overpopulation, with its attendant starvation and disease and violent death.

These are some of the reasons why it is not a mistake that man   4
dies, as the conception of death as a failure of natural processes to occur seems to imply. But even if research reveals a way to keep our bodies in perfect repair and thus avoid dying, human nature itself imposes barriers to its ever being implemented. One must assume that the above objections would be foreseen, rendering the distribution of whatever the method might be to the world population unthinkable. Who, then, will receive the fruits of this research? How will these people be chosen? Such questions raise not only moral issues, but also the issue of man's nature as a social being. Friendship is one constant

in all societies, so what will be the psychological effects upon one who receives the treatment because of, for example, his intellectual ability, if his friends and even his family die and he is left without them? The effect would certainly be one of extreme isolation, and perhaps even the severest guilt, which no contribution to humanity could allay.

The final product of immortality would be, I think, mere bore-   5
dom. One would have lived so long, done and seen the same things so often, and witnessed that "the more things change, the more they stay the same" so invariably that rather than become a misanthrope, one would simply have had enough. Because man dies he is not psychically equipped to live forever, and, aside from accidental death, the only escape we would allow one another is suicide.

Death, then, whatever its physical causes, is a necessary part of   6
nature. It cannot be altered in itself, despite advances in medicine. The first, last, and overwhelming fact is that man does die, that life is, and always will be, limited.

Questions for Study and Discussion

Meaning and Purpose

1. What is Finnegan's main idea? Do you think his essay has a purpose beyond explaining the significance of death as part of nature? If so, what might it be?
2. According to Finnegan, what are some of the "unavoidable obstacles" that human nature places in the path of our achieving physical immortality?
3. What is it about the way in which nature works that makes death necessary and unavoidable?

Strategy and Audience

1. Finnegan uses two principal rhetorical strategies in "On Death and Nature." What are these, and how and where does he use each?
2. This essay was written for a college class. To what extent does Finnegan speak directly to his fellow students, and to what extent to a wider audience? What reason might the author have for aiming at the general reader?
3. What is your reaction to Finnegan's essay?

Style and Language

1. Finnegan's style here is more formal and academic than conversational. Why do you think he chose it? Compare his overall style to that of Lewis Thomas ("To Err Is Human") in this chapter. How would the effect of Finnegan's essay change if he had used a lighter, breezier style to explain his subject?

2. In keeping with his style, Finnegan's diction leans toward formality. Identify some of the words and phrases for which plainer language might be substituted if the essay were rewritten in an informal style. For example: "as the *prospect* of one's own death, *if not wholly unimaginable,* certainly is *repugnant*" (paragraph 2). Possible revision: "since no one likes to think about dying."

Writing Ideas

1. Write your own "On _____" essay, analyzing and explaining a current problem or issue that interests you. Some sample topics: On . . .

   - Keeping up with fashion
   - Education and careers
   - Loss
   - Growing older

2. Using Finnegan's essay as a model, find an article in a current magazine and write an analytical response to it. Briefly consider its general point, and devote the rest of your essay to explaining the issues or problems the article's author doesn't address.

— Additional Writing Ideas —

Choose a problem or question that genuinely intrigues you and explore possible answers to it in an analytical or explanatory essay. Don't pick a rhetorical strategy and then find a subject to suit it; rather, start with a subject that interests you and apply to it the strategies discussed in this chapter (analyzing process or cause-and-effect; comparing and contrasting; classifying and dividing; using analogy and metaphor), remembering those covered in Chapter 2 as well (example, description, narration, definition). Sample topics:

- How or why relationships fail (or succeed)
- How you can be your own worst enemy (or best friend)
- Why emotion and reason may sometimes conflict
- Resolving personal problems
- Becoming mature
- Healthy and unhealthy life-styles
- Independence and conformity
- Starting your own business
- Choosing career goals
- Training for sport or recreation
- Learning photography, filmmaking, a musical instrument, cooking, or other avocation
- Friends and lovers
- Using technology
- Avoiding peer pressure
- Making sense of movies
- Male and female attitudes, behavior, tastes
- What made a great sports team great
- Reality and dreams
- Love, hate, and indifference

You may want to check the suggestions in Chapter 2, page 71, as well.

— 5 —

Writing to Argue or Prove

Defending Claims, Building Cases

The Argumentative Aim

If I tell you students are smoking and drinking less these days, I'm giving you neutral information—without comment. If I tell you students are smoking and drinking less because such habits have fallen out of favor or because newer generations are paying more attention to health warnings, I'm giving information with supporting analysis or explanation. But if I tell you that students, or anyone else, *should avoid* cigarettes and immoderate amounts of alcohol because they poison the body and can cause illness and death, I'm using explanation to support an *argument*—an attempt *to convince* you that you should change your opinions or actions. Essays with an argumentative aim always include information, analysis, or explanation, but they put these to service in the attempt to convince; they go beyond informing or explaining to *advocacy,* to supporting claims or assertions (the thesis of the argument) with sound reasoning and evidence.

With arguments we attempt to show the certainty or prove the validity of our claims. We can argue *for* the validity of our assertions, or we can argue *against* others' claims, but in either situation we take a position and try to defend it. We try to build a case that seems logically undeniable—as convincing as a mathematical proof or an attorney's summation in court.

People can find themselves in dispute about almost anything, of course, from the choice for president to belief in God to the pressing matter of who lost the car keys. Most arguments, however, address basic *issues* and form a few general categories: disputes over *facts* (such as attempts to prove whether a crime has been committed); disputes over *ideas, beliefs, or values* (the morality or immorality of capital punishment); and disputes over *actions or policies* (the proper course for dealing with terrorists).

Whatever the issue or dispute, authors of argumentative essays must be especially aware of their *audience*. All writers must consider their readers, as we'll continue to see, but in argument—and in any persuasive writing—the audience is a sort of target. We're aiming to move our readers in some way, and to do so requires that we know where they stand. In general, this aim means trying to gauge the distance the argument is meant to bridge, assessing the amount of *common ground*, or lack of it, between writer and reader. When you and your audience share values or opinions, basic assumptions about the nature of things, you stand on ample common ground, and you may want to use such points of agreement to bolster your case. When common ground is less, when your differences are more fundamental, you may need to first establish what *is* shared before mounting your cause. When you and your reader share little or no agreement, a successful argument will depend on how well you demonstrate the validity of your assumptions or evidence and the conclusions you draw from them.

Whether defending your own position or attacking another, however, remember that your goal is to *convince* your readers, not to turn them away. Your assertion must be *limited* or *qualified*, able to be reasonably supported—not sweeping, unlimited generalities that no one will take seriously.

We find written argument in all walks of life—government, law, business, journalism, academia—wherever people seek to influence others with reasoned discourse. As citizens, moreover, we're the target of argumentative writing and speaking, as politicians, editorial writers, activists, and our fellow citizens try to rally our support or opposition for seemingly endless decisions, attitudes, and policies. Becoming more adept at constructing sound arguments, and learning better to evaluate those of others, then, may be one of the most useful tasks in anyone's writing education.

Argument in a Paragraph

In this brief example, the author claims that women should not be exempt from a military draft. He supports his assertion with a deductive appeal to reason—that if women and men truly are to be viewed as equals, neither group can have grounds for exemption. Notice also that to make this unpopular position more acceptable, he qualifies or limits his claim at the end of this passage.

The question of women's service is the most emotionally troubling aspect of this generally emotional issue, but the progress of domestic politics over the last ten years suggests that the answer is clear. If any sexual distinctions that would deny a woman her place as a construction worker or a telephone pole climber have been forbidden by legislators and courts, what possible distinction can spare women the obligation to perform similar functions in military construction units or the Signal Corps? President Carter recognized this reality in deciding to include women in his initial draft registration order. If women are drafted, they have an ironclad case for passage of the Equal Rights Amendment. If they are not, their claim for equal treatment elsewhere becomes less compelling. At the same time, it is troubling to think of women in combat, or of mothers being drafted, and a sensible draft law would have to recognize such exceptions.

—James Fallows, "The Draft: Why the Country Needs It"*

Argumentative Strategies

We may think of arguments as strongly voiced opinions—that one argument is as good as another—but good arguments are much more than this. We have a right to our opinions, of course, but some may be illogical or even silly, unable to pass the test of rationality. Good arguments, by contrast, are attempts at *proving* our claims valid. We go about building such proofs with two basic ways of reasoning: *induction* and *deduction*. Although either induction or deduction may be used alone to support an argument, they complement each other and are usually combined in everyday writing and speaking.

The Atlantic April 1980: 47.

Inductive Reasoning

Forms of reasoning aren't abstract contrivances; they come from ordinary experience. Inductive reasoning is the natural human tendency to generalize from such experience—to infer conclusions from a body of specific evidence or individual instances. If, when I go grocery shopping, the price of food is a little higher than last time, I'll tend to infer that inflation is in progress and that I can expect even higher prices later. The evidence of individual price hikes contributes to and *supports* my general conclusion. What happens, however, if when I continue shopping and several weeks later discover that most prices haven't changed or that some have actually declined? My evidence no longer supports the same conclusion, but leads me to a revised one: the rate of inflation may be slowing, too.

Inductive reasoning indicates *probabilities*—sometimes extremely strong ones—but does not offer absolute or perfect proof. We can only conclude what is *likely* to be true, using the best evidence we can find. When we reason inductively, then, we must be careful not to *overgeneralize* or go beyond what the evidence can support. When we *qualify* or *limit* our inferences, we help to avoid such unwarranted generality. Sometimes our information can support a fairly broad statement: "It seems clear that the days of low-budget feature films are over, given audience tastes for expensive productions and special effects." It is more likely, however, that most inductive conclusions need at least some limits: "Although the days of low-budget feature films appear to be over, some new filmmakers are trying to resurrect the tradition."

It's not always easy to know when we have enough evidence to support an inductive conclusion. Most of the time, common sense must be our guide. If I poll people to see who's likely to win the coming election, my sample must be large enough to be representative. If I see one high-speed auto collision, however, I can probably infer without seeing dozens of them that they're lethal.

The *quality* of our evidence, as much as its quantity, will determine whether the argument is convincing. If our information is accurate, reliable, able to be checked, and if we have enough to support a carefully limited conclusion, chances are we'll have a convincing case, or a convincing general statement that we can apply to a deductive argument.

Here's how an essay based on inductive reasoning might be organized:

Deductive Reasoning

When we reason deductively, instead of starting with data and generalizing from them, we start with general principles or assumptions and apply them to specific situations. Deductive reasoning relies on a logical form called the *syllogism*, which dictates the relationship among premises (the assumptions we start with), the specific case at hand, and conclusions. If the premises are true and in a valid relationship with one another, the conclusion we draw from them will be true and valid—impossible to refute. Unlike induction, deductive reasoning, with the syllogism, can give us complete certainty in our arguments.

What is the proper or valid relationship between the premises in a syllogism? The *minor premise,* the specific instance, must be contained within the general class or group of instances expressed by the *major premise:*

Major premise: All citizens have specific rights and responsibilities.

Minor premise: I am a citizen.

Conclusion: I have specific rights and responsibilities.

If I accept the two premises, and if the minor premise is an instance of the major, then the conclusion *follows* logically and convinces us because it's the only one possible. For deductive arguments to work, we must grant that the premises are true and in valid form. If we don't accept the premises, we won't accept the conclusion.

The major premise of a syllogism is a "given"; we accept it without proof, as an assumption. In some cases, the assumption is a generality derived from observation or evidence, an inductive conclusion: "Wearing safety belts reduces the risk of injury in most auto accidents." In others, the assumption is a matter of belief or value, something we grant as true or self-evident: "We must always oppose injustice." In either type, we apply the generality to an individual situation in order to derive our conclusion.

Sometimes, however, we may join our major and minor premises incorrectly, or the premises themselves may be faulty. Then our arguments may be invalid, untrue, or both. What, for instance, is wrong with this syllogism?

Major premise: All rock stars are drug abusers.

Minor premise: My friend Nick is a rock star.

Conclusion: My friend Nick is a drug abuser.

Here, the major premise is obviously false; it's an unqualified generalization and can't be supported. (Drugs may be a problem in the rock world, but certainly not *all* rock stars abuse drugs.) My friend Nick may or may not use drugs, but I haven't proved anything with this argument, even though its form is valid, because I've started with an untrue premise.

What's wrong with this one?

Major premise: Distance runners are physically fit.

Minor premise: I am physically fit.

Conclusion: I am a distance runner.

Here, all the statements are true, but the argument is invalid because the premises aren't logically related—the minor premise isn't an instance of the major generality. The conclusion, therefore, has nothing to do with the premises.

Finally, what's wrong here?

Major premise: All businessmen are crooks.

Minor premise: I am a crook.

Conclusion: I am a businessman.

The argument is both untrue and invalid. Most businessmen aren't crooks, and even if they were, and I were one, too, that wouldn't make me a businessman (unrelated premises again).

When using deductive reasoning, then, remember to (1) word your major assumptions so that your reader can accept them as true, and (2) make sure that your specific instances are covered by the generality. If you can defend both the truth and validity of your arguments, your conclusions will be soundly reasoned and forcefully convincing.

Here's how an essay based on deductive reasoning might be organized:

I.   Introduction (and thesis/claim)

II. Deductive support (general assumptions)

III. Deductive support (examples of the general case)

IV. Deductive support (refute counterarguments against II and III)

V.   Conclusion (or thesis/claim at end)

Combining Induction and Deduction: Claims, Supports, Warrants

Induction and deduction are primary forms of reasoning, each an intellectual procedure based on human experience: generalizing *from* particulars, applying generalities *to* particulars. Each supports the other. When we compose arguments in everyday life, moreover, we're likely to use both reasoning processes, as we use both our hands.

We've already seen that inductive conclusions can become the major premises of deductive arguments. Just as easily, induction can provide us with minor premises. One of the best-known examples of inductive support for a minor premise is in the Declaration of Independence (included in this chapter's readings). In this classic argument, Thomas Jefferson builds the case for American autonomy from a major-premise assumption and a minor premise supported by extensive evidence:

Major premise: People have the right to abolish tyrannical governments.

Minor premise: The government of King George III is tyrannical.

Conclusion: The people of the Colonies have a right to abolish the government of George III.

Having asserted his assumptions about basic human rights, Jefferson goes on to cite the "history of repeated injuries and usurpations" of which the Crown is guilty. The conclusion—if we grant the premises and the accompanying support—is, and was, inescapable.

We find inductive and deductive logic combined in almost every form of knowledge, as we support our conclusions with both evidence and general assumptions. Scholar Stephen Toulmin describes the everyday occurrence of such reasoning in his claim-support-warrant system of argument:

- The arguer presents a *claim* or *proposition.*
- He or she *supports* the claim with *data* (such as facts and the opinions of experts—inductive evidence) or other *reasons.*
- The advocate ties the claim and support together with an underlying *warrant* or general principle that relates them (like the major premise of a syllogism). This form of argument includes *qualifiers,* limits to keep claims from going beyond what the data can reasonably support.

Most arguments, then, will include these elements:

- The *claim* or main proposition.
- *Evidence:* specific data, either fact or opinion, gathered to back the claim. Such evidence may be in the form of testimony: statements by witnesses and experts; or as documented information: facts that can be verified by other sources.
- *Reasons or motivational appeals:* appeals to the audience's needs, values, beliefs, or common sense, including explanations and analyses.
- *Assumptions or warrants:* general principles taken for granted, believed to be true without additional proof. They may be stated explicitly or left unstated.
- *Qualifiers:* limits on the claim.

Here's an example of a claim-support-warrant argument:

Claim: Regular exercise contributes to cardiovascular fitness.

Data: Published findings in medical journals, testimony by physicians.

Other support: Testimony from heart patients who've added exercise to their daily routines.

Warrant: Most scientific studies and medical opinions are reliable.

Qualifier: "Contributes to" implies that other factors are also necessary for cardiovascular fitness.

The claim-support-warrant method acknowledges that, in everyday life, people don't always construct arguments according to strict formulas. Rather, they make assertions (claims) and attempt to support them with any evidence and reasons that seem appropriate or convincing. Here, too, we see how writing argument builds on the two aims covered in Chapters 3 and 4: We support our claims with *information* and *explanation*. We try to *justify* our positions by showing that they're based on solid facts and meaningful interpretations of those facts.

Avoiding Fallacies

Even when we take pains to write logical, well-supported arguments, however, we can run into trouble. Sometimes we fall into patterns of thought that don't really make sense. If we include such errors of logic in our arguments, our readers are sure to spot them, and sure to be *unconvinced* by them. Some pitfalls to watch for:

Unqualified or hasty generalization

Here the fallacy is basing a conclusion on insufficient evidence. Few sweeping statements can stand without qualifications or limits. Example: *College students these days study only for a career, not for the love of learning.* Although the evidence may show strong interest in careers among students, the statement above drastically oversimplifies the truth by ignoring any other possibilities.

Either/or fallacy

The arguer claims that only two choices exist—good and bad—with no chance of compromise. Example: *We can be the friends of democracy, or its enemies; the lines are clearly drawn.* Unfortunately, extreme characterizations rarely hold up.

Blurring the issues

Other common errors can crop up when we lose focus or willfully attempt to cloud the issues we're addressing. Such distractions only undermine our attempts to be persuasive. Example: *Yes, I did cheat on the exam, but I wasn't the only one. Three guys had crib sheets, and two others had advance copies of the test.* Blaming others doesn't affect the question of my guilt, but only diverts attention from it.

Arguing in a circle (begging the question)

In this error, the arguer assumes the very conclusion he or she is trying to prove. Example: *Because a balanced budget is the only responsible fiscal policy, we should balance ours immediately.* Here the author appears to draw a conclusion from a premise, but the premise and conclusion are nearly the same.

Non sequitur

Here, a claim is justified by irrelevant support. Example: *The cocaine problem is the fault of the media, which have glamorized it on television and in movies.* These are separate issues; the drug culture exists apart from the way in which it's portrayed in television or film.

Attacking the person (*ad hominem* argument)

This tactic diverts attention from the issue by questioning the opponent's character. It almost always backfires. Example: *The president's policies are unfair—the product of a man who couldn't care less about ordinary people.* The fairness or unfairness of policy is the question, not whether the president himself is compassionate.

Arguing from analogy

Although analogy and metaphor (figurative comparisons) are very useful ways to explain things, basing an argument on them won't work. Example: *The moral fiber of the American people is weakening, and eventually it will break, like thread stretched beyond the limit of endurance.* Though moral character may weaken, the comparison to fiber or thread isn't literal or factual; it *proves* nothing.

Arguing from poor or inappropriate authority

It's always useful to cite expert or first-hand testimony as evidence in an argument, as in court, but the quality of the authority can make or break a case. If testimony comes from unqualified or inappropriate sources, it adds nothing and can badly damage your claim. Example: *My uncle made some money in the stock market last year, and he says it's time to sell—another crash is coming.* My uncle may be qualified to speak about the experience of investing, but he may be much less able to give learned advice. Authorities have credentials—a record of education and achievement—and even the most expert figures may disagree. We can use their words for support—as evidence, not proof.

Avoiding fallacies in argument is, like most things, a matter of common sense and concentration. If you're paying close attention to your arguments, and viewing them as an opponent would (looking for weaknesses, gaps in logic, faulty assumptions), you're much less likely to include fallacies, and more likely to write sound, convincing argumentative essays.

Process checklist: Writing to argue or prove

The task
- What is the issue or dispute? A matter of fact? Value? Policy?
- What is the goal of my argument? To argue against an opposing position? To advocate a position of my own? To do both?
- What common ground connects me to my audience?

Exploring and collecting
- What are some potential lines of argument I might pursue?
- How can I use open writing (see Chapter 1) to uncover possible arguments I haven't thought of yet?
- Of the various cases I might build, which one(s) will be the strongest or most convincing?
- How might others' opinions or experiences help my case?

Finding your thesis
- What is the claim I'm going to make?
- Does this claim best express the essential point I want my argument to support?
- Is my thesis/claim a specific statement that I can back with further specific evidence, warrants, and reasoning?

Designing
- Which introductory strategies can best attract my reader to this argument?
- What information or explanation does the reader need in order to understand my basic point?
- How should I organize my support? How can I emphasize evidence (inductive support, data) and reasoning from assumptions (warrants and reasoned appeals)?

Process checklist: Writing to argue or prove
(*continued*)
- Where should I answer potential objections or counterarguments from readers?
- How can I conclude with convincing emphasis?

Drafting
- Am I satisfied with the overall focus and design of my argument?
- Have I discovered new or better points or justification along the way?
- Does my evidence give logical support to my claim?
- Do my reasons justify my claim?

Critical reading and rewriting
- Where is my argument weakest or open to counterargument?
- Have I stated my assumptions clearly?
- Have I used legitimate, appropriate authority to bolster my case?
- Have I committed errors in logic or common sense?

The final draft
- Have I revised my sentences, paragraphs, and entire essay with care?
- Cut unnecessary language?
- Checked for specific, concrete words?
- Polished and proofread for style, grammar, mechanics?

In the following essays, look for the essential claims in each argument and how the author supports them. Ask yourself whether the cases these writers build are convincing, whether they include any logical flaws, and whether they move you to a new or revised way of thinking. Notice, too, how the authors incorporate information and explanation in their arguments—how they use fact, analysis, and logic to defend their positions.

— William Raspberry —

William Raspberry, a nationally syndicated columnist for the Washington Post, was born in Okolona, Mississippi, in 1935. He attended Indiana Central College, earning a degree in history in 1958, and was awarded a Doctorate of Humane Letters there in 1973. Raspberry has worked for the Washington Post since 1962, first as a reporter-editor, then as urban-affairs columnist. He has taught journalism at Howard University, has lectured on race relations and public education, and has been a television commentator in Washington, D.C.

Good Advice for the College-Bound

In this column, Raspberry uses reporting and analysis to support his claim against the argument that "a liberal arts education 'doesn't prepare you for anything.'" Raspberry cites findings in a recent survey of liberal-arts graduates as his main source of evidence.

High school counselors need to get their hands on a little pamphlet just published by the University of Virginia. Its 22 pages contain more useful advice, guidance and perspective than all the high school baccalaureate addresses I've heard in 35 years—including those I've made.   1

The booklet, "Life after Liberal Arts," is based on a survey of 2,000 alumni of the university's College of Arts and Sciences. And, assuming Virginia graduates are reasonably typical, it should lay to rest the myth that a liberal arts education "doesn't prepare you for anything."   2

Ninety-one percent of the survey respondents, representing an array of professions, not only believe that liberal arts prepared them for fulfilling careers but would recommend liberal arts majors to students considering those same careers.   3

At a time when too many parents and counselors are looking at college as a sort of trade school, pressing students into such "hot" majors as engineering and computer science, these undergraduate generalists offer a different view of what college should do.   4

A 1971 biology major, who later earned a master of business administration degree and is now a bank vice president, said the   5 undergraduate years "provided me with an overall understanding of people, politics and society, which are most important to the understanding of marketing."

A $60,000-a-year executive, a 1973 psychology major, said "liberal arts helped me with the ability to think and write."   6

A preponderance of the respondents, all of whom graduated between 1971 and 1981, are working in careers that have no obvious connection with their undergraduate majors or even their first full-time jobs.   7

One-fifth of the survey participants are in law, 9 percent in medicine, another 9 percent in financial services and 6 percent each in government and electronics or computer technology.   8

But more important than the revelation that undergraduate majors have essentially no bearing on ultimate careers is the advice these successful men and women offer those who would follow them: that they [and their parents] should stop thinking of college as an assembly line that automatically deposits them, after four years, into lucrative professions. Most experienced uncertainty, confusion and discouragement immediately after graduation, and only 16 percent were happy with their first jobs.   9

College, they believe, should provide a solid general education. Far more important to career success, they say, is experiential learning—extracurricular activities, internships and summer jobs—writing and thinking skills and the students' own initiative.   10

And yet the trend is toward locking into career tracks as early as the sophomore year. "It seems that college students have a sense that their future might be more happy if they were getting an undergraduate professional degree as opposed to an undergraduate liberal arts degree," said Susan Tyler Hitchcock, an assistant professor of humanities at the University of Virginia who, with Richard S. Benner of the university's Office of Career Planning and Placement, co-authored the booklet. "They'll seem more ready-made for a job, whereas they'll have to sell themselves more with liberal arts."   11

But the unsurprising fact is that most students cannot know at age 19 or 20 what they will want to be doing at age 39 or 40. Instead of a too-early commitment to a specific career, the survey consensus recommends this "winning combination": a liberal arts foundation, complemented with career-related experience and personal initiative.   12

It is, to this liberal arts graduate and father of a college-bound daughter, splendid advice.   13

Questions for Study and Discussion

Meaning and Purpose

1. What is the primary claim in Raspberry's essay? Is he attempting to affect opinion, action, or both? Explain.
2. From one perspective, Raspberry may be seen as a reporter rather than an advocate of a belief or policy. Where does he objectively inform in this essay, and where does he actually advocate?
3. According to Raspberry, why is getting a liberal-arts education better than "locking into career tracks as early as the sophomore year"? What is the "winning combination" that he recommends?

Strategy and Audience

1. Does Raspberry's case rely mostly on evidence (inductive reasoning) or assumptions (deductive reasoning)? Cite passages to support your answer.
2. What kinds of data does the author use to support his argument? What underlying general principle or warrant links the claim and the data?
3. Is the author writing for an audience of high-school counselors, prospective college students, parents, or all three groups? Explain.

Style and Language

1. Raspberry's essay appeared as a newspaper column. Often, journalistic style encourages very brief, sometimes single-sentence paragraphs. What effect do such brief paragraphs have? Although the paragraphs may be short, sentences may be relatively long. Do any of Raspberry's sentences seem longer than necessary or in any way unclear? (Check paragraph 9, for instance.) How might you revise?
2. For the dictionary: baccalaureate (paragraph 1); preponderance (7); revelation, lucrative (9); experiential (10).

Writing Ideas

1. Write a defense of early career choice in college, or challenge the view that liberal preparation is necessarily the best. What specific objections would you raise to Raspberry's points? How would you

question the assumptions that underlie the argument for liberal-arts education? What data would you use to support your case? (Such an exercise may make you an even greater believer in the liberal arts.)

2. Argue for or against the kind of educational preparation you received in high school. You may need first to describe and define your course work, but focus on specific strengths and weaknesses. What assumptions underlie your argument? What data or evidence supports your claims? How would you change the educational emphasis in your high-school preparation?

— Ellen Goodman —

*Ellen Goodman is a syndicated columnist for the Boston Globe, where
she has been since 1967. Born in 1941 in Newton, Massachusetts, Goodman earned her B.A. from Radcliffe College in 1963, and in that year
began her journalistic career as a researcher and reporter at Newsweek
magazine, in New York. She later worked as a feature writer for the
Detroit Free Press and has been a radio and television commentator. She
has received several honors for her commentary, among them the Pulitzer
Prize and a distinguished writing award from the American Society of
Newspaper Editors, both in 1980. A collection of her essays, Making
Sense, appeared in 1989.*

When Smokers Court Lung Cancer, Do Makers Share the Blame?

*Goodman's essay was written about a number of lawsuits against tobacco
companies in the mid-1980s, and before the courts had ruled. Goodman
admits that the cases will be hard to win (she was right), but insists that
although the companies may avoid legal responsibility, they must share
moral responsibility for tobacco's potential hazards.*

In the last year two people I was close to died of lung cancer. It 1
goes without saying that these two were both cigarette smokers. They
had bought their first Lucky Strike or Camel or Chesterfield as teen-
agers in the 1940s. They had smoked thousands of cartons of dozens of
brands, two packs a day, three packs a day, until they died.

One tried to quit 20 times. Another had quit, finally, in the 2
hospital because he wasn't allowed to smoke around his oxygen tank.

I don't say this to disqualify myself from writing about smoking 3
but rather to qualify. As a survivor I have to ask who is to blame for
these two deaths, or for the 350,000 other Americans—friends, un-
cles, parents—who died of smoking-related diseases last year?

The daily newspaper, the medical establishment, even the ciga- 4
rette packs these smokers opened carried warnings about the lethal
dangers of cigarettes. Some 45,000 studies documented the link between smoking and ill health. Weren't these consumers responsible for
what they inhaled? Didn't they kill themselves?

What then about the tobacco industry? Year after year the people   5
who write for the Tobacco Institute go on rebutting the medical research, trying to convince us that cigarettes are not bad. The companies have spent $1.5 billion a year in advertising to entice Americans,
especially young Americans, to smoke. Don't they bear any responsibility for manufacturing and marketing such a lethal product?

These questions of responsibility, personal and corporate, will be   6
argued in the courtroom this spring by dying smokers and/or their
survivors who are suing tobacco companies. Juries in Massachusetts,
New Jersey, Texas, California, Minnesota and West Virginia will decide whether a person who lit her own cigarettes can turn around and
collect payment from the company that made them. They will decide
whether a manufacturer who denied any smoking risks can turn around
and claim that a customer smoked at his own risk.

The spring rash of cases is not a coincidence. It comes out of the   7
current antismoking climate and out of recent changes in the liability
law. In the last few years courts have ruled that a product is unreason-
ably dangerous when the risks outweigh the benefits. Such a product,
they have said, has to carry warnings, very explicit warnings.

"The courts had looked at DES, at asbestos. Why not go after the   8
most dangerous drug of all? The law was all there, ready to be applied
to cigarettes," says Richard Daynard, a professor at Northeastern University School of Law who started the Tobacco Products Liability
Project, a group of doctors and lawyers working on the strategy for
suing tobacco companies.

It is the conviction of these advocates that smokers are not fully   9
to blame for their illnesses. Smoking isn't a free choice but an addiction. The warnings carried on the cigarette packages vastly understate
the dangers of smoking and ignore those of addiction. At the same
time the ads proffer countermessages of health and happiness.

The suit strategy is, Daynard maintains, the latest ammunition of   10
frustrated public-interest groups against the tobacco lobby.

"We would prefer to have kept the epidemic from happening,"   11
Daynard says. "But this compensates the families. It produces a lot of
very detailed publicity on just how bad cigarettes are, and if the cost of
litigation could raise the price of cigarettes to $3 or $4 a pack it would
reduce consumption in the next group of potential addicts."

These cases are not going to be won easily. Smoking is an addic-   12
tion, but there are millions who have kicked the habit. Few of us are
comfortable regarding the smoker as a helpless victim.

But the tobacco industry does have a full measure of guilt for the   13
epidemic of smoking diseases, for the $13-billion-a-year medical bill.
In most states, consumers can recover some damages from the manufac-

turer of a dangerous product even when they were partially to blame for their own injury. At the very least, cigarette makers should share the cost of the damage.

Ideally, the threat of suit even might force the tobacco industry   14 to do something truly radical, to stop denying the link between smoking and emphysema, lung cancer, heart disease. The least compensation owed to the survivors is the truth.

Questions for Study and Discussion

Meaning and Purpose

1. Goodman states her claim plainly. What is it, and where does she place it in the essay? Do you see a second, closely related claim here? If so, what is it?
2. How have changes in the liability law contributed to the increase in suits against the tobacco companies? What legal precedent in most states also makes such companies appear to be liable?
3. Does Goodman propose a specific remedy for the problem she isolates?

Strategy and Audience

1. What evidence does the author offer to support the proposition that tobacco companies are at least partly responsible for smokers' illnesses?
2. In speaking for the advocates with the Tobacco Products Liability Project, Goodman says that "smoking isn't a free choice but an addiction." How does she limit or qualify this assertion for those who would object to it as a sweeping generalization?
3. Whether you smoke or not, how do you respond to Goodman's argument? Is she convincing? Why or why not?

Style and Language

1. In paragraph 13, Goodman uses the word "guilt" in asserting tobacco-company responsibility. To what extent does this word imply moral or ethical condemnation? Does a word with such connotations strengthen or weaken Goodman's case? (We'll consider such language tactics in detail in Chapter 7, "Writing to Persuade.")
2. As a columnist for a national newspaper audience, Goodman keeps

her language plain and simple overall. Some suggestions for vocabulary study: proffer (paragraph 9); epidemic (11).

Writing Ideas

1. Build a case of advocacy or attack on another consumer issue. Some sample topics:

    • Should liquor manufacturers be held liable for alcohol-related illness or death?
    • Should liquor manufacturers be forced by law to affix warning labels to their products?
    • Should doctors or drug companies be held liable for patients who may become addicted to a drug during medication?
    • Should stockbrokers or financial advisers be held liable for giving their customers poor or costly advice?

2. Find an argumentative newspaper column or editorial with which you disagree and write a counterargument, disputing its claims and supporting your own.

— Thomas Jefferson —

Born in Virginia in 1743, Thomas Jefferson was one of the most influential and respected men of his day. A lawyer by trade, Jefferson was a politician, diplomat, architect, farmer, and writer. After the Revolutionary War, Jefferson served as governor of Virginia, secretary of state under George Washington, and vice president to John Adams. He was elected third president of the United States in 1801. Among his many accomplishments, Jefferson was architect and founder of the University of Virginia. He died July 4, 1826.

The Declaration of Independence

As a delegate to the Continental Congress, Jefferson drafted the Declaration of Independence, which was reviewed by his colleagues and revised in debate by the Congress. The document remained Jefferson's, however— especially in its clarity, eloquence, and force. In the perfect elegance of its content and form, it is a classic example of argumentative prose.

When in the course of human events, it becomes necessary for one 1 people to dissolve the political bands which have connected them with another, and to assume among the powers of the earth, the separate and equal station to which the Laws of Nature and of Nature's God entitle them, a decent respect to the opinions of mankind requires that they should declare the causes which impel them to the separation.

We hold these truths to be self-evident, that all men are created 2 equal, that they are endowed by their Creator with certain unalienable rights, that among these are life, liberty and the pursuit of happiness. That to secure these rights, governments are instituted among men, deriving their just powers from the consent of the governed. That whenever any form of government becomes destructive of these ends, it is the right of the people to alter or to abolish it, and to institute new government, laying its foundation on such principles and organizing its powers in such form, as to them shall seem most likely to effect their safety and happiness. Prudence, indeed, will dictate that governments long established should not be changed for light and transient causes; and accordingly all experience hath shown, that mankind are more disposed to suffer, while evils are sufferable, than to right themselves by abolishing the forms to which they are accustomed. But when a long train of abuses and usurpations, pursuing invariably the same object, evinces a design to reduce them under absolute despotism, it is their right, it is their duty, to throw off such government, and to provide new guards for their future security. Such has been the patient sufferance of these Colonies; and such is now the necessity which constrains them to alter their former systems of government. The history of the present King of Great Britain is a history of repeated injuries and usurpations, all having in direct object the establishment of an absolute tyranny over these States. To prove this, let facts be submitted to a candid world.

He has refused his assent to laws, the most wholesome and necessary for the public good.   3

He has forbidden his Governors to pass laws of immediate and pressing importance, unless suspended in their operation till his assent should be obtained; and when so suspended, he has utterly neglected to attend to them.   4

He has refused to pass other laws for the accommodation of large districts of people, unless those people would relinquish the right of representation in the legislature, a right inestimable to them and formidable to tyrants only.   5

He has called together legislative bodies at places unusual, uncomfortable, and distant from the depository of their public records, for the sole purpose of fatiguing them into compliance with his measures.   6

He has dissolved representative houses repeatedly, for opposing with manly firmness his invasions on the rights of the people.   7

He has refused for a long time, after such dissolutions, to cause others to be elected; whereby the legislative powers, incapable of annihilation, have returned to the people at large for their exercise; the State remaining in the meantime exposed to all the dangers of invasion from without and convulsions within.   8

He has endeavoured to prevent the population of these states; for that purpose obstructing the laws for naturalization of foreigners; refusing to pass others to encourage their migration hither, and raising the conditions of new appropriations of lands.   9

He has obstructed the administration of justice, by refusing his assent to laws for establishing judiciary powers.   10

He has made judges dependent on his will alone, for the tenure of their offices, and the amount and payment of their salaries.   11

He has erected a multitude of new offices, and sent hither swarms of officers to harass our people, and eat out their substance.   12

He has kept among us, in times of peace, standing armies without the consent of our legislatures.   13

He has affected to render the military independent of and superior to the civil power.   14

He has combined with others to subject us to a jurisdiction   15
foreign to our constitution, and unacknowledged by our laws; giving
his assent to their acts of pretended legislation:

For quartering large bodies of armed troops among us: 16

For protecting them, by a mock trial, from punishment for any   17
murders which they should commit on the inhabitants of these States:

For cutting off our trade with all parts of the world: 18

For imposing taxes on us without our consent: 19

For depriving us in many cases of the benefits of trial by jury: 20

For transporting us beyond seas to be tried for pretended offences: 21

For abolishing the free system of English laws in a neighbouring   22
Province, establishing therein an arbitrary government, and enlarging
its boundaries so as to render it at once an example and fit instrument
for introducing the same absolute rule into these Colonies:

For taking away our Charters. abolishing our most valuable laws,   23
and altering fundamentally the forms of our governments:

For suspending our own legislatures, and declaring themselves   24
invested with power to legislate for us in all cases whatsoever.

He has abdicated government here, by declaring us out of his   25
protection and waging war against us.

He has plundered our seas, ravaged our coasts, burnt our towns,   26
and destroyed the lives of our people.

He is at this time transporting large armies of foreign mercenaries   27
to complete the works of death, desolation and tyranny, already begun
with circumstances of cruelty and perfidy scarcely paralleled in the
most barbarous ages, and totally unworthy the Head of a civilized
nation.

He has constrained our fellow citizens taken captive on the high   28
seas to bear arms against their country, to become the executioners of
their friends and brethren, or to fall themselves by their hands.

He has excited domestic insurrections amongst us, and has en-   29
deavoured to bring on the inhabitants of our frontiers, the merciless
Indian savages, whose known rule of warfare, is an undistinguished
destruction of all ages, sexes, and conditions.

In every stage of these oppressions we have petitioned for redress   30
in the most humble terms: our repeated petitions have been answered
only by repeated injury. A prince whose character is thus marked by
every act which may define a tyrant is unfit to be the ruler of a free
people.

Nor have we been wanting in attention to our British brethren.   31
We have warned them from time to time of attempts by their legislature

to extend an unwarrantable jurisdiction over us. We have reminded them of the circumstances of our emigration and settlement here. We have appealed to their native justice and magnanimity, and we have conjured them by the ties of our common kindred to disavow these usurpations, which would inevitably interrupt our connections and correspondence. They too have been deaf to the voice of justice and of consanguinity. We must, therefore, acquiesce in the necessity, which denounces our separation, and hold them, as we hold the rest of mankind, enemies in war, in peace friends.

We, therefore, the Representatives of the United States of America, in General Congress assembled, appealing to the Supreme Judge of the world for the rectitude of our intentions, do, in the name, and by authority of the good people of these Colonies, solemnly publish and declare, That these United Colonies are, and of right ought to be, Free and Independent States; that they are absolved from all allegiance to the British Crown, and that all political connection between them and the state of Great Britain, is and ought to be totally dissolved; and that as Free and Independent States, they have full power to levy war, conclude peace, contract alliances, establish commerce, and to do all other acts and things which Independent States may of right do. And for the support of this declaration, with a firm reliance on the protection of Divine Providence, we mutually pledge to each other our lives, our fortunes, and our sacred honor.

Questions for Study and Discussion

Meaning and Purpose

1. According to Jefferson, from what source do governments derive their "just powers"? For what purpose do people establish governments?
2. What is the underlying assumption, or major premise, in Jefferson's argument? Do you find more than one? Explain.
3. What does Jefferson claim is the purpose of the Declaration?

Strategy and Audience

1. Why does Jefferson include specific evidence to support his case? Explain why such evidence does, or does not, justify his conclusion.
2. Point out passages in which Jefferson addresses potential opposition to his claims. How do these statements strengthen his argument?

3. Why does Jefferson temper his attack with an appeal to the common ground between British and American people? Why does he refer directly to his audience in the text?

Style and Language

1. Although the Declaration is a model of logical structure, it does include powerful language that helps to arouse bad feeling toward the Crown—calling the king a tyrant in paragraph 30, for instance. (For more on connotative language, see Chapter 7.) Find other examples of words with such negative connotations. To what extent do they help or hinder Jefferson's case?
2. Jefferson's vocabulary is rich and varied. Some suggestions for study: endowed, usurpations, evinces (paragraph 2); dissolutions, annihilation (8); abdicated (25); perfidy (27); magnanimity, consanguinity, acquiesce (31); rectitude (32).

Writing Ideas

1. Write your own declaration of principle or action about a contemporary issue that deeply interests you. Consider "self-evident" assumptions upon which you may want to base your argument, and specific evidence that can support your case. Make your argument a reasonable presentation, avoiding emotional language or exaggeration.
2. Write a condensed version of the Declaration in your own words, following Jefferson's meaning and structure but paraphrasing in today's standard English. For example, the first sentence might become: "When people decide to establish the political independence to which they are naturally entitled, they should state their reasons openly."

— Adam Smith —

*Adam Smith (pen name of George J. W. Goodman) is an author, journalist, and television commentator. Widely known for his books on the business world—*The Money Game *(1967);* Supermoney *(1972);* Paper Money *(1981); and* The Roaring Eighties *(1988)—Smith has branched out into television, as an analyst on "The Nightly Business Report" and as moderator of his own Public Broadcasting System program, "Adam Smith's Money World," the first American business program to be broadcast on Soviet television. For years Smith wrote a column for* Esquire, *"The Conventional Wisdom," in which he addressed current issues with unusual clarity and insight.*

The City as the OK Corral

In this, one of his "Conventional Wisdom" pieces, Smith examines the notorious case of Bernhard Goetz, the "subway vigilante," and builds an argument against the kind of response to crime that Goetz's actions typify. Smith combines personal information and objective analysis in this long, informal essay, allowing his argumentative point to appear at the end of his discussion, where it receives particular emphasis.

On December 22, 1984, Bernhard Hugo Goetz was riding on the 1
subway in New York. Goetz is a slight, blond, bespectacled electrical engineer. He was approached by four black youths, one of whom asked him for five dollars. Asking for five dollars is itself not a crime, but streetwise New Yorkers know how to translate it: it sometimes means "Give me your wallet," just as a seemingly innocent question like "Do you have the time?" in some circumstances means "Give me your watch."

As the world now knows, Goetz's response was to shoot the four 2
black youths, two of them in the back. Goetz turned himself in a few days later, went before a grand jury, was acquitted of attempted murder and charged only with illegally carrying a gun. The four black youths, it turned out, all had police records, and two had been carrying sharpened screwdrivers with them as casually as plumbers carry their tools to work.

Goetz quickly became a folk hero. His high forehead and wire- 3
rimmed glasses appeared on T-shirts that said GO GET 'EM GOETZ.

Bumper stickers and other T-shirts sprouted the slogan GOETZ FOUR, CROOKS ZERO. Goetz himself did not attempt to cash in but *did* begin to sound off about the right of citizens to defend themselves. The Goetz case was relentlessly flogged by the media and was finally brought before a second grand jury that indicted him for attempted murder.

It is not the purpose of this column to argue the Goetz case in particular—that may go on for years. But was this whole incident just good newspaper copy? Is crime in this country as rampant as the public support for Goetz seemed to indicate? What is at stake here, anyway?   4

The Goetz case comes under the category of "random street crime." It is random because the participants in the drama did not know each other. We are not talking about marital quarrels and family arguments. And it is a street crime because we are not talking about the Mafia on the one hand, or about white-collar criminals on the other.   5

New York City is a frontier in this category of random street crime. Now, I know people in Miami who travel with loaded guns on the front seats of their cars. I know about dangerous automatic elevators in apartments in southern California. I would not like to try to hail a cab in some areas of Washington, D.C., too late at night. But New York is a particular kind of frontier, just as the Texas hill country was a century ago. The Texans had a particularly hard time because the Commanches they faced were so fierce and so cruel—the Indians sliced the eyelids off their victims and left them to look at the sun, or they scalped them. That helped determine the character of the first wave of Texans; in Massachusetts, on the other hand, the Wampanoag tribe gave the pilgrims corn for their first Thanksgiving.   6

New York is a frontier because the predators and their victims are so close to each other, brought together by a disagreeable but effective system of public transportation. Investment bankers fold their *Wall Street Journals* on the Lexington Avenue express among youths who carry their sharpened screwdrivers to "work." I know a Wall Street lawyer who was on his way home from a black-tie dinner party with his wife and was accosted at Park Avenue and East Sixty-fourth Street—a corner where the apartments can sell for $1 million. He was shot in the face and is still being rehabilitated.   7

I don't mean to suggest that the predators prey only on the rich; the poor are always the first victims. But in New York City the predators are particularly mobile. New York does not lead the nation in felonies per thousand, but it is an amphitheater in which a predator   8 and a victim of sharply contrasting backgrounds can find themselves face to face.

In the wake of the Goetz case, New Yorkers told one another mugging stories. Here is one that is typical in several respects. A friend of mine is a distinguished writer on cities and city spaces, a former consultant to the New York City Planning Commission, and a man who has made movies examining how people use various spaces in a city.   9

"I went into the Canal Street subway station at about 11:00 in the morning, and I realized a bit too late that I wasn't in one of the well-populated entrances, but in one of those long, thin corridors leading to the station," he recalled recently. "A guy came toward me— what I remember is a leather jacket and high-top basketball shoes— and when he got about fifteen feet away he took out a .45 and said, 'Throw me your wallet.' Now, I was a platoon leader in the Marines and the .45 was what we were issued, and I was a very good shot with a .45. He was waving this weapon around uncertainly. So I spoke very calmly—they always say take command of the situation as best you can—and I threw him my wallet. Then he said, 'Turn around and walk the other way.' That was a long walk, and the only time I was really scared. I went upstairs and dialed 911, the police emergency number. It took about half an hour to get through, and when the cops did come they were very bored and very perfunctory. The next week I read in the paper that a businessman carrying a briefcase had been shot with a .45 in the subway next to Canal."   10

I asked my friend—whose Marine career included the World War II battle of Guadalcanal—whether he had been more scared in the subway or on Guadalcanal.   11

"Guadalcanal was bloody; men died," he said. "But each Marine unit was assigned a cruiser sitting offshore. If you were sent out and the Japanese pinned you, you could call up a ship like the *Astoria* and tell them where you were, and in minutes you would hear this salvo come whistling over your head. In the New York subway there's nothing like the *Astoria* to back you up."   12

The elements of my friend's subway story that are typical are: the predator arrived by public transportation and got away on foot; the police did not respond instantly; the report of the crime seemed destined for immediate burial in bureaucratic paper work; the criminal was not apprehended.   13

New Yorkers speak of these incidents as if they were traffic accidents. Most New Yorkers have not been mugged, but they are all close to a mugging story. For years I wrote a column in another magazine; an illustrator at that magazine was given a ten-speed bike by his wife and   14 children for his birthday. He rode off into Central Park on the brand-new bike one spring afternoon. He was clubbed to death by a gang of youths, who took the bike. We were stunned by the uselessness and randomness of this loss of life.

But we accepted it. A thought struck me at the time: parents in   15
the most fashionable part of New York, the Upper East Side, were instructing their children to hand over their bus pass or their lunch money to teenage muggers who prowled the streets like leopards looking for tender gazelles. It was streetwise to hand over the money quickly, lest one be knifed. People otherwise very active in their lives trained themselves to be passive on the streets.

The active approach—the most extreme active approach—is   16
now promoted by the gun lobby, which says that muggers won't hit armed citizens. The National Rifle Association mails out brochures and leaflets, many of which contain happy stories about criminals foiled by users of handguns. I say "happy" without irony. Here is an example:

> When Phoenix, Arizona, authorities responded to a breaking-and-entering call, they found a seventy-seven-year-old woman gently rocking in her favorite chair. Her favorite .38 revolver was pointed at a man obediently lying half in and half out of her "pet door."

Among the interesting statistics I got from the NRA are these: 17
nearly five million Americans say they have *used* (my italics) a handgun for defense; 65 percent of *Glamour* magazine's readers own guns, and two thirds of those own them for defense. *Glamour* is a magazine for style-conscious young women. Bernhard Goetz himself, with his new celebrity, took on the role of Cotton Mather to preach of the dangers of subway crime—he advised that citizens not only carry guns, but learn how to use them swiftly. "You've got to teach them how to get the gun out quickly," he said. "You can't have a guy fumbling with the weapon . . . crimes happen too quickly for that."

It seems to me there is a major flaw in the argument that citizens   18
must go around armed—and especially that they must learn to fire quickly. One imagines entrepreneurs renting .45s at the entrances to subways, as if everybody were getting ready for the Gunfight at the OK Corral on the way to work in the morning. I don't want to be on a subway where everyone draws quickly.

No sober urban dweller wants to live in an environment where   19
he has to wear a gun. The only reason this kind of talk is even

entertained is that *effective* criminal justice has faded from such places as the New York City subway system. James Q. Wilson is a Harvard professor of government who has specialized in the study of crime for many years. In his view, the predator in a random street crime is acting as a rational economic man. He may indeed harbor frustrations, he may be angry, but basically he wants to succeed at his crime, and he calculates the odds of success. Therefore, the job of deterring crime is one not only of stacking the odds against the criminal, but of making sure that he *knows* those odds are there.

Right now the odds are decidedly *with* him. First, he may well not   20
be apprehended. Second, if he is apprehended, his chances of escaping punishment are still high. Roger Starr, author of the recent *Rise and Fall of New York City*, studied the criminal justice system in researching his book. "The guy may have a record, but most likely no one will know it," Starr says. "The record-keeping in the justice system is terrible. We have overlapping jurisdictions everywhere: at city, county, state, and federal levels. The criminal is justified in thinking, 'They'll lose my records.' Even stupid criminals now know they can have a lawyer, and their lawyer immediately begins the tactics of delay. The more delay, the lighter the sentence; months pass, witnessses disappear, memories fade. Therefore, almost all sentences are plea-bargained."

Even with the criminal incarcerated, there is pressure on the   21
justice system to let him go so that someone else can be put into his cell; Americans want the cost of government reduced, and it costs $40,000 a year to keep a man in jail. New York State has seen its prison budget rise from $100 million a year in 1972 to more than $700 million currently.

It seems to me, even after a cursory reading of the responses to   22
the Goetz case and some of the literature on the problem, that if we accept James Q. Wilson's idea of the criminal as one who rationally calculates the odds, then we must focus attention on the *swiftness* of the system, and on *identification* of the criminals. Surely in this age of fourth-generation computers this is possible, and we already spend more than $36 billion on security and crime prevention and detection. (The criminal justice system does not need a fourth-generation computer with thirty million calculations per second—just something post-Dickensian.) If the petty criminal saw his thumbprint, picture, and record when he went to the station house, it might affect his calculations. Too often, he'll put his faith in the probability of misfiled papers.

I don't want to be simplistic. Of course better schools and more   23
jobs help cut the crime statistics. People who are in school commit fewer crimes than people who are not, and people who work commit

fewer crimes than those who are unemployed. But jobs alone are not the answer. Boston has a labor shortage so desperate that last fall, retail clerks and office workers were being bused in from as far as sixty miles away, but crime did not diminish significantly.

Rapid and certain identification of previous offenders, I'm con-   24
vinced, would go a long way toward creating a deterrence, but once again I don't want to be simplistic. What happens to the culprits after they are sentenced? Do they watch soap operas and play checkers? "Rehabilitation" implies that the jails can do something the school system has failed to do. But the school system has more resources. Should there be a work program for those who commit misdemeanors? What's important is that *something* follow the identification, trial, and sentencing, but that is too complex a subject for this particular column.

If the "law and order" response to the Goetz case was *Arm the*   25
citizens, one might characterize the liberal response as *Society is the mugger.* Kenneth Clark, a retired professor of psychology and authority on race relations, asks: What about "mugged communities," "mugged neighborhoods," and "mugged schools"? Clark sees the problem as anger. "Having been robbed of the minimum self-esteem essential to their humanity," he writes, "they [the muggers] have nothing to lose. Not able to express their frustrations in words, they express their indignation in the form of more crime."

In other words, the muggers are angry, and not totally responsi-   26
ble, because they come from bad neighborhoods and bad schools. Let us say right off that no one is *for* bad neighborhoods and bad schools and that society would be better off if education were better. But no citizens are more highly taxed than those of New York City; they pay the highest taxes in the country. A New York resident can expect to give the state and city government forty-one cents on the dollar at the highest marginal rate, compared with thirty-four cents in Miami and Dallas. No city has had a larger CETA program, and no city has more articulate citizens worrying about the problems of violent crime.

In a way it is ironic to have New York condemned for its "mugged   27
neighborhoods." It was New York's traditional role to welcome and educate poor immigrants. That made it—like some other northern cities—a magnet in the years after World War II. New York's welfare system was the most generous, and in the years when southern farms and plantations were mechanizing, the agricultural workers displaced by machines were frequently given a bus ticket, a token amount of cash, and the address of the welfare office in New York. New York's onetime glamour mayor, John Lindsay, was a congressman in those years, and his southern colleagues would clap him on the back and say,

"John, we're sending 'em right up to you." New York's original taxpayers can scarcely be accused of mugging neighborhoods, at least in terms of the level of taxes paid.

The fact is, as Harvard's James Q. Wilson points out, most poor people do *not* commit crimes, and most muggers are not stealing to put bread on the table for their starving children. 28

One response to Dr. Clark's society-is-the-mugger article was a kind of weariness. "We heard this in the Sixties, 'The criminal is the victim.' When does the criminal become responsible *himself?*" And there was a second response: "What about the Koreans?" The Koreans in New York are a more recent wave of immigrants than the blacks and Hispanics. They are most visible in brightly lit all-night fruit and grocery stores. The popular image is that, even though many can barely speak English, they work eighteen hours a day to send their children to medical school, and four Koreans on a subway would not inspire fear of a mugging. Why not? They live in "mugged neighborhoods," but ambition and family life keep them focused on the means of getting out of those mugged neighborhoods. 29

"Why shouldn't we get ourselves beaten up without a whimper?" said Bernhard Goetz. "We have already given up the streets, the trains, the city, to the criminals; it's only a matter of time before we give up our houses." 30

This is the kind of Goetz hyperbole the press loves. New York still boils with street life; it is one of the few places in the country that is open after dinner, and young people continue to flock to it for its vitality and excitement. Nobody appointed Bernhard Goetz to defend the streets and the trains. 31

But the threat of street crime—of predators—is what helps kill city life. Recently I was in south Florida, which experienced high crime rates after the Mariel boatlift. My hosts sold their house after it had been burgled three times and moved into a high-rise where they drive in, insert a plastic card into a machine, and wait to be identified on closed-circuit television. They see only friends who live in other similarly secured buildings. The predators are kept out—but so is the vitality of city life; everyone lives in sanitized packages. It is like life among the Comanches, only the forts are high-rise. 32

What is at stake here *is* city life. The words *city* and *civilization* have the same root. Cities are not merely the repository of civilization—the art and the music and the theater—they are marketplaces, crossroads, where all kinds of people come together. That's why young people head for cities. Every advanced industrial society enjoys city life, and in most of the cities citizens take for granted that they can get from their house to the corner in safety. We do not need self-appointed vigilantes, but we 33 do need a system that retires the predators instead of the rest of us. We can survive with plastic ID cards and closed-circuit surveillance, but then we will have lost part of what life is about.

Questions for Study and Discussion

Meaning and Purpose

1. What is Smith trying to persuade us to think or do? Does he make any related claims? If so, what are they? What forms of reasoning does he use for support?
2. What do you think is the underlying warrant or general principle upon which Smith builds his argument? Does he state it explicitly anywhere in the essay? To what extent might such an assumption establish common ground between Smith and his readers?
3. If Smith favors swift response to the "predators," why is he so opposed to "self-appointed vigilantes"? Is Smith's essay more a condemnation of Bernhard Goetz, or the criminal-justice system? Why?

Strategy and Audience

1. Smith uses a controlling analogy or metaphor throughout his essay—the city as wild-west frontier town, and its street criminals as Comanches attacking the settlers. How useful is this figurative comparison in explaining Smith's analysis of the problem? Does it help, or hinder, his basic argument? Is it an argumentative fallacy in the essay? Why or why not?
2. Why does Smith include anecdotes about friends of his who've been mugged—or killed? Are these stories valid supporting data? Explain.
3. Smith's audience certainly includes city dwellers. Is his argument intended to reach beyond those readers immediately affected by street crime? Why or why not?

Style and Language

1. Adam Smith is known as an expert explainer of complex subjects. Can you cite examples in which Smith's style strikes you as especially clear or easy to understand? If you agree that his style is unusually lucid, what makes it so?

2. If some of Smith's references are unfamiliar to you, check the dictionary, encyclopedia, or almanac: Guadalcanal (paragraph 11); Cotton Mather (17); OK Corral (18); CETA (26).

Writing Ideas

1. Write a counterargument supporting the proposition that citizens should be allowed to carry weapons to defend themselves against attack. Address Smith's opposing points directly in your essay. Assume that your audience agrees with Smith's position.
2. Write an argument against a belief, attitude, policy, or situation that you think is wrong. Keep your case objective (avoid too many "I think . . ." assertions), and use evidence and warranted justification to support your claims. Be careful to limit or qualify your argument where appropriate. Consider your readers' opinions and whether any common ground lies between you.

— Richard Rodriguez —

Richard Rodriguez, born in San Francisco in 1944 to Mexican parents, has become a leading opponent of bilingual education (teaching children both in English and in their native language). In his autobiography, Hunger of Memory (1982), he tells of his American education and eventual separation from his Hispanic heritage. Rodriguez argues in favor of such assimilation by non-English speakers as necessary and liberating—of joining the larger, public culture. A graduate of Stanford University and the University of California at Berkeley, Rodriguez is a professional writer, lecturer, and educational consultant.

Aria: A Memoir of a Bilingual Childhood

Here Rodriguez recalls his first experiences learning English at school while living in a Hispanic family and community. The context for this personal account, though, is the public debate about bilingual education, and he provides powerful evidence supporting his criticism of that policy.

1   I remember, to start with, that day in Sacramento, in a California now nearly thirty years past, when I first entered a classroom—able to understand about fifty stray English words. The third of four children, I had been preceded by my older brother and sister to a neighborhood Roman Catholic school. But neither of them had revealed very much about their classroom experiences. They left each morning and returned each afternoon, always together, speaking Spanish as they climbed the five steps to the porch. And their mysterious books, wrapped in brown shopping-bag paper, remained on the table next to the door, closed firmly behind them.

2   An accident of geography sent me to a school where all my classmates were white and many were the children of doctors and lawyers and business executives. On that first day of school, my classmates must certainly have been uneasy to find themselves apart from their families, in the first institution of their lives. But I was astonished. I was fated to be the "problem student" in class.

3   The nun said, in a friendly but oddly impersonal voice: "Boys and girls, this is Richard Rodriguez." (I heard her sound it out: *Rich-heard Road-ree-guess.*) It was the first time I had heard anyone say my name

in English. "Richard," the nun repeated more slowly, writing my name down in her book. Quickly I turned to see my mother's face dissolve in a watery blur behind the pebbled-glass door.

Now, many years later, I hear of something called "bilingual   4
education"—a scheme proposed in the late 1960s by Hispanic-American social activists, later endorsed by a congressional vote. It is a program that seeks to permit non-English-speaking children (many from lower class homes) to use their "family language" as the language of school. Such, at least, is the aim its supporters announce. I hear them, and am forced to say no: It is not possible for a child, any child, ever to use his family's language in school. Not to understand this is to misunderstand the public uses of schooling and to trivialize the nature of intimate life.

Memory teaches me what I know of these matters. The boy   5
reminds the adult. I was a bilingual child, but of a certain kind: "socially disadvantaged," the son of working-class parents, both Mexican immigrants.

In the early years of my boyhood, my parents coped very well in   6
America. My father had steady work. My mother managed at home. They were nobody's victims. When we moved to a house many blocks from the Mexican-American section of town, they were not intimidated by those two or three neighbors who initially tried to make us unwelcome. ("Keep your brats away from my sidewalk!") But despite all they achieved, or perhaps because they had so much to achieve, they lacked any deep feeling of ease, of belonging in public. They regarded the people at work or in crowds as being very distant from us. Those were the others, *los gringos*. That term was interchangeable in their speech with another, even more telling: *los americanos.*

I grew up in a house where the only regular guests were my   7
relations. On a certain day, enormous families of relatives would visit us, and there would be so many people that the noise and the bodies would spill out to the backyard and onto the front porch. Then for weeks no one would come. (If the doorbell rang, it was usually a salesman.) Our house stood apart—gaudy yellow in a row of white bungalows. We were the people with the noisy dog, the people who raised chickens. We were the foreigners on the block. A few neighbors would smile and wave at us. We waved back. But until I was seven years old, I did not know the name of the old couple living next door or the names of the kids living across the street.

In public, my father and mother spoke a hesitant, accented, and   8
not always grammatical English. And then they would have to strain, their bodies tense, to catch the sense of what was rapidly said by *los gringos*. At home, they returned to Spanish. The language of their

Mexican past sounded in counterpoint to the English spoken in public. The words would come quickly, with ease. Conveyed through those sounds was the pleasing, soothing, consoling reminder that one was at home.

During those years when I was first learning to speak, my mother and father addressed me only in Spanish; in Spanish I learned to reply. By contrast, English (*inglés*) was the language I came to associate with gringos, rarely heard in the house. I learned my first words of English overhearing my parents speaking to strangers. At six years of age, I knew just enough words for my mother to trust me on errands to stores one block away—but no more.

I was then a listening child, careful to hear the very different sounds of Spanish and English. Wide-eyed with hearing, I'd listen to sounds more than to words. First, there were English (gringo) sounds. So many words still were unknown to me that when the butcher or the lady at the drugstore said something, exotic polysyllabic sounds would bloom in the midst of their sentences. Often the speech of people in public seemed to me very loud, booming with confidence. The man behind the counter would literally ask, "What can I do for you?" But by being so firm and clear, the sound of his voice said that he was a gringo; he belonged in public society. There were also the high, nasal notes of middle-class American speech—which I rarely am conscious of hearing today because I hear them so often, but could not stop hearing when I was a boy. Crowds at Safeway or at bus stops were noisy with the birdlike sounds of *los gringos.* I'd move away from them all— all the chirping chatter above me.

My own sounds I was unable to hear, but I knew that I spoke English poorly. My words could not extend to form complete thoughts. And the words I did speak I didn't know well enough to make distinct sounds. (Listeners would usually lower their heads to hear better what I was trying to say.) But it was one thing for *me* to speak English with difficulty; it was more troubling to hear my parents speaking in public: their high-whining vowels and guttural consonants; their sentences that got stuck with "eh" and "ah" sounds; the confused syntax; the hesitant rhythm of sounds so different from the way gringos spoke. I'd notice, moreover, that my parents' voices were softer than those of gringos we would meet.

I am tempted to say now that none of this mattered. (In adulthood I am embarrassed by childhood fears.) And, in a way, it didn't matter very much that my parents could not speak English with ease. Their linguistic difficulties had no serious consequences. My mother and father made themselves understood at the county hospital clinic and at government offices. And yet, in another way, it mattered very much. It was unsettling to hear my parents struggle with English. Hearing them, I'd grow nervous, and my clutching trust in their protection and power would be weakened.

There were many times like the night at a brightly lit gasoline 13 station (a blaring white memory) when I stood uneasily hearing my father talk to a teenage attendant. I do not recall what they were saying, but I cannot forget the sounds my father made as he spoke. At one point his words slid together to form one long word—sounds as confused as the threads of blue and green oil in the puddle next to my shoes. His voice rushed through what he had left to say. Toward the end, he reached falsetto notes, appealing to his listener's understanding. I looked away at the lights of passing automobiles. I tried not to hear any more. But I heard only too well the attendant's reply, his calm, easy tones. Shortly afterward, headed for home, I shivered when my father put his hand on my shoulder. The very first chance that I got, I evaded his grasp and ran on ahead into the dark, skipping with feigned boyish exuberance.

But then there was Spanish: *español,* the language rarely heard 14 away from the house; *español,* the language which seemed to me therefore a private language, my family's language. To hear its sounds was to feel myself specially recognized as one of the family, apart from *los otros.* A simple remark, an inconsequential comment could convey that assurance. My parents would say something to me and I would feel embraced by the sounds of their words. Those sounds said: *I am speaking with ease in Spanish. I am addressing you in words I never use with los gringos. I recognize you as someone special, close, like no one outside. You belong with us. In the family. Ricardo.*

At the age of six, well past the time when most middle-class 15 children no longer notice the difference between sounds uttered at home and words spoken in public, I had a different experience. I lived in a world compounded of sounds. I was a child longer than most. I lived in a magical world, surrounded by sounds both pleasing and fearful. I shared with my family a language enchantingly private— different from that used in the city around us.

Just opening or closing the screen door behind me was an impor- 16 tant experience. I'd rarely leave home all alone or without feeling reluctance. Walking down the sidewalk, under the canopy of tall trees, I'd warily notice the (suddenly) silent neighborhood kids who stood warily watching me. Nervously, I'd arrive at the grocery store to hear there the sounds of the gringo, reminding me that in this so-big world I was a foreigner. But if leaving home was never routine, neither was coming back. Walking toward our house, climbing the steps from the sidewalk, in summer when the front door was open, I'd hear voices beyond the screen door talking in Spanish. For a second or two I'd stay, linger there listening. Smiling, I'd hear my mother call out, saying in Spanish, "Is that you, Richard?" Those were her words, but all the while her sounds would assure me: *You are home now. Come closer inside. With us.* "*Sí,*" I'd reply.

Once more inside the house, I would resume my place in the family. The sounds would grow harder to hear. Once more at home, I would grow less conscious of them. It required, however, no more than the blurt of the doorbell to alert me all over again to listen to sounds. The house would turn instantly quiet while my mother went to the door. I'd hear her hard English sounds. I'd wait to hear her voice turn to soft-sounding Spanish, which assured me, as surely as did the clicking tongue of the lock on the door, that the stranger was gone. 17

Plainly it is not healthy to hear such sounds so often. It is not healthy to distinguish public from private sounds so easily. I remained cloistered by sounds, timid and shy in public, too dependent on the voices at home. And yet I was a very happy child when I was at home. I remember many nights when my father would come back from work, and I'd hear him call out to my mother in Spanish, sounding relieved. In Spanish, his voice would sound the light and free notes that he never could manage in English. Some nights I'd jump up just hearing his voice. My brother and I would come running into the room where he was with our mother. Our laughing (so deep was the pleasure!) became screaming. Like others who feel the pain of public alienation, we transformed the knowledge of our public separateness into a consoling reminder of our intimacy. Excited, our voices joined in a celebration of sounds. *We are speaking now the way we never speak out in public—we are together,* the sounds told me. Some nights no one seemed willing to loosen the hold that sounds had on us. At dinner we invented new words that sounded Spanish, but made sense only to us. We pieced together new words by taking, say, an English verb and giving it Spanish endings. My mother's instructions at bedtime would be lacquered with mock-urgent tones. Or a word like *sí,* sounded in several notes, would convey added measures of feeling. Tongues lingered around the edges of words, especially fat vowels. And we happily sounded that military drum roll, the twirling roar of the Spanish *r.* Family language, my family's sounds: the voices of my parents and sisters and brother. Their voices insisting: *You belong here. We are family members. Related. Special to one another. Listen!* Voices singing and sighing, rising and straining, then surging, teeming with pleasure which burst syllables into fragments of laughter. At times it seemed there was steady quiet only when, from another room, the rustling whispers of my parents faded and I edged closer to sleep. 18

Supporters of bilingual education imply today that students like   19
me miss a great deal by not being taught in their family's language.
What they seem not to recognize is that, as a socially disadvantaged
child, I regarded Spanish as a private language. It was a ghetto language that deepened and strengthened my feeling of public separateness. What I needed to learn in school was that I had the right, and
the obligation, to speak the public language. The odd truth is that my
first-grade classmates could have become bilingual, in the conventional sense of the word, more easily than I. Had they been taught
early (as upper middle-class children often are taught) a "second language" like Spanish or French, they could have regarded it simply as
another public language. In my case, such bilingualism could not have
been so quickly achieved. What I did not believe was that I could
speak a single public language.

Without question, it would have pleased me to have heard my   20
teachers address me in Spanish when I entered the classroom. I would
have felt much less afraid. I would have imagined that my instructors
were somehow "related" to me; I would indeed have heard their Spanish as my family's language. I would have trusted them and responded
with ease. But I would have delayed—postponed for how long?—
having to learn the language of public society. I would have evaded—
and for how long?—learning the great lesson of school: that I had a
public identity.

Fortunately, my teachers were unsentimental about their responsi-   21
bility. What they understood was that I needed to speak public English. So their voices would search me out, asking me questions. Each
time I heard them I'd look up in surprise to see a nun's face frowning at
me. I'd mumble, not really meaning to answer. The nun would persist.
"Richard, stand up. Don't look at the floor. Speak up. Speak to the
entire class, not just to me!" But I couldn't believe English could be my
language to use. (In part, I did not want to believe it.) I continued to
mumble. I resisted the teacher's demands. (Did I somehow suspect
that once I learned this public language my family life would be
changed?) Silent, waiting for the bell to sound, I remained dazed,
diffident, afraid.

Because I wrongly imagined that English was intrinsically a pub-   22
lic language and Spanish was intrinsically private, I easily noted the
difference between classroom language and the language of home. At
school, words were directed to a general audience of listeners. ("Boys
and girls . . .") Words were meaningfully ordered. And the point was
not self-expression alone, but to make oneself understood by many
others. The teacher quizzed: "Boys and girls, why do we use that word
in this sentence? Could we think of a better word to use there? Would

the sentence change its meaning if the words were differently arranged? Isn't there a better way of saying much the same thing? (I couldn't say, I wouldn't try to say.)

Three months passed. Five. A half year. Unsmiling, ever watchful, my teachers noted my silence. They began to connect my behavior with the slow progress my brother and sisters were making. Until, one Saturday morning, three nuns arrived at the house to talk to our parents. Stiffly they sat on the blue living-room sofa. From the doorway of another room, spying on the visitors, I noted the incongruity, the clash of two worlds, the faces and voices of school intruding upon the familiar setting of home. I overheard one voice gently wondering, "Do your children speak only Spanish at home, Mrs. Rodriguez?" While another voice added, "That Richard especially seems so timid and shy." 23

That Rich-heard! 24

With great tact, the visitors continued, "Is it possible for you and your husband to encourage your children to practice their English when they are home?" Of course my parents complied. What would they not do for their children's well-being? And how could they question the Church's authority which those women represented? In an instant they agreed to give up the language (the sounds) which had revealed and accentuated our family's closeness. The moment after the visitors left, the change was observed. "*Ahora,* speak to us only *en inglés,*" my father and mother told us. 25

At first, it seemed a kind of game. After dinner each night, the family gathered together to practice "our" English. It was still then *inglés,* a language foreign to us, so we felt drawn to it as stangers. Laughing, we would try to define words we could not pronounce. We played with strange English sounds, often over-anglicizing our pronunciations. And we filled the smiling gaps of our sentences with familiar Spanish sounds. But that was cheating, somebody shouted, and everyone laughed. 26

In school, meanwhile, like my brother and sisters, I was required to attend a daily tutoring session. I needed a full year of this special work. I also needed my teachers to keep my attention from straying in class by calling out, "*Rich-heard!*"—their English voices slowly loosening the ties to my other name, with its three notes, *Ri-car-do.* Most of all, I needed to hear my mother and father speak to me in a moment of seriousness in "broken"—suddenly heartbreaking—English. This scene was inevitable. One Saturday morning I entered the kitchen where my parents were talking, but I did not realize that they were talking in Spanish until, the moment they saw me, their voices changed and they began speaking English. The gringo sounds they uttered startled me. 27

Pushed me away. In that moment of trivial misunderstanding and profound insight, I felt my throat twisted by unsounded grief. I simply
turned and left the room. But I had no place to escape to where I could
grieve in Spanish. My brother and sisters were speaking English in
another part of the house.

Again and again in the days following, as I grew increasingly   28
angry, I was obliged to hear my mother and father encouraging me:
"Speak to us *en inglés.*" Only then did I determine to learn classroom
English. Thus, sometime afterward it happened: one day in school, I
raised my hand to volunteer an answer to a question. I spoke out in a
loud voice and I did not think it remarkable when the entire class
understood. That day I moved very far from being the disadvantaged
child I had been only days earlier. Taken hold at last was the belief, the
calming assurance, that I *belonged* in public.

Shortly after, I stopped hearing the high, troubling sounds of *los*   29
gringos. A more and more confident speaker of English, I didn't listen
to how strangers sounded when they talked to me. With so many
English-speaking people around me, I no longer heard American accents. Conversations quickened. Listening to persons whose voices
sounded eccentrically pitched, I might note their sounds for a few
seconds, but then I'd concentrate on what they were saying. Now
when I heard someone's tone of voice—angry or questioning or sarcastic or happy or sad—I didn't distinguish it from the words it expressed.
Sound and word were thus tightly wedded. At the end of each day I
was often bemused, and always relieved, to realize how "soundless,"
though crowded with words, my day in public had been. An eight-
year-old boy, I finally came to accept what had been technically true
since my birth: I was an American citizen.

But diminished by then was the special feeling of closeness at   30
home. Gone was the desperate, urgent, intense feeling of being at
home among those with whom I felt intimate. Our family remained a
loving family, but one greatly changed. We were no longer so close, no
longer bound tightly together by the knowledge of our separateness
from *los gringos.* Neither my older brother nor my sisters rushed home
after school any more. Nor did I. When I arrived home, often there
would be neighborhood kids in the house. Or the house would be
empty of sounds.

Following the dramatic Americanization of their children, even   31
my parents grew more publicly confident—especially my mother. First
she learned the names of all the people on the block. Then she
decided we needed to have a telephone in our house. My father, for his
part, continued to use the word gringo, but it was no longer charged
with bitterness or distrust. Stripped of any emotional content, the

word simply became a name for those Americans not of Hispanic descent. Hearing him, sometimes, I wasn't sure if he was pronouncing the Spanish word *gringo*, or saying gringo in English.

There was a new silence at home. As we children learned more and more English, we shared fewer and fewer words with our parents. Sentences needed to be spoken slowly when one of us addressed our mother or father. Often the parent wouldn't understand. The child would need to repeat himself. Still the parent misunderstood. The young voice, frustrated, would end up saying, "Never mind"—the subject was closed. Dinners would be noisy with the clinking of knives and forks against dishes. My mother would smile softly between her remarks; my father, at the other end of the table, would chew and chew his food while he stared over the heads of his children.

My mother! My father! After English became my primary language, I no longer knew what words to use in addressing my parents. The old Spanish words (those tender accents of sound) I had earlier used—*mamá* and *papá*—I couldn't use any more. They would have been all-too-painful reminders of how much had changed in my life. On the other hand, the words I heard neighborhood kids call their parents seemed equally unsatisfactory. "Mother" and "father," "ma," "papa," "pa," "dad," "pop" (how I hated the all-American sound of that last word)— all these I felt were unsuitable terms of address for *my* parents. As a result, I never used them at home. Whenever I'd speak to my parents, I would try to get their attention by looking at them. In public conversations, I'd refer to them as my "parents" or my "mother" and "father."

My mother and father, for their part, responded differently, as their children spoke to them less. My mother grew restless, seemed troubled and anxious at the scarceness of words exchanged in the house. She would question me about my day when I came home from school. She smiled at my small talk. She pried at the edges of my sentences to get me to say something more. ("What . . . ?") She'd join conversations she overheard, but her intrusions often stopped her children's talking. By contrast, my father seemed to grow reconciled to the new quiet. Though his English somewhat improved, he tended more and more to retire into silence. At dinner he spoke very little. One night his children and even his wife helplessly giggled at his garbled English pronunciation of the Catholic "Grace before Meals." Thereafter he made his wife recite the prayer at the start of each meal, even on formal occasions when there were guests in the house.

Hers became the public voice of the family. On official business it was she, not my father, who would usually talk to strangers on the phone or in stores. We children grew so accustomed to his silence that years later we would routinely refer to his "shyness." (My mother often

32

33

34

35

tried to explain: both of his parents died when he was eight. He was raised by an uncle who treated him as little more than a menial servant. He was never encouraged to speak. He grew up alone—a man of few words.) But I realized my father was not shy whenever I'd watch him speaking Spanish with relatives. Using Spanish, he was quickly effusive. Especially when talking with other men, his voice would spark, flicker, flare alive with varied sounds. In Spanish he expressed ideas and feelings he rarely revealed when speaking English. With firm Spanish sounds he conveyed a confidence and authority that English would never allow him.

The silence at home, however, was not simply the result of fewer   36
words passing between parents and children. More profound for me was the silence created by my inattention to sounds. At about the time I no longer bothered to listen with care to the sounds of English in public, I grew careless about listening to the sounds made by the family when they spoke. Most of the time I would hear someone's speaking at home and didn't distinguish his sounds from the words people uttered in public. I didn't even pay much attention to my parents' accented and ungrammatical speech—at least not at home. Only when I was with them in public would I become alert to their accents. But even then their sounds caused me less and less concern. For I was growing increasingly confident of my own public identity.

I would have been happier about my public success had I not   37
recalled, sometimes, what it had been like earlier, when my family conveyed its intimacy through a set of conveniently private sounds. Sometimes in public, hearing a stranger, I'd hark back to my lost past. A Mexican farm worker approached me one day downtown. He wanted directions to some place. "*Hijito,* . . . " he said. And his voice stirred old longings. Another time I was standing beside my mother in the visiting room of a Carmelite convent, before the dense screen which rendered the nuns shadowy figures. I heard several of them speaking Spanish in their busy, singsong, overlapping voices, assuring my mother that, yes, yes, we were remembered, all our family was remembered, in their prayers. Those voices echoed faraway family sounds. Another day a dark-faced old woman touched my shoulder lightly to steady herself as she boarded a bus. She murmured something to me I couldn't quite comprehend. Her Spanish voice came near, like the face of a never-before-seen relative in the instant before I was kissed. That voice, like so many of the Spanish voices I'd hear in public, recalled the golden age of my childhood.

Bilingual educators say today that children lose a degree of "indi-   38
viduality" by becoming assimilated into public society. (Bilingual

schooling is a program popularized in the seventies, that decade when middle-class "ethnics" began to resist the process of assimilation—the "American melting pot.") But the bilingualists oversimplify when they scorn the value and necessity of assimilation. They do not seem to realize that a person is individualized in two ways. So they do not realize that, while one suffers a diminished sense of *private* individuality by being assimilated into public society, such assimilation makes possible the achievement of *public* individuality.

Simplistically again, the bilingualists insist that a student should 39
be reminded of his difference from others in mass society; of his "heritage." But they equate mere separateness with individuality. The fact is that only in private—with intimates—is separateness from the crowd a prerequisite for individuality; an intimate "tells" me that I am unique, unlike all others, apart from the crowd. In public, by contrast, full individuality is achieved, paradoxically, by those who are able to consider themselves members of the crowd. Thus it happened for me. Only when I was able to think of myself as an American, no longer an alien in gringo society, could I seek the rights and opportunities necessary for full public individuality. The social and political advantages I enjoy as a man began on the day I came to believe that my name is indeed *Rich-heard Road-ree-guess*. It is true that my public society today is often impersonal; in fact, my public society is usually mass society. But despite the anonymity of the crowd, and despite the fact that the individuality I achieve in public is often tenuous—because it depends on my being one in a crowd—I celebrate the day I acquired my new name. Those middle-class ethnics who scorn assimilation seem to me filled with decadent self-pity, obsessed by the burden of public life. Dangerously, they romanticize public separateness and trivialize the dilemma of those who are truly socially disadvantaged.

If I rehearse here the changes in my private life after my Ameri- 40
canization, it is finally to emphasize a public gain. The loss implies the gain. The house I returned to each afternoon was quiet. Intimate sounds no longer greeted me at the door. Inside there were other noises. The telephone rang. Neighborhood kids ran past the door of the bedroom where I was reading my schoolbooks—covered with brown shopping-bag paper. Once I learned the public language, it would never again be easy for me to hear intimate family voices. More and more of my day was spent hearing words, not sounds. But that may only be a way of saying that on the day I raised my hand in class and spoke loudly to an entire roomful of faces, my childhood started to end.

Questions for Study and Discussion

Meaning and Purpose

1. What is the essential claim in Rodriguez's argument? Does he state it explicitly, or imply it? What additional claims, if any, does the author make?
2. What does the author mean when he speaks of public and private identity? What does such identity depend upon? How is this definition essential to his argumentative claims?
3. Although a clear argumentative strain runs throughout the essay, Rodriguez has said that he intended merely to "describe only one life, one time, one street. . . ." What qualities of expressive writing do you find here?

Strategy and Audience

1. How does Rodriguez support his claims? To what extent does he incorporate general assumptions or warrants, specific evidence, or other argumentative strategies?
2. If it's true that Rodriguez uses personal expression here, why does he do so? What does he gain through such a strategy?
3. Who is Rodriguez's intended audience? What do you think is the most powerful or convincing element here for those who, unlike the author, *favor* bilingual education?

Style and Language

1. Throughout the essay, Rodriguez shifts between the concrete, detailed diction of memoir ("We were the people with the noisy dog, the people who raised chickens") and the more abstract language of ideas ("Supporters of bilingual education imply today that students like me miss a great deal by not being taught in their family's language"). Both styles are appropriate, depending on context, purpose, and subject. Explain how you can justify the use of each kind of language in this essay.
2. Suggestions for vocabulary study: polysyllabic (paragraph 10); guttural, syntax (11); falsetto, exuberance (13); cloistered (18); diffident (21); intrinsically (22); effusive (35); tenuous (39).

Writing Ideas

1. Write an argumentative essay using personal experience as your chief supporting evidence. Like Rodriguez, consider a blend of argument and personal expression as your aim, and let expressive uses of narration, description, scene setting, and so on, come into the essay.

2. If you have experience with the bilingual issue, write to support or refute Rodriguez's essential claim (or a variation of your own) that all citizens must learn the public language if they are to become part of the wider community.

— Dennis J. Keihn —

*Dennis J. Keihn is director of athletics at Northeastern Illinois University,
in Chicago. Formerly athletics director at California State University at
Los Angeles, he received his doctorate at the University of Indiana and has
taught there and at Macalester College. Keihn has been named coach of
the year in various midwestern divisions and for several sports, and has
published articles in* NCAA News *and the* Chronicle of Higher Education.
His book, The Effectiveness of Three Methods of Physical
Education Instruction, *appeared in 1973. He is an active member of the
National Collegiate Athletic Association.*

Balancing Academics and Athletics: It's Not an Impossible Task

*In this essay, written before the recent NCAA controversy over changes in
eligibility rules and season lengths, Keihn argues forcefully for a compromise between opposing sides in the student-athletics debate.*

These days, talking about intercollegiate athletics sparks as much   1
controversy as discussing politics or religion. Many people regard the
term "student athlete" as inherently contradictory—and with good
reason, considering past abuses. They see athletics as merely an extracurricular adjunct to higher education, which in some cases it is.
However, it seems to me that if there is an argument for college
athletics at all, the programs must be put in the context of the institution's educational framework.

Today, student athletes face demands from two separate bureau-   2
cratic worlds: the college and the National Collegiate Athletic Association. The other students have to survive only in the former, but
athletes are expected to excel in athletics and at the same time be at
least "adequate" in academics. Standards are set by each bureaucracy,
and the student athletes are expected to meet them all. To falter in
either area often means giving up both.

Colleges and universities across the country have been attempt-   3
ing, along with the N.C.A.A., to pull the two worlds closer together,
if not in fact at least in theory. That was accomplished to some extent
at the N.C.A.A.'s national convention in January, 1983, by adopting

what has become known as Rule 48—which, beginning in the fall of 1986, will prohibit students who don't meet minimum academic standards from participating in intercollegiate athletics during their freshman year—and by establishing a new "normal progress" rule, which will go into effect August 1 and apply to student athletes after their freshman year.

However, there is another important issue that has yet to be addressed, and that is the issue of integrity. Everyone who participates or works in college sports is driven constantly by one imperative. It goes by many names—accomplishment, achievement, competitiveness, success—but whatever the name, it means WINNING. Coaching careers are established on won-lost records; so, often, are institutional finances. A winning program means media attention, which in turn attracts students and dollars to the institution.

Such dependence on athletics brings up the question of integrity. It is not so much whether it is right or wrong to use student athletes to promote education, or, as the case sometimes is, to use education to promote athletics. The real issue is in reconciling athletics and academics and giving priority to academic achievement; in education, "winning" is graduating. The N.C.A.A. cannot totally address this problem with legislation, but colleges, if they are willing, can and should do so.

Institutions of higher learning must clarify their values concerning athletics and education, and evaluate and resolve any incompatibility. That is a difficult undertaking, and it means more than just setting up guidelines to promote athletic and educational integrity. It requires establishing a philosophical framework within which everyone will be expected to live.

The idea that sports and education must go hand-in-hand is a cause for concern on the campuses that separate the athletic and academic endeavors, especially those that require self-support from athletics, because if the sports program is part of the total educational process, then it follows logically that athletics should receive state or institutional financial support.

New policies are needed to govern recruiting and admission of athletes. Making exceptions for athletes who do not meet standard admissions criteria and who may lack the potential to succeed academically is an abuse common on campuses throughout the country, especially in revenue-producing sports.

A popular argument in favor of making exceptions for student athletes is that if it weren't for athletics those young people wouldn't have an opportunity to get an education. The purpose of higher education is to educate qualified people capable of successfully completing college and earning a degree. Many athletes recruited and admitted under exceptions to regular standards can be viewed, for all practical purposes, as professional athletes with amateur standing, hired to perform for the institution in the unrealistic hope that an education may rub off on a few of them in exchange for their services. Exceptions should be made only for athletes who can realistically be expected to correct their academic deficiencies.

Coaching is another area of concern. If the major criterion for   10
successful coaching continues to be a favorable won-lost record, that record needs to be redefined and expanded to include graduation of athletes in the "won" column. Any student athlete who does not graduate within a reasonable time—say five years—should be counted as a loss. Coaches should be held accountable for both the academic and athletic performance of their athletes, which would force them to be more selective in recruiting.

Requiring recruits to have both academic and athletic abilities   11
could mean that many talented athletes would be passed over by colleges. Such athletes could, however, be examined on a case-by-case basis and exceptions granted contingent on the athletic program's commitment to provide them with quality academic support.

An athletic program could also be required to subtract athletes   12
admitted as exceptions from its allowable quota and to relinquish an athletic scholarship for a stated period for each student athlete who failed to graduate.

In addition to new policies, new relationships between coaches   13
and student athletes need to be established. Currently many athletes are not held responsible by coaches for tasks as simple as completing their own application and registration forms. Such coddling in the athletic department leads the athletes to expect other people throughout the institution "to take care of things" for them. New and better support programs for student athletes, such as advising and tutoring, are needed, but at the same time the athletes must be required to take responsibility for using and profiting from such programs. If athletics are to be an integral part of the education process rather than adjunct to it, colleges must establish standards for all students and tolerate nothing less.

Many different groups—alumni, students, faculty members, ad-   14
ministrators, and members of the community—have an influence on athletics, directly or indirectly. But ultimately it is the athletic director who is responsible for maintaining a balance between sports and academics, and for setting the course for success in both endeavors.

The excitement of college athletics lies in the opportunity the   15
program gives students to excel physically; the excitement of higher
education lies in the opportunity it gives students to excel mentally.
Setting standards of excellence for both athletics and educational programs is the only acceptable course and the only one that will assure
that the term "student athlete" means what it says.

Questions for Study and Discussion

Meaning and Purpose

1. Keihn's argument is fairly complex. What is his primary claim or
   thesis, and what related points does he also support?
2. What is the broad principle upon which the author's argument rests?
   Does he state this assumption directly? Where?
3. According to Keihn, who has the final responsibility for "maintaining
   a balance between sports and academics"? Why?

Strategy and Audience

1. Keihn uses several explanatory strategies in his supporting analysis.
   What are these, and of what use are they to his argument? How does
   Keihn limit or qualify his argument?
2. What specific recommendations does Keihn propose to remedy the
   current situation? How do such recommendations affect the author's
   overall case? Why?
3. How does Keihn answer the objections of readers who believe that "if
   it weren't for athletics those young people [who don't meet admissions standards] wouldn't have an opportunity to get an education"?

Style and Language

1. Keihn's essay was written for college teachers and administrators.
   Does his style seem different from those of Goodman or Raspberry,
   who address wider audiences? If so, how?
2. For vocabulary study: inherently, contradictory, adjunct (paragraph
   1); bureaucratic (2); imperative (4); integrity, reconciling (5); contingent (11); quota, relinquish (12).

Writing Ideas

1. Compose your own pro or con argument on the subject of college sports. If you would keep the current system, how would you defend it? If you would change it, what would you recommend? You might argue for allowing "marginal" student athletes to play sports under some conditions, such as a trial period during which they must bring their academic work up to par. Or you might defend or attack this proposition: "Student athletes themselves, not their coaches or athletic directors, must have the final responsibility for maintaining a balance between sports and study."

2. Write an argumentative essay on the related issue of women's intercollegiate sports. For example, should women be allowed to play in traditionally male sports such as football or hockey? Should women's sports receive the same financial backing as men's sports?

— Student Essays —

Here author Charlotte Till argues briefly but forcefully that gifted students should have special educational programs to suit their needs. She supports her claim with data (facts, such as government backing; opinions, such as those of parents, students, and the National Education Association [paragraphs 2–4]), and ties her claim and support together with a basic assumption or warrant, that society must cultivate its children or suffer the consequences (paragraph 5). Her introduction establishes a sense of common ground—that we all believe in education and in keeping our society strong—and leads logically to the thesis; in the body of the essay she lays out the supporting evidence; the conclusion confirms the thesis with a basic principle about high-quality education—that it challenges all students according to their abilities.

Following Till's essay is another student argument, with questions and suggestions for writing.

Charlotte Till

The Importance of Gifted Programs

Introduction: Establishes context for argument—appeals to common ground

Warrant: high-quality education is vital to society

Thesis statement makes point of argument: advocacy

Education has always been a vital part of our society, and in a technological age it is more important than ever. If we want to continue to advance as we have in the past, we need capable people. Because of their different abilities, however, all students don't learn at the same rate. Slower children often have special programs to help them. *Likewise, gifted students should also have access to programs that help them learn at their own rate.*

Support for claim: factual data

In fact, federal support for the gifted already exists. As many as 5 percent of students are in this category, but critics feel that gifted programs are a misplacement of priorities for

1

2

211

Acknowledges oppos-
ing opinion and re-
futes it

such a minority (Remley 44). However, federal funding for gifted programs has increased continuously since the Office of Gifted and Talented was established in 1972, indicating general government support for the policy.

New topic, further
evidence—introduced
with transition

Evidence also suggests that the students   3
need the alternative that gifted programs offer. Parents say their gifted children are bored and unhappy with the regular classroom. One student attending the North Carolina School of Science describes her day at her previous, conventional high school: "You go to school, and you sleep through classes and make A-pluses and everything, and you go home and there's nothing to do. . . . Here you are challenged all the time" (Campbell 39). It is true that a person doesn't have to be gifted to be bored in school, but when a student is bored because he has his work done and the school doesn't challenge him, a change seems essential.

Additional data: pa-
rental and student
opinion

In the present system, the gifted simply can-   4
not reach their full potential. For many, the conventional high school serves only as a means of taking up time until they can enter college. The gifted are missing the educational opportunities that high school is supposed to provide. With accelerated programs, this loss need not happen. Research on acceleration shows that the effects are favorable rather than harmful (Anderson 61), and that they provide students with a much greater chance for intellectual development.

Further data:
research study

If gifted students aren't able to grow and   5
learn, society will suffer. All students, whatever their abilities, need a challenging environment in which they can grow to their fullest potential.

Conclusion: Con-
firms thesis with
appeal to initial
assumption

Works cited

Anderson, Kenneth E., ed. *Research on the Academically Talented Student.* Washington, D.C.: National Education Association, 1961.

Campbell, Erin E. "School for Scholars." *American Education* July 1983: 36–9, 48.

Remley, Anne Gardner. "All the Best for the Brightest." *The Progressive* May 1981: 44–47.

In this paper, student Daniel Burke argues on behalf of the Greek system for an audience of those likely to be opposed or indifferent. The author aims his essay at readers who might not see the virtues of fraternal life, and builds a convincing case that this old college institution still has a valid role on campus.

Daniel Burke

In Defense of Fraternities

A revolutionary event took place at Raleigh Tavern in 1776, an 1
event that has added an important dimension to my life at college. In fact, nearly all American undergraduates are affected in some way by the actions of several students from the College of William and Mary on December 5, 1776. The formation of the first Greek-letter fraternity, Phi Beta Kappa, started the American college fraternity-sorority tradition that today can be an important addition to your undergraduate education.

Since Phi Beta Kappa, the Greek system has grown to include 2
five types of fraternities: recognition, honor, professional, service, and social. Membership in recognition and honor fraternities is earned through achievement in the area they promote. For example, Alpha Psi Omega honor fraternity will ask you to join if you've participated in several theatrical programs. Professional fraternities are for members of a particular field of study; for example, Kappa Delta Pi is a fraternity made up of education students and alumni. And service fraternities primarily provide members with opportunities to do volunteer work and to raise money for charities.

The social fraternities, though, have become the most prevalent 3
type of Greek society. Since I believe this type offers the widest range of opportunities for undergraduates, I will limit myself to it; but this does not mean that recognition, honor, professional, and service fraternities do not share many similar opportunities.

The word "fraternity" originates from the Greek word *frater*, 4 meaning "brother." After the formation of the first women's fraternity, Alpha Delta Pi, in 1851 at Wesleyan College, in Macon, Georgia, the word "sorority" was coined from the Greek word for sister. Eventually the nonsexist term "Greek-letter society" was invented to refer to both. Because of my own experience as a member of Sigma Phi Epsilon, I feel the implication of "family" in the word "fraternity" is important, and I will refer to both sisterhoods and brotherhoods as fraternities.

Unfortunately, the word "fraternity" has gained several negative   5
connotations that no longer apply to many today, yet still cause some students to hesitate or refuse to consider joining one. The reputation for snobbishness, discrimination, conformity, and hazing still remains even though many fraternities have eliminated such practices.

In the past, snobbery and discrimination were common in frater-   6
nities. They were for the "socially favored"—the elite. They became clubs used to flaunt status, wealth, or self-proclaimed "superiority." Many college administrations disapproved of such behavior as unfair to many of the students. Concerned administrations, national fraternity headquarters, and interfraternity councils dealt with this problem by disbanding chapters that would not end their unfair exclusion policies. After ordering fraternities to halt such membership restrictions in 1946, trustees of Amherst College suspended or revoked the charters of three fraternities that did not comply. In the late nineteenth century, Princeton went so far as to abolish all national fraternities from campus. As a result of many similar actions, today social class is rarely used as a criterion for fraternity membership.

Earlier, fraternities also demanded conformity. Since member-   7
ship was composed of the same social elite, an elite reputation had to be upheld. This was accomplished by regulating what everyone did, wore, and said.

Today, diversified membership is valued more than uniformity.   8
Snobbery, discrimination, and conformity are understood to be imma-ture and unhealthy for the organization. A chapter cannot run well without many individuals of different interests, skills, and back-grounds. Those skilled in business and leadership run the business aspects and teach those who are less skilled. The "scholars" boost G.P.A.s and help bring out the academic potential of the rest. The athletes balance the group toward excellence in intramurals and physi-cal fitness. Everyone fills a niche.

The reputation fraternities have for hazing also turns away many   9
prospective members. Hazing can be defined as any situation that is dangerous or humiliating to a potential member. Hazing still is prac-ticed in some fraternities. Even at a private midwestern college, one can see the victims of "Hell Week" or hear rumors of what has been

done to them. But hazing is (or should be) damaging to a fraternity's reputation.

Most national fraternities (those with chapters located on more   10
than one campus under a central government) condemn the practice not only in the interest of reputation, but also for insurance reasons. Individual chapters can lose their charters if hazing is a proven practice. I think this rule makes sense, for it's a sad contradiction of behavior when the people who might become your future *brothers* or *sisters* first humiliate you by smearing you with Miracle Whip and then parade you in public, insult you, or endanger your life with alcohol or drugs.

I had reservations about joining "Sig Ep" until I found out that its   11
hazing practices were abolished in the mid-1970s. I was pleased to see Hell Week replaced by "Brotherhood Development Week." Instead of being demeaned as an inferior, I was treated with respect and welcomed among the members. For example, when I first went around meeting the guys in their rooms, most would shake my hand, invite me in, and start a conversation.

Some fraternities today still are snobbish, discriminatory, and   12
proconformity. Some still practice hazing. Yet this attitude emphasizes the importance of carefully choosing the right fraternity to join. Before you choose, however, ask yourself what you want the fraternity to offer. I have learned that besides the many possibilities for a good time, involvement can provide opportunities for service, job skills, stimulation of values and ideals, and strong friendships.

Social events and fellowship are the prominent purposes of a   13
social fraternity, but many also involve service projects. On our campus, for example, Lambda Xi helps the elderly, Sigma Phi Epsilon works for muscular dystrophy, and Alpha Phi does service projects for the American Heart Association.

Involvement in a fraternity can also provide experience in vari   14
ous job skills. You can learn leadership by being an executive, such as president or vice president. You might head a committee responsible for such things as fundraising or rushing (attracting new members). As a controller (treasurer) you would be involved in record keeping and correspondence.

The meetings themselves help you develop skills. If they are run   15
according to Robert's Rules of Order, you will learn parliamentary procedure. You will also learn the procedures of group goal setting and policy making. If someone suggests at a meeting that the members should plan more mixers with other "Greeks," for example, you will play a part in voting on the proposal and suggesting ways to implement it.

In many fraternities you are encouraged to adopt or strengthen   16
your values. Often fraternities emphasize a set of general ideals or
cardinal principles, such as morality, knowledge, charity, or friendship, and embody those ideals in secret, elaborate rituals which bring
them to mind. For example, the founders of Sigma Phi Epsilon chose
to emphasize virtue, diligence, and brotherly love. This means they
considered the ideal "Sig Ep" to be someone who shows strong moral
character through his behavior (virtue) and who applies himself well
to his tasks (diligence). He has the ability to form strong friendships as
well as concern for the well-being of others (brotherly love). The
ritual of Sigma Phi Epsilon, still used today, symbolizes those principles and encourages members to live by them.

I feel that modern fraternity life is an excellent way to round off an   17
undergraduate education beyond that offered by various academic studies and by other extracurriculars. The service opportunities, job skills
and experience, promotion of values and ideals, and the unique and
lifelong friendships all provide for the future but also make the present
college experience more meaningful and memorable. Some say that
fraternity life isn't for them. I agree that it may not be for everyone, but
I encourage every college student to give fraternity life a chance.

Questions for Study and Discussion

Meaning and Purpose

1. According to Burke, what makes fraternities worth joining? What are
   their best features? Does he mention any negatives? If so, what are
   they?
2. What do today's fraternities value most? Why have many abandoned earlier practices, such as hazing, snob appeal, or racial or
   class exclusion?
3. What is the main point of Burke's argument? That everyone should
   join a Greek society? That students should at least accept fraternities
   and sororities as a legitimate part of campus life? That all frats are
   good?

Strategy and Audience

1. Where does Burke establish common ground between himself and the
   reader? Why do you think he felt such a gesture necessary?

2. What methods does the author use to support his claim? Why do you think he includes background on the history and development of fraternities? What does this tactic add to his case?
3. What is your position on the Greek issue? Do you agree with Burke? Where are his points strongest, in your opinion, and where weakest?

Style and Language

1. One of Burke's real strengths as a writer here is his control of his material. Point out where he uses key words, transitions, and clarity of style to make his case easy to follow.
2. How would you describe the tone of Burke's essay? How does the feeling or attitude of the author help the argument?

Writing Ideas

1. Write your own "In Defense of————" essay, in which you make a logical case for a sometimes controversial campus activity. Some sample topics: intramurals, clubs, dorm parties, and fraternity or sorority rushing practices.
2. Take the other side of Burke's argument and write a condemnation of the Greek system as a part of campus experience. Who will be your audience? How will you support your negative claims?

— *Additional Writing Ideas* —

Argue for or against a specific proposal of your own on a topic that you know something about. Assume your audience to be fairly broad—students, teachers, the reading public—and that your case must appeal primarily to those who hold contrary opinions. (Check the topics at the end of Chapter 7 as well.) Sample proposal or claim: "Convicted drug smugglers should receive mandatory life sentences." Sample topics:

- The minimum wage
- Sex in advertising
- Censoring rock lyrics
- Prayer or free speech in school
- Drug testing on the job
- Voluntary withdrawal of life support for the terminally ill
- The rights of animals in medical research
- The homeless or chronically unemployed
- States' rights to pass abortion laws
- The "Star Wars" nuclear defense system
- Banning smoking in public places
- Immigration quotas
- Merit pay raises for teachers (or any employees)
- Drafting both men and women
- The drinking age
- Random highway checks for drunken drivers
- Crimes committed by juveniles
- Longer school years
- Stiffer penalties for white-collar criminals
- The movie rating system
- Banning controversial books from public libraries
- Sex education
- Dormitory or campus rules
- Electronic spying in the workplace
- Salaries of professional athletes

— 6 —

Writing to Criticize or Evaluate

Arguing Meaning and Merit

The Critical Aim

In Chapter 5, we saw that writers of argumentative essays can address greatly varied subjects—the whole range of human experience and belief. Such essayists attempt to convince us with logic and evidence, reasoned justification of specific claims. The methods of argument—because they can be so persuasive—also are useful in writing about another, narrower group of subjects. When we argue the meaning and merit of created works, as in literature, film, music, theatrical performances, television or radio programs, and works of art or architecture, we engage in *criticism.* We try to form a knowledgeable opinion about our subject, to convince readers that the opinion is valid, and, often, to bring our audience closer to our view.

No one likes to receive criticism, of course, perhaps because we misunderstand the word to mean only "cutting something down." Just as arguments in general may be for *or* against a claim, criticism isn't always negative. Think of the last glowing review you read in your favorite newspaper or magazine; the reviewer may have praised the subject to the skies. Criticism, when it's honest and reasonable, presents our full understanding or judgment of a subject (poem, short story, movie, television show) and *justifies* our interpretation or evaluation with logic and evidence.

As in almost all the writing we do, our objectivity or subjectivity will be a matter of degree. In criticism, too, especially in popular reviews, we often find writers using a very personal approach, openly admitting that any critical response begins with a subjective or personal reaction. (Siskel and Ebert, the battling television movie reviewers, never hide such feelings.) But however much our private views affect our critical attitude, good critical writing doesn't just express the author's reaction. Rather, it builds a convincing case—as in any sound argument—*about the thing itself*: what it is, what it does, where it succeeds and fails, whether and why it's well or poorly done.

One of the reasons for this is that criticism is often quite practical. Reviews can give us useful information—facts we'll need to make up our mind whether to attend the film, buy the book, visit the art gallery, or see the show. In the criticism you'll write in college—in literature, film, music, and art courses—you'll want not only to demonstrate your grasp of subjects but to contribute your own ideas and perspectives, which may change others' views.

Because criticism is a kind of argument, finally, it pays to remember that not all claims are equally valid—nor are all critical opinions. Just as in other occasions of argument, we need to be wary of *fallacy* (condemning a book because its author is a convicted criminal, perhaps, or assuming a movie is good because it stars our favorite actor), basing our arguments on *questionable assumptions* (all movies that include sex or violence are bad), or *using inadequate or inappropriate evidence* (the novel was well written because it didn't bore me). The claim, or thesis, in a critical essay should be as precise and substantial as the claim in any solid argument, and it should be supported with the best evidence you can find, the best rationale you can construct.

We find critical arguments common in the world of writing, as reviews of films, books, dramatic performances, concerts, and art exhibits, and in the scholarship we study in college humanities classes. Often, too, you may find yourself writing critical essays and debating with friends about the merits of new movies, television programs, books, record albums, and theatrical or musical performances.

Critical arguments typically follow the same thesis-and-support design we've been studying. Here's a sample outline for a critical essay on popular television melodrama. The thesis: "Although some may consider television cop shows gritty and realistic, the world they portray is a fantasy, with rock music, high-fashion style, and Hollywood heroics the dominant elements."

I. Introduction: Brief description of a typical action melo-drama with these three elements; thesis

II. The world as rock video
   A. Examples of how shows use technique
   B. Rock videos like dreams or fantasies

III. The world as fashion magazine
   A. Description of clothing and visual style
   B. Such styles meant to be exaggerated, unrealistic

IV. The world as adventure movie
   A. Analysis of characters' heroism
   B. Stylized heroics typical of Hollywood movies

V. Conclusion: Cop shows are popular because they use these elements very skilfully to create a fantasy world.

Criticism in a Paragraph

In this example, a critic of mass culture evaluates the Beatles' influence on popular music. He makes his claim in his opening line and defends it with detailed supporting evidence. Notice also that he includes expert testimony from a famous American composer for additional support.

> The Beatles made rhythm and blues into a complex, challenging, open-ended musical genre. Lennon, McCartney, and Harrison proved to be talented and ingenious musicians who surprised the public with new ideas in every record release. By their use of startling rhythmic devices such as abrupt time changes, metrical alterations, and extended rubatos; by instrumental experimentation involving baroque trumpet, harpsichord, organ, celli, or sitars; by daring chord progressions, dissonances, shifting key signatures and the like, they extended the boundaries of popular music. Their success—both musical and commercial—encouraged a creative, spontaneous, and exciting kind of music for a new generation of composers and performers. "When people ask to re-create the mood of the sixties," remarked composer Aaron Copland in 1968, "they will play Beatles music."
>
> —Russel Nye, *The Unembarrassed Muse: The Popular Arts in America**

*(New York: Dial, 1970): 354.

Critical Strategies

We've seen that arguments build upon information and explanation, that they can use both to justify claims. When putting together a critical argument, then, you'll be writing to inform, to explain and analyze, and to prove your point. The strategies you use will depend on which kind of writing you're doing at the time.

Presenting Information

What will your readers want or need to know about your subject so that your evaluation makes sense? In a critical essay for your literature class, you may not need to spend much time on summary or general background; you and your readers will share that knowledge. Instead, you'll emphasize specific references to the text or other critics' opinions. In a movie review for the school newspaper, on the other hand, you'll want to include some information that provides a *context* for the subject:

- What kind of movie is it (thriller, comedy, adventure, drama)?
- Who's responsible for it or involved with it (director, screenwriter, actors, cinematographer, costume designer)?
- What's it about, or what happens (sketch general story outline without revealing major plot points)?
- What, if anything, is notable about it (new work by a major director, particularly fresh approach to the subject, controversy surrounding the film, or debut of a striking new actor)?

Usually, such information will supplement your essay but won't be its exclusive focus. In your critical analysis you will consider the meaning, and often the worth, of your subject, beyond giving essential information about it.

Any of the informative strategies we discussed in Chapter 3 can be useful in criticism: *examples* (evidence illustrating or supporting your critical points); *description* (the makeup, physical appearance, or other features of your subject); *narration* (what happens during the story, movie, play); and *definition* of key terms.

Explaining Information and Evidence

As you study your subject, however, you'll want to find ways to open it to even closer scrutiny—to understand it from the inside.

You'll also want to explain what you've found—to interpret or evalu-ate your subject and to justify your conclusions about it. Here the analytical and explanatory tools covered in Chapter 4 will serve you well:

Process analysis can help you to better understand or explain *how* your subject works, especially when it takes place over a period of time. We experience films, musical or theatrical performances, even short stories or poems, as processes or step-by-step events, and such works may proceed in unique or particularly effective ways. A movie or story might open with one mood or situation, shift focus to another, introduce a new character, flash back to an earlier time, jumble or reorder chronology, and so on. As we study how the film or fiction unfolds and analyze how it is put together, we may gain insight about its meaning, quality, originality, and significance.

Comparison and contrast, pinpointing significant similarities or differences, can be one of criticism's most useful strategies, especially if we're looking at more than one work, or comparable elements within one work. We might compare poems or stories by the same author, films with similar themes by different directors, paintings from one period by different artists, or characters, themes, or actions within a story. Such comparison-or-contrast writing can not only help us to understand more about what works contain, but it can also provide additional evidence—in the form of analysis and explanation—to sup-port our critical position.

Division and classification, like comparison and contrast, can help us to draw distinct lines in our critical study, to sort or group subjects for greater clarity. We might divide stories into parts (establishing situation, growing tension, crisis, climax, resolution), music or art into periods (classical, romantic, modern). We might classify architec-ture according to its function (domestic, commercial, religious), or films by their genre (gangster movies, westerns, slapstick farces). On a smaller scale, we might classify characters' traits or actions (brave, neurotic, passive), or a poem's images (violent or pastoral, taken from city life or from nature).

Cause-and-effect analysis can help us understand the actions or motives of characters, or the effects of plot, style, form, or other artistic choices, on the audience. It can help us gauge our initial response to the work as well as our continuing reaction and evaluation.

Finally, *analogy and metaphor* can give us ways to interpret or explain our understanding to our readers, if not to prove our critical points. Seeing a good adventure film might be like riding a roller coaster or visiting the fun house at the carnival. Seeing a bad comedy might be like being chained to your seat for an all-day amateur show.

Proving Your Point

No matter what informative or explanatory devices you use, your goal in writing a critical essay will be to mount a convincing case—a logical argument. You'll want to construct your essay according to basic rules of argument for presenting a claim, and supporting and justifying it with evidence and reason.

The *evidence* you'll use to support or justify your critical point may be any of these:

- References to the thing itself, such as quoted passages
- Your descriptions of character, style, setting, action, or other features of the object
- Statements by other critics

The *assumptions* you'll cite to justify your interpretation or evaluation are criteria, *critical warrants* or general principles appropriate to your subject. (The criteria for judging poetry, for example, are different from those for film.)

The vast range of subjects open to critical inquiry, and their accompanying standards, are beyond our scope here. We can, however, look at some basic approaches to criticism and at the kind of warrants that critics in all fields use to support their claims.

Critics consider created works from two general perspectives: from the inside, and from the outside. That is, they may look at the work itself, as if it were unrelated to anything else, or they may look at the work as it relates to the world around it. In critical essays we may stress one or the other, or both, of these views.

Intrinsic criticism

When we focus on the poem, story, or play, without regard to its author's intentions, its history, its social context, we look at its intrinsic nature, at the thing itself. We try to understand and evaluate the object's specific qualities, flaws, successes, or failures. Much of the criticism we read daily in popular reviews, and a good deal of scholarly criticism as well, is of this type. If you think about it, most of us practice this sort of critical analysis in our everyday encounters with television shows, movies, books, and records; we see them as independent objects, things with or without value.

But how do we arrive at such judgments? We evaluate objects by applying general critical principles or assumptions about what we ex-

pect from created works. No matter what kind of object we're studying, we'll consider some or all of these matters:

The overall *effect* of the work, or our reaction to it.   What were
our first and later reactions? Was our response favorable, or not? Did it
change? Were we attracted to the work? Did it make us feel something—
anger, sorrow, terror, joy? Why did it or why did it not give us pleasure?
Would we recommend it to others? Did we try to understand it even if
we didn't like it?

The work's *form* or design, its qualities of *beauty*.   Did we find
the pattern or composition pleasing or meaningful? Is the work unified, without unrelated or useless elements? Does it fit together in a
pattern that makes sense? Does it seem finished or complete, so that
nothing can be added or changed to improve it? Or, on the other
hand, is it *lacking* any of these qualities?

The *meaning* of the work.   Does the object give us a new or
interesting way of looking at the world? Does it add to our knowledge
or awareness, provide us with compelling experience? Does it enrich
our lives in any way?

The work's *craft*.   Is the object made well, with care and skill?
Does the maker seem to be in control of the work's various elements?
Is the work designed to appeal only to passing interest—to be here
today and gone tomorrow—or to last a long time?

These kinds of general questions can point us toward decisions
common to any form of intrinsic criticism. Beyond them, however,
we'll want to look at our subject's *specific* elements—the unique components that make it up. Here's a sample:

Fiction, film, drama
>   Character, setting, plot, point of view, theme, tone, style
>   Direction, acting, cinematography, set design, special effects

Poetry, music
>   Language, imagery, style, form, theme
>   Sound, rhythm, lyrics, melody, texture

Art, architecture
>   Composition, form, style, scale, materials

Extrinsic criticism

Close examination of stories, poems, films, and so on, certainly
tells us much about their quality, importance, or meaning. The intrinsic
perspective, however, has limits. Sometimes we must stand outside the

work, to place it in a larger context. Extrinsic criticism evaluates the work in relation to such outside forces or influences. Though this approach doesn't ignore the object's internal nature, it uses other fields of knowledge as frames of reference. Some of the usual ones:

Biography.   Here the critic evaluates the object in relation to its maker's personal and public life. The critic looks for the potential influences of life upon art, how personal experience or belief may have affected the artist's choices.

History.   In a similar approach, writers of historical criticism try to relate works to the specific times and places from which they come. They treat literature, art, music, and so on, as outgrowths or reflections of historical forces—defined by the periods in which they are created.

Theory or ideology.   Some critics use even narrower frames of reference, interpreting created works according to specific theories or social or political beliefs. Such systems of thought include psychology, philosophy, language study, and political ideology.

Myth or religion.   Here, critics look for relationships between works and religious or mythical traditions. They ask whether such works express, or question, or otherwise reflect religious themes or ideas, such as Judeo-Christian ethics and beliefs.

Whether your critical argument emphasizes internal or external elements, you'll build it as you would any argumentative essay—qualifying your claims, backing them with specific evidence and rationale, seeking to convince your audience that your judgment is soundly reasoned, fair, and worth hearing.

Process checklist: Writing to criticize or evaluate

The task
- What object will I attempt to criticize?
- Who is my audience?
- What will my readers want to know about the work and my reaction to it?

Exploring and collecting
- What can I learn by studying the work's internal makeup?

Process checklist: Writing to criticize or evaluate (*continued*)

- What's my initial reaction to it? Did my reaction change?
- Is the work pleasing or meaningful to me? Why?
- What are its obvious strengths or weaknesses?
- What specific elements might I examine more closely?
- Could I use an external frame of reference to enhance my criticism?

Finding your thesis

- Have I narrowed my analysis to a specific critical judgment?
- Is this the best or most interesting assessment I can make? Will the reader profit from it?
- Does the claim best express my overall understanding of the object's meaning or value?

Designing

- What kind of supporting evidence or reasoning do I plan to use?
- How can I present this support in the clearest, most convincing way?
- What information and explanation best support my argument, and where should I include them?

Drafting

- Have I executed my design fully?
- Has my focus or design changed in any way?
- Have I included all necessary material?

Critical reading and rewriting

- Have I expressed my view exactly as I intend?
- Have I supported my claim thoroughly and answered readers' possible questions or objections?
- Are my sentences and paragraphs clear, concise, logical?
- Are there gaps in my argument?

The final draft

- Have I checked the entire essay for spelling, grammar, style, mechanics?

In the following essays, study the kinds of critical claims the authors make, and the methods they use to justify them. Notice where and how the writers present information, explain or analyze it, and offer reasons for their interpretations. Is their focus mostly on the object itself, or on its relation to outside forces? Do they consider the effect of the work, its design, its meaning, its craft? What elements of the work do they isolate for analysis? If they consider outside factors, is the context one of biography, history, theory, or religion? Finally, ask yourself if you're convinced by their discussions, if you do or don't agree.

— Martha Bayles —

Martha Bayles is a freelance writer as well as television critic for the Wall Street Journal. *Born in Boston in 1948, Bayles grew up in Weston, Massachusetts, and is a 1970 graduate of Harvard University with a master's in education from the University of Pennsylvania. She has taught in the Philadelphia and Boston public schools and has been a college writing teacher at Syracuse, Cornell, Fordham, and Harvard. From 1981 to 1985 she was film critic for* American Spectator *and a book critic for* The New York Times. *She has been the* Journal's *television writer since inception of the "Arts & Leisure" page in 1984. Bayles has published fiction and essays in* The New Republic, Harper's, The Atlantic, *the* New Criterion, *and* Public Interest, *among other magazines, and was a contributor to the book* Political Passages *(1988). She is currently at work on a book about American popular music.*

The Wonder of The Wonder Years

In this review, Bayles argues in praise of an especially well-crafted, well-acted, and well-written television situation comedy, a show that has gathered wide critical acclaim.

Even in these nostalgic days, it's hard to get misty-eyed about the TV sitcoms of the 1960s. To borrow a phrase from TV historian David Marc, the tube's chief response to the turmoil of the times was "deep escapism." On the one hand, there were witless military shows like *Hogan's Heroes* and *McHale's Navy*. On the other hand, there was the witlessness of what Mr. Marc calls "magicoms": *The Addams Family, Bewitched, I Dream of Jeannie* and *My Favorite Martian*.

In the early 1970s, it was Norman Lear to the rescue. With shows like *All in the Family* and *Maude*, Mr. Lear yanked the genre out of deep escapism and plunged it into deep didacticism. Until quite recently, the Lear legacy has been unmistakably present every time an episode of what is supposed to be a comedy ends not with a laugh but a lesson—as this or that controversial issue gets illuminated by a big, bright Hollywood spotlight, usually located well to the left.

It's no wonder, given the choice between airhead fluff and political heavy breathing, that the sitcom was pronounced dead by the early

229

1980s. Then it was Bill Cosby to the rescue, with a show that found comic inspiration not in the headlines but in the humble stuff of everyday life—grocery lists, kids' allowances, geometry homework. But despite its apparent reversion to deep domesticity, *The Cosby Show* and the slew of family shows it inspired still partake, in subtle ways, of the Lear legacy.

Here's how. In true 1960s fashion, *All in the Family* assumed the   4
moral superiority of the younger generation, thus setting a precedent for sitcoms pitting enlightened children against benighted parents. *Cosby* restored the authority of parents, but only at the price of making them even wiser and wittier than the kids, who remain just as wise and witty as ever. Such preternaturally wonderful families become examples for the rest of us poor bums, in the latest sitcom formula: didactic domesticity.

Now it's *The Wonder Years* to the rescue. In a way, this blossom-   5
ing new show . . . is as much a reaction to didactic domesticity as the sloppy-but-happy sitcoms *Roseanne* and *Married . . . with Children.* But unlike them, it doesn't offer blue-collar slovenliness as the flip side of the upper-middle class perfection of *Cosby.* The families depicted in *The Wonder Years* are strictly middle class, something rarely seen on TV nowadays—except in docudramas about white males busily abusing their spouses, their children and illegal substances.

The first thing the viewer notices about *The Wonder Years* is that   6
it isn't "filmed before a live studio audience"—or a dead one, for that matter. Instead, it follows its 13-year-old hero, Kevin (Fred Savage), hither and thither in the pleasant suburb where he is growing up in the late 1960s. This cinematic freedom is the show's first departure from the Lear legacy. Canned messages are harder to deliver when the show itself doesn't feel canned.

The second departure is even simpler. There's plenty of wit and   7
wisdom in *The Wonder Years,* but it doesn't come directly out of the characters' mouths. Instead, it comes from the adult Kevin, never seen but frequently heard (in voice-overs read by Daniel Stern). Like the rest of us poor bums, young Kevin doesn't always have a witticism for life's vicissitudes. But also like the rest of us, his older self's 20/20 hindsight sees all the humor that was hidden at the time. This neat device keeps us laughing while also keeping the characters natural and believable.

Perhaps the most tiresome aspect of the Lear legacy is its habit of   8
trying to evoke tender sentiment while driving home the lesson of each week's episode. Veteran comedy writers have an unprintable term for this sudden upsurge of mush. They call it the "M.O.S.," or "Moment of S---." Whatever the name, it's always recognizable as that all-

too-predictable pause when we are expected to quit laughing and squeeze out a tear. Or more likely, a groan: "Why am I watching this stuff?"

Again, *The Wonder Years* has a simple solution. You want senti-   9
ment? You'll get it, the easy way. Instead of forcing its characters to recite the Moral of the Story before the final commercial, *The Wonder Years* just spins a golden oldie. Of course, plenty of TV shows and movies do that nowadays. But in most cases, the music is slathered on as a substitute for real character or dialogue. *The Wonder Years*, by contrast, uses it sparingly, and only as a substitute for the dreaded M.O.S.

All these departures worked their magic in a recent episode in   10
which Kevin and his best friend, Paul (Josh Saviano), both turn 13. Paul, who is Jewish, relishes being the center of attention at his bar mitzvah. Kevin, who lacks strong ethnic roots, is so consumed by envy that he refuses to attend, telling Paul that his family is giving him a big party, too. Then, at the half-hearted get-together his mother does arrange, Kevin mugs thanks for her gift of a thesaurus. The voice-over quips: "Any synonyms for 'extremely disappointed' in there?"

Meanwhile, the dialogue between the 13-year-olds stays true.   11
Having bottomed out on self-pity, Kevin finally shows up at the bar mitzvah—to Paul's evident joy. After the service, Paul beams: "I felt like such a jerk up there." And Kevin beams back: "No, you were good. You had this big thing hanging from your nose, but you were good." The next thing we know, the two friends are helping the band destroy "Hava Nagila."

All without a single sermon about family, tradition or productive   12
coexistence between Christians and Jews. All without a mawkish scene in which Kevin's own family reaffirms some last-minute tradi-tion that makes everything all right. They're good people, but they're not perfect, and Kevin's disappointment is real. But that is precisely what gives the story its bittersweet poignancy. By the time "Hava Nagila" fades out, replaced by a mellow Simon and Garfunkel ballad, even the most jaded sitcom viewer will be gazing through mist.

Questions for Study and Discussion

Meaning and Purpose

1. In her critique, Bayles gives us a brief history of the television situa-tion comedy over three decades. What traditions does she isolate, and how does she use them in her evaluation of *The Wonder Years*?

2. What is the "Lear legacy"? What is "didactic domesticity," and which show best exemplifies it?
3. According to Bayles, what are some unique features of *The Wonder Years*? How does the author set it apart from its past *and* its current competition?

Strategy and Audience

1. Which specific production elements (character, setting, plot, and so on) of the show does Bayles evaluate? To what extent does she analyze the program's effect on viewers, its qualities of design or beauty, its meaning and craft?
2. Other than setting the historical context, does Bayles bring any external perspectives to the show?
3. If you know the program, how do you react to Bayles's criticism? Where do you agree or disagree? What, if anything, has Bayles left out that merits attention?

Language and Style

1. The *Wall Street Journal*, in which this review first appeared, is a national business newspaper with a reputation for holding politically conservative editorial views. To what extent does Bayles's essay reflect such views? Where in her language do you find indications that reveal her politics?
2. Suggestions for vocabulary study: didacticism (paragraph 2); reversion (3); benighted, preternaturally (4); slovenliness (5); witticism, vicissitudes (7); mawkish (12).

Writing Ideas

1. Write a review of your favorite television program—or one whose qualities or freshness you especially admire. What specific things make the show worth watching? What makes it better than average, different, moving, or captivating? What underlying critical assumptions do you bring to any consideration of television? What's your sense of the show's effect, truthfulness, beauty, or craft?
2. Review a program, as above, but turn your critical eye toward a show you consider truly awful—but which is undeniably popular. Write to convince viewers that they are misguided in their appreciation of this wretched program.

— Mark Moses —

Mark Moses, who died in 1989, was a freelance popular-music critic for The New Yorker *magazine. For many years a staff member on the* Boston Phoenix—*that city's weekly alternative newspaper*—*Moses was an especially articulate writer about the contemporary music scene, bringing to it a sense of intelligence and elegance of prose style that elevated the subject to serious critical consideration.*

Wise Guy

In this, excerpted from Moses's last review for The New Yorker, *he evaluates a recent album from one of rock music's most notorious and flamboyant figures—a former "bad boy" who in middle age still writes, plays, and sings with a distinctive urban style.*

Lou Reed's "New York" (Sire) has been treated as a tour de force, 1 most suspiciously by the singer himself, who on the back of the album instructs us to listen to it "in one 58-minute (14 songs!) sitting as though it were a book or a movie." It's surprising that Reed still feels he has to make a case for his literary reputation, after more than two decades of stunning, though erratic, work. Straining for a masterpiece, as he has done periodically during his solo career (1973's "Berlin," 1978's "Street Hassle"), he misses (fortunately), and comes up with something more vital: a talky bull session as full of insight and preposterousness as anything he has done. For all the vaunted topical seriousness of the album, the secret premise here is refreshingly loose: Reed scanning the morning paper, mouthing off about everything from crack dealers to the environment. Instead of responding to the correctness of any of the views that the songs put forth, you respond to the tone of the proclamations, which is alternately haughty, deadpan, and hilarious.

On his previous album, 1986's hodgepodge "Mistrial," Reed made 2 shaky moves toward blunt social commentary in songs such as "Video Violence" and "The Original Wrapper." Aside from the fact that they weren't particularly good songs, what was disheartening about them was how they abandoned Reed's trademark dispassion in favor of the blandly responsible carping of your average, dutiful citizens, most of

233

whom don't make records to air their mild discontent. Even in the ostensibly confessional "The Blue Mask" and "Legendary Hearts" (which might be the genuine masterworks of his solo career), the madly shifting points of view would have been unthinkable without Reed's ability to observe everything in a full circle around the subject, even when he was that subject. When he proclaimed, in "The Blue Mask," that he was just "an average guy," the irony was so broad it was almost beside the point, and his distance from his own claim was what made the song cut.

The worst songs on "New York" seem like afterthoughts, at-   3 tempts to give the project a completeness that it doesn't need. "Xmas in February" is a soggy Vietnam-slice-of-life story so flat you could swear that it was cribbed from any of the rush of war movies from three or four years ago. Neither "There Is No Time" nor "Strawman" can make much out of the pounding, anthemlike forward motion of its setting. Framing an attack on Jesse Jackson with images of Kurt Waldheim meeting with the Pope has gratuitousness written all over it, but the worse trouble with "Good Evening Mr. Waldheim" is that when Reed expresses doubts about Jackson's "Common Ground" speech with the query "Is 'common ground' a word or just a sound?" he falls into the old trap of claiming that black oratory has more to do with feeling than with sense.

For the most part, though, the songs rise or fall not on Reed's   4 beliefs but on the slangy, sneaky way he draws you into his one-sided conversations. "Last Great American Whale" ought to be an unbear-able idea for a song; instead, as it widens to include the perils of media faith (and, possibly, the stubbornness of Reed's career), it takes on an offhand majesty. "Halloween Parade" casts Reed as a bemused by-stander at Greenwich Village's annual bacchanalia, quietly noticing the absence of familiar characters lost to AIDS. The jarring tribute to Andy Warhol (whose neutral stare influenced much of Reed's song-writing), "Dime Store Mystery," interlaces images of the human (the title phrase) and the divine (Christ's last temptation) to comment on the artist's icy elusiveness. And no one but Reed would begin a song about prospective fatherhood ("Beginning of a Great Adventure") with the line "It might be great to have a kid that I could kick around / A little me to fill up with my thoughts."

What shoves the album along just as much as Reed's talking-   5 blues, beat-infected vocals is the stark force of the band's playing. Since "The Blue Mask," Reed has been rediscovering the joys of the lineup of two guitars, bass, and drums, and here, even though he doesn't have the wiry scrawl of the guitarist Robert Quine this time around, the band applies a lean, echoey sheen to even the most raging tunes, without simply reverting to the pent-up rhythmic fury of the Velvet Underground. The sound it gets, full of light and unguarded movement, is as appropriate a musical counterpart as Reed has ever had, well suited to the lyrics' sprawl. The grand intentions of "New York" may turn out to have been a sop to Reed's newfound quizzical status as a grand old man of rock, a perch that has risen ever since "The Blue Mask" and "Legendary Hearts" announced him to be a happily married man who lets off steam on his motorbike, and not the sexual question mark who liked to simulate shooting up onstage. Yet, making melodies out of the barest handful of chords, talking trash with the best of them (including his former selves), Reed gives "New York" the spin of much of his most scabrous work, in which you can never tell what he's going to say next.

Questions for Study and Discussion

Meaning and Purpose

1. According to Moses, why is "New York" a praiseworthy record album? What are the album's main strengths? What are its flaws?
2. What does the author claim are Reed's strengths and weaknesses as a performer? How are these traits revealed in the "New York" album?
3. What do you learn about Reed's work in general here?

Strategy and Audience

1. Does Moses devote most of his attention to the content of Reed's songs or to the music itself? Why would he choose one element over the other?
2. To what extent would a reader uninterested in or unfamiliar with rock music be persuaded to take a look at this record or at other work by its composer? Why?
3. Do you know the album being reviewed here? What is your opinion of it, or of Lou Reed? Where do you agree, or disagree, with Moses?

Style and Language

1. Moses's style mixes general theorizing about the singer ("Reed's trademark dispassion") with vivid, sometimes metaphorical, description of

the music ("the band applies a lean, echoey sheen to even the most raging tunes"). Point out other instances where Moses's language moves in one direction or the other. What is the effect of this blend of styles?

2. Vocabulary: tour de force, preposterousness, vaunted (paragraph 1); dispassion, carping, ostensibly (2); gratuitousness (3); bemused, bacchanalia (4); sop, scabrous (5).

Writing Ideas

1. Write a positive or negative critical review of a recent or classic record album, paying particular attention to musical elements (texture, melody, beat, instrumentation, lyrics, phrasing, and so on). Write for an audience who may not know your subject intimately, but whom you want to persuade to accept or reject the record.

2. Write a review of a recent live performance of a musical act. Consider the elements mentioned in the first suggestion, but widen your focus to take in elements of the performance itself: staging, lighting, energy or skill of performance, originality.

— Roger Ebert —

Roger Ebert, born in 1942 in Urbana, Illinois, is one of a select group of writers who make their living watching movies. Chief film critic for the Chicago Sun-Times since 1967, Ebert is a nationally syndicated columnist, university lecturer, author of books and screenplays, and perhaps best known as co-host, with his Chicago Tribune rival Gene Siskel, of "Siskel & Ebert & the Movies" (originally "Sneak Previews," on PBS, and later "At the Movies"), a weekly movie-review television program. Ebert has been a juror at major film festivals, a consultant to the National Endowment for the Arts, and has won many writing awards, including the Pulitzer Prize (he is the only movie critic ever to win that award) for distinguished criticism, in 1975. He is the author of A Kiss Is Still a Kiss (1984) and Roget Ebert's Movie Home Companion (1985 and later yearly editions), among other books, and has contributed to Esquire, Film Comment, American Film, and Rolling Stone.

Batman

In this column from the Chicago Sun-Times, Ebert gives a careful, insightful, and decidedly mixed review to one of the great movie blockbusters of all time. As you read Ebert, ask yourself where you agree with him, and where, if you had the chance to talk, you'd challenge his criticism.

The Gotham City created in *Batman* is one of the most distinctive and atmospheric places I've seen in the movies. It's a shame something more memorable doesn't happen there. *Batman* is a triumph of design over story, style over substance—a great-looking movie with a plot you can't care much about. All of the big moments in the movie are pounded home with ear-shattering sound effects and a jackhammer cutting style, but that just serves to underline the movie's problem, which is a curious lack of suspense and intrinsic interest.

Batman discards some of the recent cultural history of the Batman character—the camp 1960s TV series, the in-joke comic books—and returns to the mood of the 1940s, the decade of film noir and fascism. The movie is set at the present moment, more or less, but looks as if little has happened in architecture or city planning since the classic DC comic books created that architectural style you could call

237

Comic Book Moderne. The streets of Gotham City are lined with bizarre skyscrapers that climb cancerously toward the sky, held up (or apart) by sky bridges and stresswork that look like webs against the night sky.

At street level, gray and anonymous people scurry fearfully   3
through the shadows, and the city cancels its 200th anniversary cele-bration because the streets are not safe enough to hold it. Gotham is in the midst of a wave of crime and murder orchestrated by The Joker (Jack Nicholson), and civilization is defended only by Batman (Mi-chael Keaton). The screenplay takes a bow in the direction of the origin of the Batman story (young Bruce Wayne saw his parents mur-dered by a thug and vowed to use their fortune to dedicate his life to crime-fighting), and it also explains how The Joker got his fearsome grimace. Then it turns into a gloomy showdown between the two bizarre characters.

Nicholson's Joker is really the most important character in the   4
movie—in impact and screen time—and Keaton's Batman and Bruce Wayne characters are so monosyllabic and impenetrable that we have to remind ourselves to cheer for them. Kim Basinger strides in as Vicki Vale, a famous photographer assigned to the Gotham City crime wave, but although she and Wayne carry on a courtship and Batman rescues her from certain death more than once, there's no chemistry and little eroticism. The strangest scene in the movie may be the one where Vicki is brought into the Batcave by Alfred, the faithful valet, and realizes for the first time that Bruce Wayne and Batman are the same person. How does she react? She doesn't react. The movie forgets to allow her to be astonished.

Remembering the movie, I find that the visuals remain strong   5
in my mind, but I have trouble caring about what happened in front of them. I remember an astonishing special effects shot that travels up, up to the penthouse of a towering, ugly skyscraper, and I remem-ber the armor slamming shut on the Batmobile as if it were a high-tech armadillo. I remember The Joker grinning beneath a hideous giant balloon as he dispenses free cash in his own travesty of the Macy's parade, and I remember a really vile scene in which he defaces art masterpieces in the local museum before Batman crashes in through the skylight.

But did I care about the relationship between these two carica-   6
tures? Did either one have the depth of even a comic book character? Not really. And there was something off-putting about the anger be-neath the movie's violence. This is a hostile, mean-spirited movie about ugly, evil people, and it doesn't generate the liberating euphoria

of the Superman or Indiana Jones pictures. It's classified PG-13, but it's not for kids.

Should it be seen, anyway? Probably. Director Tim Burton and his special effects team have created a visual place that has some of the same strength as Fritz Lang's Metropolis or Ridley Scott's futuristic Los Angeles in *Blade Runner*. The gloominess of the visuals has a haunting power. Nicholson has one or two of his patented moments of inspiration, although not as many as I would have expected. And the music by Prince, intercut with classics, is effectively joined in the images. The movie's problem is that no one seemed to have any fun making it, and it's hard to have much fun watching it. It's a depressing experience. Is the opposite of comic book "tragic book"?

7

Questions for Study and Discussion

Meaning and Purpose

1. What is Ebert's essential argument about *Batman*? How does his subjective response to the film influence his final opinion?
2. What are the film's major strengths, according to Ebert? What are its flaws? What does he admire most about this movie, and why? What, finally, is its biggest weakness?
3. Ebert broadens his discussion by including references to other films. What critical points does this outside evidence support? How vital is it to his overall evaluation?

Strategy and Audience

1. Which production elements (plot, character, cinematography, action sequences, music, and so on) does Ebert consider? What does he say about each?
2. Chances are you've seen this film. Where do you agree with Ebert, and where do you disagree? Why? Has he changed your opinion of the movie in any way?
3. How influential are the film reviews you read or see on the weekly "sneak-preview" programs in determining the movies you'll attend? What sparks your interest in new films? Reviewers' comments? Word-of-mouth opinions of friends? The cast? The story or subject?

Style and Language

1. Ebert writes for a national audience of readers of all ages and levels of education. How would you compare his language and style to those of the Moses *New Yorker* review in this chapter, or Oates's essay from a small literary magazine?
2. Throughout his essay, Ebert refers to himself, his opinions, his thoughts. How does this first person technique affect you? Does it damage or enhance Ebert's credibility?

Writing Ideas

1. Write a critical essay in which you make a case for or against a film that had a particularly strong effect on you. You'll first want to establish some criteria of your own for evaluating your subject. What qualities do you expect in memorable films? What movies provide supporting examples of the qualities you admire or dislike?
2. Write a movie review for your student newspaper in which you defend or argue critically against a recent film. Consider the elements of the film itself—its plot, characters, setting, execution, believability, coherence, and so on—as well as its more general qualities such as meaning, truthfulness, importance.

— Joyce Carol Oates —

Joyce Carol Oates—known for being both versatile and prolific—is a poet, novelist, short-story writer, essayist, critic, and editor. Born in 1938 and first published as an undergraduate at Syracuse University, Oates earned an M.A. degree at the University of Wisconsin in 1961 and has taught at the universities of Detroit and Windsor and at Princeton. Author of close to two dozen novels, Oates won the National Book Award for them (1969). Other works include The Wheel of Love *(1970),* Wonderland *(1971),* Do with Me What You Will *(1973),* The Profane Art *(1983),* Solstice *(1985),* Marya: A Life *(1987),* American Appetites *(1989), and* Because It Is Bitter, and Because It Is My Heart *(1990).*

Ernest Hemingway

In this article from the Ontario Review, *Oates wears her critic's hat to consider the life and art of one of America's best-known twentieth-century writers. The essay illustrates the frequent and typical use of the biographical perspective on an author's work. Oates first reviews Hemingway's life and personal characteristics, and then applies her findings to one of his most memorable novels,* The Sun Also Rises.

Nearly a quarter-century after his violent, self-inflicted death in 1961, Ernest Hemingway remains the most controversial and very likely the most influential of American writers. His influence has been both literary and personal—and therefore incalculable. The ear, if not the eye, can detect Hemingwayesque cadences in the elliptical dialogue of Harold Pinter; the swift, declarative sentences of the young Gabriel Garcia Márquez; the laconic first-person narratives of Albert Camus; the carefully honed, ironic prose of Joan Didion. Norman Mailer, strongly influenced by Hemingway's work in his early career, remains under the not altogether beneficent influence of the man: the Hemingway who believed that *aficion* (passion) justified the expenditure of the self in public.

Like all major artists, Hemingway arouses a diversity of critical responses, ranging from adulation to loathing. But in Hemingway's case the situation is confused by the highly visible presence—one might almost say the embarrassing intrusion—of the writer-as-celebrity, the flamboyant "Papa" Hemingway of the popular media, whose advertisements for himself (as big-game hunter, deep-sea fisherman, grizzled sage, man among men) approached self-parody in the 1950s. (It is interesting to note that the expatriated Hemingway, long a derisory critic of American culture, succumbed to a distinctly American pathology, like Mark Twain and Jack London before him, and more recently Truman Capote: the surrender of the self to the public image, to the inevitable debasement of the self.) Perhaps because media celebrity came early and unbidden to Hemingway—at the age of 18, as a driver for the Red Cross Ambulance Corps, he was wounded in Italy, cited for his extraordinary bravery under fire, and taken up for a time by American wire services and newsreels as a hero—he accepted fame as his due, and believed that, though writing was, in itself, a pure activity, it might also be the means to an end: the enshrinement and immortalization of Ernest Hemingway.

As a consequence, attitudes toward Hemingway's considerable   3
achievement now come sharply conditioned by attitudes toward Hemingway the man: how one feels, for instance, about his highly stylized religion of *machismo* (the glorification of the bullfight as a ritual of beauty, the camaraderie of men who are bonded by their "superiority" not only to women, but to most other men as well); his rites of personal risk and exotic adventure ("It is certainly valuable to a trained writer to crash in an airplane that burns"); the equation of masculinity with greatness in literature.

More than one acquaintance of Hemingway's made the observa-   4
tion that, despite his several wives and liaisons, he seemed to dislike women, and since he rarely wrote of women with sympathy, and virtually never with subtlety and understanding, feminist charges of misogyny are surely justified. (Yet in the context of American literature, this is simply to accuse Hemingway of being a male writer. William Faulkner's more insidious misogyny passes largely unnoted, perhaps because Faulkner's prose is less accessible than Hemingway's and his manner more self-consciously "visionary.") It cannot be surprising that Jewish readers have been disconcerted by the casual anti-Semitism that pervades his work; or that the sensitive are offended by his fascination with blood sports, like bullfighting and boxing, and that general air of indifference to the suffering of others that seems the more pitiless for being expressed in short, blunt, declarative sentences.

Writers have always admired and learned from Hemingway, as   5
Hemingway in his time admired and learned from any number of other older writers, but critics have been doubtful of his overall worth. Indeed, critical reassessment of Hemingway in the past two or three

decades has been so harsh that Malcolm Cowley, in a sympathetic essay titled "Papa and the Parricides," analyzed the phenomenon in terms of Freud's highly speculative "Totem and Taboo"—the notion, never substantiated by anthropologists, that there might exist a primitive rite of murder, dismemberment and devouring of the "primal" father by his own sons. Yet even the most severe critics have granted Hemingway a few classic books—*In Our Time* (1925), *The Sun Also Rises* (1926), *A Farewell to Arms* (1929), *Green Hills of Africa* (1935), the posthumously published *A Moveable Feast* (1964), and a number of masterly short stories.

The Sun Also Rises, written in Paris and published when Hemingway was 27 years old, immediately established his reputation as one of the most brilliant and original writers of his generation; he was lauded as an unsentimental, if not pitiless, interpreter of post-World War I society. The novel's idle, self-absorbed characters are American and English expatriates in Paris in the early 1920s, veterans in one way or another of the war: the newspaperman-narrator Jake Barnes was wounded on the Italian front and is sexually impotent ("No," Jake says self-mockingly, "I just had an accident"); the woman he loves, Brett Ashley, estranged from an English baronet who became mentally deranged during his service in the Royal Navy, is something of a nymphomaniac-alcoholic ("I've always done just what I wanted," Brett says helplessly to Jake. "I do feel such a bitch"). 6

The novel's title, perfectly chosen, taken from Ecclesiastes ("One generation passeth away, and another cometh; but the earth abideth forever. . . . The sun also ariseth, and the sun goeth down, and hasteth to the place where he arose. . . ."), strikes exactly the right chord of ennui and resignation, and succeeds in lifting Hemingway's story of drifting, alienated, rather superficial men and women to a mythopoeic level. And the novel's other epigraph, long since famous, is Gertrude Stein's: "You are all a lost generation." (In fact, as Hemingway discloses in *A Moveable Feast,* Stein appropriated the remark from the manager of a Parisian gas station.) 7

Reading Hemingway's first novel today, one is likely to be struck by its "modern" sound; the affectless, meiotic prose, confrontations that purposefully eschew emotion, the circular and even desultory movement of its narrative. The generation of the 1920s was perhaps no more lost than many another postwar generation, but the self-consciousness of being lost, being special, "damned," casually committed to self-destruction (Jake and his friends are virtually all alcoholics or on their way to becoming so), sounds a new note in prose fiction. Jake's impotence is, of course, not accidental. Being estranged from conventional society (that is, one's family back home) and religion 8 (for Jake, Catholicism: a "grand" religion) establishes the primary bond between the novel's characters. Brett says defensively at the novel's end, after she has made a surely minimal gesture of doing good, "It makes one feel rather good deciding not to be a bitch. . . . It's sort of what we have instead of God." As for morality—Jakes wonders if it isn't simply what goads a man to feel self-disgust after he has done something shameful.

It seems not to be generally recognized that Hemingway's classic   9
novel owes a good deal to F. Scott Fitzgerald's *The Great Gatsby,* which Hemingway read in 1925 and admired greatly. Each novel is narrated by a disaffected young man who observes but does not participate centrally in the action; each novel traces the quixotic love of an outsider for a beautiful if infantile woman; each is an excoriation from within of the "lost generation" and the "fiesta concept of life"— Hemingway's phrase denoting the aristocratic rich "who give each day the quality of a festival and who, when they have passed and taken the nourishment they need, leave everything dead. . . ."

Fitzgerald's Daisy is unhappily married to the wealthy Tom Bu-   10
chanan, whom Gatsby bravely challenges for her love; Hemingway's Brett intends to marry the drunkard, wealthy-bankrupt Mike Campbell, whom the hapless Robert Cohn fights with his fists. (Cohn knocks the inebriated Campbell down but loses Brett all the same—not to Campbell, but to a 19-year-old bullfighter.) In each novel, men and women set themselves the task of being entertained, absorbed, diverted, not by work (though Jake Barnes is a newspaperman of a literary sort), but primarily by drinking and talking. Hemingway's people in particular are obsessed with various forms of sport—golfing, tennis, swimming, hiking, trout fishing, attending boxing matches and bullfights. And drinking. Only in Malcolm Lowry's *Under the Volcano* are drinks so rigorously catalogued and described—whiskey, brandy, champagne, wines of various kinds, absinthe, liqueurs. After a long, drunken sequence, Jake thinks: "Under the wine I lost the disgusted feeling and was happy. It seemed they were all such nice people."

As a story, *The Sun Also Rises* depends primarily upon the reader's   11
acceptance of Jake Barnes as an intelligent and reliable observer, and of Brett in the role of a 34-year-old Circe awash in alcohol and cheery despair. Though based, like many of Hemingway's characters, on a real person (Lady Twysden, a "legend" in Montparnasse during the time Hemingway and his first wife, Hadley, lived there), Brett is sketchily portrayed; she is "nice," "damned nice," "lovely," "of a very good family," "built with curves like the hull of a racing yacht," but the reader has difficulty envisioning her. Hemingway gives her so little to say that we cannot come to know her. (Whereas Duff Twysden was

evidently an artist of some talent and seems to have been an unusually vivacious and intelligent woman.)

Another problematic character is the Jew, Robert Cohn, who 12 evokes everyone's scorn by "behaving badly"—he follows Brett around and intrudes where he isn't wanted. Cohn is so much the scapegoat for the others' cruelty ("That kike!" "He's just so awful!" "Was I rude enough to him?" "He doesn't add much to the gaiety." "[He has] a wonderful quality of bringing out the worst in anybody") that most readers will end up feeling sympathy for him. The fact that Cohn cannot drink as heavily as the others, that the bullfight sickens him (especially the disemboweling of the picador's horse), that in this noisy *macho* milieu he finally breaks down and cries—these things seem altogether to his credit; he emerges as the novel's most distinctly drawn character. One waits in vain, however, for Jake Barnes to rise to Nick Carraway's judgment of Jay Gatsby: "You're worth the whole damn bunch put together."

The Sun Also Rises is a novel of manners and a homoerotic 13 (though not homosexual) romance, merely in outline a "love story" of unconsummated passion. Like most of Hemingway's books, fiction and nonfiction, it celebrates the mysterious bonds of masculine friendship, sometimes ritualized and sometimes spontaneous. Women are viewed with suspicion and an exaggerated awe that readily turns to contempt. Jake is happiest when he and his friend Bill are away from the company of women altogether and fishing alone in the Rio de la Fabrica valley in Spain. There they achieve a degree of intimacy impossible else-where. ("Listen," says Bill. "You're a hell of a good guy, and I'm fonder of you than anybody on earth. I couldn't tell you that in New York. It'd mean I was a faggot.") Of equal importance with male friendship is the worship of the matador, the master of the bull, the only person (in Hemingway's judgment) to live his life to the full.

Afición means passion and an *aficionado* is one who feels intense 14 passion for the bullfight. Says Jake: "Somehow it was taken for granted that an American could not have *afición.* He might simulate it or con-fuse it with excitement, but he could not really have it. When they saw that I had *afición,* and there was no password, no set questions that could bring it out, rather it was a sort of oral spiritual examination . . . there was this same embarrassed putting the hand on the shoulder, or a '*Buen hombre.*' But nearly always there was the actual touching." Only at cer-tain rigorously defined moments are men allowed to touch one another, just as, in the ritual of the bullfight (bloody and barbarous to those of us who are not *aficionados*), the tormented bull and the matador "become one" (in Hemingway's repeated phrase) at the moment of the kill. These are quite clearly sacred rites in Hemingway's private cosmology.

If many men are disturbed by Hemingway's code of ethics—as,   15
surely, many women are disturbed by it—it is because Hemingway's
exaggerated sense of maleness really excludes most men. The less than
exemplary bullfighter is jeered in the ring, even if he has been gored;
poor Robert Cohn, whose flaw seems to have been to have felt too
deeply and too openly, is ridiculed, broken, and finally banished from
the clique.

If it seems to us highly unjust that Hemingway's men and women   16
derive their sense of themselves by excluding others and by establishing
codes of behavior that enforce these exclusions, it should be recalled
that Hemingway prided himself on his ability to write of things as they
are, not as they might, or should, be. One can object that he does not
rise above his prejudices; he celebrates *aficion* where he finds it, in the
postwar malaise of the 1920s and in his own heart. *The Sun Also Rises*
remains a distinctly American work, a classic of its time and ours, like its
author, controversial and disturbing, but certainly compelling.

Questions for Study and Discussion

Meaning and Purpose

1. What is Oates's overall assessment of Ernest Hemingway? How much
    of what we remember of him has to do with his life, and how much
    with his work? What relationship does she see between them?
2. Oates uses the novel *The Sun Also Rises* as a prime example of Heming-
    way's work. What is her critical judgment of the book? What are its
    major strengths and weaknesses?
3. What was Hemingway's apparent attitude toward women? How sig-
    nificant is this attitude in Oates's evaluation? Similarly, how does his
    attitude toward men figure in Oates's critique?

Strategy and Audience

1. Why does Oates open her essay with a consideration of Hemingway's
    biography? How does this historical background set the stage for her
    critique of the novel?
2. Why does the author compare *The Sun Also Rises* with another well-
    known novel of the period, F. Scott Fitzgerald's *The Great Gatsby*?
    How does the comparison affect Oates's view of Hemingway's book?
3. Hemingway and his novel, both subjects frequently taught in high-

school literature classes, should be familiar to you. Do you agree with Oates's evaluation of the author or his book? Where would you dispute her comments?

Style and Language

1. Oates, herself a novelist, poet, and critic, writes here in a style suitable for a literary or academic audience. Compare her prose with that of Martha Bayles or Roger Ebert in this chapter. What major differences do you find?

2. Suggestions for vocabulary study: incalculable, elliptical, laconic (paragraph 1); adulation, derisory (2); camaraderie (3); liaisons, misogyny (4); lauded (6); ennui, mythopoeic (7); meiotic, eschew, desultory (8); quixotic, excoriation (9); homoerotic (13).

Writing Ideas

1. Write a critical review of a novel or short story by an author whose life is generally familiar to you. What biographical influences seem apparent in the fiction? How would you judge the overall merit of the author or of his or her most prominent work?

2. Find a review of a recent book, either fiction or nonfiction, whose author's opinion about it differs from yours. Examine the review carefully and write a counterargument, addressing the other critic's main points with your own detailed views.

— Alicia Ostriker —

Alicia Ostriker was born in 1937 and is a poet and professor of English at Rutgers University. Educated at Brandeis University and the University of Wisconsin (Ph.D., 1964), she has written several books of poetry and has been awarded Guggenheim and Rockefeller fellowships. Her book of essays, Writing Like a Woman, *appeared in 1983, and her* Stealing the Language: The Emergence of Women's Poetry in America *was published in 1986.*

American Poetry, Now Shaped by Women

Here Ostriker argues that there is such a thing as women's poetry, and that the work of American women poets over the past twenty-five years constitutes a significant literary movement that will affect the future of poetic literature. In making her case, Ostriker reviews works by several prominent writers, allowing her essay to serve as a corrective, and as an introduction to a neglected literary tradition.

In her pathbreaking autobiographical essay "When We Dead Awaken," the poet Adrienne Rich describes growing up in the 1940's and 1950's under the tutelage of male literary masters from whom she learned "that poetry should be 'universal'—which meant, of course, nonfemale." My own education, in the late 50's and early 60's, was similar. When I was a student, there were six Romantic poets: Blake, Wordsworth and Coleridge in the first generation, followed by Byron, Shelley and Keats in the second. Then came the Victorians, of whom Tennyson, Browning and Matthew Arnold were the major figures. After that, one would read Hardy perhaps, Hopkins certainly. During long years of undergraduate loneliness, I solaced myself reciting long mouthfuls of Hopkins, savoring those resonant cadences so full of ecstasy and despair. It made no difference that Hopkins was a Jesuit priest and I was a Jewish coed. Thanks to the magic of poetry, he was I, I was he. Finally, there were the supernovas of the moderns: Yeats, Eliot, Frost, Stevens, Pound, Williams. That was literary history as my professors taught it—and it became my own history. In turn they lit up my sky; I was they, they were I.

Needless to say, I read few women poets. The wicked and hilarious Aphra Behn, who should have been snuggling next to the wicked and hilarious Lord Rochester in my 17th-century text, wasn't in the book at all. Poor Dorothy Wordsworth, devoted sister and secretary to William, was absent from among the Romantics, though the prose poetry of her Grasmere journals—which William mined for his poems—is as fresh as new grass. Elizabeth Barrett Browning's love sonnets were considered sentimental, and nobody mentioned her political poetry or her feminist novel in verse, "Aurora Leigh." Christina Rossetti was in the anthologies as a minor figure, so nobody noticed that her tormented religious sensibility and exquisite lyric gift were the equal of Coleridge's or that her "Goblin Market" is as strange and compelling as "The Rime of the Ancient Mariner."

The women poets who could not be ignored could be subtly   3
diminished. Thus the eminent critic R. P. Blackmur wrote of Emily Dickinson that "she was neither a professional poet nor an amateur; she was a private poet who wrote indefatigably as some women cook or knit. Her gift for words and the cultural predicament of her time drove her to poetry instead of antimacassars." This is a bit like saying that Ezra Pound wrote the "Cantos" as indefatigably as some men work on an assembly line and that his gift for words and his cultural predicament drove him to poetry instead of bowling. Writing of Marianne Moore, Randall Jarrell complained that her work lacked "the live vulgarity of life" and was "divorced from sexuality and power." Yet a sexual and powerful Marianne Moore would scarcely have met with the respect accorded the chaste, ladylike and self-effacing spinster. Moore's more assertive and less respectable modernist sisters, Gertrude Stein, Mina Loy and H.D., were somehow a bit outside the professional pale; and I remember the afternoon when the distinguished poet-scholar J. V. Cunningham, of whom we were all in awe, made it clear that Edna St. Vincent Millay was not to be taken seriously as a poet for reasons that seemed to have something to do with the excesses of her private life.

Today the poetic landscape has changed. Some of our literary   4
mothers are being admitted to equal status in the curriculum and the literary consciousness. More important, we are in the midst of an explosion of brilliant and powerful poetry by American women in our own time. The searching intellect of Adrienne Rich, the flamelike rage of Sylvia Plath, the shameless earthiness and anguish of Anne Sexton, have stirred countless readers and influenced countless writers. Denise Levertov, Mona Van Duyn, May Swenson, Maxine Kumin and Carolyn Kizer are in their prime. Diane Wakoski is an American Surrealist, Margaret Atwood's pen drips vitriol, Marge

Piercy delineates connections between the body and the body politic, Sharon Olds enacts an erotics of family love and pain, black women writers like Gwendolyn Brooks, Lucille Clifton, Audre Lorde, Nikki Giovanni, June Jordan, Ntozake Shange give us sex and love, anger and vision in pungent language—and all these poets, with many others, portray explicitly female experience as if it were exactly as universal as men's experience.

There is reason to believe that American women poets writing   5
in the last 25 years constitute a literary movement comparable to Romanticism or modernism in our literary past and that their work is destined not only to enter the mainstream but to change the stream's future course. To be sure, the idea of "women's poetry" is still distressing in some quarters, as is the whole notion of a female literary tradition. Most critics and professors of literature deny that women's poetry, as distinct from poetry by individual women, exists. Some women writers agree. Some—for instance, Louise Glück and the late Elizabeth Bishop—have been reluctant to appear in women's anthologies.

The superficial plausibility of this position rests partly upon the   6
residual conviction that "woman poet" means "inferior poet" and partly on the undeniable fact that women writers are a diverse lot, adhering to no single set of beliefs, doctrines, styles or subjects. Yet we do not hesitate to use the term "American poetry" (or "French poetry" or "Russian poetry") on the grounds that American (or French or Russian) poets are diverse. From a global perspective, we are well aware that the more deeply an artist represents the ethos of a nation, the more likely that artist is to represent humanity, as witness Homer, Dante, Shakespeare, Goethe. The belief that true poetry is genderless—which is a disguised form of believing that true poetry is masculine—fails to recognize that writers necessarily articulate gendered experience just as they necessarily articulate the spirit of a nationality, an age, a language. What, then, happens when "we who are writing women and strange monsters," in May Sarton's phrase, begin to write with a freedom and boldness that no generation of women in history has ever known?

In part the answer is obvious. "I have a self to recover, a queen,"   7
cries Sylvia Plath. Marge Piercy imagines a women who is "like a handgrenade set to explode, / like goldenrod ready to bloom." Carolyn Kizer notes that women poets "are the custodians of the world's best-kept secret, / Merely the private lives of one-half of humanity." "No more masks! No more mythologies!" exclaims Muriel Rukeyser. Adrienne Rich in her quest poem "Diving into the Wreck" insists that we

seek "the wreck and not the story of the wreck / the thing itself and not the myth."

When the republic of letters annexes a new province, it is immediately revealed to be different from, and more complex than, what we thought while it was a blank spot, like Conrad's Congo, on the cultural map. Who would have thought love was so complicated, before Petrarch and Dante? Who would have thought little boys were so sensitive, before Rousseau and Dickens? Woman in poetry for millenniums has been a sort of blank, a screen upon which the male poet could project his fantasies of the muse, the elusive love object, the virgin, the whore, the *femme fatale*, the victim. Plath's "Lady Lazarus" perhaps summarizes this history: "I am your opus, / I am your valuable. / The pure gold baby / That melts to a shriek." Gauguin's "Soyez Mystérieuses" is, as the West Coast poet Kathleen Fraser notes, a motto engraved above the backside of a nude female lying "perfectly / voluptuous / in mud." When this female turns over, Miss Fraser suggests, she will want "to re-write" herself and her environment. The tragic and comic roles of daughter, wife, lover, mother, the routines of domesticity, the classroom, the job market, relationships with heroines, female precursors, the insulted and injured of the present and the past—to explore such themes is to release imprisoned stratums of experience into the daylight of language.

Women's poetry now is generating an enriched stock of tropes for bodily experience, augmenting humanity's array of images to define the human condition. Sharon Olds's "Language of the Brag" celebrates childbirth as a "proud American boast" equivalent to Whitman's or Ginsberg's visions of literary valor. One of the nicest compliments I ever received was when a male colleague told me that a long poem I had written on pregnancy had captured what he felt when he was pregnant with a new idea. May not such responses be as normal as my girlhood identification with a Jesuit priest? Women have proposed fresh metaphors for spiritual quests (usually employing images of descent, not ascent), for God (and an array of goddesses) and for our relation to nature. Compare Robert Frost's account of man's division from the animal world in "The Most of It" with Elizabeth Bishop's account of a reunion in "The Moose" or A. Ammons's cerebral analyses of nature with May Swenson's and Maxine Kumin's equally intelligent but more intimate tactilities. Women have also, of course, demystified some ancient poetic values like heroism and conquest ("Don't you get tired of wanting to live forever?" Margaret Atwood's Circe asks Ulysses. "Don't you get tired of saying Onward?") and romance ("Every man I have loved / was like an army," remarks Marge Piercy).

To the reader trained in postwar literary values, with their stress   10
on control and distance (the cooler the tone the warmer the critical
reception, is a good rule of thumb), women's poetry may well be
disturbing. The best women writers tend to be intimate rather than
remote, passionate rather than distant, and to defy divisions between
emotion and intellect, private and public, life and art, writer and
reader. Urged not to publish her early poems about breakdown and
"the commonplaces of the asylum," Anne Sexton insisted that her
suffering and struggle were shared:

> *it was you, or your house*
> *or your kitchen . . .*
> *although your fear is anyone's fear,*
> *like an invisible veil between us all.*

Many women poets besides Sexton are attempting to rip through that
veil, to arrive at a sense of a communal self, an "I" that is also a "we."
Marge Piercy's preface to "Circles in the Water" declares, "I imagine
that I speak for a constituency, living and dead, and that I give utter-
ance to energy, experience, insight, words flowing from many lives."
Ntozake Shange in a self-interview she calls "a conversation with all
my selves" announces:

> *quite simply a poem shd fill you up with something*
> *cd make you swoon, stop in yr tracks, change yr*
> *mind, or make it up, a poem shd happen to you like*
> *cold water or a kiss.*

June Jordan in the prefatory poem to "Things That I Do in the Dark"
identifies language with the darkness of eros and exploration:

> *These poems*
> *they are things that I do*
> *in the dark*
> *reaching for you*
> *whoever you are*
> *and*
> *are you ready? . . .*
>
> *whoever you are*
> *whoever I may become.*

Robin Morgan polemically defines and defends paranoia to her audience in the performance poem "Phobophilia":

> *Do you smell smoke?*
> *If you don't, it's not*
> *because a tenement isn't burning—*
> *down the street, in Derry, Beirut or San Salvador.*
> *Did you just hear a scream?*
> *If you didn't, it's not*
> *because a woman wasn't raped*
> *since I asked if you smelled smoke.*

Kathleen Fraser provocatively defends the poetics of intimacy to a reader-lover-critic: "Dear other, I address you in sentences. I need your nods and I hear your echoes. . . . You are against confession because it's embarrassing. I want to embarrass you." Denise Levertov in the essay "The Origins of a Poem" describes "the communion . . . between the maker and the needer within the poet; between the maker and the needers outside him." A consensus exists among women poets that "the true nature of poetry" is, as Adrienne Rich claims, "the drive / to connect. The dream of a common language." As the poet refuses to distance herself from her emotion, so she prevents us from distancing ourselves.

Ezra Pound in "The ABC of Reading" remarks that when poetry 11 moves too far from its origins in music and dance, it atrophies and needs renewal. We should add that when poetry and the poet move too far from their origins in communal expression—too far from the expectation of shared human feeling and need, too far into a regulated and predictable literacy bound to academic role playing, where the poem becomes an artifact and the reader becomes a judge and scorekeeper—they are again in need of reinvigoration.

Today our schools for the most part train poets and critics into 12 postures of detachment and impersonality, as if our encounters with the life of poetry ought to resemble our encounters with law and bureaucracy. The training no doubt has its uses but also its limitations. Walt Whitman, who wrote, "Camerado, this is no book, / Who touches this touches a man" and "What I assume you shall assume," articulated an abiding impulse latent within all poetry. At the present moment the women's poetry movement is a carrier of that same impulse, enabling its audience to assume more than we did before. If poetry written by contemporary women demands that we read as participants, it may help us discover not only more of what it means to be a woman but more of what it means to be human.

Questions for Study and Discussion

Meaning and Purpose

1. In surveying contemporary women's poetry, Ostriker argues several related points. What are these? If you were to summarize the essay's claims in one sentence, what would it be?
2. According to Ostriker, why may women's poetry be "disturbing" to readers "trained in postwar literary values"? Why does she claim that "the belief that true poetry is genderless" is a fallacy?
3. To what extent does the author explain or justify the fact that her education in literary history generally ignored women poets? According to her, how were those "who could not be ignored" regarded by her professors?

Strategy and Audience

1. From what external perspectives (biography, history, theory or ideology, myth or religion) does Ostriker view her subject? How do these affect her overall argument? Explain.
2. What intrinsic characteristics of women's poetry (effect, style, language, meaning, and so on) does the author consider? How do these help shape her argument?
3. Who is Ostriker's intended audience? How successful should her case be with readers either indifferent to or hostile to her main proposition? What likely objections of this audience does the author answer?

Style and Language

1. Ostriker's essay is written in a fairly formal, academic style. Still, there's some room for the playfulness we've seen in other critical reviews. What is it about her subject that makes formal style appropriate? What has style to do with the effect the author wants to have on her audience?
2. Ostriker's prose is direct and clear, but she does employ a large vocabulary and refers to persons who may be new to you. In reading this essay, much of which is self-explanatory, you'll want to look up any

words you don't know and check names of historical figures in the biographical section of your dictionary.

Writing Ideas

1. Write a critical argument defending or attacking the work of a poet (or small group of poets) with whom you're familiar. Why is the work important or meaningful, trivial or clichéd? Why is it good, or bad? Support your position with specific details about the poetry itself and your general assumptions about what makes for value in poetry.
2. Follow the suggestion above, but base your argument on references to outside factors, such as the poet's life or your own political or religious perspective.

Here author Jim Roddy concisely appraises a contemporary novel, claiming that the book challenges our traditional or "sentimental" view of American history. Defending his claim primarily with evidence from the text, he focuses on the novel's meaning, especially its elements of theme and character. To explain his thesis, he divides the novel's characters into two groups—the indifferent and the heroic—analyzing representatives of each category. For additional supporting data, he includes the views of two professional critics. The warrant or unstated critical assumption that underlies this argument is that a writer's personal view can be known through his fictional constructions—in this case that E. L. Doctorow clearly favors his heroic characters and clearly condemns those either responsible for or indifferent to the social conditions his novel depicts.

Following Roddy's essay is another critical argument, with questions and suggestions for writing.

Jim Roddy

Images of America in Doctorow's Ragtime

Introduction: Opens generally with background information, then narrows to critical thesis

E. L. Doctorow's *Ragtime* is considered a classic of American contemporary literature. Set at the turn of the century, it is a unique and innovative look at American transformation. The fact that *Ragtime* was published the year before the American bicentennial might lead some to believe that it is a celebration of our great American culture. However, large portions of the book deal with some of the more atrocious and barbarous elements of our society. One cannot help feeling that Doctorow wants to remind us of the many inhumane aspects of life in the United States. *Indeed,* Ragtime *challenges the*

1

<table>
<tr><td>

Thesis makes point of interpretation

Topic 1—first element considered

</td><td>

view that much of white America has toward this country.

One of the obvious atrocities Doctorow brings to life is poverty. The book portrays the lives of three families, one of which is poor Jewish immigrants. Doctorow goes to great lengths to describe the conditions under which this family had to live:

</td><td>2</td></tr>
</table>

Evidence from text of novel—supporting data

> This was early in the month of June and at the end of the month a serious heat wave had begun to kill infants all over the slums. . . . Families slept on stoops in the doorways. Horses collapsed and died in the streets. The Department of Sanitation sent drays around the city to drag away horses that had died. But it was not an efficient service. Horses exploded in the heat. Their exposed intestines heaved with rats.

Topic 2—second element: unfavorable characters

Another aspect of our society that Doctorow criticizes is the oppression of the working class by the capitalists. J. P. Morgan ironically sees "a reincarnation of pharaohism" in Henry Ford's use of men. Ford, the great entrepreneur, applied the idea of the assembly line to the mass production of cars. This great innovation was based on Ford's assumption that the people who produced his products should themselves be interchangeable—certainly a dehumanizing idea.

3

Explanation of evidence

Subtopic under 2—more evidence from novel

Ford is not the only person who has this detached view of the oppression of the working class. Doctorow claims that many shared it, in this alarming and matter-of-fact passage about working conditions:

4

> In the mines they [children] worked as sorters of coal and sometimes were smothered in the coal chutes; they were warned to keep their wits about them. One hundred Negroes a year were lynched. One hundred miners were burned alive. One hundred children were mutilated. There seemed to be quotas for these

things. There seemed to be quotas for death by starvation.

The wealthy Mrs. Stuyvesant Fish held poverty balls to honor the poor while "Children died on beds made from two kitchen chairs pulled together." And Father, the epitome of the detached WASP, "foundered in his soul" upon seeing an incoming immigrant ship.

Topic 3—introduced with contrast to earlier material, transition to favorable characters

While this theme of detachment runs   5 throughout the story, it should not be inferred that all of the characters are so indifferent to the struggles and hardships of the poor and oppressed. There are three characters who recognize the atrocities that the poor and black must endure, and all three are shown favorably by Doctorow.

Subtopic under 3—first character

More data—support from professional critic

Although Younger Brother is the butt of a   6 hilarious incident in Emma Goldman's hotel room, one senses that Doctorow holds him in high regard. Critic Martin Green agrees, saying that "Younger Brother, the 'passionately sullen,' as we are often told, is painted in a blurred halo of heavy-breathing enthusiasm" (843). Near the end of the novel, Younger Brother tells Father:

> You are a complacent man with no thought of history. You pay your employees poorly and are insensitive to their needs. . . . The fact that you think of yourself as a gentleman in all your dealings is the simple self-delusion of all those who oppress humanity. You have travelled everywhere and learned nothing.

Younger Brother sees the atrocities and becomes a revolutionary, a man unwilling to accept the injustices of the society he lives in.

Subtopic under 3—second character

The anarchist Emma Goldman, one of Doc-   7 torow's "real" historical figures, is also portrayed favorably. Early in the story, Doctorow symbolically reveals Goldman's unique perception of society: "And though the newspapers called the

Supporting
explanation

shooting [of Stanford White by Harry K. Thaw] the Crime of the Century, Goldman knew it was only 1906, and there were ninety-four years to go." Throughout, Doctorow seems to be applauding Goldman for her belief that "wealth is the oppressor."

Subtopic under 3—
third character

Finally, Coalhouse Walker, an innocent   8
black man turned revolutionary, is portrayed as a martyr. He is shown as a man of stubborn principle, who, unwilling to bend against the racism and injustice of his day, must die for his beliefs.

Further critical
support

Doctorow's characterization of Coalhouse, according to Martin Green, is "uncritically romantic" (842). If there is a hero in this novel, it is Coalhouse Walker.

Summary of major
points

What we have in *Ragtime* then is a portrait   9
of American society at the turn of the century, in which there is poverty, racism, and injustice, along with the wealth that accompanies the American Dream. Those in the story who are living this dream are distorting and repressing the obvious injustices that are occurring around them. Those who recognize the abomination of the society are put forth as heroes.

Conclusion: More
critical testimony and
emphatic restatement
of thesis

What message is Doctorow trying to get   10
across? Another critic, David Gross, feels that *Ragtime* is an attempt to "debunk the sentimental nostalgia of American schoolbook history" (133). Doctorow apparently thinks that, just as white America ignored the atrocities that existed during the time of *Ragtime,* so too has American history ignored such atrocities.

Works cited

Green, Martin. "Nostalgia Politics." *American Scholar* 45 (Winter 1975–76): 841–845.

Gross, David. "Tales of Obscene Power: Money and Culture, Modernism and History in the Fiction of E. L. Doctorow." *E. L. Doctorow: Essays and Conversations.* Ed. Richard Trenner. Princeton, New Jersey: The Ontario Review Press, 1983: 120–150.

Student Michael Miller presents a witty and perceptive critique of contemporary horror films—particularly the "slasher" movies that have been such a hit with young audiences. Miller examines the intrinsic features of the films (plot, characterization, acting, and direction), lamenting their pandering attitude and lack of imagination, and comparing them unfavorably to those in the classic tradition of Hollywood horror movies.

Michael J. Miller

Horrors!

One of the first horror movies I ever saw was James Whale's 1931 version of *Frankenstein*. The moment that made the greatest impression on my (then) six-year-old mind was the famous "He's alive!" scene. If you don't already know it, here's how it went. With a furious thunderstorm raging outside his castle, Dr. Frankenstein has levitated his "creation" up into the heart of the storm. The body of the monster is assaulted by tremendous bolts of lightning and eventually lowered into the laboratory. Colin Clive, who plays Dr. Frankenstein, approaches the still-unmoving, sheet-covered body, his eyes wild, searching for some movement. Time seems frozen as Clive appears about to burst with nervous energy. Then, the sheet now pulled back, the monster's right hand motions ever so slightly, as if reaching out to touch the alien air with its fingertips. Clive's eyes balloon still larger, and an insane smile of triumph appears on his face. Hunched over, watching each barely perceptible twitch of the creature's fingers, Clive is overcome by the knowledge that he has created life. On the apparent verge of a breakdown, Clive cries, "He's alive! He's ALIIIVE! . . . He's ALIIIVE!"

The sheer emotion and wonder of that scene galvanized me. Though I was quite young, I knew I was watching greatness in quality and craftsmanship, of both acting and directing. I couldn't have used those big words back then, but somehow this scene made me *feel* something, a kind of awe mixed with excitement. The film was entertaining, to be sure, but beyond that it had a great Gothic quality to it. I felt like I *knew* Dr. Frankenstein, his passionate quest for knowledge, his all-too-fallible ego. And I felt for the monster as well: his mockery of a life, and his tragic but poignant search for a place where he could belong. Something had been awakened in me, something that could not be denied. I had been exposed to such marvels as corpses rising from the grave, lightning and thunder, hunchbacked assistants, stolen brains . . . and before long I was hooked. I became that rare breed of filmgoer, the horror-movie lover. Werewolves, vampires, zombies, and mummies lumbered, crawled, and slithered across my TV screen for the next few years until the mid-70's when "Creature Features" was taken off the air. Still, horror movies had become a part of me, something I would never turn my back on, something that would always entertain me . . . or so I thought.

Recently, I saw a film called *Silent Night, Deadly Night*, a contemporary horror movie. Like *Frankenstein*, *Silent Night, Deadly Night* had one particularly memorable scene, albeit of a slightly different flavor. A young couple are sprawled across a billiard table, engaged in a fairly heavy necking episode. The girl, hearing something, pushes her paramour away and, clad only in a skintight pair of cut-off jeans, strides nonchalantly toward the door. She opens it, standing half-naked in the well-lit doorway, displaying complete disregard for the heavy snow falling outside in the cold December night. A few seconds later, a cat scurries past the girl into the house. The girl, satisfied that the cat was the source of the noise, turns and readies herself for another romp on the pool table. Suddenly, there is another noise at the door. The girl, puzzled, returns to the door and cautiously opens it. In the doorway stands a crazed teenager in a Santa Claus suit with a large axe. He proceeds to smash the door to bits, and chases the hysterically screeching girl around the living room, all the while growling "Naughty! Punish! Must punish!" At last catching the girl, he hoists her above his head, and, utilizing what is quite possibly the most unusual murder weapon I have ever seen, impales her on the horns of a deer head mounted above the living-room fireplace. Colin Clive, were are you when we need you?

The above example is pretty representative of the celluloid trash masquerading as horror films these days. I have suffered through hours and hours of those little screen gems, via the modern miracle of pay-TV. Titles like *Mother's Day*, *Graduation Day*, *My Bloody Valentine*, *New Year's Evil*, *Prom Night*, *The Dorm that Dripped Blood*, *Final Exam*, *Night School*, and *Friday the 13th*, ad nauseam, pop up constantly in the cable guide. Each time I will watch, hoping to catch some shred of creativity, some morsel of imagination that was missing in all the others, and each time I disgustedly flick off the set, another hour and a half of my life down the tubes.

Gone are the days of originality in plotting, depth of characterization, the rich Gothic atmosphere of the Universal horror movies of the 30s and 40s. Worse yet, gone are all the scares! These elements have been replaced by one-dimensional characters played by wooden actors, inventive but often laughable murder techniques, ridiculously predictable plots, and of course, gobs of blood and guts.

The plot of most modern horror movies is almost invariably the same: a teenage psycho with a wide assortment of kitchen utensils and/ or tools hacks, gouges, and garrotes about eight or ten other teenagers at (A) a cabin in the woods, (B) a small town, (C) a deserted school-house, or (D) a summer camp. The entire film is really a ghoulish "Ten Little Indians" with the cardboard teens falling one by one, their quickly forgettable performances finally coming to an end. "Who will survive?" the creators of the movie apparently want us to ask. Who *cares?* I ask. Near the ending (which for me is generally long overdue), there is usually one girl still alive who must try to outwit (and for these characters *any* use of wit is an extremely difficult task) the killer. The killer usually dies, but the movie invariably leaves room for a sequel, as if to entice this probably sleeping moviegoer. 6

The characters of today's "mad-slasher" films can almost always be neatly placed in one of several categories. There is the Practical Joker, usually a kid who enjoys such subtleties as rubber knives, fake blood, and the like. There is the Horny Couple (no need to explain further). There is the Evil Adult, usually a ridiculously caricatured authority figure, often a sheriff, schoolteacher, etc. (In *Silent Night, Deadly Night,* it was a nun.) Also always on hand is the Virtuous Couple, with whom we are supposed to identify. The Virtuous Couple doesn't smoke, drink, swear, or have sex. They are given the most lines, since only those who play the Virtuous Couple have any chance of furthering their acting career beyond this movie. Another staple of these movies is the Nerd. Often a well-intentioned young man, he is also incredibly naive. He usually has short hair and glasses, and uses too many big words. Occasionally the Nerd and the Practical Joker are the same character. And, of course, there is the killer himself. Generally a teenager, the Killer is male and has been deformed either physically or mentally by some traumatic incident from his past. The Killer is just a normal human, but can somehow survive wounds that would be fatal to any other human being. For instance, the character of Jason in the *Friday the 13th* series (none of which I have missed, I am ashamed to add) was stabbed in the neck with a butcher knife, had his neck broken in a hanging, had his left hand cut in half, suffered the indignity of an axe being implanted in his head, and was electrocuted by a large television set. Did any of these injuries kill good ol' Jason? I should say not! Remember now, Jason is just as human as you or me. Uh, yeah. 7

The real problem with these killers is that they are presented as 8 simple humans, yet display superhuman endurance and strength. No explanation is ever given for this seeming inconsistency. Dracula, Frankenstein, and the other horror greats from the past were also invulnerable, but they were supernatural characters who, accordingly, had supernatural qualities. Realistically, if the movie played by its own rules, these modern slashers should be just as susceptible to injury as anyone else. Yet they emerge unscathed from a barrage of surely fatal injuries. This inconsistency completely destroys the movie's suspension of disbelief because it tells us one thing (the killers are human) but shows us another (they are invulnerable).

Certainly, I would rank characters and plot as integral elements 9 in any horror film. But, to me at least, the most probing depth of characterization and the most complex and involving plotting is useless to a horror film if it lacks one essential ingredient: ability to scare the hell out of the audience. To me, a horror movie without scares is like a comedy without laughs. If I don't feel that familiar tingle of fear that somehow seems to electrify my whole body, or if I don't keep turning around to look over my shoulder as I walk home, the horror movie just didn't deliver. I defy anyone who has seen more than two of these "mad-slasher" movies to claim that he is *frightened* by them. The murders can be anticipated at least a minute before they occur, and the unbelievable indestructibleness of the killers makes suspense regarding the victim's potential escapes impossible. The killers themselves are about as frightening as a Halloween mask. For all their invulnerability, they are basically little boys in search of something that was denied them as children. They are as one-dimensional as their victims. The fear they instill in us (if any) comes not from their basic evilness, but from the knives and axes they carry. Remove them from the dark corners of the woods they always seem to inhabit and they become all-too-accessible figures: screwed-up human beings. Remove Dracula from the mountains of Transylvania and he is still a vampire. He retains his otherworldliness, his aura of mystery and evil. Dracula and his ilk represent the unknown, a quality that invariably instills fear in man. Aside from their inexplicable endurance, Jason and his ilk represent the known, a quality that instills fear in no one.

Since modern horror directors don't seem to care about *scaring* 10 the audience, they take another, easier, route: they attempt to gross the audience out. These directors forever dwell on the end result of the suspense, the murder itself. Instead of building suspense and making that the frightening element, these directors give us gratuitous close-ups of shattered skulls, gouged-out eyes, and endless rivers of blood. This sort of scene doesn't scare me. In fact, after continued exposure, it doesn't even nauseate me any more. It simply *bores* me. What is much more frightening to me is the tension before the act, the feeling that something awful is going to happen, only you don't know what or when. The shadow that appears suddenly behind the girl walking home alone on an empty street is much more chilling than her scattered remains the next morning, and, ultimately, more creative.

Now, before I am labeled a reactionary, let me try to clarify my 11 gripe against these films. Graphic violence is not the problem. Many horror movies have made excellent use of graphic violence, incorporating it into the film as a necessary element. *The Exorcist,* for example, contained such explicit scenes as Linda Blair's head pivoting 360 degrees, and a priest being thrown out of a window and dying a quite bloody death on the ground below. But these scenes were merely components of the whole film. They weren't the reason for making the film in the first place. Many so-called horror films seem to be little more than auditions for makeup artists hoping to impress the Hollywood fat cats.

I don't even really detest the "teenage-psycho" plot as such. John 12 Carpenter's 1978 *Halloween,* the movie that gave birth to this whole subgenre, is one of my all-time favorites. Its plot concerned the return of a very anti-social teenager (well, he was 21, close enough) to Haddonfield, Illinois, on Halloween night. Like its many clones, this movie featured a lot of violent deaths, teenage victims, and a speechless, heavy-breathing slasher. But it was an *original.* Its plot wasn't copied from a dozen other movies, so it had a style all its own. *Halloween* also had characters you cared about, people you didn't want to see die. Most of the trashy *Halloween* rip-offs contain characters so brainless and shallow I almost hope they *do* get picked off. But such characters aren't even developed well enough to elicit hate from an audience, so my general reaction is to sit back disinterestedly, not caring much who gets killed, hoping only for a merciful and swift ending to the film itself.

Actually, if I had my way, this whole subgenre of horror films 13 would gradually die out in popularity, leaving room for some truly imaginative and "horrific" ones. But I must be realistic about the subject and address myself to some depressing questions. Will America ever tire of such banal, repetitive, and, most of all, scareless, horror films? Or will these movies continue to be incredible financial successes, goading the ever-opportunistic Hollywood to produce more and more of them?

Obviously, I cannot answer these questions, but I *can* remember 14 some hard facts. One recent "mad-slasher" movie, *Friday the 13th, the Final Chapter,* opened on March 13th (a Friday) and briefly achieved the largest first-weekend gross of any film in the history of cinema (though it later fell behind *Indiana Jones*). It appears that as long as these movies attract people and continue to be very marketable, the creative horror-movie scripts will *remain* scripts in deference to the "slash-em-up," "crank-em-out," "cash-em-in" gorefests. And, this, to me, is the *real* horror story.

Questions for Study and Discussion

Meaning and Purpose

1. What are Miller's main objections to contemporary horror films? What does he say are the chief differences between such movies and their "classic" predecessors?
2. Are his criticisms based primarily on intrinsic, or extrinsic, elements? Explain. To what extent does he address issues of the films' effect, form, meaning, and craft?
3. Is Miller's essay aimed more at making us avoid such films, or at increasing our awareness of their quality (or lack thereof)?

Strategy and Audience

1. What kinds of informative and analytical strategies does Miller use to substantiate his argument? Cite specific examples.
2. Why does Miller introduce his critical argument with two anecdotes from his moviegoing past and a confession of his love for horror films? Does this fairly long opening enhance or detract from his overall argument? Why?
3. Who is Miller's intended audience? Who else besides this group might find the essay of interest? Why?

Style and Language

1. Miller writes in an expressive, easygoing way, with vivid description and a sense of humor. Cite several passages that exhibit his descriptive or humorous language. What, if anything, do these passages add to the essay? Do they make his case more convincing, or merely more fun to read?
2. Vocabulary: galvanized, poignant (paragraph 2); albeit, paramour (3); susceptible, unscathed (8); inexplicable (9); gratuitous (10); banal (12).

Writing Ideas

1. Write your own blanket review of assorted recent films of one type (comedies, action-adventures, thrillers). Try, as Miller does, to gain some perspective about the type itself, seeing beyond the individual examples. What common characteristics do you find? Can you defend or attack the whole group, or are some films clearly better than others of the same type?

2. Review a recent (or classic) film in depth, giving detailed criticism of plot, character, subject, or theme. Consider the guiding principles of the work's effect, design, meaning, and craft in your essay.

— *Additional Writing Ideas* —

Write a critical argument on one of these subjects for a general audience. Keep in mind whether you'll focus primarily on the thing itself, or view it in relation to external criteria. You may wish to write your essay as a for-publication review for your student or local newspaper. Express your opinions freely, but remember to justify them with evidence and reasoning.

- A favorite novel, story, or poem
- The last good (or bad) movie you saw
- A current record album
- A theatrical or musical performance
- A television or radio program or series
- The work of a student artist or photographer
- An architectural work
- A current pop or film star
- A hopeful or discouraging trend or fad in popular culture
- The artistic or cultural life of your school or home town
- What television really needs (or doesn't need)
- The work of a film or theatrical director or writer
- A stand-up comic or comedy team
- An influential band or recording artist
- Music videos
- Cable television networks
- Video games, as artistic creations
- Current subjects, themes, or styles in television or film
- An underappreciated writer, artist, or actor

− 7 −

Writing to Persuade

Using Emotional and Ethical Appeals

The Persuasive Aim

One January evening a few years ago, during the second half of the Super Bowl game, the American viewing public witnessed a strange moment in advertising history. It saw a dramatic commercial in which an oppressive, impersonal futuristic world dominated by a giant corporation (IBM) was saved by a then much smaller and supposedly more humane one (Apple). The ad said little about the new product that was going to vanquish IBM's market supremacy. Instead, IBM was portrayed as a menacing bureaucracy with obvious resemblances to the totalitarian state in George Orwell's nightmare novel *1984*, and Apple as the young, hammer-throwing hero who would bring it to its knees. The commercial cost more than $500,000 to produce, yet it was aired only once. (It was later voted by *Advertising Age* the best commercial of the 1980s.)

The smaller company's marketing staff believed that the ad's *emotional appeal*—to the audience's dread of totalitarian authority—was strong enough to convince viewers they should abandon IBM. The commercial didn't argue *logically* for the merits of the new product or against IBM. Rather, it skirted rational argument in favor of a metaphor: that the business world was, as in Orwell's story, a place where good and evil were pitted against each other, where huge organizations could extinguish individual freedom.

The ad, like much everyday advertising, went beyond logic to a *nonrational* attempt to persuade or influence. In fact, it was built upon basic argumentative fallacies (see Chapter 5): either/or reasoning— implying that people had only two choices in the computer world— and argument from analogy. Why didn't the company just run a campaign backing its new products with evidence of their high quality and testimony from satisfied users? Certainly such logic should have appealed to the business people watching the Super Bowl that Sunday. But Apple wanted something potentially more powerful than mere common sense. It wanted to change the way people *felt* about IBM, to change the audience's perceptions—and so its behavior—by appealing to deep-seated emotions.

If the rational approach to convincing audiences were always the best choice, there'd be no need for advertising slogans, political rhetoric, sermons by religious leaders, appeals by fundraising and lobbying groups, heartfelt sentiments in love letters, or the many other forms of persuasive language in everyday life. Like it or not, human beings aren't purely rational creatures. Sometimes, in our attempts to convince others, it can be more appropriate, or more effective, to speak directly to our readers' emotions, sense of ethics or morals, or self-interest. Persuasive writing and speaking, in other words, are often aimed at the heart or the stomach instead of the head.

Persuasive writing needn't abandon logic altogether, of course. We can support rational arguments with appeals to belief, value, or desirable or undesirable emotions. It's just that persuasive rhetoric isn't *limited* to tests of rationality or logic. Persuasive writing allows us to use strategies *in addition to* the purely rational ones appropriate to argument.

We find persuasive writing and speaking throughout everyday discourse, as we cajole, entice, or exhort others to do as we would like, and as others, from friends and family to fundraisers, advertisers, and politicians, do the same to us. Although nonrational persuasion may not have a big role in your academic writing, it certainly does in the larger world. Knowing such persuasive techniques can, at the very least, make us smarter consumers and citizens, less likely to be automatically influenced by the smooth or inflammatory talk in the marketplace of things and ideas.

Persuasion in a Paragraph

Here is a famous passage from a presidential inaugural address that is said to have profoundly affected a whole generation of Americans and to have helped create the political conditions of the ensuing decade. The speech is a clear, forthright appeal to patriotic loyalty, to every citizen's feeling of belonging to the national community, even to the ordinary person's sense of his or her own heroism. Above all else, its author tells us in stirring language, we are to be brave. Notice the strong emotional tone in these sentences, their direct appeal to patri-otic feeling:

> Let the word go forth from this time and place, to friend and foe alike, that the torch has been passed to a new generation of Americans—born in this century, tempered by war, disciplined by a cold and bitter peace, proud of our ancient heritage—and unwilling to witness or permit the slow undoing of those human rights to which this nation has always been committed, and to which we are committed today.
>
> Let every nation know, whether it wish us well or ill, that we shall pay any price, bear any burden, meet any hardship, support any friend or oppose any foe in order to assure the survival and success of liberty.
>
> —John F. Kennedy, January 1961

Persuasive Strategies

In argumentative writing, we try to win our readers' assent or agreement by proving a logical case. In persuasive writing, we try to win that assent by moving readers toward emotional or ethical agree-ment with our position. Often, that may mean convincing our audi-ence of something it *already* knows or accepts "on a gut level," or arousing powerful feelings of right or wrong that the reader finds hard to ignore.

Emotional Appeals

Appeals based on emotions attempt to move readers by making them feel something strongly. The feeling may be anything in the range of human experience and temperament: *fear, greed, envy, anger, joy, hope, sympathy,* or *love.* Commercial advertisers, in their attempts to persuade us to spend money, almost always appeal to our emotions—often to a sense of *longing* or *desire* (for beauty, wealth, luxury); to *passion* (for thrills, excitement, the sensual life); and to *sentimental feelings* (love of family, love of animals, love of country). Emotional appeals also have a part in much everyday public and private discourse—from persuading a teacher to take pity on you for flunking a test to the president's whipping up support for increased military spending. Emotional appeals persuade us to *act* on our feelings, or at least to listen to them—on the assumption that feelings can guide us as well as can rational thought.

In this passage of emotionally based persuasion, author Jonathan Schell gives a nightmarish inventory of death by nuclear war:

> Let us consider, for example, some of the possible ways in which a person in a targeted country might die. He might be incinerated by the fireball or the thermal pulse. He might be lethally irradiated by the initial nuclear radiation. He might be crushed to death or hurled to his death by the blast wave or its debris. He might be lethally irradiated by the local fallout. He might be burned to death in a firestorm. He might be injured by one or another of these effects and then die of his wounds before he was able to make his way out of the devastated zone in which he found himself. He might die of starvation, because the economy had collapsed and no food was being grown or delivered, or because existing local crops had been killed by radiation, or because the local ecosystem had been ruined, or because the ecosphere of the earth as a whole was collapsing. He might die of cold, for lack of heat and clothing, or of exposure, for lack of shelter. He might be killed by people seeking food or shelter that he had obtained. He might die of an illness spread by an epidemic. He might be killed by exposure to the sun if he stayed outside too long following serious ozone depletion. Or he might be killed by some combination of these perils. . . .
>
> —Jonathan Schell, *The Fate of the Earth**

Not only do the horrid possibilities themselves make us fearful, but the author's relentless repetition of such words as *killed, die, lethally,* and so on, and of the phrase "he might be," drives the point home. He wants us to be afraid of what could happen, and to act to thwart such possibilities.

Ethical Appeals

With appeals based on ethics, we attempt to move readers by their sense of right or wrong. (Ethical appeals may have an emotional base, too, for such views are often a matter of feeling or belief.) The

---

*(New York: Knopf, 1982): 24.

ethical appeal often rests on the *author's moral character:* we're persuaded because we believe in the writer's sincerity and ethical convictions. We can also appeal to our *readers'* own sense of morality, calling
upon them to be conscientious citizens, to think or act according to
principles they know to be correct. It's possible, however, that successful ethical persuasion can't ignore either side of the equation. We may
need to speak from our own moral convictions in order to convince
others that they should obey theirs.

Here's a brief example of ethically based persuasion from a prophetic science writer and naturalist:

> It is not my contention that chemical insecticides must never
> be used. I do contend that we have put poisonous and biologi-
> cally potent chemicals indiscriminately into the hands of persons
> largely or wholly ignorant of their potentials for harm. We have
> subjected enormous numbers of people to contact with these
> poisons, without their consent and often without their knowl-
> edge. . . . I contend, furthermore, that we have allowed these
> chemicals to be used with little or no advance investigation of
> their effect on soil, water, wildlife, and man himself. Future
> generations are unlikely to condone our lack of prudent concern
> for the integrity of the natural world that supports all life.
>
> —Rachel Carson, *Silent Spring**

Although this appeal does have an emotional element—our sense of
dread about the effects of environmental contamination—it is aimed
to persuade us that opposing reckless pollution is ethically just.

Other Persuasive Strategies

Whether our persuasive case is chiefly emotional, ethical, or a
blend of the two, we must present it vividly, concretely—in words that
arouse the reader's feelings or moral intent. To do that, writers employ
a number of techniques, some of which we've seen applied to other
purposes.

Connotative language

One of the most common persuasive strategies is to use connotative
language—words rich in positive or negative meaning or association.

*(New York: Milestone Editions, 1960): 10–11.

Connotative language elicits definite feelings from us. In the excerpt from Kennedy's inaugural address, for instance, we see words such as *friend, foe* (each used twice in the brief passage), *torch, war, peace, ancient heritage, human rights,* and *liberty.* All reinforce one of the speech's themes: it's "us against them" in the cruel world of global politics, and we must be willing to confront our enemies. An isolationist president, on the other hand, might have talked about avoiding "mindless conflict," "the waste of young men's precious lives," the "suicidal danger" of being the world's police force.

Connotative language *colors* writing, gives it deeper or richer shades of meaning. It can be a powerful tool for affecting an audience's perceptions. Strong language, however, can backfire if used carelessly or in excess. Most readers will see through exaggeration, inflated claims or criticisms, and appeals to bias or prejudice. When everybody on welfare is a bum, when the country is being run by dupes of Moscow, or when all music videos rot the minds of youth, the loaded words probably have been *over*loaded and may collapse of their own weight.

Notice the persuasive difference in these two sentences:

Neutral language: We should give military aid to the rebels because it is in our best interest to do so.

Connotative language: We must help the freedom fighters, those brave and selfless patriots who are willing to sacrifice their lives so that their children may live free of bloody oppression.

The first statement is a flat proposition—either we agree or we don't. The second, however, appeals emotionally to our admiration for courage—implying that the rebels are like our own soldiers, whom we'd be likely to support without question.

Figurative language

Like connotative language, *figurative language* (metaphor and simile) can be an effective persuasive tool. Although metaphor can't prove a case logically, figurative language can be convincing in its power of suggestion. When Kennedy said that "the torch has been passed to a new generation," he spoke metaphorically—the torch of liberty being a symbol of values that each generation must protect. Figurative language usually appeals to our senses, makes us see an *image* or picture that illustrates meaning. The phrase "nuclear winter" conjures an image of a cold, barren earth after nuclear war. Opponents of wasteful government spending talk of Congress "picking the taxpayers' pockets." Advocates of an economic policy want to "make America stand tall again." According to the old saying, "A picture is worth a thousand words," and though that may be an exaggeration, language presenting a visual image can be especially persuasive.

Description and narration

We saw in Chapters 2 and 3 that description and narration can be effective methods of expressing experience and of conveying information. Well-written description and narration use concrete language to evoke the texture of life, and, because they depend on the writer's choice of detail, they can be *slanted* for positive or negative effect. Read the real-estate ads in your newspaper, for instance. Can you find any that mention warped floors, sagging rafters, poor insulation? Opponents of abortion, likewise, confront us with grisly descriptions of the operation's aftermath, and the pro-choice camp tells stories of pregnant teenagers and back-alley butchery. Description and narration appeal directly to our sense of the ways things are, or should be, and thus can be powerful means of swaying opinion.

Tone and style

Finally, the way we use persuasive language reveals our attitude toward our subject and our audience and will affect our results. Choosing an appropriate style and tone means putting ourselves in our reader's shoes, asking what the audience will or won't accept.

Our tone may be serious and straightforward, the no-nonsense approach: "*It's time we face facts and raise taxes. Otherwise, we'll drown in this sea of debt.*" We may be sarcastic or mocking, criticizing a position with ridicule: "*Maybe our Congressmen know something we don't, but judging from their past performance, I doubt it.*" We may employ an upbeat or optimistic voice, hoping to instill confidence in the reader: "*Let's get behind this fund drive—and make our neighborhood the great place it really deserves to be!*" Or we may use a dark or menacing tone, trying to arouse the audience's fear or concern: "*There's something wrong at City Hall. Something very wrong. The mayor says he's innocent of the bribery charges, but the mayor may not be telling us the truth.*" Likewise, the style we choose to achieve an appropriate tone or mood may range from the simple, plain, and understated to the flowery and ornate, though it is usually best to avoid overwriting.

Persuasion, like argument, is intended to win consent or agreement—to bridge the gap between opposing sides. It makes sense, then, to temper your strategies, your choices of language, content, and style, to appeal to your audience, not to drive a wedge between you. Consider possible common ground—shared feelings or beliefs—and build your persuasive case with these in mind. Address your readers with respect; let them know that although you may not agree with them, you value their right to hold contrary opinions. And, as always, write with common sense. Even though persuasion can move beyond pure rationality, don't abandon it completely. Your emotional or ethical appeals must seem true and valid, despite their highly charged language.

Process checklist: Writing to persuade

The task
- What do I want to persuade my audience to think, feel, or do?
- Is my goal advocacy or opposition?
- What common ground do I share with my readers?

Exploring and collecting
- What kinds of persuasive strategies might work best in this situation—an appeal based on ethics, emotions, or self-interest?
- Can I use connotative or figurative language to enhance my persuasive content?
- Can description or narration be useful in swaying my audience?
- What tone and style are most appropriate for this essay?

Finding your thesis
- What is my persuasive point?
- Will my intended strategies support it clearly and appropriately?
- Is it the most persuasive claim I can devise?

Designing
- What kinds of introductory strategies will appeal to my audience?

Process checklist: Writing to persuade (*continued*)
- Do I need to include other material, such as basic information and explanation, in my design? If so, how can I best integrate it?
- What kind of conclusion will be most emphatic and memorable?

Drafting
- Have I included all that I wanted to say, in understandable order?
- Have I uncovered new or better material that I should include or substitute?
- Have I stayed close to my primary appeal?

Critical reading and rewriting
- Where are the weak points in my persuasive case?
- Have I considered audience questions and objections?
- Have I tempered my language and tone to avoid alienating my readers?
- Have I clearly appealed to their character, emotions, or self-interest in this subject?

The final draft
- Have I revised and proofread carefully for my best possible execution of style, grammar, mechanics?

In the following readings, notice how the writers use nonrational strategies to support their persuasive positions. Consider the degree of emotion, ethical, or self-interest appeal in each, and how the author's use of colorful language, description, narration, tone, and style does or does not contribute to the persuasive aim.

— Anna Quindlen —

*Anna Quindlen writes a weekly syndicated column, "Public & Private,"
for* The New York Times. *Former reporter, deputy metropolitan editor,
and author of the "About New York," "Hers," and "Life in the 30s"
columns, Quindlen is a 1974 graduate of Barnard College and winner of
several awards, including honors from the Newswomen's Club of New
York, the Associated Press, and Columbia University. The mother of three
children, Quindlen is especially known for her essays and articles about
family life, child rearing, and life in New York City neighborhoods. Her
work has appeared in* Ms., McCalls, Woman's Day, Vogue, Glamour,
and other magazines. She is the author of Living Out Loud *(1988), a
collection of her columns, as well as a forthcoming novel.*

A City's Needy

In this article from The New York Times *annual Christmas charity
appeal, Quindlen uses her reporter's skills to evoke the plight of the city's
poor. Her appeal is effective not only because she lets the sad facts speak
for themselves in blunt, vivid, descriptive language, but because her tone
conveys her great seriousness and concern.*

The formica counter was so white, the apples so red, the veins in   1
her hand as she touched one so blue, that it might have been some
modern still life: three apples, one elderly woman, the 27th of the
month.

"I have always loved apples," she said in her slightly accented   2
English, looking at them lined up on the kitchen counter, shiny as
trophies, the only thing left in the apartment to eat until the next
Social Security check arrived on the first day of the next month.

The most singular thing about need in New York City is not how   3
much of it there is, for in a city as large as this one, in times as hard as
these, it is inevitable and, sadly, somehow accepted that pain will be
legion. It is that need here is often so private, and so proud. Behind
the brick walls of thousands of apartment buildings, beneath the shin-
gled roofs of thousands of homes, people live with hunger and deprivation just a wall away from those who have plenty.

Need is also so various there. The woman of the apples lived in a   4 lovely senior citizens housing project on the Lower East Side, only a few blocks from an abandoned building in which a teen-age couple had camped out with their infant son, rigging complicated systems of electrical wires from the street to the ceiling for lights, tucking the baby into a box, beating off the rats with a folded newspaper. The old woman had come from Germany at the beginning of the century, the young couple from Puerto Rico 10 years ago. Only the baby had been born in the United States, but like the rest, he was hungry.

There are whole neighborhoods of the needy in New York, areas   5 where the buildings with sheet metal where the windows used to be tell you that there are people in trouble there. But they are proud neighborhoods as well as poor ones, and inside apartments with very little in the way of furniture mothers will stand over old stoves and tell you how far you can stretch rice and dried beans and a paper envelope of soup mix. And when it is on the table the children will dig in as though there were really meat in it.

And there are neighborhoods that are obviously a source of pride   6 to their citizens where the unlikeliest residents eke out an existence day by day just this side of desperation. I spent a day once in a kind of stage set of turn-of-the-century plenty on the West Side, in an apartment large enough for a family of 10 inhabited by one very old lady. The armoires, the mirrors, the prints, the china, the silver—the contents of the apartment at auction would have garnered hundreds of thousands of dollars, but, like most memories, they were not for sale. I was the first visitor my hostess had had in three years. She was living on instant oatmeal and tea; her one extravagance was aspirin, which she took almost every hour to relieve the pain of her arthritis.

There are more-visible people in need. There are the legions of   7 the homeless, lying on the benches in Grand Central Terminal, huddled in doorways against the cold, carrying their lives on their backs, trading subsistence for life. In soup kitchens they lean over their meals as though in prayer and use the broth to warm as well as feed them, and use their dinnertime to stoke their beaten souls as well as their empty innards.

And there are more-helpless people in need, too: the children.   8 There are the ones who come into the world with heroin or cocaine in their frail bodies, who flail in their cribs with the poison in their veins. There are the ones who are born with acquired immune deficiency syndrome, born to die because their parents used dirty needles. There are the ones who are left in hospitals to lie in the metal cribs, their only stimulation the occasional visit from a nurse. There are those who are freezing, and starving, and those who are beaten and bruised.

A doctor in the neonatal intensive care unit at one city hospital   9
looked around at the incubators one afternoon and wondered aloud
about the tubes, the medicines, the machines needed to make the
premature thrive and the sickly ones bloom. It was not at all uncommon, she said, to find that an infant who had been coaxed from near
death to life in the confines of that overly warm room, in one of those
little plastic wombs, had turned up two or three years later in the
emergency room with cigarette burns, broken bones, or malnutrition.

It is all horrible to contemplate until the day you first see some-   10
one, in some small way, doing something about it: finding a meal
ticket at a senior citizens center for the lady of the apples; getting the
teen-agers into a sweat equity project that will end with a new apartment; sending a neighborhood college student to fix meals and listen
to old anecdotes amid the faded splendors of the Upper West Side
apartment.

There are good people in this city, people who peel the vegeta-   11
bles in soup kitchens and cuddle the babies who are diseased and
discarded, who see, not still lifes or half lives, but lives in search of
sustenance, and who give it.

Questions for Study and Discussion

Meaning and Purpose

1. What is the basis for Quindlen's appeal? What feelings or emotions
    does the author seek to arouse in us? To what end?
2. What kinds of need does Quindlen illustrate in her survey?
3. Does Quindlen imply why homelessness and poverty are such serious
    problems in New York City? Does she place blame? Why or why not?

Strategy and Audience

1. Quindlen uses a number of forceful strategies to draw us into her
    essay. Find examples of description, brief narration, repetition, and
    vivid, concrete details that seem especially effective to you. To what
    extent are these objective facts or selected, slanted observations?
2. Why does Quindlen choose to focus partly on a specific person, the
    "woman of the apples"? What is the effect of this technique?
3. Who is the target audience for Quindlen's appeal? How did you
    respond to it? Why?

Style and Language

1. In one sense, Quindlen is acting as a reporter here, observing stark reality. Where does her prose seem objective and informational, and where does it seem more personal and subjective?
2. Suggestions for vocabulary study: deprivation (paragraph 3); eke, armoires, garnered (6); neonatal (9); sustenance (11).

Writing Ideas

1. Ever since the political reform movements of the late nineteenth century, an American muckraking tradition has been exposing corruption and other social evils. Try your hand at writing a persuasive appeal that arouses strong sympathy or outrage toward a pressing social problem: poverty, homelessness, crime, AIDS, or drug use among teens. Your audience may include those who usually ignore or reject such requests. How will you make them take notice? How will you make them feel compelled to do something?
2. Consider the needy in your own community. Who are they? What is their plight? What is being done to address the problem? Write an emotional or ethical call for action in which you evoke their situation in precise, descriptive detail. (You may want to do some first-hand observation to gather impressions.)

The Iowa City Press-Citizen, *formed in 1920, traces its lineage through a long line of southeast Iowa newspapers dating to 1841. Serving a seven-county area around Iowa City, Iowa, the* Press-Citizen *has a daily circulation of 17,000. Editorially, the paper maintains an independent political perspective.*

A Heartland Tragedy

Dale Burr, about whom this editorial is written, was a sixty-three-year-old Hills, Iowa, farmer faced with possible loss of his land, equipment, livestock, and grain. Despondent, he killed his wife and a bank president (who had long been a neighbor), and then himself. For many, the Burr case symbolized much of what the farming community had experienced during the agricultural depression in the mid-1980s. The editorial writer here makes a plea on behalf of that community.

Imagine for a minute that tomorrow, your boss tells you that for the next 12 months, you're going to earn only two-thirds of your salary. You can't quit your job.

What would you do? Quick.

The mortgage payment is already a week overdue. The kids need boots, and it's snowing. Quick.

The last two checks you wrote bounced, and the bank wouldn't pay them. The pediatrician's bill is overdue. The corner grocery store won't let you put anything on your charge account. Quick.

Your spouse is angry; you're not holding up your end of the deal. What are you going to do? Quick.

Your father and grandfather have done the same job as you're doing now. They went through the Depression. They lived on pork and potatoes, and they made it. You are the third generation. You're blowing it. You're blowing it. Think fast. You don't have much time. Weeks, maybe months.

The pressure builds, the stress is stronger. You keep going to work, hanging on. It doesn't matter. Nothing you do matters. You are powerless.

This is the kind of thing Dale Burr probably felt. And it is the 8
kind of thing many other Iowa farmers feel every day.

There are accounts of bank transactions and economic explana- 9
tions and other hypotheses as the murder and suicide story unravels.
But that's not what it is really all about. It's about people—alone,
desperate and powerless with nowhere to turn.

Once the Burrs were one of the wealthier families in the county. 10
They were well-thought-of people. Salt of the earth. Churchgoers. A
family of farmers carrying on a tradition. That was a year or two ago.
That's how fast things crumble.

Target prices, price supports, ceilings, sealing crops. The termi- 11
nology doesn't matter. It's welfare. Farmers know it. And farmers are
proud people. Nobody really wants to live that way. But for now, there
is no choice.

Many Iowa farmers already have taken deep pay cuts. They've 12
scaled down operations. They've swallowed their pride—gone to stress
clinics, sought therapy, stood in line at the market with food stamps in
their pockets.

Some of it was bad judgment. Some of it was bad luck. The mid- 13
1970s was a boom time for Iowa agriculture, but everyone else caught
on. Physicians' fees rose, hospital costs rose, the cost of cars and homes
and tractors and loans and mortgages and a college education rose.
Then the bottom fell out—for farmers. Now things are so out of kilter
that people who once were pillars of their communities are falling into
poverty, depression and disrepute.

This is the farm crisis—the people who are alive and hanging on, 14
and those who have died at the hands of anger, frustration, humiliation. And they are here.

Politicians tell us it is only a matter of balancing the books. That 15
if we can reduce the deficit, deflate the value of the dollar, increase
exports and give the market free rein—then, everything will be all
right.

But if there's one thing that is clear from Monday's tragic series 16
of murder and suicide, it is that the farm crisis is *not* numbers and
deficits and bushels of corn. It is people and pride and tears and
blood.

The time has come for the state and the county to reach to the 17
farmers who are suffering—not because they are failed businessmen
and women, but because they are human beings whose lives are falling
apart—fast.

Questions for Study and Discussion

Meaning and Purpose

1. What does this editorial writer attempt to make us think or feel about the farm crisis? To what extent does the writer expect us to have sympathy for a murderer?
2. Although it may be emotionally appropriate to base this appeal on the plight of Dale Burr, how does the essay stand up as rational argument? Does it have a rational core, or is it entirely emotional in its execution? Explain.
3. Does the writer place blame for the farm crisis? If so, upon whom or what?

Strategy and Audience

1. Apart from appealing to our sympathy for a desperate man, to what other emotions does this writer appeal? Cite examples to support your answer. Does this essayist also appeal to the reader's sense of right and wrong? If so, how?
2. To what extent does the writer use connotative or figurative language, slanted description and narration, or variations in tone, to affect us? Give examples.
3. Who is the audience for this editorial? How likely are the intended readers to be moved by its content?

Style and Language

1. This editorial writer uses several stylistic devices to involve us in the essay. Why does the writer repeat the word "quick" at the end of paragraphs 2–5? What is the effect of a series of very short sentences, as in paragraph 7? What is the effect of using the second person in the early paragraphs ("Your spouse is angry; you're not holding up your end of the deal . . .")?
2. For the most part, this essayist uses elemental, concrete language. Why has the writer kept abstraction to a minimum?

Writing Ideas

1. Write an emotion-based editorial on a current economic or social problem you know something about. You might want to refer to a

specific case that illustrates the seriousness of your subject. Keep your language as concrete as possible, to evoke the experience of those about whom you're writing.

2. As in the suggestion above, write an emotion-based editorial for a campus audience about a policy issue at your school. Decide whether you'll pitch your essay at those in power (administration and faculty) or at those who may be able to influence the authorities (students, parents).

— Roger Simon —

Roger Simon is a columnist for the Baltimore Sun. *Born in Chicago in 1948, Simon earned his B.A. from the University of Illinois in 1970 and got his first professional job with the Chicago City News Bureau. He became a columnist for the* Chicago Sun-Times *in 1972, later moving to the* Tribune. *He has been a humor columnist for* Chicago Magazine, *and contributed articles to several popular periodicals. His work is collected in* Simon Says: The Best of Roger Simon *(1985), and he has written an account of the 1988 presidential campaign,* Road Show *(1989). Among his honors are several United Press International public-service awards, and the Peter Lisagor Award.*

No Compassion for Drunk Drivers

In this essay, Simon writes an outraged reply to a television program about drunken driving (produced and narrated by the guilty party, a Washington, D.C., television reporter, as part of his punishment), condemning the show as self-serving and dishonest. Simon's real target, however, is drunken drivers themselves. His view is angry and uncompromising in the extreme.

1   I would like to make an admission up front: I have a thing about drunken drivers.

2   I hate them. I really hate them. Every time I read about another innocent person slaughtered by a drunken driver, I become enraged.

3   So when I saw the nationally broadcast PBS special on drunken driving last week, I did not react as many did. I did not think it was sensitive and forthright.

4   I did not react as Phil Donahue, the host, did when he came on at the end and said: "I was enormously moved by this documentary, as I'm sure you were."

5   Not me, Phil. I wanted to kick in the set.

6   I was plenty moved for the victims. I was plenty moved for the people who were crippled, paralyzed, reduced to vegetables or killed. But the drunken drivers themselves did not move me. I thought most got off real easy.

7   First, let me tell you about the magnitude of the problem. Someone is killed by a drunken driver every 20 minutes in this country. On

286

any given weekend night, on any road in America, 1 out of every 10 drivers is drunk.

Which is why drunken drivers will continue to get off easy.   8
Because so many of the lawmakers, so many of the jurors, so many of the judges have driven drunk themselves. They have a certain amount of sympathy for those who get caught.

The purpose of the documentary, called "Drinking and Driving: 9
The Toll, The Tears," was to show that drunken drivers don't get off easy. Sometimes they go to jail and sometimes they lose their licenses and sometimes they lose their jobs, we were told.

But, in reality, they rarely do. Most drunken drivers get away   10
with it. If they are caught, and few are, most go out and hire the best lawyers they can afford in order to beat the rap.

The element that made this documentary special is that it was   11
produced and written by Kelly Burke, 39, a Washington, D.C., television reporter. At 6:17 A.M. on July 1, 1984, after having 6 to 11 glasses of wine, Burke crossed the center line in his van and crashed head-on into a pick-up truck driven by Dennis Crouch, 32, who was on his way to Army Reserve training.

Crouch was killed, leaving behind a son and a wife who was 8   12
months pregnant.

After the accident, Burke's lawyer told reporters: "It's our feeling   13
that there's a defense no matter what charges come down." That line wasn't in the documentary, of course.

Burke's lawyer did a heck of a fine job, by the way. He was worth   14
whatever he cost, because Burke's case was plea-bargained. In return for a guilty plea, the charge of homicide with a motor vehicle while intoxicated was dropped. Instead, Burke pleaded guilty to charges of driving under the influence and failing to stay in the proper lane.

His driver's license was revoked. He was sentenced to two years   15
of unsupervised probation, fined $500 and ordered to produce a documentary on the results of drinking and driving.

But having seen his documentary, I get the impression that one   16
of the big results of drinking and driving for Burke was getting exposure on national TV.

The show, which he also narrates, uses a lot of euphemisms.   17
Drivers are "impaired" after "imbibing." In one case, we are told that a drunken driver who killed a family of five "didn't mean it; he didn't even remember it happening."

But didn't he mean it? Don't all drunken drivers mean it? If you   18
drink 6 to 11 glasses of wine, as Burke did, and then get behind the wheel, just what is it you do mean?

In the last segment, Burke comes on the screen. He stands there   19 in a nice suit and there is very dramatic background music. He tells us about a driver who pleaded guilty to driving under the influence of alcohol. This driver had worked "long hours and began celebrating." And then this driver crashed into a guy and he now suffers a "melancholy paradoxically like that of the victims."

And, Burke tells us, this driver now is "bumming rides" and   20
taking "buses and the subway" because his license was revoked. Legal fees are high. If this weren't enough, "social activists kept saying he hadn't suffered enough."

Then Burke tells us: "I was the driver."   21

Wrong, Mr. Burke. You were the killer. So why don't you just   22
say it?

A guy is dead, a woman widowed, two children orphaned, and   23
Kelly Burke is telling me what agony it is to take public transportation.

As I said, I wanted to kick in the set. I admit my reaction to   24
drunken driving is extreme. But Burke and I do agree on one thing: "I've said many times," he told the judge at his sentencing, "I wished it had been me."

If these self-indulgent slobs would just maim and kill each other, 25
drunken driving wouldn't upset me as much.

In fact, it wouldn't upset me at all.   26

Questions for Study and Discussion

Meaning and Purpose

1. What is Simon trying to persuade his readers to think or feel about drunken drivers? Has this essay in any way changed your attitude about such people? If so, how, and why?
2. What is Simon's chief complaint about how the documentary television program portrayed the problem of drunk driving?
3. Is Simon's attack on Burke, the narrator of the documentary, fair? Why or why not? Do you think Simon has picked an easy target?

Strategy and Audience

1. To what extent does Simon appeal to both emotional and ethical interests in his essay? Explain.
2. What's the effect of Simon's admission in paragraph 2? Does he damage his appeal in any way by speaking so strongly so soon?

3. As a columnist, Simon addresses a large audience. How pointed do you think this essay is toward drunk drivers themselves? Why?

Style and Language

1. Simon's style in this essay is blunt, no-nonsense ("Not me, Phil. I wanted to kick in the set."). What persuasive effect does such a style have? What, if anything, makes it right for this subject?
2. Simon tells us that the television documentary used "a lot of euphemisms." What is the main euphemism Simon wants to expose in this essay?

Writing Ideas

1. Write your own strongly-worded attack on a policy or behavior you "hate." Who will be your intended audience—those responsible for the problem, or a wider audience whom you want to arouse to your pitch of anger?
2. If you feel that Simon is at all unfair in condemning Kelly Burke (who apparently wanted to atone for his crime by participating in the documentary), write an impassioned defense of his willingness to stand in the spotlight as a drunk driver. How will you make your audience feel sympathy for an admitted criminal?

— Wendell Berry —

Wendell Berry is a farmer, writer, teacher, and leading American advocate of agricultural reform. Born in 1934, he was educated at the University of Kentucky, and taught there from 1964 to 1977. Berry has written many books, among them A Place on Earth *(fiction; 1967, revised 1983);* A Continuous Harmony: Essays Cultural and Agricultural *(1972);* The Unsettling of America *(1977); and* The Gift of Good Land *(1981), from which this essay is reproduced. His most recent book is* What Are People For? *(1990).*

Home of the Free

Here Berry makes an ethical appeal for us to reject the shallow values of contemporary society—the yearning to be "set free from . . . the natural conditions of the world and the necessary work of human life," the "desire for comfort, convenience, remote control, and the rest of it"—and to embrace hard work and responsibility. In going against the grain of so much that we may take for granted, Berry challenges us to rethink our everyday values and attitudes.

I was writing not long ago about a team of Purdue engineers who 1
foresaw that by 2001 practically everything would be done by remote
control. The question I asked—because such a "projection" *forces* one
to ask it—was, *Where does satisfaction come from?* I concluded that
there probably wouldn't be much satisfaction in such a world. There
would be a lot of what passes for "efficiency," a lot of "production" and
"consumption," but little satisfaction.

What I failed to acknowledge was that this "world of the future" 2
is already established among us, and is growing. Two advertisements
that I have lately received from correspondents make this clear, and
raise the question about the sources of satisfaction more immediately
and urgently than any abstract "projection" can do.

The first is the legend from a John Deere display at Waterloo 3
Municipal Airport:

INTRODUCING SOUND-GARD BODY . . .

A DOWN TO EARTH SPACE CAPSULE.

New Sound-Gard body from John Deere, an "earth space capsule"
to protect and encourage the American farmer at his job of being
"Breadwinner to a world of families."

290

> *Outside: dust, noise, heat, storm, fumes.*
> *Inside: all's quiet, comfortable, safe.*

Features include a 4 post Roll Gard, space-age metals, plastics, and fibers to isolate driver from noise, vibration, and jolts. He dials 'inside weather', to his liking . . . he push buttons radio or stereo tape entertainment. He breathes filtered, conditioned air in his pressurized compartment. He has remote control over multi-ton and multi-hookups, with control tower visibility . . . from his scientifically padded seat.

The second is an ad for a condominium housing development:

HOME OF THE FREE.

We do the things you hate. You do the things you like. We mow the lawn, shovel the walks, paint and repair and do all exterior maintenance.

You cross-country ski, play tennis, hike, swim, work out, read or nap. Or advise our permanent maintenance staff as they do the things you hate.

Different as they may seem at first, these two ads make the same appeal, and they represent two aspects of the same problem: the widespread, and still spreading, assumption that we somehow have the right to be set free from anything whatsoever that we "hate" or don't want to do. According to this view, what we want to be set free from are the natural conditions of the world and the necessary work of human life; we do not want to experience temperatures that are the least bit too hot or too cold, or to work in the sun, or be exposed to wind or rain, or come in personal contact with anything describable as dirt, or provide for any of our own needs, or clean up after ourselves. Implicit in all this is the desire to be free of the "hassles" of mortality, to be "safe" from the life cycle. Such freedom and safety are always for sale. It is proposed that if we put all earthly obligations and the rites of passage into the charge of experts and machines, then life will become a permanent holiday.

What these people are really selling is insulation—cushions of technology, "space age" materials, and the menial work of other people—to keep fantasy in and reality out. The condominium ad says flat out that it is addressed to people who "hate" the handwork of household maintenance, and who will enjoy "advising" the people who do it for them; it is addressed, in other words, to those who think themselves too good to do work that other people are not too good to do. But it is a little surprising to realize that the John Deere ad is addressed to farmers who not only hate farming (that is, any physical contact with the ground or the weather or the crops), but also hate tractors, from the "dust," "fumes," "noise, vibration, and jolts" of which they wish to be protected by an "earth space capsule" and a "scientifically padded seat."

Of course, the only real way to get this sort of freedom and   6
safety—to escape the hassles of earthly life—is to die. And what I think we see in these advertisements is an appeal to a desire to be dead that is evidently felt by many people. These ads are addressed to the perfect consumers—the self-consumers, who have found nothing of interest here on earth, nothing to do, and are impatient to be shed of earthly concerns. And so I am at a loss to explain the delay. Why hasn't some super salesman sold every one of these people a coffin—an "earth space capsule" in which they would experience no discomfort or inconvenience whatsoever, would have to do no work that they hate, would be spared all extremes of weather and all noises, fumes, vibrations, and jolts?

I wish it were possible for us to let these living dead bury them-   7
selves in the earth space capsules of their choice and think no more about them. The problem is that with their insatiable desire for comfort, convenience, remote control, and the rest of it, they cause an unconscionable amount of trouble for the rest of us, who would like a fair crack at living the rest of our lives within the terms and conditions of the real world. Speaking for myself, I acknowledge that the world, the weather, and the life cycle have caused me no end of trouble, and yet I look forward to putting in another forty or so years with them because they have also given me no end of pleasure and instruction. They interest me. I want to see them thrive on their own terms. I hate to see them abused and interfered with for the comfort and convenience of a lot of spoiled people who presume to "hate" the more necessary kinds of work and all the natural consequences of working outdoors.

When people begin to "hate" the life cycle and to try to live   8
outside it and to escape its responsibilities, then the corpses begin to pile up and to get into the wrong places. One of the laws that the world imposes on us is that everything must be returned to its source to be used again. But one of the first principles of the haters is to violate this law in the name of convenience or efficiency. Because it is "inconvenient" to return bottles to the beverage manufacturers, "dead soldiers" pile up in the road ditches and in the waterways. Because it is "inconvenient" to be responsible for wastes, the rivers are polluted with everything from human excrement to various carcinogens and poisons. Because it is "efficient" (by what standard?) to mass-produce

meat and milk in food "factories," the animal manures that once would have fertilized the fields have instead become wastes and pollutants. And so to be "free" of "inconvenience" and "inefficiency" we are paying a high price—which the haters among us are happy to charge to posterity.

And what a putrid (and profitable) use they have made of the   9
idea of freedom! What a tragic evolution has taken place when the inheritors of the Bill of Rights are told, and when some of them believe, that "the home of the free" is where somebody else will do your work!

Let me set beside those advertisements a sentence that I consider   10
a responsible statement about freedom: "To be free is precisely the same thing as to be pious, wise, just and temperate, careful of one's own, abstinent from what is another's, and thence, in fine, magnanimous and brave." That is John Milton. He is speaking out of the mainstream of our culture. Reading his sentence after those advertisements is coming home. His words have an atmosphere around them that a living human can breathe in.

How do you get free in Milton's sense of the word? I don't think   11
you can do it in an earth space capsule or a space space capsule or a capsule of any kind. What Milton is saying is that you can do it only by living in this world as you find it, and by taking responsibility for the consequences of your life in it. And that means doing some chores that, highly objectionable in anybody's capsule, may not be at all unpleasant in the world.

Just a few days ago I finished up one of the heaviest of my spring   12
jobs: hauling manure. On a feed lot I think this must be real drudgery even with modern labor-saving equipment—all that "waste" and no fields to put it on! But instead of a feed lot I have a small farm—what would probably be called a subsistence farm. My labor-saving equipment consists of a team of horses and a forty-year-old manure spreader. We forked the manure on by hand—forty-five loads. I made my back tired and my hands sore, but I got a considerable amount of pleasure out of it. Everywhere I spread that manure I knew it was needed. What would have been a nuisance in a feed lot was an opportunity and a benefit here. I enjoyed seeing it go out onto the ground. I was working some two-year-olds in the spreader for the first time, and I enjoyed that—mostly. And, since there were no noises, fumes, or vibrations the loading times were socially pleasant. I had some help from neighbors, from my son, and, toward the end, from my daughter who arrived home well rested from college. She helped me load, and then read *The Portrait of a Lady* while I drove up the hill to empty the spreader. I don't think many young women have

read Henry James while forking manure. I enjoyed working with my daughter, and I enjoyed wondering what Henry James would have thought of her.

Questions for Study and Discussion

Meaning and Purpose

1. One of the ways that we persuade others is by setting a good example ourselves. What kind of example does Berry want to set? How does he convince us that he's telling the truth about himself?
2. What ideas or values in contemporary life is Berry opposed to? How are these illustrated by the two advertisements he quotes?
3. What is the "tragic evolution" that Berry claims has occurred in our way of thinking? Why is the phrase "home of the free" especially ironic as a title for Berry's essay?

Strategy and Audience

1. In building his persuasive case, Berry divides the world into two camps—the "haters" and the rest of us. Does such a division imply a logical fallacy (see Chapter 5)? If so, what is it?
2. What is the effect of Berry's sardonic humor in this essay—especially his claim that he wishes "it were possible for us to let these living dead bury themselves in the earth space capsules of their choice and think no more about them"?
3. Whom is Berry trying to convince? On what grounds, if any, are those committed to the values of leisure and fantasy likely to change their minds?

Style and Language

1. Berry adopts a folksy, down-to-earth persona, yet there's a sophisticated debater's wit in what he says. How does he turn the language of "the enemy" into his own persuasive weapon?
2. Vocabulary: insatiable, unconscionable (paragraph 7); putrid (9); pious, abstinent, magnanimous (10).

Writing Ideas

1. Following Berry's example, write a moral or ethical criticism of a value or group of values you find objectionable. Some suggestions: selfishness, disloyalty, ambition, laziness, conformity.
2. If you disagree with Berry's position or think he overstates the problem, write an ethically based rebuttal in which you defend an opposite, or at least less radical, view of contemporary notions of progress, efficiency, leisure, freedom, and the like.

— Jonathan Swift —

Jonathan Swift (1667–1745) was an Anglican priest and writer, perhaps best known as the author of Gulliver's Travels *(1726), a masterpiece of satire sometimes mistaken for a children's book. Born in Dublin, Ireland, of Anglo-Irish parents, he was schooled there and later became a political activist and spokesman for the Tory party. Swift became famous in Ireland in 1729 when he published this essay as a pamphlet. He was throughout his life a defender of the Irish in a world dominated by English power.*

A Modest Proposal

"A Modest Proposal for Preventing the Children of Poor People in Ireland from Being a Burden to Their Parents or Country, and for Making Them Beneficial to the Public" is an outraged cry for justice framed in savage irony. Swift's heartlessly callous speaker, apparently advocating an indefensible brutality, in effect exposes as equally horrible the very conditions for which he claims to offer remedy.

It is a melancholy object to those who walk through this great town or travel in the country, when they see the streets, the roads, and cabin doors, crowded with beggars of the female-sex, followed by three, four, or six children, all in rags and importuning every passenger for an alms. These mothers, instead of being able to work for their honest livelihood, are forced to employ all their time in strolling to beg sustenance for their helpless infants, who, as they grow up, either turn thieves for want of work, or leave their dear native country to fight for the Pretender in Spain, or sell themselves to the Barbadoes.

I think it is agreed by all parties that this prodigious number of children in the arms, or on the backs, or at the heels of their mothers, and frequently of their fathers, is in the present deplorable state of the kingdom a very great additional grievance; and therefore whoever could find out a fair, cheap, and easy method of making these children sound, useful members of the commonwealth would deserve so well of the public as to have his statue set up for a preserver of the nation.

But my intention is very far from being confined to provide only for the children of professed beggars; it is of a much greater extent, and shall take in the whole number of infants at a certain age who are born of parents in effect as little able to support them as those who demand our charity in the streets.

As to my own part, having turned my thoughts for many years   4
upon this important subject, and maturely weighed the several schemes of other projectors, I have always found them grossly mistaken in their computation. It is true, a child just dropped from its dam may be supported by her milk for a solar year, with little other nourishment; at most not above the value of two shillings, which the mother may certainly get, or the value in scraps, by her lawful occupation of begging; and it is exactly at one year old that I propose to provide for them in such a manner as instead of being a charge upon their parents or the parish, or wanting food and raiment for the rest of their lives, they shall on the contrary contribute to the feeding, and partly to the clothing, of many thousands.

There is likewise another great advantage in my scheme, that it   5
will prevent those voluntary abortions, and that horrid practice of women murdering their bastard children, alas, too frequent among us, sacrificing the poor innocent babes, I doubt, more to avoid the expense than the shame, which would move tears and pity in the most savage and inhuman breast.

The number of souls in this kingdom being usually reckoned one   6
million and a half, of these I calculate there may be about two hundred thousand couple whose wives are breeders; from which number I subtract thirty thousand couples who are able to maintain their own children, although I apprehend there cannot be so many under the present distresses of the kingdom; but this being granted, there will remain an hundred and seventy thousand breeders. I again subtract fifty thousand for those women who miscarry, or whose children die by accident or disease within the year. There only remain an hundred and twenty thousand children of poor parents annually born. The question therefore is, how this number shall be reared and provided for, which, as I have already said, under the present situation of affairs, is utterly impossible by all the methods hitherto proposed. For we can neither employ them in handicraft or agriculture; we neither build houses (I mean in the country) nor cultivate land. They can very seldom pick up a livelihood by stealing till they arrive at six years old, except where they are of towardly parts; although I confess they learn the rudiments much earlier, during which time they can however be looked upon only as probationers, as I have been informed by a principal gentleman in the county of Cavan, who protested to me that he never knew above one or two instances under the age of six, even in a part of the kingdom so renowned for the quickest proficiency in that art.

I am assured by our merchants that a boy or girl before twelve   7 years old is no salable commodity; and even when they come to this age they will not yield above three pounds, or three pounds and half a crown at most on the Exchange; which cannot turn to account either to the parents or the kingdom, the charge of nutriment and rags having been at least four times that value.

I shall now therefore humbly propose my own thoughts, which I   8
hope will not be liable to the least objection.

I have been assured by a very knowing American of my acquain-   9
tance in London, that a young healthy child well nursed is at a year old a most delicious, nourishing, and wholesome food, whether stewed, roasted, baked or boiled; and I make no doubt that it will equally serve in a fricassee or a ragout.

I do therefore humbly offer it to public consideration that of the   10
hundred and twenty thousand children, already computed, twenty thousand may be reserved for breed, whereof only one fourth part to be males, which is more than we allow to sheep, black cattle, or swine; and my reason is that these children are seldom the fruits of marriage, a circumstance not much regarded by our savages, therefore one male will be sufficient to serve four females. That the remaining hundred thousand may at a year old be offered in sale to the persons of quality and fortune through the kingdom, always advising the mother to let them suck plentifully in the last month, so as to render them plump and fat for a good table. A child will make two dishes at an entertainment for friends; and when the family dines alone, the fore or hind quarter will make a reasonable dish, and seasoned with a little pepper or salt will be very good boiled on the fourth day, especially in winter.

I have reckoned upon a medium that a child just born will weigh   11
twelve pounds, and in a solar year if tolerably nursed increaseth to twenty-eight pounds.

I grant this food will be somewhat dear; and therefore very proper   12
for landlords, who, as they have already devoured most of the parents, seem to have the best title to the children.

Infant's flesh will be in season throughout the year, but more   13
plentiful in March, and a little before and after. For we are told by a grave author, an eminent French physician, that fish being a prolific diet, there are more children born in Roman Catholic countries about nine months after Lent than at any other season: therefore, reckoning a year after Lent, the markets will be more glutted than usual, because the number of popish infants is at least three to one in this kingdom; and therefore it will have one other collateral advantage, by lessening the number of Papists among us.

I have already computed the charge of nursing a beggar's child   14
(in which list I reckon all cottagers, laborers, and four fifths of the

farmers) to be about two shillings per annum, rags included: and I believe no gentleman would repine to give ten shillings for the carcass of a good fat child, which, as I have said, will make four dishes of excellent nutritive meat, when he hath only some particular friend or his own family to dine with him. Thus the squire will learn to be a good landlord, and grow popular among the tenants; the mother will have eight shillings net profit, and be fit for work till she produces another child.

Those who are more thrifty (as I must confess the times require) 15 may flay the carcass; the skin of which artificially dressed will make admirable gloves for ladies, and summer boots for fine gentlemen.

As to our city of Dublin, shambles may be appointed for this 16 purpose in the most convenient parts of it, and butchers we may be assured will not be wanting; although I rather recommend buying the children alive, and dressing them hot from the knife as we do roasting pigs.

A very worthy person, a true lover of his country, and whose 17 virtues I highly esteem, was lately pleased in discoursing on this matter to offer a refinement upon my scheme. He said that many gentlemen of this kingdom, having of late destroyed their deer, he conceived that the want of venison might be well supplied by the bodies of young lads and maidens, not exceeding fourteen years of age nor under twelve, so great a number of both sexes in every county being now ready to starve for want of work and service; and these to be disposed of by their parents, if alive, or otherwise by their nearest relations. But with due deference to so excellent a friend and so deserving a patriot, I cannot be altogether in his sentiments; for as to the males, my American acquaintance assured me from frequent experience that their flesh was generally tough and lean; like that of our schoolboys, by continual exercise, and their taste disagreeable; and to fatten them would not answer the charge. Then as to the females, it would, I think with humble submission, be a loss to the public, because they soon would become breeders themselves: and besides, it is not improbable that some scrupulous people might be apt to censure such a practice (although indeed very unjustly) as a little bordering upon cruelty; which, I confess, hath always been with me the strongest objection against any project, how well soever intended.

But in order to justify my friend, he confessed that this expedient 18 was put into his head by the famous Psalmanazar, a native of the island Formosa, who came from thence to London above twenty years ago, and in conversation told my friend that in his country when any young person happened to be put to death, the executioner sold the carcass to persons of quality as a prime dainty; and that in his time the body of a plump girl of fifteen, who was crucified for an attempt to poison the emperor, was sold to his Imperial Majesty's prime minister of state, and other great mandarins of the court, in joints from the gibbet, at four hundred crowns. Neither indeed can I deny that if the same use were made of several plump young girls in this town, who without one single groat to their fortunes cannot stir abroad without a chair, and appear at the playhouse and assemblies in foreign fineries which they never will pay for, the kingdom would not be the worse.

Some persons of a desponding spirit are in great concern about   19
that vast number of poor people who are aged, diseased, or maimed, and I have been desired to employ my thoughts what course may be taken to ease the nation of so grievous an encumbrance. But I am not in the least pain upon that matter, because it is very well known that they are every day dying and rotting by cold and famine, and filth and vermin, as fast as can be reasonably expected. And as to the younger laborers, they are now in almost as hopeful a condition. They cannot get work, and consequently pine away for want of nourishment to a degree that if at any time they are accidentally hired to common labor, they have not strength to perform it; and thus the country and themselves are happily delivered from the evils to come.

I have too long digressed, and therefore shall return to my sub-   20
ject. I think the advantages by the proposal which I have made are obvious and many, as well as of the highest importance.

For first, as I have already observed, it would greatly lessen the   21
number of Papists, which whom we are yearly overrun, being the principal breeders of the nation as well as our most dangerous enemies; and who stay at home on purpose to deliver the kingdom to the Pretender, hoping to take their advantage by the absence of so many good Protestants, who have chosen rather to leave their country than to stay at home and pay tithes against their conscience to an idolatrous Episcopal curate.

Secondly, the poorer tenants will have something valuable of   22
their own, which by law may be made liable to distress, and help to pay their landlord's rent, their corn and cattle being already seized and money a thing unknown.

Thirdly, whereas the maintenance of an hundred thousand chil-   23
dren, from two years old and upwards, cannot be computed at less than ten shillings a piece per annum, the nation's stock will be thereby increased fifty thousand pounds per annum, besides the profit of a new dish introduced to the tables of all gentlemen of fortune in the kingdom who have any refinement in taste. And the money will circulate among ourselves, the goods being entirely of our own growth and manufacture.

Fourthly, the constant breeders, besides the gain of eight shillings 24 sterling per annum by the sale of their children, will be rid of the charge of maintaining them after the first year.

Fifthly, this food would likewise bring great custom to taverns, 25 where the vintners will certainly be so prudent as to procure the best receipts for dressing it to perfection, and consequently have their houses frequented by all the fine gentlemen, who justly value themselves upon their knowledge in good eating; and a skillful cook, who understands how to oblige his guests, will contrive to make it as expensive as they please.

Sixthly, this would be a great inducement to marriage, which all 26 wise nations have either encouraged by rewards or enforced by laws and penalties. It would increase the care and tenderness of mothers toward their children, when they were sure of a settlement for life to the poor babes, provided in some sort by the public, to their annual profit instead of expense. We should see an honest emulation among the married women, which of them could bring the fattest child to the market. Men would become as fond of their wives during the time of their pregnancy as they are now of their mares in foal, their cows in calf, or sows when they are ready to farrow; nor offer to beat or kick them (as is too frequent a practice) for fear of a miscarriage.

Many other advantages might be enumerated. For instance, the 27 addition of some thousand carcasses in our exportation of barreled beef, the propagation of swine's flesh, and improvement in the art of making good bacon, so much wanted among us by the great destruction of pigs, too frequent at our tables, which are no way comparable in taste or magnificence to a well-grown, fat yearling child, which roasted whole will make a considerable figure at a lord mayor's feast or any other public entertainment. But this and many others I omit, being studious of brevity.

Supposing that one thousand families in this city would be con- 28 stant customers for infants' flesh, besides others who might have it at merry meetings, particularly weddings and christenings, I compute that Dublin would take off annually about twenty thousand carcasses, and the rest of the kingdom (where probably they will be sold somewhat cheaper) the remaining eighty thousand.

I can think of no one objection that will possibly be raised against 29 this proposal, unless it should be urged that the number of people will be thereby much lessened in the kingdom. This I freely own, and it was indeed one principal design in offering it to the world. I desire the reader will observe, that I calculate my remedy for this one individual kingdom of Ireland and for no other that ever was, is, or I think ever can be upon earth. Therefore let no man talk to me of other expedients:

of taxing our absentees at five shillings a pound: of using neither clothes nor household furniture except what is of our own growth and manufacture: of utterly rejecting the materials and instruments that promote foreign luxury: of curing the expensiveness of pride, vanity, idleness, and gaming in our women: of introducing a vein of parsimony, prudence, and temperance: of learning to love our country, in the want of which we differ even from Laplanders and the inhabitants of Topinamboo: of quitting our animosities and factions, nor acting any longer like the Jews, who were murdering one another at the very moment their city was taken: of being a little cautious not to sell our country and conscience for nothing: of teaching landlords to have at least one degree of mercy toward their tenants: lastly, of putting a spirit of honesty, industry, and skill into our shopkeepers; who, if a resolution could be now taken to buy only our native goods, would immediately unite to cheat and exact upon us in the price, the measure and the goodness, nor could ever yet be brought to make one fair proposal of just dealing, though often and earnestly invited to it.

Therefore I repeat, let no man talk to me of these and the like   30
expedients, till he hath at least some glimpse of hope that there will ever be some hearty and sincere attempt to put them in practice.

But as to myself, having been wearied out for many years with   31
offering vain, idle, visionary thoughts, and at length utterly despairing of success, I fortunately fell upon this proposal, which, as it is wholly new, so it hath something solid and real, of no expense and little trouble, full in our own power, and whereby we can incur no danger in disobliging England. For this kind of commodity will not bear exportation, the flesh being of too tender a consistence to admit a long continuance in salt, although perhaps I could name a country which would be glad to eat up our whole nation without it.

After all, I am not so violently bent upon my own opinion as to   32
reject any offer proposed by wise men, which shall be found equally innocent, cheap, easy, and effectual. But before something of that kind shall be advanced in contradiction to my scheme, and offering a better, I desire the author or authors will be pleased maturely to consider two points. First, as things now stand, how they will be able to find food and raiment for an hundred thousand useless mouths and backs. And secondly, there being a round million of creatures in human figure throughout this kingdom, whose sole subsistence put into a common stock would leave them in debt two millions of pounds sterling, adding those who are beggars by profession to the bulk of farmers, cottagers, and laborers, with their wives and children who are beggars in effect; I desire those politicians who dislike my overture, and may perhaps be so bold to attempt an answer, that they will first ask the parents of these

mortals whether they would not at this day think it a great happiness to have been sold for food at a year old in the manner I prescribe, and thereby have avoided such a perpetual scene of misfortunes as they have since gone through by the oppression of landlords, the impossibility of paying rent without money or trade, the want of common sustenance, with neither house nor clothes to cover them from the inclemencies of the weather, and the most inevitable prospect of entailing the like or greater miseries upon their breed forever.

I profess, in the sincerity of my heart, that I have not the least   33
personal interest in endeavoring to promote this necessary work, having no other motive than the public good of my country, by advancing our trade, providing for infants, relieving the poor, and giving some pleasure to the rich. I have no children by which I can propose to get a single penny; the youngest being nine years old, and my wife past childbearing.

Questions for Study and Discussion

Meaning and Purpose

1. Although published more than 250 years ago, "A Modest Proposal" remains timely in its expression of Irish bitterness toward England. What does Swift's essay tell you about the relationship between the two nations in the eighteenth century?
2. Against what is Swift protesting? What does his "proposal" say about the plight of Ireland and about English attitudes toward it?
3. What is the real purpose in "A Modest Proposal"? How do you know?

Strategy and Audience

1. How would you describe the speaking voice or persona (created by Swift, the author) of this essay? Do you take him seriously? Why or why not? Where does it become clear that the speaker is not Swift himself but a mask?
2. In what ways does Swift's essay appeal either to ethics or emotions? What ethical principles underlie Swift's attack? What specific emotions does the essay arouse? Cite examples.
3. Why did Swift choose to write in such an indirect, ironic way— saying precisely the opposite of what he really means? How did the

essay affect you, and how might the effect have changed if Swift had made a straightforward appeal?

Style and Language

1. Does Swift's style seem appropriate for his subject? What effect may such a combination of style and subject have on readers?
2. Swift's essay holds many words that may send you to the dictionary; among them: melancholy, importuning, sustenance (paragraph 1); prodigious, deplorable (2); rudiments (6); collateral (13); inducement (26); propagation (27); parsimony, animosities (29).

Writing Ideas

1. Write your own "modest proposal" in which you call attention to and address a serious problem with irony and satire. You may wish, like Swift, to invent a persona or voice to enforce the distance between your ironic proposal and your real self.
2. Swift's satire is bitter and angry. Write a persuasive essay in which you reveal similar feelings about your subject through heightened language, and direct appeals to your readers' emotions.

— Student Essays —

Here author Lisa Rodden combines some striking information (her statistics on illiteracy) with an outraged tone that is at once angry, sarcastic, and sympathetic. She opens with an appeal to the audience's sympathy before citing the figures and stating her position. She goes on to give more informational backing in paragraph 2, but changes the tone to sarcasm and indignation. She returns to a sense of sympathy for the illiterate worker, and concludes with emphatic, highly charged language, both literal and figurative. She writes in a conversational, informal style, and mixes appeals to emotion and ethics—she wants us to join her in her anger about the problem and to support aid for it because of the implied morality of such action.

Following Rodden's essay is another student's work, with questions and suggestions for writing.

Lisa Rodden

A Nation of Illiterates

Introduction: Appeals to readers' sympathy

Imagine yourself not being able to travel to unfamiliar places because you cannot read street signs. Think of trying to shop for groceries, selecting products by the pictures on the labels. What if you weren't able to read the newspaper, fill out a job application, or read a simple story to your child? These are only some of the problems faced every day by twenty-three million adults in the United States. According to the Department of Education, one of every five adults in this country isn't able to read and write—an amazing 20 percent of our population. *While some federal programs do exist, it's time our government did more to fight illiteracy in the United States.* 1

Supporting information

Thesis makes point of advocacy

Further informative backing

In our country, the land of freedom and opportunity, people seem to be ignorant of illiteracy. Thinking ourselves a cut above the rest of 2

305

Tone changes to
sarcasm

the world, we can't imagine that illiterates are among us—but they are. The Department of Education also estimates that there is a "shadow" group of 47 million more adults who are borderline illiterates, barely able to function. Also each year a crippling 2.3 million people over the age of sixteen join the pool of illiterates. Not only are these statistics astounding, but they are shameful.

Additional supporting
data

Indignant tone

One area feeling the impact of this problem   3
is the ever-delicate economy, where America's high illiteracy rate is clearly taking a toll. If people can't read and write, how can they be expected to function properly on the job, or even obtain one? Some people insist that in a technological era reading and writing are disappearing skills, that computers can do anything and everything for us, but computers are not the answer to our problems. According to one recent article, "We must remember that computers will process error at the same bewildering speed at which they process truth." High tech doesn't replace books and pens. In fact, it relies on them.

Rhetorical question
continues appeal to
sympathy

Direct address to
reader in informal
language

Well, you might say, illiteracy isn't a prob-   4
lem in the white-collar world. But what about the blue-collar workers? What difference does it make if they can't read and write? Many of our working-class forefathers were illiterate, weren't they? Maybe so, but today literacy is much more a precondition of employment. Employers won't knowingly hire people who can't read and write. Think about it: Part of one of America's biggest economic assets, its work force, is going to waste. In fact, employers are reporting that there simply aren't enough qualified people to fill available jobs. If so many potential workers are incompetent or uneducated, where does the economy go? We're supposed to believe that the government wants to keep the economy healthy. Working to raise the literacy rate might be a great place to invest our tax dollars.

Strong, blunt
language

It's sad. Illiteracy is destroying many Ameri-   5
cans, damaging them physically, socially, and

emotionally. Each day millions of us have to suffer the shame and personal agony of not being able to read and write. Put yourself in their place. It's a frightening feeling, isn't it?

Conclusion: Opens with figurative language—strongly negative connotation; closes with a final question that implies author's answer

Why are we letting this disease destroy us? There is no reason for it. Sure, spending money on literacy is less glamorous than putting people into space or building bigger and better bombs, but shouldn't we be spending our money to build up people instead?

6

In this essay, student John Irvin makes a persuasive ethical and emotional plea for us to become more responsible in our international economic behavior. Irvin backs his case with disturbing statistics but lets forceful, connotative language take the lead.

John Irvin

The Imbalance in World Consumption

There is a great crime of inequity in the world today in the form of resource consumption, and the United States is its biggest perpetrator. The statistics that support this contention are undeniable. Moreover, their implications are disturbing, if not disastrous. If our country is living a life of plenty at the expense of other nations, we should reevaluate our methods of resource acquisition, and adopt more equitable and self-sufficient energy sources.

1

The facts that point to America's gluttony are hard to ignore. According to John Baldwin, in his book *Environmental Planning and Management*, the United States constitutes slightly more than 5 percent of the world's population, yet it consumes nearly 33 percent of its resources. In one lifetime, the average American uses 623 tons of coal, oil, and natural gas; 613 tons of sand, gravel, and stone; 21,000 gallons of gasoline; 50 tons of food, and 19 tons of paper. The list is seemingly endless. Out of this mammoth consumption, each American also generates 840 tons of domestic and industrial waste; 7 million

2

gallons of polluted water; and 70 tons of air pollution. In that time, the average American also disposes of 19,250 bottles, 19,000 cans, and 8 automobiles (1, 91).

These figures are astounding. While most of the Third World countries starve, the United States takes pride in its abundance. Yet since we consume one-third of the world's resources, we can hardly be considered a self-sufficient nation. Rather, our worldwide corporate policy could be blamed for the exploitation of the human and natural resources of these Third World countries for selfish gain. While we hide behind the guise of "Big Brother," our nation, by exploiting these countries, may only be contributing to their rampant hunger and social chaos. If a country uses more than its share of available resources, then other countries will be forced to give up some of theirs, which is bound to cause serious consequences. Instead of the "Big Brother," the United States might more appropriately be called the "Big Leech," or the "Big Bully."

What right do we have to take more than our share? Isn't our basic ethic founded on the right of individuals to reap what they sow? The problem can easily be blamed on "government policy" or "big business," yet you and I, the American public, sanction such repression. Not only through our voting habits, but also through our thirst for materialistic advancement, do we perpetuate the problem. In our loftiness, we prance about the world as if it were our playground, blind to the fact that our country has a widespread reputation, even with its allies, as being little more than a monstrous parasite that roams the world consuming everything in sight while leaving a long and stinking trail of waste behind it.

As an alternative, couldn't we band together and demand that world resource utilization be more evenly distributed? Could we, as individuals, learn to be more efficient consumers? Could we demand that our consumer products be manufactured for durability and longevity? While preserving our abundance, couldn't we rely more on our local resources rather than on foreign imports? Finally, wouldn't it be better for all if we, as a nation, were to adopt a more respectful attitude toward the other nations of the world, especially those of the Third World?

The imbalance in world consumption is a menacing problem and needs to be reevaluated. The United States should no longer continue to monopolize the world's resources while other countries starve. If we could focus our tremendous technology on a redistribution of the world's assets, perhaps we could create a new and better world for everyone.

Works cited

John H. Baldwin. *Environmental Planning and Management.* Boulder and London: Westview, 1985.

Questions for Study and Discussion

Meaning and Purpose

1. What is the imbalance the author claims to see? How does he support his contention?
2. Who, if anyone, is to blame for the problem Irvin points out? What does the author propose we do about it?
3. What specific moral value or ethical principle underlies Irvin's persuasive appeal? Of what is he trying to convince us?

Strategy and Audience

1. Which persuasive strategies does Irvin use here? Find examples of inflated rhetoric, connotative language, appeals to emotion, ethics, or self-interest.
2. Irvin uses a number of economic statistics as evidence for his claims. What is the effect of including such concrete facts?
3. Who is Irvin's intended audience? How do you respond to his appeal?

Style and Language

1. Irvin isn't shy about using loaded words and phrases to accomplish his goal. In paragraph 4, he portrays the United States as a "monstrous parasite that roams the world consuming everything in sight while leaving a long and stinking trail of waste behind it." How are readers likely to react to such pointed, even insulting, language? Would you tone down Irvin's language anywhere, or let it stand? Why or why not?
2. Vocabulary: perpetrator (paragraph 1); gluttony (2); repression, perpetuate (4); monopolize (6).

Writing Ideas

1. Write an ethically based essay in which you appeal to your readers to resolve a dilemma by doing what you consider to be morally correct. What ethical assumptions will you bring to bear? What factual support may bolster your persuasive appeal?

2. Take a position to which you are morally or ethically opposed and see whether you can defend it as an advocate. What kinds of assumptions must you accept? Writing as an advocate for the other side, how would you persuade yourself to change your mind? Some sample controversies: capital punishment, abortion, animal experimentation, drug testing.

— Additional Writing Ideas —

For an audience of your fellow students, write an emotion- or ethics-based attack or defense on a topic you feel strongly about. Avoid illogical extremes, but include vivid, powerful language where fitting. (You might review the suggestions at the end of Chapter 5 as well.) Sample topics:

- Alcoholism or drug abuse among the young
- Racial or ethnic bigotry
- Patriotism and personal conscience
- Nuclear waste disposal
- Welfare policy
- The influence of the media in our lives
- Liberalism and conservatism
- The money mentality
- Prison reform
- What parents should (or shouldn't) teach their children
- Moral heroes or villains (individuals or organizations) in contemporary life
- A controversial campus issue
- Current government economic or social policy
- A worthy (or unworthy) public service or charitable cause
- The environment
- Animal rights
- Capital punishment
- Censorship
- Divorce
- Child abuse
- White-collar crime
- Religious or moral hypocrisy

— 8 —

Writing to Entertain

Using Humor to Delight and Amuse

The Humorous Aim

Few among us don't love to laugh. We flock to the latest movie comedies, stay up for David Letterman or "Saturday Night Live," attend concerts by our favorite stand-up comedians or theatrical troupes, follow the daily satire in "Doonesbury," or read humorous essays in newspapers and magazines. Americans have always valued comedy and humor—from the tall tales about frontier life to the movies of Charlie Chaplin or the Marx Brothers, from scathing editorial cartoons of Thomas Nast to popular diversions like "The Cosby Show." Humor gives us comic relief from life's day-to-day seriousness, gives us new ways of looking at ourselves and the world. It can be a vehicle for criticism, a way to redeem life's mistakes and misfortunes, or pure delight for its own sake. For many of us, in fact, humor may be one of the most precious things in life—a very special and elevating human quality.

It is no surprise, then, that writing to entertain or delight our readers and ourselves is an essential aim for essays. The word entertain also means to hold in mind or consider, or to play against, as in a game. In this sense, our work can entertain in many ways; we can be held by sad and serious ideas. Here, though, we speak of the lighter side of essay writing—one that can influence all the writing you do as you become better able to express your sense of humor even about serious subjects.

Writing humor is different—and perhaps more demanding—because our *sense* of humor is so personal. A passage that may seem absolutely hysterical to me may leave my readers scratching their heads. Being funny is risky. The audience holds the ultimate weapon—refusal to laugh—and they may use it at any time. Writers, of course, have a distinct advantage over other humorists, such as stand-up comics, who must suffer humiliation, if it comes, face-to-face. Writers don't always know if their readers are laughing or groaning. Still, we put ourselves on the line with humor, perhaps more than in any other kind of prose we write.

If that's true, why do it? Why stick out our necks? Because, as in expressive writing, it can be an extremely satisfying, rewarding accomplishment. Humor affects us in ways that no other kind of writing can.

As we've seen in the readings throughout this book, essays are a nonfiction form; their content cannot be wholly imaginary. When we write essays with a humorous or entertaining aim, likewise, we usually must avoid making up material outright. Some kinds of humor, such as parody and satire, are fictional, giving us mocking *imitations* of life (in the form of theatrical skits, movies, or short stories, for instance). Humorous essays, on the other hand, although they may use many types of comic strategies, remain rooted in the real world, in references to actual people, situations, or ideas. The line between fiction and nonfiction isn't always clear, however; jokes, imaginary examples, and other bits of fictionalizing have been known to sneak into the essays.

Our definitions of humor will differ, depending on personal taste. Despite such preferences, however, humor does have several basic characteristics. One of these, perhaps the most common one, is the element of *surprise*—the unexpected. We laugh, often, because we've been caught off guard.

The surprises humorous writers spring on us can be just about anything, but most fall into one of two categories: the coupling of things that typically don't go together—the incongruous or incompatible; and the shock of recognition—something that delights us with its unexpected truth. You'll see examples of both in the readings for this chapter.

The surprises of humor, too, may arise from *language*, such as wit, wordplay, irony, sarcasm, or exaggeration and understatement, or from *character* and *situation*—unusual people, and odd or surprising events or reactions to them. It's likely that you'll use both sources in your humorous writing, perhaps emphasizing one or the other but not relying exclusively on only one.

Whatever your subjects or humorous strategies, however, you must believe in your own comic instincts. Humor is best when it is unique, your own honest expression. Successful comedians and humorists, though they may be influenced by one another in style or choice of subjects, try to find their individual, special way of being funny. As with expressive writing in general, then, look for subjects that affect you strongly, be open with yourself in the writing process, and stay alert for discoveries that seem original, useful, surprising. Make yourself laugh, first, and there's a good chance your reader will do the same.

Humor in a Paragraph

Here's an example from a writer known for his dry wit and wry observation of the human condition. In this brief narrative passage from a humorous autobiography about a night of hopeless confusion in the family household, we see subtle humor arising from character and situation:

> Father, farthest away and soundest sleeper of all, had by this time been awakened by the battering on the attic door. He decided that the house was on fire. "I'm coming, I'm coming!" he wailed in a slow, sleepy voice—it took him many minutes to regain full consciousness. My mother, still believing he was caught under the bed, detected in his "I'm coming!" the mournful, resigned note of one who is preparing to meet his Maker. "He's dying!" she shouted.
>
> "I'm all right!" [cousin] Briggs yelled to reassure her. "I'm all right!" He still believed that it was his own closeness to death that was worrying mother. I found at last the light switch in my room, unlocked the door, and Briggs and I joined the others at the attic door. The dog, who never did like Briggs, jumped for him. . . .
>
> —James Thurber, "The Night the Bed Fell"*

---

*My *Life and Hard Times* (New York: Bantam, 1961): 24.

Humorous Strategies

Narration and description are natural devices for writing humor.

Narration, of course, is ideally useful when your subject is a comic situation or event, when you may wish to shape all or most of the essay as a funny story. Brief narration, as a paragraph or two, also may support essays that aren't focused on a story line. Narrative may also underlie verbal or character humor, or the narrative itself may be the comic subject, the source of surprise.

Description, we've seen, has many uses, and can be particularly helpful in humor. Not only will description enhance your narrative passages, but you can also use it to portray character, evoke a setting or mood, or reveal objects in a new light. Also, descriptive language may carry much of your verbal playfulness.

Here are some other common humorous techniques:

Understatement

We understate when we deliberately *play down* what we say, or represent something as less than it is in a sort of reverse exaggeration. The humor in understatement comes from the apparent gap between what is and the way in which it's characterized. Here's Woody Allen:

> It is no secret that organized crime in America takes in over forty billion dollars a year. This is quite a profitable sum, especially when one considers that the Mafia spends very little for office supplies.
>
> —Woody Allen, "A Look at Organized Crime"*

Allen uses understatement twice in this passage, first calling $40 billion "a profitable sum," then compounding the understatement with a wildly inappropriate reference to office supplies, as if the mob were merely a small business like any other. What we know about organized crime is in extreme contrast to what Allen says about it.

Overstatement or Exaggeration

When we exaggerate or overstate, on the other hand, we make *more* of something than is warranted. We use this device regularly in

*(New York: Random House, 1971): 13.

conversation, for emphasis, for criticism, or for mockery. Like understatement, exaggeration uses the discrepancy between what is and
what is said for comic effect:

> One stifling summer afternoon last August, in the attic of a
> tiny stone house in Pennsylvania, I made a most interesting dis-
> covery: the shortest, cheapest method of inducing a nervous
> breakdown ever perfected. In this technique (eventually adopted
> by the psychology department of Duke University, which will
> adopt anything), the subject is placed in a sharply sloping attic
> heated to 340°F. and given a mothproof closet known as the Jiffy-
> Cloz to assemble. . . .
>
> —S. J. Perelman, "Insert Flap 'A' and Throw Away"*

Perelman clearly exaggerates his description of the situation to evoke
his frustration. Most writers keep such overstatements from going *too*
far, however. It's usually a mistake to exaggerate so much that the
point, and thus the humor, is lost.

Ridicule

Another everyday device, ridicule simply means *making fun* of
something. It isn't so much a separate technique as a goal or object of
some kinds of humor. We may mock something or someone in a
friendly way, as in gentle kidding or teasing, or we may be much more
aggressive in our attack. Ridicule leans toward strong mockery and
satire—the goal being to undermine the object, to make it laughable.
Here are two brief examples, mocking definitions from the American
satirist Ambrose Bierce's *The Devil's Dictionary†*:

> *Faith:* Belief without evidence in what is told by one who speaks
> without knowledge of things without parallel.
>
> *History:* An account mostly false, of events mostly unimportant,
> which are brought about by rulers mostly knaves, and soldiers
> mostly fools.

*The Best of S. J. Perelman (New York: Modern Library, 1947): 285.
†(New York: Dover, 1958): 40, 57.

Bierce wants to make us laugh, but he wants also to explode our pieties about these hallowed subjects. Notice that he achieves his ridicule partly by exaggeration.

Wordplay

In a sense, all humor is wordplay—arranging language so that it makes us laugh. Sometimes, however, we use words themselves as a source of humor; such verbal wit is another tool at the humorist's disposal. Perhaps the most usual type of wordplay is the *pun,* which has two forms (apart from good and bad): (1) suggesting different meanings of the same word, or (2) substituting a similar-sounding word for one with a different meaning. The philosophical balding man says, "Hair today, gone tomorrow!" The convict about to be hanged, seeing that the rope is missing, says, "No noose is good noose."

As a rule, wordplay arises spontaneously in our speaking and writing, as we stumble upon illogical, silly, clever, or surprising turns of phrase. For most of us, however, it's nearly impossible to create puns and clever witticisms on command. Watch for opportunities for verbal wit in your humor, but don't worry too much if it doesn't come easily to you. If you do have a facility for verbal cleverness, however, use it judiciously. Like exaggeration, it can quickly become too much of a good thing.

Tone and Style

As in any of our writing, the tone we employ affects our readers' responses. In humor, tone may be *sarcastic, whimsical, deadpan, tongue-in-cheek, falsely naive,* and so on, reflecting the writer's attitude toward subject and audience. As in the other humorous strategies we've considered, it's generally wise to avoid extremes. Tone should color a piece of writing, not completely dominate it.

Style, likewise, seems to work best when it's subtle, not a glaring characteristic of our prose. Humorous styles range from the *fancy* or *elaborate* (funny in their high-toned extravagance) to the *blunt, plain-spoken,* and *folksy.* Again, however, remember to keep control of your style, whatever it may be in a piece of humor. Style and tone should be appropriate to the subject, both supporting and enhancing a unified treatment.

Surprise

Because humor so often depends on *the unexpected*—the bizarre twist, the clever remark—it pays to use the element of surprise to its best advantage. Avoid "telegraphing"—warning your readers that they're supposed to laugh at what comes next. Instead, keep them in suspense, so that your surprises aren't anticipated. Laughter is the release of tension. Keep your readers in some doubt about where you're going and how you'll get there.

Finally, we've said that humor has two essential elements; keeping them in mind can be a strategy unto itself.

First is the *joining of things that don't normally go together*—a man wearing a business suit and rabbit ears. Combining incongruous or incompatible elements produces tension, conflict, and the potential for humor. Look for subjects—whether from your own experience or from what you observe around you—that provide such opportunities.

The other element in our definition is the pleasing *shock of recognition* we experience when humor surprises us with sharp perception, keen observation. Humor can be much more than gags, jokes, or a pie in the face. It can be memorable writing when it startles us with its truthfulness. In your work, then, try to be as honest and accurate as you would in any of your writing. Avoid the easy or predictable. Try to discover something funny, to surprise yourself. If you do, it's likely that your reader will laugh with you.

Process checklist: Writing to entertain

The task
- What kinds of humorous subjects attract me?
- Are there ones I've already considered as potential sources of humor?
- How can I use humor as a way to express myself?

Exploring and collecting
- Can I recall specific incidents, details, or remarks that seem funny or memorable?
- Can I use narrative or description to express my humorous material?

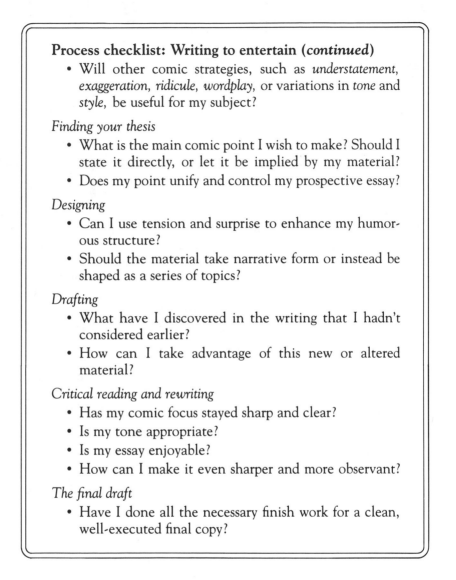

Process checklist: Writing to entertain (*continued*)

- Will other comic strategies, such as *understatement, exaggeration, ridicule, wordplay,* or variations in *tone* and *style,* be useful for my subject?

Finding your thesis

- What is the main comic point I wish to make? Should I state it directly, or let it be implied by my material?
- Does my point unify and control my prospective essay?

Designing

- Can I use tension and surprise to enhance my humorous structure?
- Should the material take narrative form or instead be shaped as a series of topics?

Drafting

- What have I discovered in the writing that I hadn't considered earlier?
- How can I take advantage of this new or altered material?

Critical reading and rewriting

- Has my comic focus stayed sharp and clear?
- Is my tone appropriate?
- Is my essay enjoyable?
- How can I make it even sharper and more observant?

The final draft

- Have I done all the necessary finish work for a clean, well-executed final copy?

In the humorous readings that follow, notice the variety of comic attitudes, targets, and styles, and ask yourself which pieces are funniest, truest, or most entertaining. Study the writers' comic strategies, especially the ones that appeal to you, and see if you can't use them yourself in your humorous essays.

— Bob Greene —

Bob Greene, a columnist for the Chicago Tribune, *was born in 1947 in Columbus, Ohio, and was educated at Northwestern University. Greene started as a reporter for the* Chicago Sun-Times *in 1969, becoming a columnist for that paper in 1971. He moved to the* Tribune *in 1978. He has received awards from the Associated Press, the Chicago Newspaper Guild, and other journalistic organizations. Greene has written several books, including* Billion Dollar Baby *(1974), the story of his experience touring with the Alice Cooper rock band, and has published several collections of his columns:* Johnny Deadline, Reporter *(1976);* American Beat *(1983);* Cheeseburgers: The Best of Bob Greene *(1985).* Homecoming, *a book about Vietnam veterans, appeared in 1989. Greene is also a former columnist for* Esquire, *and has been an occasional contributor to ABC News "Nightline."*

Bob—A Name Spurned by History

In this column, Greene expresses his frustration that he was given a "dumb" first name. Using many examples of names from history, literature, sports, and the movies, Greene shows us how different things would be if Bob hadn't been spurned, at the same time speaking for those among us whose name seems ill-fitted. Greene's essay also reveals that self-expression need not always be solemn or serious.

I got pretty depressed last week when a big storm in the Atlantic 1
was upgraded to Hurricane Bob.

You may have noticed that every TV weatherman and newscaster 2
had a little smirk on his face every time he mentioned Hurricane Bob.
The broadcasters couldn't help it; there was something funny about
Hurricane Bob.

And I don't blame the newscasters. Bob is a dumb name. It's a 3
clunky name. Bob is the plain, boring, sensible shoe of names. Bob
sounds like a cork dipping up and down in the ocean.

I have never been able to escape this, of course, and Hurricane 4
Bob only served to remind me of it. On our computer system at work,
when I log on every morning the screen flashes a message at me:
"Welcome to the Editorial System, Bob." I always feel that the screen
is laughing.

Bob. Bob. Bob. Down through history, men of valor and 5

achievement have seldom been named Bob. The great figures in literature are not named Bob. Think about it. There's Bob Cratchit in
Dickens' "A Christmas Carol"—and let's face it, Cratchit was not
exactly a dashing, dream-inspiring vagabond. After Cratchit the list of
literary Bobs grows pretty short.

There has never been a President of the United States named   6
Bob. Thomas, yes. John, yes. James, yes. Martin and Zachary and
Millard and Warren and Ulysses and Rutherford and Chester and
Grover and Woodrow—yes. But never a President Bob. In all of our
200-plus years as a nation, the people of America have never taken it
upon themselves to make a Bob their president.

I'm not much of a student of English history, but if there ever was   7
a King Bob, I'm not aware of it. And it's no wonder; the name is not
the stuff of legends, which is why we have never heard about the
exploits of Bob the Lionhearted.

The main anchormen for the three big commercial television   8
networks' evening news programs have never been named Bob, either.
Walter and Dan and Tom and John and Peter and Chet and David—
over the years all of them have read the evening news. Not Bob,
though. In television terms, Bob is just the guy who flies up from
Washington to substitute on the weekend newscasts.

The most dashing movie stars have not been Bobs, either. Cary,   9
Kirk, Errol—of course. Think about a Bob in the movies, and you
come up with Bob Cummings. Those talented actors who have been
born with the name Robert have taken the wise course and not short-
ened it—Robert Mitchum is one example. But if a movie star wants to
be memorable, he is best advised to stay away from Bob. James Dean
would have caused nary a ripple if he would have called himself Bob
Dean. In the world of popular culture, who ever would have screamed
for Bob Presley? When you think of Crosbys, Bing is the one who
immediately comes to mind. There was a Bob Crosby, but he sort of
fades into your brain. That's how it is with Bobs.

One way out for Bobs is to go with Bobby. A lot of teen-idol   10
rock-and-roll stars did that in the early years, with remarkable success.
Bobby Vee sold millions of records; Bob Vee sounds like a small-time
embezzler. Bobby is also a good name for athletes; a Bobby is a scram-
bling quarterback or an elusive running back. Bob? The team trainer.

But grown men, if they aren't singers or athletes, have trouble   11
going around calling themselves Bobby. There is probably a book in all
this; it could be called "The Bob Dilemma." But potential readers
would take one look at the title and decide not to buy it. Too boring.

Our history would be so much duller had the great men of fiction   12
and real-life accomplishment been named Bob. F. Scott Fitzgerald's

The Great Gatsby is often called the finest novel of all time; had Fitzgerald decided to make Jay Gatsby into Bob Gatsby, no one would have paid any attention. The memory of Franklin Delano Roosevelt still brings tears to many people's eyes; do you think Bob Roosevelt would have attracted a dozen votes? Joe DiMaggio was perhaps the greatest sports figure of his time; how many fans do you think would have lined up to see Joltin' Bob DiMaggio?

Here's a typical twist: Hurricane Bob, which got me started think- 13
ing about all this, was downgraded after one day to a tropical depression. That figures.

By the way, this is only the beginning of my problems. 14

My middle name is Bernard. 15

Questions for Study and Discussion

Meaning and Purpose

1. Why does Greene make fun of his name? Do you think he really means it when he says, "Bob is a dumb name. It's a clunky name"? Why or why not?
2. Though Greene's essay is funny and obviously meant to entertain, to what extent is he trying to express something serious about himself? Explain.
3. Can you contradict Greene's case with examples of "men of valor and achievement" who've been named Bob?

Strategy and Audience

1. What is the effect of Greene's substituting Bob for the first names of famous people and fictional characters? Why does he search for presidents, kings, television anchormen, and movie stars with this first name?
2. Why does Greene frame his essay with references to Hurricane Bob? How does he use this frame to reinforce the essay in his conclusion?
3. Why would anyone not named Bob be interested in this essay?

Style and Language

1. Greene's style is appropriately relaxed and informal, typical of humor writing. Find examples of his everyday language and sentence

structure, such as his opening remark: "I got pretty depressed last week. . . ." Why does Greene choose to write in such a breezy way? If this style works, what are its strengths? Why wouldn't it be right for every writing task?

2. Where does Greene use slang, irony, understatement or overstatement, wordplay, or other humorous language strategies?

Writing Ideas

1. Do you have a name with which you're especially happy, or unhappy? What is it about the name that thrills or disappoints you? How has it helped (or hindered) your identity? Write a humorous essay in which you consider your name, the role it has played in your life, what your name should have been (or what you'd change it to), why it's the perfect name for you, and so on.

2. Write about another aspect of yourself that seems to have had an important part in your life: your size, your physical features, your personality type (shy, outgoing, serious, happy-go-lucky) from a humorous or self-mocking perspective.

— Mark Twain —

Mark Twain (Samuel Clemens, 1835–1910), one of America's most beloved writers, was born in Missouri and grew up in Hannibal, where he fell in love with the Mississippi River. At twelve, when his father died, Twain left school to make his way in the world, working as a printer, journalist, and riverboat pilot. Perhaps best known as the author of The Adventures of Huckleberry Finn *(1884), a landmark in the development of the American novel, Twain wrote many books, among them:* The Innocents Abroad *(1869),* The Gilded Age *(1873),* The Adventures of Tom Sawyer *(1876),* Life on the Mississippi *(1876), and* A Connecticut Yankee in King Arthur's Court *(1889).*

Advice to Youth

Though certainly one of our most pungent humorists, Twain was a moralist who wished to expose human folly and vice to ridicule. In this essay, he offers guidance tailored to his young audience—tongue-in-cheek, sharply ironic, funny, but ultimately serious in its message.

Being told I would be expected to talk here, I inquired what sort of a talk I ought to make. They said it should be something suitable to youth—something didactic, instructive, or something in the nature of good advice. Very well. I have a few things in my mind which I have often longed to say for the instruction of the young, for it is in one's tender early years that such things will best take root and be most enduring and most valuable. First, then, I will say to you, my young friends—and I say it beseechingly, urgingly—

Always obey your parents, when they are present. This is the best policy in the long run, because if you don't they will make you. Most parents think they know better than you do, and you can generally make more by humoring that superstition than you can by acting on your own better judgment.

Be respectful to your superiors, if you have any, also to strangers, and sometimes to others. If a person offend you, and you are in doubt as to whether it was intentional or not, do not resort to extreme measures; simply watch your chance and hit him with a brick. That will be sufficient. If you shall find that he had not intended any offense, come out frankly and confess yourself in the wrong when you struck him; acknowledge it like a man and say you didn't mean to. Yes, always avoid violence; in this age of charity and kindliness, the time has gone by for such things. Leave dynamite to the low and unrefined.

Go to bed early, get up early—this is wise. Some authorities say   4
get up with the sun; some others say get up with one thing, some with another. But a lark is really the best thing to get up with. It gives you a splendid reputation with everybody to know that you get up with the lark; and if you get the right kind of a lark, and work at him right, you can easily train him to get up at half past nine, every time—it is no trick at all.

Now as to the matter of lying. You want to be very careful about   5
lying; otherwise you are nearly sure to get caught. Once caught, you can never again be, in the eyes of the good and the pure, what you were before. Many a young person has injured himself permanently through a single clumsy and illfinished lie, the result of carelessness born of incomplete training. Some authorities hold that the young ought not to lie at all. That, of course, is putting it rather stronger than necessary; still, while I cannot go quite so far as that, I do maintain, and I believe I am right, that the young ought to be temperate in the use of this great art until practice and experience shall give them that confidence, elegance, and precision which alone can make the accomplishment graceful and profitable. Patience, diligence, painstaking attention to detail—these are the requirements; these, in time, will make the student perfect; upon these, and upon these only, may he rely as the sure foundation for future eminence. Think what tedious years of study, thought, practice, experience, went to the equipment of that peerless old master who was able to impose upon the whole world the lofty and sounding maxim that "truth is mighty and will prevail"— the most majestic compound fracture of fact which any of woman born has yet achieved. For the history of our race, and each individual's experience, are sown thick with evidence that a truth is not hard to kill and that a lie told well is immortal. There is in Boston a monument of the man who discovered anaesthesia; many people are aware, in these latter days, that that man didn't discover it at all, but stole the discovery from another man. Is this truth mighty, and will it prevail? Ah no, my hearers, the monument is made of hardy material, but the lie it tells will outlast it a million years. An awkward, feeble, leaky lie is a thing which you ought to make it your unceasing study to avoid; such a lie as that has no more real permanence than an average truth. Why, you might as well tell the truth at once and be done with it. A feeble, stupid, preposterous lie will not live two years—except it be a

slander upon somebody. It is indestructible, then, of course, but that is no merit of yours. A final word: begin your practice of this gracious and beautiful art early—begin now. If I had begun earlier, I could have learned how.

Never handle firearms carelessly. The sorrow and suffering that have been caused through the innocent but heedless handling of firearms by the young! Only four days ago, right in the next farm-house to the one where I am spending the summer, a grandmother, old and gray and sweet, one of the loveliest spirits in the land, was sitting at her work, when her young grandson crept in and got down an old, battered, rusty gun which had not been touched for many years and was supposed not to be loaded, and pointed it at her, laughing and threatening to shoot. In her fright she ran screaming and pleading toward the door on the other side of the room; but as she passed him he placed the gun almost against her very breast and pulled the trigger! He had supposed it was not loaded. And he was right—it wasn't. So there wasn't any harm done. It is the only case of that kind I ever heard of. Therefore, just the same, don't you meddle with old unloaded firearms; they are the most deadly and unerring things that have ever been created by man. You don't have to take any pains at all with them; you don't have to have a rest, you don't have to have any sights on the gun, you don't have to take aim, even. No, you just pick out a relative and bang away, and you are sure to get him. A youth who can't hit a cathedral at thirty yards with a Gatling gun in three-quarters of an hour, can take up an old empty musket and bag his grandmother every time, at a hundred. Think what Waterloo would have been if one of the armies had been boys armed with old muskets supposed not be loaded, and the other army had been composed of their female relations. The very thought of it makes one shudder.

There are many sorts of books; but good ones are the sort for the young to read. Remember that. They are a great, an inestimable, an unspeakable means of improvement. Therefore be careful in your selection, my young friends; be very careful; confine yourselves exclusively to Robertson's Sermons, Baxter's *Saint's Rest*, *The Innocents Abroad*, and works of that kind.

But I have said enough. I hope you will treasure up the instructions which I have given you, and make them a guide to your feet and a light to your understanding. Build your character thoughtfully and painstakingly upon these precepts, and by and by, when you have got it built, you will be surprised and gratified to see how nicely and sharply it resembles everybody else's.

Questions for Study and Discussion

Meaning and Purpose

1. Twain is poking fun at a number of things in this essay. What are they?
2. What does "Advice to Youth" imply about its author? Characterize the attitudes likely to produce such an essay.
3. Does Twain's humorous essay have an underlying serious purpose? If so, what might it be?

Strategy and Audience

1. Twain was a master of verbal irony—saying the opposite of what you mean. Point out some ironic statements in Twain's essay. What is their effect?
2. Does Twain use any other humorous strategies? Which ones?
3. How are Twain's remarks likely to be received by adult readers serious about giving moral advice to youths? Is anything there that some readers may find in bad taste? Explain.

Style and Language

1. Humorous style often moves from the serious or lofty to the ridiculous. Find sentences (or sequences of them) where Twain begins in the voice of mature authority, only to undercut himself with wild, exaggerated, or ludicrous advice.
2. Vocabulary: didactic, beseechingly (paragraph 1); diligence, eminence, maxim, preposterous (5).

Writing Ideas

1. Write your own humorous "Advice" essay, in which you present a brief guide to so-called proper conduct. Like Twain, try your hand at using irony, overstatement, and understatement for comic effect.
2. As above, write an essay in which you advise your elders (parents, teachers, and so on) about how to behave.

— Garrison Keillor —

Garrison Keillor is a writer, radio entertainer, and inventor of the now famous Lake Wobegon, Minnesota, an imaginary "little town that time forgot and the decades could not improve." Keillor, born Gary Edward in 1942, grew up in Minnesota and now lives in New York City as a staff writer for The New Yorker Magazine. *Keillor's former National Public Radio program, "A Prairie Home Companion," which ended in 1987 after thirteen years, won the Peabody Award for distinguished broadcasting in 1980. A new radio program, "The American Radio Company of the Air," now broadcasts live from New York City every Saturday night. Keillor has written humorous essays and stories for a number of magazines and has published several books:* Happy to Be Here *(1982),* Lake Wobegon Days *(1985),* Leaving Home *(1987), and* We Are Still Married *(1989).*

Attitude

Keillor here gives us a funny, friendly lecture about the value of correct behavior and style in slow-pitch softball. It's not hard to see this essay as being about something bigger than a sandlot game, however, as Keillor's observant humor and disarming wit reveal.

Long ago I passed the point in life when major-league ballplayers begin to be younger than yourself. Now all of them are, except for a few aging trigenarians and a couple of quadros who don't get around on the fastball as well as they used to and who sit out the second games of doubleheaders. However, despite my age (thirty-nine), I am still active and have a lot of interests. One of them is slow-pitch softball, a game that lets me go through the motions of baseball without getting beaned or having to run too hard. I play on a pretty casual team, one that drinks beer on the bench and substitutes freely. If a player's wife or girlfriend wants to play, we give her a glove and send her out to right field, no questions asked, and if she lets a pop fly drop six feet in front of her, nobody agonizes over it.

Except me. This year. For the first time in my life, just as I am entering the dark twilight of my slow-pitch career, I find myself taking the game seriously. It isn't the bonehead play that bothers me especially—the pop fly that drops untouched, the slow roller juggled and the ball then heaved ten feet over the first baseman's head and into the next diamond, the routine singles that go through outfielders' legs for doubles and triples with gloves flung after them. No, it isn't our stone-glove fielding or pussyfoot base-running or limp-wristed hitting that gives me fits, though these have put us on the short end of some mighty ridiculous scores this summer. It's our attitude.

Bottom of the ninth, down 18–3, two outs, a man on first and a woman on third, and our third baseman strikes out. *Strikes out!* In slow-pitch, not even your grandmother strikes out, but this guy does, and after his third strike—a wild swing at a ball that bounces on the plate—he topples over in the dirt and lies flat on his back, laughing. *Laughing!*

Same game, earlier. They have the bases loaded. A weak grounder is hit toward our second baseperson. The runners are running. She picks up the ball, and she looks at them. She looks at first, at second, at home. We yell, "Throw it! Throw it!" and she throws it, underhand, at the pitcher, who has turned and run to back up the catcher. The ball rolls across the third-base line and under the bench. Three runs score. The batter, a fatso, chugs into second. The other team hoots and hollers, and what does she do? She shrugs and smiles ("Oh, silly me"); after all, it's only a game. Like the aforementioned strikeout artist, she treats her error as a joke. They have forgiven themselves instantly, which is unforgivable. It is *we* who should forgive them, who can say, "It's all right, it's only a game." They are supposed to throw up their hands and kick the dirt and hang their heads, as if this boner, even if it is their sixteenth of the afternoon— *this* is the one that really and truly breaks their hearts.

That attitude sweetens the game for everyone. The sinner feels sweet remorse. The fatso feels some sense of accomplishment; this is no bunch of rumdums he forced into an error but a team with some class. We, the sinner's teammates, feel momentary anger at her— dumb! dumb play!—but then, seeing her grief, we sympathize with her in our hearts (any one of us might have made that mistake or one worse), and we yell encouragement, including the shortstop, who, moments before, dropped an easy throw for a force at second. "That's all right! Come on! We got 'em!" we yell. "Shake it off! These turkeys can't hit!" This makes us all feel good, even though the turkeys now lead us by ten runs. We're getting clobbered, but we have a winning attitude.

Let me say this about attitude: Each player is responsible for his or her own attitude, and to a considerable degree you can *create* a good attitude by doing certain little things on the field. These are certain little things that ballplayers do in the Bigs, and we ought to be doing them in the Slows.

1. When going up to bat, don't step right into the batter's box as if it were an elevator. The box is your turf, your stage. Take possession of it slowly and deliberately, starting with a lot of back-bending, knee-stretching, and torso-revolving in the on-deck circle. Then, approaching the box, stop outside it and tap the dirt off your spikes with your bat. You don't have spikes, you have sneakers, of course, but the significance of the tapping is the same. Then, upon entering the box, spit on the ground. It's a way of saying, "This here is mine. This is where I get my hits." 7

2. Spit frequently. Spit at all crucial moments. Spit correctly. Spit should be *blown,* not ptuied weakly with the lips, which often results in dribble. Spitting should convey forcefulness of purpose, concentration, pride. Spit down, not in the direction of others. Spit in the glove and on the fingers, especially after making a real knucklehead play; it's a way of saying, "I dropped the ball because my glove was dry." 8

3. At bat and in the field, pick up dirt. Rub dirt in the fingers (especially after spitting on them). Toss dirt, as if testing the wind for velocity and direction. Smooth the dirt. Be involved with dirt. If no dirt is available (e.g., in the outfield), pluck tufts of grass. Fielders should be grooming their areas constantly between plays, flicking away tiny sticks and bits of gravel. 9

4. Take your time. Tie your laces. Confer with your teammates about possible situations that may arise and conceivable options in dealing with them. Extend the game. Three errors on three consecutive plays can be humiliating if the plays occur within the space of a couple of minutes, but if each error is separated from the next by extensive conferences on the mound, lace-tying, glove adjustments, and arguing close calls (if any), the effect on morale is minimized. 10

5. Talk. Not just an occasional "Let's get a hit now" but continuous rhythmic chatter, a flow of syllables: "Hey babe hey babe c'mon babe good stick now hey babe long tater take him downtown babe . . . hey good eye good eye." 11

Infield chatter is harder to maintain. Since the slow-pitch pitch is required to be a soft underhand lob, infielders hesitate to say, "Smoke him babe hey low heat hey throw it on the black babe chuck it in there back him up babe no hit no hit." Say it anyway. 12

6. One final rule, perhaps the most important of all: When your team is up and has made the third out, the batter and the players who were left on base do not come back to the bench for their gloves. *They* 13

remain on the field, and their teammates bring their gloves out to them. This requires some organization and discipline, but it pays off big in morale. It says, "Although we're getting our pants knocked off, still we must conserve our energy."

Imagine that you have bobbled two fly balls in this rout and now   14
you have just tried to stretch a single into a double and have been easily thrown out sliding into second base, where the base runner ahead of you had stopped. It was the third out and a dumb play, and your opponents smirk at you as they run off the field. You are the goat, a lonely and tragic figure sitting in the dirt. You curse yourself, jerking your head sharply forward. You stand up and kick the base. How miserable! How degrading! Your utter shame, though brief, bears silent testimony to the worthiness of your teammates, whom you have let down, and they appreciate it. They call out to you now as they take the field, and as the second baseman runs to his position he says, "Let's get 'em now," and tosses you your glove. Lowering your head, you trot slowly out to right. There you do some deep knee bends. You pick grass. You find a pebble and fling it into foul territory. As the first batter comes to the plate, you check the sun. You get set in your stance, poised to fly. Feet spread, hands on hips, you bend slightly at the waist and spit the expert spit of a veteran ballplayer—a player who has known the agony of defeat but who always bounces back, a player who has lost a stride on the base paths but can still make the big play.

This is *ball*, ladies and gentlemen. This is what it's all about.   15

Questions for Study and Discussion

Meaning and Purpose

1. Keillor writes about proper attitude in slow-pitch softball, but his ideas might be extended to the larger arena of life. Review his rules (paragraphs 7–13); can any be translated and applied to life in general? How so?
2. According to Keillor, why does maintaining a winning attitude matter so, even in defeat? Is he sincere in his belief, or is he making fun of such an attitude? How do you know?
3. What is Keillor's real attitude toward sport? To what extent is this entertainment also a persuasive essay aimed at convincing us that we should behave "correctly"?

Strategy and Audience

1. Where and how does Keillor use narration and description for humorous intent? How does he use sharp observation and detail to surprise and delight his readers? Cite examples.
2. What other humorous devices does Keillor use in this essay? Find examples of understatement, exaggeration, and ridicule.
3. Can this essay be entertaining for those not interested in slow-pitch softball or regular baseball? Why or why not?

Style and Language

1. Keillor blends folksy diction ("The fatso feels some sense of accomplishment; this is no bunch of rumdums he forced into an error . . .") with mock seriousness ("Spit should be *blown,* not ptuied weakly with the lips, which often results in dribble"). Find other examples of Keillor's use of slang and colloquial language, and his deadpan tone. Does this sort of humor appeal to you? Why or why not?
2. Keillor builds much of his humor from baseball language. Where does he turn the terminology of the sport and the players' language to humorous advantage?

Writing Ideas

1. Write your own rules for behaving or performing correctly in a specific situation, but do so with a light touch. Try to see what's funny about being serious in taking tests, asking someone for a date, eating dinner with your parents or your boss, asking a teacher for a higher grade, and so on.
2. Write an affectionate, or mocking, tribute to your favorite sport, game, or other group activity. Use the concrete details and language of the pastime to give your readers a vivid, entertaining look at its funny side.

Woody Allen is one of America's most prolific and talented film directors and writers. Born in 1935, Allen grew up in Brooklyn, New York, dropping out of college to try his hand at show business. He started as a gag writer, working for such luminaries of the day as Sid Caesar, Art Carney, and Jack Paar (an early host of the "Tonight Show"). Branching out into stand-up comedy, Allen was an immediate hit with his offbeat, intellectual humor and wild sense of the absurd. He recorded several bestselling albums, and started writing for the stage and the screen. Since his movies began appearing in the late 1960s, Allen has gathered a worldwide following with such films as Play It Again, Sam *(1972, based on his Broadway play);* Annie Hall *(1977);* Zelig *(1983);* Hannah and Her Sisters *(1986);* Radio Days *(1987); and* Crimes and Misdemeanors *(1989), among many others. Allen has also published three books of his collected humorous pieces:* Getting Even *(1971);* Without Feathers *(1975); and* Side Effects *(1980), from which the following is taken.*

My Speech to the Graduates

This selection is a perfect example of Allen's bizarre humor, summed up in the essay's first four sentences. Is Allen making light of very serious subjects? Yes—but he's also satirizing the clichés and platitudes with which we discuss such matters, the kind of canned language it has been said sometimes turns up in commencement addresses.

More than any other time in history, mankind faces a crossroads. One path leads to despair and utter hopelessness. The other, to total extinction. Let us pray we have the wisdom to choose correctly. I speak, by the way, not with any sense of futility, but with a panicky conviction of the absolute meaninglessness of existence which could easily be misinterpreted as pessimism. It is not. It is merely a healthy concern for the predicament of modern man. (Modern man is here defined as any person born after Nietzsche's edict that "God is dead," but before the hit recording "I Wanna Hold Your Hand.") This "predicament" can be stated one of two ways, though certain linguistic philosophers prefer to reduce it to a mathmatical equation where it can be easily solved and even carried around in the wallet.

Put in its simplest form, the problem is: How is it possible to find meaning in a finite world given my waist and shirt size? This is a very difficult question when we realize that science has failed us. True, it has conquered many diseases, broken the genetic code, and even placed human beings on the moon, and yet when a man of eighty is left in a room with two eighteen-year-old cocktail waitresses nothing happens. Because the real problems never change. After all, can the human soul be glimpsed through a microscope? Maybe—but you'd definitely need one of those very good ones with two eyepieces. We know that the most advanced computer in the world does not have a brain as sophisticated as that of an ant. True, we could say that of many of our relatives but we only have to put up with them at weddings or special occasions. Science is something we depend on all the time. If I develop a pain in the chest I must take an X-ray. But what if the radiation from the X-ray causes me deeper problems? Before I know it, I'm going in for surgery. Naturally, while they're giving me oxygen an intern decides to light up a cigarette. The next thing you know I'm rocketing over the World Trade Center in bed clothes. Is this science? True, science has taught us how to pasteurize cheese. And true, this can be fun in mixed company—but what of the H-bomb? Have you ever seen what happens when one of those things falls off a desk accidentally? And where is science when one ponders the eternal riddles? How did the cosmos originate? How long has it been around? Did matter begin with an explosion or by the word of God? And if by the latter, could He not have begun it just two weeks earlier to take advantage of some of the warmer weather? Exactly what do we mean when we say, man is mortal? Obviously it's not a compliment.

Religion too has unfortunately let us down. Miguel de Unamuno writes blithely of the "eternal persistence of consciousness," but this is no easy feat. Particularly when reading Thackeray. I often think how comforting life must have been for early man because he believed in a powerful, benevolent Creator who looked after all things. Imagine his disappointment when he saw his wife putting on weight. Contemporary man, of course, has no such peace of mind. He finds himself in the midst of a crisis of faith. He is what we fashionably call "alienated." He has seen the ravages of war, he has known natural catastrophes, he has been to singles bars. My good friend Jacques Monod spoke often of the randomness of the cosmos. He believed everything in existence occurred by pure chance with the possible exception of his breakfast, which he felt certain was made by his housekeeper. Naturally belief in a divine intelligence inspires tranquillity. But this does not free us from our human responsibilities. Am I my brother's keeper? Yes. Interestingly, in my case I share that honor with the Prospect Park Zoo.

Feeling godless then, what we have done is made technology God. And yet can technology really be the answer when a brand new Buick, driven by my close associate, Nat Zipsky, winds up in the window of Chicken Delight causing hundreds of customers to scatter? My toaster has never once worked properly in four years. I follow the instructions and push two slices of bread down in the slots and seconds later they rifle upward. Once they broke the nose of a woman I loved very dearly. Are we counting on nuts and bolts and electricity to solve our problems? Yes, the telephone is a good thing—and the refrigerator—and the air conditioner. But not every air conditioner. Not my sister Henny's, for instance. Hers makes a loud noise and still doesn't cool. When the man comes over to fix it, it gets worse. Either that or he tells her she needs a new one. When she complains, he says not to bother him. This man is truly alienated. Not only is he alienated but he can't stop smiling.

The trouble is, our leaders have not adequately prepared us for a   4
mechanized society. Unfortunately our politicians are either incompetent or corrupt. Sometimes both on the same day. The Government is unresponsive to the needs of the little man. Under five-seven, it is impossible to get your Congressman on the phone. I am not denying that democracy is still the finest form of government. In a democracy at least, civil liberties are upheld. No citizen can be wantonly tortured, imprisoned, or made to sit through certain Broadway shows. And yet this is a far cry from what goes on in the Soviet Union. Under their form of totalitarianism, a person merely caught whistling is sentenced to thirty years in a labor camp. If, after fifteen years, he still will not stop whistling, they shoot him. Along with this brutal fascism we find its handmaiden, terrorism. At no other time in history has man been so afraid to cut into his veal chop for fear that it will explode. Violence breeds more violence and it is predicted that by 1990 kidnapping will be the dominant mode of social interaction. Overpopulation will exacerbate problems to the breaking point. Figures tell us there are already more people on earth than we need to move even the heaviest piano. If we do not call a halt to breeding, by the year 2000 there will be no room to serve dinner unless one is willing to set the table on the heads of strangers. Then they must not move for an hour while we eat. Of course energy will be in short supply and each car owner will be allowed only enough gasoline to back up a few inches.

Instead of facing these challenges we turn instead to distractions   5
like drugs and sex. We live in far too permissive a society. Never before has pornography been this rampant. And those films are lit so badly! We are a people who lack defined goals. We have never learned to love. We lack leaders and coherent programs. We have no spiritual

center. We are adrift alone in the cosmos wreaking monstrous violence on one another out of frustration and pain. Fortunately, we have not lost our sense of proportion. Summing up, it is clear the future holds great opportunities. It also holds pitfalls. The trick will be to avoid the pitfalls, seize the opportunities, and get back home by six o'clock.

Questions for Study and Discussion

Meaning and Purpose

1. Allen makes a mockery of the ceremony of advice-giving we've come to expect at graduation. What specific characteristics of commencement addresses does he ridicule?
2. In his speech Allen considers the state of the modern world. What elements of modern life does he attack? What do you think is his real or unspoken attitude toward these subjects? Explain.
3. Does Allen have any aims besides humorous satire in his essay? What makes you think so?

Strategy and Audience

1. Allen's "speech" seems to be the product of a demented mind. Is this essay merely a rambling, chaotic string of weird remarks, or is there some overall logic or order to it? Explain.
2. Allen's humor often startles us with strange combinations of incompatible elements—the sublime and the ridiculous. For instance (paragraph 3): "I often think how comforting life must have been for early man because he believed in a powerful, benevolent Creator who looked after all things. Imagine his disappointment when he saw his wife putting on weight." Find other examples of this strategy. Which of these are funniest or most meaningful? Why?
3. To whom is Allen's humor directed? How close does he come to addressing your interests? How do you respond to his essay?

Style and Language

1. Allen's style comes from stand-up comedy, where he began as a writer for other performers before going on stage himself. His absurd flights of fancy often take the form of one-liners, very brief jokes or gags.

How does Allen tie his jokes together so that his prose is coherent (or at least semicoherent)?

2. Allen uses the vocabulary of modern philosophy ("the predicament of modern man," "meaning in a finite world," "crisis of faith," and so on) throughout "My Speech." Can you understand enough of this from its context to make the essay meaningful, or is the terminology a problem for you? Upon rereading, do the troublesome passages become clearer?

Writing Ideas

1. Write a humorous essay in which you wax ridiculous about the state of the world as you see it. What absurdities do you perceive? How can you turn them to comic advantage? Is your audience likely to share your opinions about what is crazy and what isn't?

2. Write an essay of humorous advice to your fellow students, or to an audience of high-school students about to enter college. What in the college experience seems a good subject for comedy? Avoid easy or clichéd targets (bad cafeteria food, for instance) unless you can add a fresh twist.

— Judith Martin —

Judith Martin, also known as Miss Manners, is a nationally syndicated columnist and author of three witty and ironic books on etiquette: Miss Manners' Guide to Excruciatingly Correct Behavior *(1982),* Miss Manners' Guide to Rearing Perfect Children *(1984), and* Miss Manners' Guide for the Turn-of-the-Millennium *(1990). Born in 1938, Martin earned her B.A. at Wellesley College and in 1960 joined the* Washington Post *as a reporter. A collection of her columns on the Washington social scene,* The Name on the White House Floor, *was published in 1973. Miss Manners came to life in 1978, and has since become a huge success, doubtless helping to spawn the recent revival of interest in proper, and improper, etiquette.*

Undergraduate Romance

In this excerpt, Martin presents a brief but painfully funny and accurate statement about the heartbreak in college relationships. True to her mock disdain for those imperfect persons among us, Miss Manners chides youth for its immaturity (a somehwat circular line of thought, perhaps) and counsels the only "sure cure" for what she calls "an endless chain of misery."

The Prerequisite Heartbreak

What a marvelous, carefree time college is. There is nothing to do but read and write, all in beautiful and dignified surroundings, in the company of unattached and attractive people of one's own age, interests, and abilities. 1

It is too bad that such an idyllic existence is confined to the reveries of those who are not matriculated. Not content with this ironic discovery, and recognizing that it is not quite nice to take amusement in finding that youth has its troubles, too, Miss Manners has long puzzled about why clouds of human suffering should hang over such pretty institutions. 2

It was long ago, as a student herself, that Miss Manners first noticed a pattern to undergraduate romance. Just about every young person, she observed, had a passion for some other young person, who treated the admirer with callous cruelty. In turn each of these victims of love commanded the passions of another person, known as the 3

Creep, who was treated, in turn, disdainfully. Thus, an endless chain of misery was formed.

Why anyone would want to live that way, Miss Manners could not   4
imagine. Why was unrequited love such a powerful force, and why was anyone with a passion for oneself considered contemptible? Miss Manners would have thought that someone's being madly in love with one's own dear self would be a most alluring demonstration of good taste.

And so it is, in the mature. After people have attained full   5
emotional growth, which is unfortunately never for a great proportion of the population, they can actually enjoy being truly loved. When you hear of someone who can't be happy if allowed to become secure about a partner's affections, you know that such a stage has not yet been reached. Miss Manners is always suspicious of the concept of "being taken for granted," used to explain the demise of a romance. It either means that the person subscribes to the heinous idea that it is not necessary to be mannerly to those who are committed to one, or that someone is unable to sustain interest in anyone who does not provide the cheap excitement of uncertainty. To the real grown-up, knowing that one can rely on another person's love is one of the greatest joys of life.

Miss Manners does not expect such wisdom to appear in, say, the   6
first third of life. It is quite reasonable then, she believes, to be interested in finding out, in a variety of ways, how one measures up in the society. Grades and careers are one way of doing this. Another is considered to be the ability to attract someone worth attracting. What makes all that trouble is deciding who is in that category.

In elementary and secondary schools, the children are notori-   7
ously incapable of judging one another individually. The whole class agrees that this or that child is the most beautiful, much to the amazement of parents, who notice that this person may be quite homely and a truly good-looking child goes unnoticed. That is because the very young recognize only self-confidence, and render group judgments based on accepting people at their own high or low evaluation.

In the late teens, there tend to be more distinctions based on   8
objective standards or individual preferences. Still, the idea often hangs on that only a person who thinks he or she is too good for you is good enough. Conversely, on the Groucho Marx principle of not wanting to join a club that would accept members like him, there is the feeling that a person who loves you can't be worth loving.

Miss Manners tries hard to sympathize with this state of affairs as   9
a necessary part of social development. She understands that the state of life devoted to "How am I doing?" is a necessary prelude to the more interesting (to her, anyway) state of "What do I want to accomplish?"

She cannot, however, help wanting to alleviate gloom and despair when she sees it. And there is an awful lot of it to be seen in the love lives of young adults.

For one's own relief, she advises examining the state of one's 10 affections in terms of the pattern she has described. Does the loved one have any quality to offer other than that paradoxically compelling one of rejection? Admittedly, this is not an easy cure, but it might help along the development of the maturity that leads to romantic happiness. A sure cure is only promised to those with the nerve to reverse the process and begin acting superior to the one who has been doing it to one. If everyone did that, the entire chain would be flipped.

That piece of advice, which Miss Manners doesn't expect anyone 11 but the most daring to try, uses up Miss Manners' sympathy, and she has none left for the meanness with which people in the same state treat their own admirers. There, a realization of the pattern also helps; it is possible that a perfectly nice person has the misfortune to admire you. Believe that or not, however, it is necessary to be polite to those so afflicted. (It is not necessary to return the affections; the gift of romantic love cannot ever presume to create an obligation in kind.) They may, upon mature reflection, turn out to be not so completely devoid of taste as you had supposed, or to have nice friends.

Questions for Study and Discussion

Meaning and Purpose

1. What is Martin's point? Does she mean for the advice in her essay to be taken seriously despite its ironic delivery? Explain.
2. What is Miss Manners' apparent attitude toward the age group about whom she writes? What is Martin's real attitude? How do you know?
3. Do you agree with Martin that young people believe that "only a person who thinks he or she is too good for you is good enough" and that, conversely, "they feel that a person who loves you can't be worth loving"? Explain.

Strategy and Audience

1. Martin makes Miss Manners a master of ironic understatement, as in this sentence from paragraph 5: "After people have attained full emotional growth, which is unfortunately never for a great proportion of

the population, they can actually enjoy being truly loved." Find other examples of Martin's dry, subtle, or ironic wit.

2. Where do Martin's observations about student behavior seem especially accurate or perceptive? Cite examples.

3. Martin's essay appeared in her book *Miss Manners' Guide to Rearing Perfect Children*. Is this essay clearly aimed at older readers—who've survived the "endless chain of misery" that is college romance? How are younger readers likely to respond to it? Why?

Style and Language

1. As Miss Manners, Martin writes in a self-consciously mannered style, in a voice that makes fun of the same snobby propriety Miss Manners herself appears to advocate. How does Martin's elaborate, formal prose contribute to her comic intensions? Do you think it is effective? Why or why not?

2. Some of Martin's sentences may require a second or third reading to be fully understood or appreciated. Can you find examples where such rereading is rewarded? Explain your choices.

Writing Ideas

1. Write a humorous or ironic essay on undergraduate romance. Try, as Miss Manners does, to view it from a distance, as an observer who sees it clearly for what it is. Look for details that will be pleasingly recognizable or surprising to your readers.

2. Reread Martin's opening paragraph about college. Do you agree with her admittedly dreamy assessment? Write a humorous essay in which you characterize campus life. You might use Martin's implied categories—daily schedules, environment, and character of one's fellow students—as a starting point, but don't necessarily limit yourself to them.

— Student Essays —

Author Teresa Freund here takes a humorous shot at the social pressure to be thin that faces us all. She constructs a narrative in a single scene, with much of the humor coming from precise observation and self-mocking commentary. The natural conflict between the author and her skinny roommate, and the author's desire to continue snacking despite her nagging conscience, give the essay comic tension. We laugh (and perhaps cringe a bit) because we see the truth in these words, that the difficulty in dieting is as much a problem of losing weight as it is of meeting others' expectations.

Following Freund's essay is another piece of student humor, with questions and suggestions for writing.

Teresa Freund

Diet Is a Four-Letter Word

Introduction: Announces subject with descriptive language

Sarcastic tone

Self-mocking details

No formal thesis announced, but subject is clear

Situation established, story begins

Potential dramatic conflict with roommate introduced

As I was driving home from McDonald's the other evening I saw a woman pictured on a huge billboard advertising Diet Pepsi. Of course, she was blond, blue-eyed, tan, and her thermometer hips disappeared in a size-five string bikini. Entering my apartment, I wondered how she would look in the Big Mac, large fries, hot apple pie, and large Coke that I had just consumed. I plopped in front of the television set, just in time to hear Bill Bixby announce that "Fat has become a national obsession." Diet pills? I'd probably gain weight on those, too.

Turning the TV off, I wandered into the kitchen for a post-dinner snack, but the cupboard was bare except for my anorectic roommate's Carnation Instant and a box of Figurines. I was so depressed I went to the refrigerator, but I found only an apple, a grapefruit, some celery and carrot sticks, and a jug of water. Desperate,

343

Descriptive detail

I continued on to the freezer: Weight Watcher's lasagna and a tray of ice cubes! Not a drop of starch in the place. God, I can't stand this, I thought on my way out of the apartment, heading to the store for a box of Twinkies and a bag of potato chips.

Self-mocking tone

Conflict developed

Hurrying to the door, I opened it just in time to let my roommate in with her arms laden with groceries.   3

Dialogue moves story forward, reveals character

"Where are you going in such a rush?" she asked.   4

"I'm on my way to the store."   5

"Oh, no need," she said, smiling as if she'd just done me the biggest favor of my life. "I just came from there, and I'm sure we'll have enough to last at least a week."   6

Great, I thought. As we unpacked the food, I kept rustling the bags to muffle the sounds of my growling stomach. Not an ounce of chocolate! How did she expect me to live?   7

Exaggeration

She must have noticed the look on my face. "What's the matter?" she asked, pulling out a head of lettuce and some bean sprouts. "Did I forget something?"   8

Details

"Yeah," I snapped, "the Twinkies and potato chips."   9

More conflict

"When are you going to quit eating that junk? No wonder you can't lose weight. Your body's never going to be the same—it will never recover from all the damage you do to it by eating all that poison!" She walked away in disgust, wiggling her itsy bitsy body around the corner and into her room.   10

Playful language

I contemplated the words she had just flung in my face. It's easy to give advice on dieting when your metabolism burns calories before they enter your body.   11

Description

A few minutes later she sat down in a chair across from me, her bony knees sticking out between a pair of shorts and sweat socks. She was tying her tennis shoes.   12

"Where are you going now?" I asked.   13

"Exercise class. Why don't you come with me? It's really a lot of fun."   14

Fun? "No thanks," I replied. "I don't feel   15
like going anywhere. I think I'll just stay here."

She looked annoyed. "How come twenty   16
minutes ago you had enough energy to go to the
store for some snacks, but now you don't feel up
to doing anything? You're always complaining
about your weight, so why don't you try to do
something about it? Here I've given you the perfect opportunity to get some exercise. . . ." She
continued her lecture for a while.

Conflict heightened

I stared at her. Her face was red. She   17
looked hot. She was angry and drained from her
dramatic speech. She'd probably burned off another pound or two. I sat calmly, unmoved.

Sarcasm

"There's only one thing that could really   18
help me lose weight," I said, "and it can be
summed up in one four-letter word." I was thinking of l-o-v-e. Yes, the pounds would shed
themselves.

"D-i-e-t," she said, walking out the door.   19

No, I thought. That is not the word. I   20
watched out the window to make sure her car
had left before I ran to get my keys.

*Crisis resolved: room-
mate leaves, story
ends having implied
several themes*

Here student Pat Healy writes a funny and warmhearted account
of life in the dormitory. His portrait may exaggerate for comic effect,
but the underlying truth of what he says will be apparent to all those
who have experienced the dorm world.

Pat Healy

The Poor Slob

College teaches a person many things. Some of the lessons are   1
seemingly unimportant, such as using a verb in a sentence. Other
lessons are vital, such as how to tap a keg. But college learning extends

beyond the classroom and the bar, and into the dormitory. The dormitory is where the freshman must adjust. The college freshman has been going to school for at least twelve years, but he has never had to live with a whole floor and sometimes a whole dorm of roommates. It doesn't take long for the college freshman to learn. After one week, or one month, or certainly after one semester, the college freshman becomes aware of a basic truth—the world is made up of a number of types of people.

Colleges attract all kinds who must reside in dorms. Fruitcakes, eggheads, jocks, burnouts, and lushes are just a few of the categories that students may fit into. Invariably, some from each category find their way into each dormitory floor, where they are usually tolerated by other fruitcakes, eggheads, etc. But, one type of student is almost always liked by the other dormmates. This student is affectionately known as "the slob." 2

Funk and Wagnall's Standard Dictionary defines slob as, "A stupid, careless, or unclean person." This is an accurate description, especially if you ask any slob's roommate. Slobs are usually stupid or at least lazy. There are very few slobs who bring home a straight-A (let alone a straight-C) report card to mom and dad. Slobs are also careless, or even better, carefree. Slobs are not easily riled by what other people do because they are not riled about what they themselves do or don't do. For instance, if a slob forgets to do his laundry, he'll just wear whatever's lying around, which brings us to the last part of the definition. Slobs are unclean. Oh sure, they take showers; some even use soap. However, a slob's attire often leaves something to be desired. A slob's shirt is often wrinkled. In fact a slob's shirt sometimes looks like it was on the slob when he fell asleep the night before. A slob's socks are often stiff from being worn three days in a row. A slob's pants are ripped, torn, or filthy with caked-on grass or mud stains. A slob's shoes are often his roommate's. 3

At first dirty glance, then, a slob would not seem to be very likable or popular. Nothing could be farther from the truth. There are a number of reasons why a slob is liked by everyone, with the possible exception of his roommate. The reason is the uplifting mood the slob can give to an unhappy dormmate. For example, a fruitcake may be having trouble in school. He may have just flunked a test that he'd studied for. The fruitcake tells the slob his troubles, and leaves with a grin. The fruitcake realizes that compared to the slob, he's got it made. And so, one reason the slob is liked is because he makes others feel good. He makes others feel good because he always finds himself in predicaments. He always finds himself in predicaments because he procrastinates. The slob is constantly cramming—writing overdue pa- 4 pers or unpreparedly taking tests. Why he procrastinates leads us to another likable aspect of the slob.

Slobs, on the whole, are gullible or easily persuaded. Whenever someone, anyone, needs a friend to go out with, they call the slob. This trait would probably fall under the stupid section of the slob definition. Although slobs do not really enjoy procrastinating, they enjoy *not* procrastinating even less. All a slob needs is an excuse or a nudge of an arm (not even a twist) as to why he should not study. Once he hears an excuse, a slob is convinced. An excuse to a slob is like candy to a baby, Ripple to a wino, hair dye to Ronald Reagan. The slob enjoys kidding himself. He enjoys and lives by the motto, "It's the thought that counts." He subscribes to that motto because his thoughts rank considerably higher than his tests scores.

Another reason a slob is popular is that he is fun to go out with. Slobs can adapt to just about any social situation. For instance, on one night a jock may want to go to the bars with the boys. He brings the slob with him. The slob fits in well. The next night, the lush brings the slob with him when he tries to pick up girls. The slob fits in equally well. The slob fits in because of his appearance. Nobody takes the slob seriously. Everyone puts the slob on a lower rung of the social ladder. The slob is thought to be harmless. Give him a beer and he's happy. Girls don't take the slob seriously because of his unkempt appearance. The slob, being carefree, is not out to impress anyone, so he doesn't. Guys enjoy being around the slob. He's always a good butt for jokes. "I had a shirt like that once. Then my dad got a job." The slob laughs it off.

Slobs play another important role in dorm life. On those nights when no one feels like going out, slobs make the very best hosts. Quite often, the slob's room is the meeting place for everyone on the floor, if not the dorm. The slob's room is easy to find. It's the room that day-in and day-out best typifies a post-tornado scene. The slob's room often smells like a dirty sweat sock. There is a good reason for this. Dirty sweat socks are strewn all over the room. Anyone needing last Thursday's stock market report need only go as far as the slob's dorm-room floor. Why, you might ask, would anyone want to enter a room inhabited by a slob? Because everyone feels at home there. People feel free to chew tobacco, eat pizza, flick their ashes, shoot pop-tops, belch, or do just about anything that a slob would do.

There are many other positive qualities exhibited by slobs. Slobs, in general, have a good sense of humor. There is a reason for this. If slobs worried about all their troubles, they'd all come up with ulcers. Slobs aren't fussy. Give a slob his pillow and a blanket, and do what you want to the rest of the room. Slobs are easy to get along with.

Slobs realize that they aren't perfect, and they don't expect anyone else to be.

Despite all this, people don't really appreciate slobs. It's not   9
glamorous. They are always being yelled at by their mothers, grounded by their fathers, scolded by their teachers. On TV, slobs are constantly being portrayed as stupid, careless, and unclean. The sole source of pride for slobs was Oscar Madison, of the "Odd Couple." But on the whole, slobs get no respect.

Just once, I'd like to see slobs get the recognition they deserve.   10
Slobs help everyone's problems seems less serious, if not actually funny. Slobs help people feel good about themselves. They are, in a stupid, careless, unclean way, the psychiatrists of the dormitories.

Questions for Study and Discussion

Meaning and Purpose

1. What are some of the slob's chief characteristics? Why is he nice to have around? According to Healy, why do slobs deserve to be recognized and even respected? Should we feel sorry for the poor slob?
2. Healy's essay may be seen as a gentle satire on life in the college dorm. Does "The Poor Slob" have any other target? If so, what is it?
3. What picture of college life arises from this essay? How accurate, overall, do you think it is? Is there a potentially serious satirical point here about students squandering their college experience? Why or why not?

Strategy and Audience

1. Much of Healy's humor comes from surprise, and from matter-of-fact observation. Which of his details provide a pleasant (or unpleasant) shock of recognition? Why? Where does he clearly exaggerate for comic effect?
2. How does Healy use the dictionary definition (paragraph 3) as a controlling device throughout the essay? Where does he return to his definition unexpectedly?
3. Healy's essay was written for a college audience. To what extent would it appeal to the general reader? Why? How much might it have to say to female college students? Why?

Style and Language

1. Healy writes in a mock-academic style with a straight face throughout and keeps surprising us with its possibilities. Point out passages that sound as if they could have been lifted from a typical nonhumorous college paper but for their incongruous or incompatible content. (An example from paragraph 1: "Other lessons are vital, such as how to tap a keg.")
2. What is the effect of Healy's repetition of the word "slob" throughout the essay? (It's in most of the sentences.) Does he go too far with this stylistic device? Why or why not?

Writing Ideas

1. Write a satiric defense of, or attack on, another college type with which you're familiar. You might want to borrow some of Healy's, or determine your own.
2. Write a humorous treatment of an aspect of college life, or life in general, that seems silly or ridiculous to you. Why is it funny in your eyes? Do others share your view? If not, can you make it funny for them?

— *Additional Writing Ideas* —

For a general audience, write a humorous essay or essay-story on a topic that strikes you as potentially funny. (Be sure to review the suggestions in preceding chapters, especially Chapter 2, for humorous treatment.) Sample topics:

- Social life
- Sports and games
- Your most humiliating or frightening experience
- The funniest story you know
- First love
- Really bad movies or television shows
- Your biggest mistake
- The most ridiculous thing in the world
- The funny side of a serious or sad subject
- Laughable characters in public or private life
- Money
- Families
- Contemporary moral values
- Pets
- Politics and current events
- Education
- Business behavior
- Television commercials or ad campaigns
- Fashions in dress or music
- Leisure pastimes
- Speech or language
- Parents
- Friendships
- Material possessions
- Status
- The human condition

— 9 —

```
┌─────────────────────────────────────────┐
│                                         │
│           For Further Reading           │
│                                         │
│           Writers on Writing            │
│                                         │
└─────────────────────────────────────────┘
```

These additional readings all are focused on one subject: writing itself, how writers feel and think about their craft and its challenges. These essays give you a glimpse into the minds of some contemporary professionals considering what they know best.

Moreover, these essays illustrate the controlling idea in this book—that we write for varied aims, no matter what our subjects may be. Though every author in this section considers writing, language, or the creative process, you'll see that each has different purposes in mind.

Here then is a brief anthology of writers on writing—aiming to express themselves, to inform and explain, to argue, to persuade, and to entertain. Enjoy them for their insights, their inspiration, their understanding and humor.

— Nora Ephron —

Nora Ephron was born in 1941 in New York and grew up in Beverly Hills, California. From a family of writers, Ephron began freelancing after college and was a regular contributor to Esquire *and* New York *magazines. She has written several books, among them* Wallflower at the Orgy *(1970),* Crazy Salad *(1975), and a novel,* Heartburn *(1983). Following in her parents' footsteps, Ephron now devotes most of her time to screenwriting. Among her screen credits are* Silkwood *(1983),* Cookie, *and* When Harry Met Sally. . . . *(both 1989).*

Revision and Life: Take It from the Top—Again

Ephron tells in this self-expressive essay about her own experiences with writing, tracing her career history and reflecting on her way of being a writer and a person. Typically, Ephron uses a breezy, very informal style that captures her irreverent voice and perspective.

I have been asked to write something for a textbook that is meant to teach college students something about writing and revision. I am happy to do this because I believe in revision. I have also been asked to save the early drafts of whatever I write, presumably to show these students the actual process of revision. This too I am happy to do. On the other hand, I suspect that there is just so much you can teach college students about revision; a gift for revision may be a developmental stage—like a 2-year-old's sudden ability to place one block on top of another—that comes along somewhat later, in one's mid-20's, say; most people may not be particularly good at it, or even interested in it, until then.

When I was in college, I revised nothing. I wrote out my papers in longhand, typed them up and turned them in. It would never have crossed my mind that what I had produced was only a first draft and that I had more work to do; the idea was to get to the end, and once you had got to the end you were finished. The same thinking, I might add, applied in life: I went pell-mell through my four years in college without a thought about whether I ought to do anything differently; the idea was to get to the end—to get out of school and become a journalist.

Which I became, in fairly short order. I learned as a journalist to   3
revise on deadline. I learned to write an article a paragraph at a time—
and to turn it in a paragraph at a time—and I arrived at the kind of
writing and revising I do, which is basically a kind of typing and
retyping. I am a great believer in this technique for the simple reason
that I type faster than the wind. What I generally do is to start an
article and get as far as I can—sometimes no farther in than a sentence
or two—before running out of steam, ripping the piece of paper from
the typewriter and starting all over again. I type over and over until I
have got the beginning of the piece to the point where I am happy
with it. I then am ready to plunge into the body of the article itself.
This plunge usually requires something known as a transition. I approach a transition by completely retyping the opening of the article
leading up to it in the hope that the ferocious speed of my typing will
somehow catapult me into the next section of the piece. This does not
work—what in fact catapults me into the next section is a concrete
thought about what the next section ought to be about—but until I
have the thought the typing keeps me busy, and keeps me from feeling
something known as blocked.

Typing and retyping as if you know where you're going is a ver-   4
sion of what therapists tell you to do when they suggest that you try
changing from the outside in—that if you can't master the total commitment to whatever change you want to make, you can at least do all
the extraneous things connected with it, which make it that much
easier to get there. I was 25 years old the first time a therapist suggested that I try changing from the outside in. In those days, I used to
spend quite a lot of time lying awake at night wondering what I should
have said earlier in the evening and revising my lines. I mention this
not just because it's a way of illustrating that a gift for revision is
practically instinctive, but also (once again) because it's possible that a
genuine ability at it doesn't really come into play until one is older—or
at least older than 25, when it seemed to me that all that was required
in my life and my work was the chance to change a few lines.

In my 30's, I began to write essays, one a month for *Esquire*   5
magazine, and I am not exaggerating when I say that in the course of
writing a short essay—1,500 words, that's only six double-spaced type-
written pages—I often used 300 or 400 pieces of typing paper, so often
did I type and retype and catapult and recatapult myself, sometimes on
each retyping moving not even a sentence farther from the spot I had
reached the last time through. At the same time, though, I was polishing what I had already written: as I struggled with the middle of the
article, I kept putting the beginning through the typewriter; as I
approached the ending, the middle got its turn. (This is a kind of

polishing that the word processor all but eliminates, which is why I don't use one. Word processors make it possible for a writer to change the sentences that clearly need changing without having to retype the rest, but I believe that you can't always tell whether a sentence needs work until it rises up in revolt against your fingers as you retype it.) By the time I had produced what you might call a first draft—an entire article with a beginning, middle and end—the beginning was in more like 45th draft, the middle in 20th, and the end was almost newborn. For this reason, the beginnings of my essays are considerably better written than the ends, although I like to think no one ever notices this but me.

As I learned the essay form, writing became harder for me. I was   6
finding a personal style, a voice if you will, a way of writing that looked chatty and informal. That wasn't the hard part—the hard part was that having found a voice, I had to work hard month to month not to seem as if I were repeating myself. At this point in this essay it will not surprise you to learn that the same sort of thing was operating in my life. I don't mean that my life had become harder—but that it was becoming clear that I had many more choices than had occurred to me when I was marching through my 20's. I no longer lost sleep over what I should have said. Not that I didn't care—it was just that I had moved to a new plane of late-night anxiety: I now wondered what I should have done. Whole areas of possible revision opened before me. What should I have done instead? What could I have done? What if I hadn't done it the way I did? What if I had a chance to do it over? What if I had a chance to do it over as a different person? These were the sorts of questions that kept me awake and led me into fiction, which at the very least (the level at which I practice it) is a chance to rework the events of your life so that you give the illusion of being the intelligence at the center of it, simultaneously managing to slip in all the lines that occurred to you later. Fiction, I suppose, is the ultimate shot at revision.

Now I am in my 40's and I write screenplays. Screenplays—if   7
they are made into movies—are essentially collaborations, and movies are not a writer's medium, we all know this, and I don't want to dwell on the craft of screenwriting except insofar as it relates to revision. Because the moment you stop work on a script seems to be determined not by whether you think the draft is good but simply by whether shooting is about to begin: if it is, you get to call your script a final draft; and if it's not, you can always write another revision. This might seem to be a hateful way to live, but the odd thing is that it's somehow comforting; as long as you're revising, the project isn't dead. And by the same token, neither are you.

It was, as it happens, while thinking about all this one recent   8
sleepless night that I figured out how to write this particular essay. I say
"recent" in order to give a sense of immediacy and energy to the
preceding sentence, but the truth is that I am finishing this article four
months after the sleepless night in question, and the letter asking me
to write it, from George Miller of the University of Delaware, arrived
almost two years ago, so for all I know Mr. Miller has managed to
assemble his textbook on revision without me.

Oh, well. That's how it goes when you start thinking about   9
revision. That's the danger of it, in fact. You can spend so much time
thinking about how to switch things around that the main event has
passed you by. But it doesn't matter. Because by the time you reach
middle age, you want more than anything for things not to come to an
end; and as long as you're still revising, they don't.

I'm sorry to end so morbidly—dancing as I am around the subject   10
of death—but there are advantages to it. For one thing, I have managed to move fairly effortlessly and logically from the beginning of this
piece through the middle and to the end. And for another, I am able
to close with an exhortation, something I rarely manage, which is this:
Revise now, before it's too late.

— Kurt Vonnegut —

Kurt Vonnegut, Jr., an acclaimed American novelist, was born in 1922 in Indianapolis, Indiana. He attended Cornell University, Carnegie Institute (now Carnegie-Mellon University) and the University of Chicago, earning his M.A. there in 1971. Vonnegut served in the Army Infantry in World War II, was a prisoner of war in Germany, and received the Purple Heart. He was later to use these experiences in one of his best-known novels, Slaughterhouse-Five *(1969). Starting out as a reporter for the Chicago City News Bureau in 1947, Vonnegut has worked as a public-relations writer for General Electric, a teacher, and a lecturer at the Iowa Writers' Workshop and Harvard University. A prolific writer, Vonnegut has written many books, plays, and essays, including* Player Piano *(1952),* The Sirens of Titan *(1959),* Mother Night *(1962),* Cat's Cradle *(1963),* God Bless You Mr. Rosewater *(1965),* Breakfast of Champions *(1973),* Slapstick *(1976),* Jailbird *(1979),* Dead-Eye Dick *(1982),* Galápagos *(1985), and* Bluebeard *(1987).*

How to Write with Style

In this essay, originally part of a series of advertisements about writing prepared for the International Paper Company, Vonnegut gives us some simple, straightforward, and enduring advice, explaining how good writing comes from honesty, concern for your readers, and a sincere attempt to say something worthwhile.

Newspaper reporters and technical writers are trained to reveal almost nothing about themselves in their writings. This makes them freaks in the world of writers, since almost all of the other ink-stained wretches in that world reveal a lot about themselves to readers. We call these revelations, accidental and intentional, elements of style. 1

These revelations tell us as readers what sort of person it is with whom we are spending time. Does the writer sound ignorant or informed, stupid or bright, crooked or honest, humorless or playful—? And on and on. 2

Why should you examine your writing style with the idea of improving it? Do so as a mark of respect for your readers, whatever you're writing. If you scribble your thoughts any which way, your readers will surely feel that you care nothing about them. They will 3 mark you down as an egomaniac or a chowderhead—or, worse, they will stop reading you.

The most damning revelation you can make about yourself is that you do not know what is interesting and what is not. Don't you yourself like or dislike writers mainly for what they choose to show you or make you think about? Did you ever admire an empty-headed writer for his or her mastery of the language? No. 4

So your own winning style must begin with the ideas in your head. 5

1. Find a subject you care about   Find a subject you care about and which you in your heart feel others should care about. It is this genuine caring, and not your games with language, which will be the most compelling and seductive element in your style. 6

I am not urging you to write a novel, by the way—although I would not be sorry if you wrote one, provided you genuinely cared about something. A petition to the mayor about a pothole in front of your house or a love letter to the girl next door will do. 7

2. Do not ramble, though   I won't ramble on about that. 8

3. Keep it simple   As for your use of language: Remember that two great masters of language, William Shakespeare and James Joyce, wrote sentences which were almost childlike when their subjects were most profound. "To be or not to be?" asks Shakespeare's Hamlet. The longest word is three letters long. Joyce, when he was frisky, could put together a sentence as intricate and as glittering as a necklace for Cleopatra, but my favorite sentence in his short story "Eveline" is this one: "She was tired." At that point in the story, no other words could break the heart of a reader as those three words do. 9

Simplicity of language is not only reputable, but perhaps even sacred. The *Bible* opens with a sentence well within the writing skills of a lively fourteen-year-old: "In the beginning God created the heaven and the earth." 10

4. Have the guts to cut   It may be that you, too, are capable of making necklaces for Cleopatra, so to speak. But your eloquence should be the servant of the ideas in your head. Your rule might be this: If a sentence, no matter how excellent, does not illuminate your subject in some new and useful way, scratch it out. 11

5. Sound like yourself   The writing style which is most natural for you is bound to echo the speech you heard when a child. English was the novelist Joseph Conrad's third language, and much that seems piquant in his use of English was no doubt colored by his first language, 12 which was Polish. And lucky indeed is the writer who has grown up in Ireland, for the English spoken there is so amusing and musical. I myself grew up in Indianapolis, where common speech sounds like a band saw cutting galvanized tin, and employs a vocabulary as unornamental as a monkey wrench.

In some of the more remote hollows of Appalachia, children still 13 grow up hearing songs and locutions of Elizabethan times. Yes, and many Americans grow up hearing a language other than English, or an English dialect a majority of Americans cannot understand.

All these varieties of speech are beautiful, just as the varieties of 14 butterflies are beautiful. No matter what your first language, you should treasure it all your life. If it happens not to be standard English, and if it shows itself when you write standard English, the result is usually delightful, like a very pretty girl with one eye that is green and one that is blue.

I myself find that I trust my own writing most, and others 15 seem to trust it most, too, when I sound most like a person from Indianapolis, which is what I am. What alternatives do I have? The one most vehemently recommended by teachers has no doubt been pressed on you, as well: to write like cultivated Englishmen of a century or more ago.

6. Say what you mean to say   I used to be exasperated by such 16 teachers, but am no more. I understand now that all those antique essays and stories with which I was to compare my own work were not magnificent for their datedness or foreignness, but for saying precisely what their authors meant them to say. My teachers wished me to write accurately, always selecting the most effective words, and relating the words to one another unambiguously, rigidly, like parts of a machine. The teachers did not want to turn me into an Englishman after all. They hoped that I would become understandable—and therefore understood. And there went my dream of doing with words what Pablo Picasso did with paint or what any number of jazz idols did with music. If I broke all the rules of punctuation, had words mean whatever I wanted them to mean, and strung them together higgledy-piggledy, I would simply not be understood. So you, too, had better avoid Picasso-style or jazz-style writing, if you have something worth saying and wish to be understood.

Readers want our pages to look very much like pages they have 17 seen before. Why? This is because they themselves have a tough job to do, and they need all the help they can get from us.

7. Pity the readers   They have to identify thousands of little 18 marks on paper, and make sense of them immediately. They have to *read*, an art so difficult that most people don't really master it even after having studied it all through grade school and high school—twelve long years.

So this discussion must finally acknowledge that our stylistic   19
options as writers are neither numerous nor glamorous, since our readers are bound to be such imperfect artists. Our audience requires us to be sympathetic and patient teachers, ever willing to simplify and clarify—whereas we would rather soar high above the crowd, singing like nightingales.

That is the bad news. The good news is that we Americans are   20
governed under a unique Constitution, which allows us to write whatever we please without fear of punishment. So the most meaningful aspect of our styles, which is what we choose to write about, is utterly unlimited.

8. For really detailed advice   For a discussion of literary style in   21
a narrower sense, in a more technical sense, I commend to your attention *The Elements of Style*, by William Strunk, Jr., and E. B. White. E. B. White is, of course, one of the most admirable literary stylists this country has so far produced.

You should realize, too, that no one would care how well or badly   22
Mr. White expressed himself, if he did not have perfectly enchanting things to say.

— Donald Hall —

Donald Hall, born in 1928, is a poet, prose writer, and editor. Educated at Harvard and Oxford universities, Hall has been a teacher and editorial consultant, has lectured widely, has received numerous awards and honors, and is a frequent contributor to a number of magazines. Among his many books are Exiles and Marriages *(1955),* Man and Boy *(1968),* Writing Well *(1973, and subsequent editions),* To Read Literature *(1982),* The Contemporary Essay *(1984),* The Happy Man: Poems *(1986),* Poetry and Ambition: Essays 1982–88 *(1988), and* Old and New Poems *(1990).*

A Fear of Metaphors

Hall here makes the case that, in our fear of potential imprecision in figurative speech, we have reduced our everyday language to a dry and lifeless literalism. Instead, Hall argues, we should recapture our sense of the language's metaphorical richness and its natural expressiveness.

The American language, long praised for its vigor, is now tired and feeble. Old energies of metaphor and image depart from educated speech and the language of editorial writers—to endure on the sports page or in street talk. Most of us talk and write so faintly, with such passivity, that our guiding spirit seems to be the stylist who writes directions on medicine bottles.

Tropophobia rules and inhibits us. This word, worked up for the occasion, may be defined as "fear and loathing of metaphor." Tropes are figures of speech, and it is not only metaphor but all extravagance of language that tropophobics abhor—including, heaven knows, neologism.

Our pale time distrusts original metaphor, prefers abstract language to concrete, and takes literal over figurative. Modern translators provide examples I cherish. In his 55th chapter, Isaiah asks, in the King James: "Wherefore do ye spend money for that which is not bread? And your labor for that which satisfieth not?" To the contemporary translators of *The Living Bible*, "bread" must seem obscure, as if it implied that Old Testament peoples lived by Pepperidge Farm alone. In *The Living Bible*, the straight-talking prophet asks, "Why spend your money on foodstuffs that don't give you strength?"

Tropophobia correcteth other sacred texts. Although people   4
have rewritten Shakespeare ever since Shakespeare, they have not
always deleted metaphor. A decade ago, a publisher issued textbooks
of four plays "in the original and modern English." Because "styles of
discourse . . . have gone out of fashion"—an introduction told us—
and "exuberance of expression [is] no longer appropriate in modern
English," these texts explain metaphors by abstractions. Macbeth
cries: "Burn out, burn out, you short candle of life."

Tropophobia is not, however, a modern invention. In 1670, an   5
English legislator proposed an act of Parliament that would outlaw
"fulsome and luscious" metaphors—collapsing into a food-trope as he
moved to proscribe troping. Distrust of colorful language has thrived
among philosophers. A dream of reason foresees evolution in language
from infantile figures of speech to civilized, reasonable, scientific,
pallid discourse. Hobbes defined "words used metaphorically" as employed to "deceive others." Locke continued: "The artificial and figurative application of words . . . [is] for nothing else but to insinuate
wrong ideas, move the passions, and thereby mislead the judgment."

Not all tropophobia calls itself progressive. Some textbook   6
authors—when they footnote poetic metaphor, turning energetic
speech into boring paraphrase—apologize by pleading that today's students are unsophisticated. Were Isaiah's contemporaries really more
sophisticated than our students? Apparently they understood "bread"
for "food in general." But our street talk does similar tricks—and
automobiles turn into "wheels." Only the disadvantaged talk like
Shakespeare.

Although distrust of metaphor is ancient, I suspect that the   7
contemporary variety has different causes and purposes. Tropophobia
issues not from philosophy class but from the department of English,
and its source is not a dream of reason but a fear of being taken in.
When George Orwell wrote "Politics and the English Language," in
1946, he praised the energy of metaphor while he exposed its misuse
for purposes of propaganda. His essay described the assault of deceptive
rhetoric from left and right, with radio's onslaught added to the onslaught of cheap print; his skepticism shouted louder in our ears than
his praise of metaphor's energy.

In the decades since 1946, the quantity of language-with-designs-   8
on-us has increased exponentially. Advertising in print, amplified
voices, radio and television: all promote the languages of commerce
and government. While our President calls a missile a "Peacekeeper,"
the trope-troops reinforce themselves until we are each a city under
rhetoric's siege. In order to preserve our independence, we may be
directing our energies entirely to the negative. Thus, in composition

class, teachers lecture about "loaded language." The original metaphor
referred to a crooked game of dice, but increasingly it seems to imply
bullets and guns.

But poetry is loaded language: loaded not with corruption but   9
with complex feelings, which it expresses mostly by metaphor. Faced
with a metaphor in a poem or a story or—God forbid—in a textbook,
too many teachers stiffen their backs and hiss: "What's *that* supposed to
mean? Why can't you say it *plain?*" Resisting propaganda, we deny
poetry; seeking clarity, we forbid energy—and the baby goes out with
the bath water; worse still, "bread" becomes "foodstuffs."

But while tropophobia reigns, there is a reaction to the reac-   10
tion. The study of metaphor flourishes. Linguists and philosophers
argue—often, alas, in medicine-bottle prose—that metaphors generate or embody concepts, and that thought is impossible without
metaphor. Although progressive developmental notions gain support
from psychological experiments—young children make metaphors
without inhibition, and become inhibited during adolescence—the
same experiments suggest a dialectic:

Thinking adults must recover metaphorical abilities in order to   11
intuit, in order to make connections that reason may not generate.
The capacity for metaphor is not a substitute for reason, but a way of
thinking. The road past tropophobia leads to the valley of connections: where body and mind, emotion and concept are one.

Computer-Trope

In our culture, lethargic prose is taken as evidence of seriousness   12
or sincerity. The heavier the subject, the paler the prose. This style
lacks not only original metaphor but vigorous syntax, conciseness,
puns—anything like *wit.* Instead, we find dead metaphors and clichés,
weak verbs and passives, pomposity and jargon. When we find a
metaphoric conceit, it is familiar. Usually it assembles the trope of the
moment; right now, it compares all activity to the business world,
which is the bottom line.

The latest parody—by Ross Baker, professor of political science   13
at Rutgers University—of the Declaration of Independence chooses its
diction well: "When at a given point in time in the human-events
cycle, the phase-out of political relationships is mandated, a clear
signal needs to be communicated to the world as to why we are putting
independence on-line."

Of course, this parody includes the ineluctable computer-trope of   14
the moment. By a culture's pet clichés, we know a culture's values and
anxieties, and the vogue of computer analogies shows something dan-

gerous about us: it denies free will—just like astrology, just like biorhythms—and thus it is comforting because it removes responsibility. *We are programmed this way*, it says, *don't blame us*. The computer metaphor, in a tropophobic time, embodies Calvinist predestination: *It's useless to struggle; everything was decided before we were born.*

A free and energetic society requires free and energetic language. 15 Bread nurtures us; foodstuffs starve like feedback.

— Annie Dillard —

Annie Dillard is one of our most accomplished nonfiction writers, winning the Pulitzer Prize in 1974 for her widely praised Pilgrim at Tinker Creek, *the story of a year spent observing nature at very close range. More than a nature writer, however, Dillard combines her stunningly detailed knowledge of the natural world with a genuine sense of awe, so that her work often has a religious or philosophical depth unusual in much contemporary writing. Dillard is also a poet (her volume,* Tickets for a Prayer Wheel, *appeared in 1973), critic (a collection of critical essays,* Living by Fiction, *was published in 1982), and writing teacher. Her most recent books are* An American Childhood *(1987) and* The Writing Life *(1989), from which this piece is taken. Another of her essays, "The Chase," appears on page 53.*

Push It

Dillard here makes an impassioned plea for each of us to commit ourselves to the heroic task of writing as if our life depended on it. Although her examples are from fiction and other arts, what she says applies to anyone trying to make the world new by the act of writing.

People love pretty much the same things best. A writer looking for subjects inquires not after what he loves best, but after what he alone loves at all. Strange seizures beset us. Frank Conroy loves his yo-yo tricks, Emily Dickinson her slant of light; Richard Selzer loves the glistening peritoneum, Faulkner the muddy bottom of a little girl's drawers visible when she's up a pear tree. "Each student of the ferns," I once read, "will have his own list of plants that for some reason or another stir his emotions." 1

Why do you never find anything written about that idiosyncratic thought you advert to, about your fascination with something no one else understands? Because it is up to you. There is something you find interesting, for a reason hard to explain. It is hard to explain because you have never read it on any page; there you begin. You were made and set here to give voice to this, your own astonishment. 2

Write as if you were dying. At the same time, assume you write for an audience consisting solely of terminal patients. That is, after all, the case. What would you begin writing if you knew you would die 3 soon? What could you say to a dying person that would not enrage by its triviality?

Write about winter in the summer. Describe Norway as Ibsen did, from a desk in Italy; describe Dublin as James Joyce did, from a desk in Paris. Willa Cather wrote her prairie novels in New York City; Mark Twain wrote *Huckleberry Finn* in Hartford. Recently scholars learned that Walt Whitman rarely left his room.   4

The writer studies literature, not the world. She lives in the world; she cannot miss it. If she has ever bought a hamburger, or taken a commercial airplane flight, she spares her readers a report of her experience. She is careful of what she reads, for that is what she will write. She is careful of what she learns, because that is what she will know.   5

The writer knows her field—what has been done, what could be done, the limits—the way a tennis player knows the court. And like that expert, she, too, plays the edges. That is where the exhilaration is. She hits up the line. In writing, she can push the edges. Beyond this limit, here, the reader must recoil. Reason balks, poetry snaps; some madness enters, or strain. Now gingerly, can she enlarge it, can she nudge the bounds? And enclose what wild power?   6

A well-known writer got collared by a university student who asked, "Do you think I could be a writer?"   7

"Well," the writer said, "I don't know. . . . Do you like sentences?"   8

The writer could see the student's amazement. Sentences? Do I like sentences? I am 20 years old and do I like sentences? If he had liked sentences, of course, he could begin, like a joyful painter I knew. I asked him how he came to be a painter. He said, "I liked the smell of the paint."   9

Hemingway studied, as models, the novels of Knut Hamsun and Ivan Turgenev. Isaac Bashevis Singer, as it happened, also chose Hamsun and Turgenev as models. Ralph Ellison studied Hemingway and Gertrude Stein. Thoreau loved Homer; Eudora Welty loved Chekhov. Faulkner described his debt to Sherwood Anderson and Joyce; E. M. Forster, his debt to Jane Austen and Proust. By contrast, if you ask a 21-year-old poet whose poetry he likes, he might say, unblushing, "Nobody's." He has not yet understood that poets like poetry, and novelists like novels; he himself likes only the role, the thought of himself in a hat. Rembrandt and Shakespeare, Bohr and Gauguin, possessed powerful hearts, not powerful wills. They loved the range of materials they used. The work's possibilities excited them; the field's complexities fired their imaginations. The caring suggested the tasks; the tasks suggested the schedules. They learned their fields and then loved them. They worked, respectfully, out of their love and knowledge, and they   10 produced complex bodies of work that endure. Then, and only then, the world harassed them with some sort of wretched hat, which, if they were still living, they knocked away as well as they could, to keep at their tasks.

It makes more sense to write one big book—a novel or nonfiction narrative—than to write many stories or essays. Into a long, ambitious project you can fit or pour all you possess and learn. A project that takes five years will accumulate those years' inventions and richnesses. Much of those years' reading will feed the work. Further, writing sentences is difficult whatever their subject. It is no less difficult to write sentences in a recipe than sentences in *Moby-Dick*. So you might as well write *Moby-Dick*. Similarly, since every original work requires a unique form, it is more prudent to struggle with the outcome of only one form—that of a long work—than to struggle with the many forms of a collection. 11

Every book has an intrinsic impossibility, which its writer discovers as soon as his first excitement dwindles. The problem is structural; it is insoluble; it is why no one can ever write this book. Complex stories, essays and poems have this problem, too—the prohibitive structural defect the writer wishes he had never noticed. He writes it in spite of that. He finds ways to minimize the difficulty; he strengthens other virtues; he cantilevers the whole narrative out into thin air and it holds. 12

Why are we reading, if not in hope of beauty laid bare, life heightened and its deepest mystery probed? Can the writer isolate and vivify all in experience that most deeply engages our intellects and our hearts? Can the writer renew our hopes for literary forms? Why are we reading, if not in hope that the writer will magnify and dramatize our days, will illuminate and inspire us with wisdom, courage and the hope of meaningfulness, and press upon our minds the deepest mysteries, so we may feel again their majesty and power? What do we ever know that is higher than that power which, from time to time, seizes our lives, and which reveals us startlingly to ourselves as creatures set down here bewildered? Why does death so catch us by surprise, and why love? We still and always want waking. If we are reading for these things, why would anyone read books with advertising slogans and brand names in them? Why would anyone write such books? We should mass half-dressed in long lines like tribesmen and shake gourds at each other, to wake up; instead we watch television and miss the show. 13

No manipulation is possible in a work of art, but every miracle is. Those artists who dabble in eternity, or who aim never to manipulate but only to lay out hard truths, grow accustomed to miracles. Their 14 sureness is hard won. "Given a large canvas," said Veronese, "I enriched it as I saw fit."

The sensation of writing a book is the sensation of spinning, blinded by love and daring. It is the sensation of a stunt pilot's turning barrel rolls, or an inchworm's blind rearing from a stem in search of a route. At its worst, it feels like alligator wrestling, at the level of the sentence. 15

At its best, the sensation of writing is that of any unmerited grace. It is handed to you, but only if you look for it. You search, you break your fists, your back, your brain, and then—and only then—it is handed to you. From the corner of your eye you see motion. Something is moving through the air and headed your way. It is a parcel bound in ribbons and bows; it has two white wings. It flies directly at you; you can read your name on it. If it were a baseball, you would hit it out of the park. It is that one pitch in a thousand you see in slow motion; its wings beat slowly as a hawk's. 16

One line of a poem, the poet said—only one line, but thank God for that one line—drops from the ceiling. Thornton Wilder cited this unnamed writer of sonnets: one line of a sonnet falls from the ceiling, and you tap in the others around it with a jeweler's hammer. Nobody whispers it in your ear. It is like something you memorized once and forgot. Now it comes back and rips away your breath. You find and finger a phrase at a time; you lay it down as if with tongs, restraining your strength, and wait suspended and fierce until the next one finds you: yes, this; and yes, praise be, then this. 17

Einstein likened the generation of a new idea to a chicken's laying an egg: "*Kieks—auf einmal ist es da.*" Cheep—and all at once there it is. Of course, Einstein was not above playing to the crowd. 18

Push it. Examine all things intensely and relentlessly. Probe and search each object in a piece of art; do not leave it, do not course over it, as if it were understood, but instead follow it down until you see it in the mystery of its own specificity and strength. Giacometti's drawings and paintings show his bewilderment and persistence. If he had not acknowledged his bewilderment, he would not have persisted. A master of drawing, Rico Lebrun, discovered that "the draftsman must aggress; only by persistent assault will the live image capitulate and give up its secret to an unrelenting line." Who but an artist fierce to know—not fierce to seem to know—would suppose that a live image possessed a secret? The artist is willing to give all his or her strength and life to probing with blunt instruments those same secrets no one can describe any way but with the instruments' faint tracks. 19

Admire the world for never ending on you as you would admire   20
an opponent, without taking your eyes off him, or walking away.

One of the few things I know about writing is this: spend it all,   21
shoot it, play it, lose it, all, right away, every time. Do not hoard what
seems good for a later place in the book, or for another book; give it,
give it all, give it now. The impulse to save something good for a better
place later is the signal to spend it now. Something more will arise for
later, something better. These things fill from behind, from beneath,
like well water. Similarly, the impulse to keep to yourself what you
have learned is not only shameful, it is destructive. Anything you do
not give freely and abundantly becomes lost to you. You open your safe
and find ashes.

After Michelangelo died, someone found in his studio a piece of   22
paper on which he had written a note to his apprentice, in the hand-
writing of his old age: "Draw, Antonio, draw, Antonio, draw and do
not waste time."

— Dave Barry —

Dave Barry, a humorist and newspaper columnist who has been called one of the funniest men in America, was born in Armonk, New York. He got his start in journalism as a reporter on the Westchester, Pennsylvania, Daily Local News but was frustrated by his editors' demands that his writing remain factual. Barry began freelancing a humor column for $22 a week, all of which he got to keep. He became a syndicated columnist for the Miami Herald in 1986 (his work appears in 150 United States newspapers) and won the Pulitzer Prize for distinguished commentary ("as opposed to the undistinguished kind," Barry says) in 1988. He is the author of many books of humor, including Babies and Other Hazards of Sex (1984), Stay Fit and Healthy Until You're Dead (1985), Bad Habits (1987), Claw Your Way to the Top (1987), Homes and Other Black Holes (1988), Dave Barry's Greatest Hits (1988), Dave Barry Slept Here (1989), and most recently, Dave Barry Turns 40 (1990). He lives in Coral Gables, Florida, with his wife and family in a house "surrounded by giant mutant spiders."

Insights into the Creative Process—or, Genius at Play

In this, one of his newspaper pieces, Barry gives a hilariously honest portrait of the frustrations every writer faces, in his case made all the more embarrassing by his being a "professional" with a supposedly finely-honed work routine.

I frequently get letters from people who have no purpose in life and are devoid of any useful skill and who would therefore like to become writers. "I have a lot of ideas," these people always say, "but I can never seem to get anything down on paper!"

That is their first mistake. We modern professional writers never use paper for any purpose except to fill out loan applications. We do all our writing on electronic computers, which we like because they have a little light on the screen, called a "cursor," invented by Nazis, which goes like this (and I quote): "Blink." All day long it does this, serving as a helpful reminder that time is passing and you are not producing squat. We professional writers take a great deal of pleasure in sitting in front of our computer screens, hour after hour, trying to think of something professional to write and watching our cursors go blink, blink, blink, blink, BLINK, BLINK, BLINK, BLINK, IIIIEEEEEEEEEEEEEEE

What we are experiencing here is Cursor Madness, a problem   3
that has afflicted many great writers, such as Fyodor Dostoyevsky, who was driven totally insane by his own word processor and, in a famous literary anecdote, cut off Vincent Van Gogh's ear. This need-less tragedy could have been averted if Dostoyevsky had owned "Flight Simulator," a computer game that is extremely popular with people all over America who are supposed to be competing with Japan. Whenever you get tired of doing your actual job, you just pop "Flight Simulator" into your computer, and it puts you "at the con-trols" of a small aircraft so you can simulate all the basic activities of a real pilot: taking off, steering and crashing into the Statue of Liberty. At least that's what I generally do because I am feeling hostile from caffeine.

Crashing into the Statue of Liberty is a basic part of my daily   4
writing routine, which is something that all of us professional writers have. Let's say it's 9 A.M. and I have a humor column due at 5 P.M. Here's the routine I follow:

First I get a good, solid start on some humorous topic. For exam-   5
ple, I'll write:

"One topic that has always struck me as being very humorous is"   6

Then I usually stare at the cursor for two hours. To the untutored   7
eye, it would appear that I'm not accomplishing anything, but a trained professional writer would notice that I am in fact picking at my toenails with a small jeweler's screwdriver.

Eleven o'clock already! Time for lunch! After a nutritious yet   8
easy-to-prepare meal of peanut butter gouged out of the jar with a forefinger, I'm back at my computer with a fresh new idea for the introduction:

"I have always been struck by the humorousness of a certain   9
topic, namely"

There! Now we are really achieving some professional results!   10
Time to play "Flight Simulator."

What? One o'clock already? Time for lunch!   11

Okay, now it's 2:15, and I'm back at the computer, ready to   12
pound this sucker out, starting with a revolutionary new concept for the introduction:

"If you're looking for a funny topic, you have to go a long way to   13
find one better than"

I'll be darned! It's 2:18! Time for lunch!   14

Okay, I'm back on the job, and it's 3 P.M., giving me, let's see,   15
two hours to deadline. Time to begin the process we professional

writers call "polishing," starting with some minor revisions to the introduction:

"Humor can be found almost anywhere you look for it, with one   16
obvious example being"

Suddenly I realize that I am very hungry. But it is now almost 4   17
P.M. This is not a time for lunch. This is a time to get out my electric guitar and learn to play the part at the end of the chorus to the song "Sock it to Me Baby," by Mitch Ryder and the Detroit Wheels, where the guitar player goes, and I quote: "Deet deet-deet deet-da-leet DEET deet deet." It is hard work. Harder even than "Flight Simulator." But I do it because I am a professional writer.

And now it is 10 minutes to 5. I'm in the final stage of the   18
creative process, the stage where I look at what I have done so far and change it to:

"The other day I was thinking of humorous topics, and what   19
came immediately to mind was"

Okay, I admit it's not totally 100 percent FINALIZED, but the   20
basic format is definitely there. I think I'll knock off for today and put the finishing touches on it first thing tomorrow morning. Right now I need to get out of this office and have some meaningful social contact. Maybe cut off somebody's ear.

Glossary

Aim(s)   The aims of writing are the underlying reasons or motives that call a writer's work into being, the goals the writer hopes to accomplish. In this book we examine *general* aims: the wish to express oneself, to inform others, to explain facts or ideas, to convince others with argument and persuasion, to criticize created works, and to entertain. Every writer will also have *specific* aims, depending on the context of the writing: to recall one's childhood, to report the results of a meeting, to help win an election. Our specific aims are concrete manifestations or expressions of the general ones. (*Chapter 1*)

Analogy   Analogy is a method of explanation in which we compare similar features of dissimilar things in order to better understand the unfamiliar. (*Chapter 4*)

Analysis   By analysis, we investigate the parts of a subject, and the relation of those parts in its internal structure, to better understand how it works or what it means. (*Chapter 4*)

Anecdote   An anecdote is a brief story or narrative usually used to illustrate a more general point. Anecdotes often serve as introductory and concluding strategies, or as supporting evidence.

Argumentative aim   Argument can be seen as both a goal and a way of achieving a goal. Argument itself is a form of writing whose aim is to move readers to belief or action with logic, reason, and evidence. The argumentative aim is the writer's effort to convince her audience that her thesis is logically undeniable—to prove her claim or to make the strongest possible case for it. (*Chapter 5*)

Assumption   An assumption is an underlying general principle that we take for granted in deductive argument (also called a *warrant*). The assumption describes the general situation within which we place the specific issue in order to reach our conclusion; it ties the *claim* and the supporting *data* together. (*Chapter 5*)

373

Audience   A writer's audience consists of his or her readers. Awareness of the audience's knowledge, attitudes, and needs helps to determine which strategies writers will use. All public writing (see below) is produced for a specific audience—whether an individual (as in a letter to an editor) or group (all citizens of voting age).

Body   The body of an essay or other piece of writing is its largest and most essential part—the long middle that includes the evidence and other support for the point the essayist makes.

Cause and effect   Cause and effect is a strategy for analysis and explanation in which the writer considers the reasons for, or the consequences of, an event or decision. (*Chapter 4*)

Claim   In argument, the claim is the main point or proposition the writer makes and then backs with evidence, logic, and reason. Claims address disputes and usually are about matters of fact, value, or policy. (*Chapter 5*)

Classification   Classification is a strategy for analysis and explanation in which the writer separates subjects or their parts (types of sports cars, forms of movement in dance) into distinct categories in order to gain a clearer sense of their meaning or relation. (*Chapter 4*)

Coherence   Coherence is the principle of clear, logical links among all the parts of a piece of writing, so that they fit together and make sense. (*Chapter 1*)

Comparison and contrast   Comparison and contrast is a strategy for analysis and explanation in which the writer considers important similarities and differences between two subjects in order to understand them in depth. (*Chapter 4*)

Conclusion   The effective conclusion of an essay ends it with a memorable and emphatic final point, one that is logical and appropriate to that which has gone before. (*Chapter 1*)

Concreteness   In language, concreteness is the principle of naming the specific qualities of an object rather than its general or *abstract* nature. Concrete language refers to things we actually perceive (*a ham and Swiss cheese sandwich on rye*), and abstract language refers to broad categories or conditions (*lunch*).

Criticism   Criticism is a form of explanatory and argumentative writing in which the writer considers the merits of created works such as music, poetry, fiction, painting, or film. (*Chapter 6*)

Deductive reasoning   Deduction or deductive reasoning is one of the two essential forms of logic, in which we apply specific cases to general principles or assumptions in order to reach conclusions. If all candy is fattening, and the object in my hand is a large chocolate bar, then the object in my hand is fattening. (*Chapter 5*)

Definition   When we define, we seek to establish the essential nature or characteristics of a thing or idea. Definition in writing can be used briefly to stipulate meanings of words or terms, or as extended strategy of development. (*Chapter 3*)

Description   Descriptive writing appeals to our senses (sight, sound, taste) in order to evoke the *concreteness* (see above) of experience and perception. Description may be objective, emphasizing detached or scientific observation; or it may be subjective, emphasizing the writer's own thoughts and feelings. (*Chapter 2*)

Design   Design is a stage in the writing process and the shape we give to our unique thoughts and ideas as we seek the most effective and logical order for our material. (*Chapter 1*)

Dialogue   In narrative writing or storytelling, dialogue is use of characters' conversation in order to reveal themselves to us or to advance the action.

Diction   The term diction refers to the kinds of words we choose, how we use them, and the effect they have on our readers. Scholars divide diction into levels or categories:
- Standard and nonstandard: the conventional language of a majority of speakers (*It doesn't matter to me*), on the one hand, and the unconventional usage of smaller groups (*It don't matter to me*), on the other.
- Informal or colloquial: the conversational language considered part of standard conventions (*Wow, what a great stereo!*).
- Slang: the most informal or colloquial speech, often arising from special groups (criminals, show-business people) or the language of the street (*Chill out, dude!*). Americans use slang all the time and often find it hard to distinguish between slang and more standard or conventional usages. Slang is usually omitted from most writing in college, business, and the professions.

Draft   A draft is a *version* of your written work. It may be an early, incomplete rendering of your ideas, a more highly developed and polished later draft, or the final draft—the one to which you've committed yourself as a product for your audience.

Economy   In all writing, the notion of economy means cutting anything that's unnecessary, keeping your sentences, paragraphs, and whole essays clean and elegant. (See Style, below.)

Emotional appeal   In persuasive writing, an emotional appeal is one designed to arouse emotions or feelings in the audience and thereby move it toward the writer's position. (*Chapter 7*)

Essay   An essay is a writer's unique selection, design, and emphasis of nonfiction material devoted to asserting and supporting a specific idea or claim. Every finished essay, whatever its aim or length, gives its audience the results of the writer's discovery, selection, shaping, and presentation of a clear and unified view of a subject. (*Chapter 1*)

Ethical appeal   In argumentative and persuasive writing, an ethical appeal is one which addresses the reader's sense of right and wrong, or which presents the writer as a person of respectable moral character, to encourage readers to emulate him or her in thinking or action. (*Chapter 7*)

Evidence   In all forms of essay writing, evidence is the *support,* the *backing,* we give our thesis or claim. It is the material (first-hand knowledge, facts gathered by research, testimony by witnesses or experts) that we present to make our assertions convincing. (*Chapters 5 and 6*)

Example   Providing examples or illustrations—"for instances"—is one way in which we offer support for our explanations, arguments, and self-expressive essays. (*Chapter 3*)

Explanatory aim   When we seek to explain, we want to do more than merely provide facts to our readers; we want to tell them what those facts mean or how or why they are otherwise important or significant. (*Chapter 4*)

Expressive aim   The expressive aim in writing is one focused on our own need to say something. Self-expression arises from feelings, thoughts, or experiences that we are compelled to tell others (or ourselves) about. (*Chapter 2*)

Fallacy   In writing, speaking, or thinking, a fallacy is a logical mistake. (See Chapter 5 for a complete explanation.) The effective writer, speaker, and thinker seeks to avoid muddled or wrongheaded logic for his own sake and for the sake of his readers.

Figurative language   Figurative language (figures of speech) is a natural aspect of human thought and expression, as we make connections among things we see. Some typical types:
- Simile: a direct or stated comparison (*He had a mind like a steel trap*).
- Metaphor: an indirect or unstated comparison, equating both terms (*This class is a zoo*).
- Personification: a kind of metaphor that gives human characteristics to objects or ideas (*the grim face of poverty*).
- Hyperbole: a deliberate exaggeration for effect (*I'd walk a million miles for one of your smiles*).
- Understatement: the opposite of hyperbole, a deliberate playing down for ironic or humorous effect (*My boss is so nice—he almost said hello this morning*).

Generalization   Broad statements meant to include many particulars, generalizations are abstractions that may or may not hold up. Sweeping or unqualified statements can be contradicted easily: *I've never met an honest man.* Qualifications or limits help make general statements more convincing: *Some students, it's true, will do almost anything to avoid school work.* (*Chapter 5*)

Humor   A strategy for entertaining our readers, humor is the playful, imaginative, and sometimes irreverant or satirical, treatment of subjects in order to provoke laughter. (*Chapter 8*)

Illustration   (See Example, above.)

Image   An image is a concrete, descriptive picture in language that appeals to our senses. Images can be *literal* (her pale blue-gray eyes) or *figurative* (the air as sweet as perfume).

Inductive reasoning   In argument, induction is one of the two essential forms of logic (see Deductive reasoning, above), in which we survey particulars and generalize from them. Induction is a principal form of reasoning in science, as in this example: If I discover that a pattern of illness appears among smokers more than nonsmokers, I may conclude (with sufficient evidence) that smoking is a risk factor in such illness.

Informative aim   The informative aim is the writer's wish to convey useful or necessary information to her audience. Informing and reporting are basic nonfiction purposes, the core of journalism. Gathering facts and presenting them accurately is an essential component in almost all writing. (*Chapter 3*)

Introduction   The introduction is our opening gesture to our readers, an invitation to meet us and our subject. Effective introductions appeal to readers' interest and usually state or imply the essential aim and content of the essay to follow. (*Chapter 1*)

Metaphor   Metaphor, like *analogy* (above), is also a way of explaining through indirect comparison: *For some people, learning to drive is a kind of torture; for others, it's a joyful, soaring flight.*

Narrative   Narratives are stories. We may tell them in brief, as *anecdotes* (see above) or in *extended narration.* Nonfiction stories can add much to our essays with concrete illustrations of our ideas and experiences. (*Chapter 2*)

Objectivity   In all writing, objectivity is the principle of being as truthful and accurate as possible in conveying facts, of not letting our personal views prevent solid, trustworthy reporting. (*Chapter 3*)

Persuasive aim   Persuasion is often a blanket label for any writing meant to convince us of anything. Just as often, though, persuasion means the writing that differs from argument because it's not limited to tests of logic and reason. Advertising uses persuasive appeals as much as or more than it uses logic. The persuasive aim is the writer's wish to convince readers by any means available, not just rational argument. (*Chapter 7*)

Point of view   All writers adopt a point of view, the vantage or position from which they speak. Depending on our relation to the subject, our point of view may be close or distant, knowledgeable or innocent. Similarly, we may write about our subjects in the *first person*, from the "I/we" point of view; in the *second person* or "you" perspective (used mainly for instructive writing); or the *third person* or "he/she/they" vantage. We have few strict rules about point of view, but formal, objective writing tends toward the third person, and personal, subjective writing inclines toward the first person.

Process analysis   Process analysis is a method of analysis and explanation in which we examine phenomena in their steps or stages, to observe how they develop or to provide instruction. (*Chapter 4*)

Public versus private writing   Public writing is any work intended for an audience, whether in school, the community, the workplace, or by publication. Private writing is that which we withhold from public view, in the form of personal letters (usually intended to remain private), diaries, journals, or even as early drafts of our public work. Essays are a form of public writing in that they address others for public purposes.

Purpose   (See Aims, above.)

Revision   The writing process is the method of exploring, inventing, shaping, and reexamining what we've produced until we're satisfied with it. Revision means re-seeing, taking a fresh look, asking hard questions, making necessary improvements—keeping at it until we have something worth reading. (*Chapter 1*)

Rhetoric   The study of how language works and can be made to work effectively, rhetoric covers the whole range of human experience through the writing process: the aims, forms, and strategies of writing and speaking well.

Satire   Satire uses wit and ridicule to attack individuals or actions the writer deems wrong. Unlike humor, with satire we seek more than entertainment; it is meant to undermine or discredit its target, sometimes to make way for change.

Scene   In narrative writing, a scene is a self-contained part of the story in which we see a portion of the action dramatized. A scene usually includes descriptive language and may have *dialogue* (see above) to advance the story.

Slang   (See Diction, above.)

Style   Every writer has his or her own way of saying things, a unique style. Beyond that, some general styles, each with its own values or sense of beauty, are tied to their subjects or fields. The plain style, for instance, is a straightforward, unadorned kind of prose writing many professional writers (especially journalists) use. But styles may vary, becoming more elaborate or complex, fancy, abstract or theoretical, academic, or even, at times, unreadable. Your style is almost always a product not only of your own manner of writing but also of the context in which the writing takes place.

Subjective point of view   The subjective point of view openly acknowledges the writer's presence in a piece of writing. (See Objectivity, above.)

Support   (See Evidence, above.)

Syllogism   The syllogism is the principal form of deductive reasoning, in which we begin with a major premise (*All men are human*), apply to it a specific case covered by the premise (*Hitler was a man*), and deduce a conclusion (*Hitler was human*). (*Chapter 5*)

Thesis   Your thesis is your essay's main point, controlling idea, or claim. It is the core statement that everything else in your essay supports or elaborates. (*Chapter 1*)

Tone   Like style, tone often conveys the writer's unique attitude toward his or her subject. And tones, like styles, can vary. Depending on the situation, your tone can be serious, sarcastic, ironic, angry, sympathetic, detached, and so on.

Topic (or topic sentence)   Topics are the secondary points or ideas used to back your main idea, and writers usually state them directly in *topic sentences*, which introduce supporting paragraphs. Topics *develop* your thesis in depth, helping to provide detail, evidence, and other material designed to convince your reader that you know what you're talking about and have something to say.

Transition   Transitions are the links we use to achieve *coherence* (see above). Transitions bridge words, sentences, paragraphs, and sections of longer essays in a continuous, logical stream. Repetition of important words, linking expressions (*in addition to, next, furthermore, consequently, likewise*), and clear statements showing how your thoughts flow together, all contribute to your reader's ease and understanding.

Unity   Unity is the rhetorical principle of staying on or close to the point. Essays are unified when the parts relate to and support the thesis, and when stray thoughts or unnecessary material are cut. (See Economy, above.)

Warrant   In argument, warrants are assumptions, underlying general principles that link the claim or proposition with its supporting evidence.

Rhetorical Contents

Example and Illustration

Definition

Process Analysis

Comparison and Contrast

Classification and Division

Cause and Effect

Analogy and Metaphor

Argument and Persuasion

Thematic Contents

Science and Nature

Business, Careers, and Technology

History

Language and Writing

Culture and the Arts

Education and College Life

Sports and Games

Current Affairs and Politics

Ethics, Religion, and Philosophy

Index of Authors, Titles, and Terms

Chapter 5

Chapter 6

Chapter 7

Page 278. Anna Quindlen, "A City's Needy," *The New York Times*, November 30, 1986. Copyright © 1986 by The New York Times Company. Reprinted by permission.

Page 282. *Iowa City Press-Citizen* editorial, "A Heartland Tragedy," published December 10, 1985. Reprinted with permission of the Press-Citizen Co., Inc., a subsidiary of Gannett Co., Inc.

Page 286. Roger Simon, "No Compassion for Drunk Drivers," *Los Angeles Times*, May 12, 1986. Copyright © 1986, Los Angeles Times Syndicate. Reprinted by permission.

Page 290. Wendell Berry, "Home of the Free." From *The Gift of Good Land*, copyright © 1981 by Wendell Berry. Published by North Point Press and reprinted by permission.

Page 305. Lisa Rodden, "A Nation of Illiterates." Reprinted by permission of the author.

Page 307. John Irvin, "The Imbalance in World Consumption." Reprinted by permission of the author.

Chapter 8

Page 321. Bob Greene, "Bob—A Name Spurned by History," *Chicago Tribune*, July 29, 1985. Reprinted by permission: Tribune Media Services.

Page 329. Garrison Keillor, "Attitude." Reprinted by permission of Atheneum Publishers, an imprint of Macmillan Publishing Company, from *Happy to Be Here* by Garrison Keillor. Copyright © Garrison Keillor.

Page 334. Woody Allen, "My Speech to the Graduates." Copyright © 1980 by Woody Allen. Reprinted from *Side Effects*, by Woody Allen, by permission of Random House, Inc.

Page 339. Judith Martin, "Undergraduate Romance." Reprinted with permission of Atheneum Publishers, an imprint of Macmillan Publishing Company, from *Miss Manners' Guide to Rearing Perfect Children* by Judith Martin. Copyright © 1984 United Feature Syndicate.

Page 343. Teresa Freund, "Diet Is a Four-Letter Word." Reprinted by permission of the author.

Page 345. Pat Healy, "The Poor Slob." Reprinted by permission of the author.

Chapter 9

Page 352. Nora Ephron, "Revision and Life: Take It from the Top—Again," *New York Times Book Review*, November 9, 1986. Reprinted by permission of International Creative Management, Inc. Copyright © 1986 by Nora Ephron.

Page 356. Kurt Vonnegut, "How to Write with Style." Reprinted with permission of International Paper.

Page 360. Donald Hall, "A Fear of Metaphors," *New York Times Magazine*, July 14, 1985. Copyright © 1985 by The New York Times Company. Reprinted by permission.

Page 364. "Push It," from *The Writing Life* by Annie Dillard. Copyright © 1989 by Annie Dillard. Reprinted by permission of Harper & Row Publishers, Inc.

Page 369. Dave Barry, "Insights into the Creative Process—or, Genius at Play," *Chicago Tribune*, October 25, 1987. Copyright 1987 by Dave Barry. Reprinted by permission.